INFORMATION SECURITY AND CYBER LAWS

Information Security and Cyber Laws

Editor:

Prof. Dr. Zoran Gacovski, Ph.D.

ArclerPress

www.arclerpress.com

Information Security and Cyber Laws
Editor: Prof. Dr. Zoran Gacovski, Ph.D.

708 3rd Avenue, 6th Floor
New York
NY 10017
United States of America
www.arclerpress.com

ISBN: 978-1-68094-456-3

Library of Congress Control Number: 2016951154

About the Editor

Prof. Dr. Zoran Gacovski, Ph.D.

A native of Rhode Island, in the U.S., Alexandra obtained her Bachelor's degree in History from Johns Hopkins University and her Master's in Media and Communications from the London School of Economics. Her Master's dissertation examined blogs through the lens of psychoanalysis. Alexandra has worked internationally in Prague, Marseille, Tel Aviv, New York and Seattle in various communications and marketing positions in industries such as consumer goods, technology and event production. Her current interests lie in editing and corporate content development.

Contents

Section III: Cyber Laws

Section IV: Cyber Terrorism

List of Contributors

K. K. Sindhu
Computer Engineering Department, Shah and Anchor Kutchhi Engineering College, Mumbai, India

B. B. Meshram
Computer Engineering Department, Veermata Jijabai Technological Institute, Mumbai, India

Fredrik Johansson
Swedish Defence Research Agency (FOI), Stockholm, Sweden

Lisa Kaati
Swedish Defence Research Agency (FOI), Stockholm, Sweden
Uppsala University, Uppsala, Sweden.

Amendra Shrestha
Uppsala University, Uppsala, Sweden.

Jiexun Li
College of Business, Oregon State University

Alan G. Wang
Pamplin College of Business, Virginia Tec

Bogdan Denny Czejdo
Department of Mathematics and Computer Science, Fayetteville State University, Fayetteville, USA

Erik M. Ferragut
CSIIR Group, CSE Division, Oak Ridge National Laboratory, Oak Ridge, USA

John R. Goodall
CSIIR Group, CSE Division, Oak Ridge National Laboratory, Oak Ridge, USA

Jason Laska
CSIIR Group, CSE Division, Oak Ridge National Laboratory, Oak Ridge, USA

Huansheng Ning
School of Electronic and Information Engineering, Beihang University, Beijing, China

Hong Liu
School of Electronic and Information Engineering, Beihang University, Beijing, China

Shuai Yuan
SUNY at Buffalo, Buffalo, NY 14260, USA

Raghav H Rao
SUNY at Buffalo, Buffalo, NY 14260, USA

Shambhu Upadhyaya
SUNY at Buffalo, Buffalo, NY 14260, USA

Hongxu Yin
The Power Company of Dezhou, Shandong, Dezhou, China
Rui Xiao
College of Mechanical & Electrical Engineering, Jiaxing University, Jiaxing, China

Fenfei Lv
The Power Company of Dezhou, Shandong, Dezhou, China

Shengxuan Wei
School of Electric Power, South China University of Technology, Guangzhou, China

Qianjin Liu
School of Electric Power, South China University of Technology, Guangzhou, China

Goutham K. Chalamasetty
Department of Electrical and Computer Engineering, The University of Texas at El Paso, El Paso, TX, USA

Paras Mandal[1]
Department of Electrical and Computer Engineering, The University of Texas at El Paso, El Paso, TX, USA

Tzu-Liang (Bill) Tseng[2]
Department of Industrial, Manufacturing, and Systems Engineering, The University of Texas at El Paso, El Paso, TX, USA

Bruce Wardhaugh
University of Manchester School of Law

Claire Bessant
Principal Lecturer, Northumbria Law School

Samson Yoseph Esayas
Norwegian Research Center for Computers and Law (NRCCL), Department of Private Law, University of Oslo

Yohannes Eneyew Ayalew
School of Law, Samara University, Samara, Ethiopia

Rabiah Ahmad
Center for Advanced Computing Technology, Faculty of Information and Communication Technology, Universiti Teknikal Malaysia Melaka (UTeM), Melaka, Malaysia

Zahri Yunos
Center for Advanced Computing Technology, Faculty of Information and Communication Technology, Universiti Teknikal Malaysia Melaka (UTeM), Melaka, Malaysia

Shahrin Sahib
Center for Advanced Computing Technology, Faculty of Information and Communication Technology, Universiti Teknikal Malaysia Melaka (UTeM), Melaka, Malaysia

Mariana Yusoff
Centre for Languages and Human Development, Universiti Teknikal Malaysia Melaka (UTeM), Melaka, Malaysia

Rabiah Ahmad
Center for Advanced Computing Technology, Faculty of Information and Communication Technology, Universiti Teknikal Malaysia Melaka (UTeM), Melaka, Malaysia

Zahri Yunos
Center for Advanced Computing Technology, Faculty of Information and Communication Technology, Universiti Teknikal Malaysia Melaka (UTeM), Melaka, Malaysia

Jacob R Scanlon*
Predictive Technology Laboratory, Department of Systems and Information Engineering, University of Virginia, Charlottesville VA, USA

Matthew S Gerber
Predictive Technology Laboratory, Department of Systems and Information Engineering, University of Virginia, Charlottesville VA, USA

Lorraine Bowman-Grieve
School of PsychologyUniversity of Lincoln

Robyn Torok
Security Research Institute, Edith Cowan University, Perth, Australia

Preface

In today's inter-connected world, the security and the privacy of digital data are primary concerns for all governments and businesses. Virtually no one is protected from the cybercrime on the internet. The term cybercrime originates since the year 2000 when the book with the same name was first published (edited by Thomas and Loader). Cybercrime is defined as computer-initiated illegal activity realized over the global electronic network. Many national governments have adopted their own legislations in the areas of cybercrime and information security. These laws cover different sectors of the economy and the society, such as banking and e-commerce, telecommunications, health, transport (air, sea, rail and road), power and water supply, and education. The adopted laws and standards define different information security measures. Some of these involve security checks, physical security, data safety, security of information systems, and industrial security measures. Importantly, the adopted national information security and cyber laws make sure that all attackers (intruders) who initiate and/or realize attacks are sued and accordingly punished. There are also regional cyber laws, such as European Union's Network and Information Security Directive (NISD), which extend national borders and apply to all the associated member states. This edition covers different topics from cyber security and anti-cybercrime laws, including cyber-criminal detection and prevention, cyber security in different society segments, cyber laws, and cyber terrorism.

Section 1 focuses on cyber-criminal detection and prevention, describing digital forensics and cybercrime data mining, time prints for identifying social media users, a framework of identity resolution, and network intrusion detection and visualization using aggregations.

Section 2 focuses on cyber security in different society segments, describing cyber-physical-social based security architecture for Internet of Things (IoT), emerging issues for education in electronic health records, analysis of causes and events on electric power infrastructure impacted by cyber attacks, quantitative methodology to assess cyber security risk of smart grid, and SCADA framework incorporating MANET and IDP.

Section 3 focuses on cyber laws, describing regimes and mobile telecoms regulation in the twenty-first century, the directive 95/46/EC and the data protection act 1998, the role of anonymization and pseudo-nymisation under the EU data privacy rules, and cyber warfare under the International Humanitarian law.

Section 4 focuses on cyber terrorism, describing the perception on the cyber terrorism, an application of mixed method in developing a cyber terrorism framework, an automatic detection of cyber-recruitment by violent extremists, a psychological perspective on virtual communities supporting terrorists, and an explanatory model for the process of online radicalization and terrorism.

Editor

Prof. Dr. Zoran Gacovski, Ph.D.

INTRODUCTION

Information security, sometimes shortened to InfoSec, is the practice of defending information from unauthorized access, use, disclosure, disruption, modification, inspection, recording or destruction. It is a general term that can be used regardless of the form the data may take (e.g. electronic, physical).

IT security

Sometimes referred to as computer security, information technology security is information security applied to technology (most often some form of computer system). It is worthwhile to note that a computer does not necessarily mean a home desktop. A computer is any device with a processor and some memory. Such devices can range from non-networked standalone devices as simple as calculators, to networked mobile computing devices such as smartphones and tablet computers. IT security specialists are almost always found in any major enterprise/establishment due to the nature and value of the data within larger businesses. They are responsible for keeping all of the technology within the company secure from malicious cyber-attacks that often attempt to breach into critical private information or gain control of the internal systems.

Threats

Computer system threats come in many different forms. Some of the most common threats today are software attacks, theft of intellectual property, identity theft, theft of equipment or information, sabotage, and information extortion. Most people have experienced software attacks of some sort. Viruses, worms, phishing attacks, and Trojan horses are a few common examples of software attacks. The theft of intellectual property has also been an extensive issue for many businesses in the IT field. Intellectual property is the ownership of property usually consisting of some form of protection. Theft of software is probably the most common in IT businesses today. Identity theft is the attempt to act as someone else usually to obtain that person's personal information or to take advantage of their access to vital information. Theft of equipment or information is becoming more prevalent today due to the fact that most devices today are mobile.

Cell phones are prone to theft and have also become far more desirable as the amount of data capacity increases. Sabotage usually consists of the destruction of an organization's website in an attempt to cause loss of confidence to its customers. Information extortion consists of theft of a company's property or information as an attempt to receive a payment in exchange for returning the information or property back to its owner. There are many ways to help protect yourself from some of these attacks but one of the most functional precautions is user carefulness.

Information Security Consultant

An information security consultant is also called a cyber or information technology (IT) security professional. Workers in this job are responsible for safeguarding computer systems. Information security personnel often work for governmental agencies and corporations, as well as non-profit organizations. Common tasks for IT security consultants include securing networks from hackers and preventing viruses from harvesting or damaging computer files.

In the modern world, businesses and organizations often depend on computer networks and the Internet to operate. While these connections can bring many opportunities, they also expose computers to potential threats. Malicious attacks on computer systems are not uncommon, and can occur as both automated viruses and targeted security breaches. Regardless of the source, computer security problems can result in sensitive data such as customer credit card numbers and business records being stolen.

IT security experts are retained by organizations and paid to locate and fix vulnerabilities. Consultants often work as independent freelancers, and advise several different clients simultaneously. An information security consultant does not need to have a formal education, and many are self-taught. A degree in computer science and industry-recognized certification in system security is often helpful, however. Many consultants depend on referrals for business, and the previous track record of a cyber-expert is very important.

The technical duties of an information security consultant can vary widely, depending on the needs of a client. Many cyber professionals provide general security services, such as installing antivirus programs and network firewalls for customers.

If a client is concerned about a specific type of breach, such as the theft of financial data, security consultants may focus on proactively testing a system for security flaws. Viewing a network through the eyes of a hacker allows consultants to fix security holes before a vulnerability is exploited.

While the major focus of an information security consultant is to prevent computer attacks before they occur, cyber experts can also take action after a breach has been discovered. Some IT professionals provide services to stop malicious hacking while it is still in progress. These individuals must work against the clock to isolate and fix a detected security leak quickly. An information security consultant might also be tasked with investigating an event after data theft has occurred. Like other types of investigators, IT experts must methodically collect evidence to find the perpetrator of a cybercrime and provide advice to prevent the offense from reoccurring.

Cyberspace

Cyberspace can be defined as an intricate environment that involves interactions between people, software, and services. It is maintained by the worldwide distribution of information and communication technology devices and networks. With the benefits carried by the technological advancements, the cyberspace today has become a common pool used by citizens, businesses, critical information infrastructure, military and governments in a fashion that makes it hard to induce clear boundaries among these different groups. The cyberspace is anticipated to become even more complex in the upcoming years, with the increase in networks and devices connected to it.

Cyber security

Cyber security denotes the technologies and procedures intended to safeguard computers, networks, and data from unlawful admittance, weaknesses, and attacks transported through the Internet by cyber delinquents. ISO 27001 (ISO27001) is the international Cyber security Standard that delivers a model for creating, applying, functioning, monitoring, reviewing, preserving, and improving an Information Security Management System.

Cyber security Policy

The cyber security policy is a developing mission that caters to the entire field of Information and Communication Technology (ICT) users and providers. It includes –

- Home users
- Small, medium, and large Enterprises
- Government and non-government entities

It serves as an authority framework that defines and guides the activities associated with the security of cyberspace. It allows all sectors and organizations in designing suitable cybersecurity policies to meet their requirements. The policy provides an outline to effectively protect information, information systems and networks.

It gives an understanding into the Government's approach and strategy for security of cyber space in the country. It also sketches some pointers to allow collaborative working across the public and private sectors to safeguard information and information systems. Therefore, the aim of this policy is to create a cybersecurity framework, which leads to detailed actions and programs to increase the security carriage of cyberspace.

Cybercrime

Cybercrimes are generally defined as any type of illegal activity that makes use of the Internet, a private or public network, or an in-house computer system. While many forms of cybercrime revolve around the appropriation of proprietary information for unauthorized use, other examples are focused more on an invasion of privacy. As a growing problem around the world, many countries are beginning to implement laws and other regulatory mechanisms in an attempt to minimize the incidence of cybercrime.

Sometimes referred to as electronic crime, one of the most prolific examples involves utilizing a computer connection and specially developed software in order to steal identities, credit card numbers, or other data that the criminal can use to his or her advantage. Using illegally obtained data, the criminal can open accounts, charge a wide range of goods and services, and then abandon the accounts. This leaves the victim in the position of having to deal with huge debts that he or she did not generate.

Blackmail is a long-established illegal act that has been given a new twist in the modern age. The blackmailer may threaten to release embarrassing or other harmful information via the Internet or a private network if the victim does not comply with the demands of the criminal. A cybercrime of this type may go as far as having the victim transfer funds to an untraceable bank account using some type of online payment program, thus making full use of modern technology to commit the crime.

Cybercrime can also involve illegal access to company information. Just as with individuals, criminals can steal financial information and make purchases using the data. The criminal may also withdraw funds from company reserves, transferring the stolen funds through a variety of accounts and making it virtually impossible to locate the stolen assets. In other cases, it is not money or credit information the criminal seeks; obtaining proprietary client information and selling it to competitors is another example of this type of high tech criminal activity.

In many countries around the world, nations have passed cybercrime law packages that make the issuance of spam a criminal act. Spam is loosely defined as unsolicited emails that are simultaneously sent to thousands or even millions of email accounts. Some nations have enacted specific conditions that must apply in order for the spam to not be considered a cybercrime, such as providing a means for the recipient to opt out of receiving further email solicitations from the sender. As the problem grows, more politicians promote the idea of some sort of national or international cybercrime act that would specifically address the use of spam and either limit or eliminate the practice altogether.

Obtaining authoritative cybercrime statistics is not as easy as it would seem. As with many criminal acts, some incidents of electronic crime go unreported. This makes it hard to compile any type of cybercrime report that tells the whole story for a given period of time. However, many law enforcement agencies around the world cooperate in an effort to provide as complete a picture as possible. In the United States, FBI cybercrime documentation seeks to identify any and all examples of electronic crime, including actions that may involve terrorist activity as well as crimes such as fraud, identity theft, or embezzlement.

Cyber Crime Investigation

Computer crime encompasses a wide variety, and ever-growing, array of crimes. As a result of the many different types of computer crimes, the techniques and procedures used in cybercrime investigation are varied as well. Often, cybercrime investigation involves law enforcement agencies in multiple jurisdictions. Traditional law enforcement detectives, forensic accountants, and experts in information technologies are all frequently involved in investigating cybercrimes.

Common examples of crimes that may be classified as a cybercrime, or that may have a cyber-component to them, include fraud, phishing, and identity theft, as well as terrorist activities and child pornography. Crimes such as fraud and identify theft are often accomplished through phishing. "Phishing" is the term used to describe the illegal acquisition of personal information over the internet. Cyber criminals often hack into personal files, or trick people into giving away personal data and/or account information, over the internet which they later use to make illegal purchases or transfer money from bank accounts.

Aside from financial and identity crimes, a cybercrime investigation may also target terrorist activities or child pornography activity that is carried out over the internet. Terrorists, as well as child pornographers, often use the anonymity of the internet to aid in the commission of their crimes. The internet also provides an endless supply of potential buyers of pornographic videos or photos for child pornographers.

Much like traditional crimes that leave a paper trail, cybercrimes often lead a digital trail. The first place to look in a cybercrime investigation, then, is to follow the digital trail. All internet correspondence or transactions must have a point of origination. Finding where the communication or transaction originated is the job of the law enforcement officials who work in cybercrime investigation.

Cybercrime investigation often requires investigators to sift through massive computer files trying to connect all the dots. Often, the suspect has attempted to delete incriminating files or communications. For this reason, information technology experts are frequently used to retrieve deleted files or communications from computers to ascertain what information the suspect was trying to hide.

Once the information is located, a forensic accountant is often called upon to make sense of the information located when the crime is a financial crime. Cybercrimes such as fraud or embezzlement often entail very complex banking transactions that require an expert to understand and follow. A forensic accountant is someone who is trained to discover even the smallest inconsistency in financial records.

Types of Cybercrime

Some cybercrimes create substantial amounts of financial damage, such as software piracy and credit card fraud. Phishing is a cybercrime that involves fraudulently acquiring personal information. Cyberstalking and credit card fraud are two offenses that can include a wide range of actions.

Phishing is a cybercrime that is used to obtain information under false pretenses. Criminals who phish usually achieve their goals by sending emails or instant messages that seem to come from legitimate companies. These messages often communicate the need for victims to disclose or confirm some type of information, and links will be included that will redirect the readers to a website that appears to belong to a company. After information such as passwords, personal details, or credit card information is entered, phishers use it for illicit purposes.

Cyber stalking is much like stalking in the real world. It can encompass a wide range of actions that are directed toward a particular individual. This can include behaviors such as sending threatening emails, following an individual from one forum to another and leaving messages along the way, and using social media sites to generate fear. The common element is the use of electronic communication.

Credit card fraud costs businesses phenomenal amounts of money each year. For fraudsters, the Internet often proves to be an ideal place to use stolen credit cards to make purchases and to obtain cash. These schemes are often carried out in a manner that makes it difficult to track the location of the goods or money. This is a crime where a single act can have multiple victims, including the merchant, the consumer, and the card issuer.

Software piracy is another cybercrime that has done a lot of economic damage. This intellectual property violation deprives the deserving parties of the financial compensation that they deserve. Software piracy generally involves a criminal illegally acquiring one or more programs. He may then keep them for personal use or may distribute them to others.

When individuals use a computer to gain unauthorized access to items such as other computers, servers, or networks, they are committing the cybercrime referred to as hacking. Individuals commit this crime for a wide range of reasons, including to get money, to access classified information, and to commit acts of online vandalism. Some people claim that they hack for no other reason than the challenge it poses.

Convention on Cybercrime

The Convention on Cybercrime is an international treaty ratified by more than 30 countries. The treaty was drafted by the Council of Europe in 2001. The main purpose of the Convention on Cybercrime was to foster cooperation among nations to combat Internet and computer crimes on a global level. The most common types of cybercrimes include copyright infringement, child pornography, and pirating of privileged information. Since cybercrimes can take place across multiple countries and jurisdictions, the Council of Europe, in conjunction with the United States, Canada, and Japan, crafted a treaty that used the law enforcement resources of multiple nations.

On 23 November 2001, the Committee of Ministers of the Council of Europe met in Budapest, Hungary, to discuss the issue of international cybercrime. Discussion centered on the legal challenges that emerged from attempted application of traditional criminal laws and statutes to an evolving global society. It was determined that traditional criminal procedures in member countries were inadequate, when operating separately, to handle new challenges emerging due to increased use and dependence on Internet technology.

The Council of Europe designated a specific committee called the European Committee on Crime Problems (CDPC) to analyze specific points of law and policy in an international context. Areas examined included specific types of crimes that the Convention on Cybercrime could address, issues of criminal law in member countries, international jurisdictional issues, and cooperation among member states regarding investigations and evidence. The Council of Europe gave the CDPC authority to draft a legally binding agreement for these specific points of law and policy. This agreement became the Convention on Cybercrime, which was later adopted and ratified by many member countries.

The Convention on Cybercrime consists of four chapters and 48 articles that detail the scope and extent of the treaty. The specific crimes or computer-related offenses outlined in the treaty include misuse of technological devices, fraud, forgery, child pornography, copyright violations, aiding and abetting, and issues of corporate liability. The treaty specifies under Article 13 that member countries must enact statutes to punish offenders.

Cyber Intelligence

Cyber intelligence is the tracking, analyzing and countering of digital security threats. This type of intelligence is a blend of physical espionage and defense with modern information technology. Various cyber intelligence efforts help to combat viruses, hackers and terrorists that exist on the Internet with the aim to steal sensitive information. Protecting parties, like a government, from these threats is a major part of this field, but so is aggressively fighting these threats.

There are many different forms of cyber terrorism that constantly threaten the cyber intelligence field. Identity theft is a common form of cybercrime that sees hackers infiltrating computer systems, ranging from personal computers to governmental networks, in order to retrieve personal data. Viruses are another common attack method that can be covertly installed on computers or entire networks in order to cause them to malfunction. Governmental and business secrets are routinely hunted down by cyber terrorists, using the Internet to uncover restricted information that could be used in negative ways.

One of the biggest duties of the cyber intelligence community is providing security against these digital threats. An intelligence professional will likely have a dual background in espionage and Internet security or information technology. Setting up firewalls, virus scanning programs, and routinely checking for breaches in security are important roles that keep a computer system secure from outside forces.

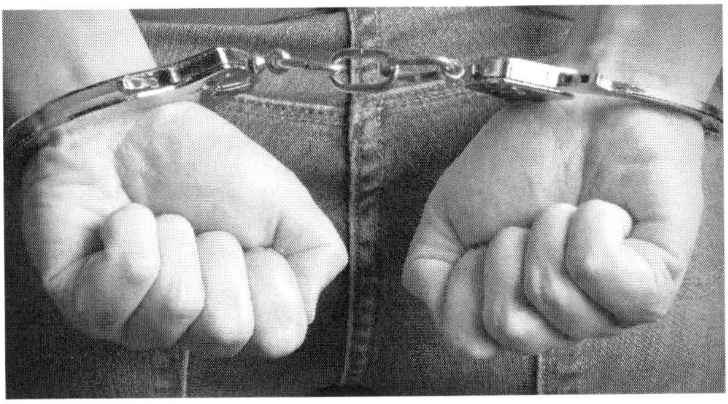

Analyzing terror threats is another important aspect of cyber intelligence. This aspect of the field is most like traditional intelligence and espionage tactics of information gathering. Using third party sources, either informants or one of the many independent companies that help identify cyber threats, professionals must gather this data and determine how it threatens what is being protected. Often, creating reports and recommendations for others is more common in this area than electronic work.

A third aspect of cyber intelligence is fighting these threats. Professionals with the proper computer training and armed with intelligence reports from analysts are able to seek out offenders and neutralize them. From teenage hackers to worldwide terrorist organizations, this arm of intelligence is dedicated to tracking down offenders and, often using law enforcement, stopping dangerous schemes. Many times, these intelligence workers will also have the authority to take aggressive action against terrorists by using counter terrorism measures to end a combatant's ability to operate.

SECTION I: CYBER-CRIMINAL DETECTION AND PREVENTION

1

CHAPTER

DIGITAL FORENSICS AND CYBER CRIME DATAMINING

K. K. Sindhu, B. B. Meshram

Keywords: Cyber Forensic, Digital Forensic Tool, Network Forensic Tool, Crime Data Mining

INTRODUCTION

Computer forensics is the process that applies computer science and technology to collect and analyze evidence which is crucial and admissible to cyber investigations. Network forensics is used to find out attackers' behaviours and trace them by collecting and analyzing log and status information. A digital forensic investigation is an inquiry into the unfamiliar or questionable activities in the Cyber space or digital world. The investigation process is as follows (As per National Institute of Standards and Technology) [1]. Figure 1 shows the complete phases of Digital Forensic investigation processes. Collection phase: The first step in the forensic process is to identify potential sources of data and acquire forensic data from them. Major sources of data are desktops, storage media, Routers, Cell Phones, Digital Camera etc. A plan is developed to acquire data according to their importance, volatility and amount of effort to collect [2]. Examination: Once data has been collected, the next phase is to examine it, which involves assessing and extracting the relevant pieces of information from the collected data [2]. Analysis: Extracted and relevant data has been analysed to draw conclusions. If additional data is sought for detail investigation will call for in depth data collection.

Citation: K. K. Sindhu, B. B. Meshram, Digital Forensics and Cyber Crime Datamining, http://dx.doi.org/10.4236/jis.2012.33024

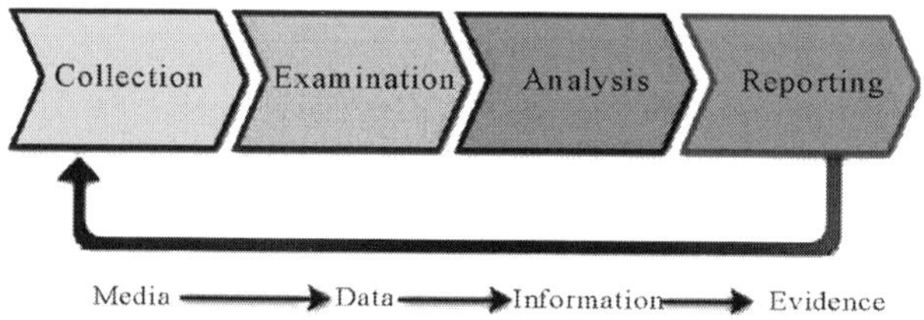

Figure 1. The digital forensic investigation processes [1].

Reporting: This is the process of preparing and presenting the outcome of the Analysis phase. Digital Forensic Science covers Computer forensics, Disk forensics, Network forensics, Firewall forensics, Device forensics, Database forensics, Mobile device forensics, Software forensics, live systems forensics etc.

File System Forensics

The File system investigation is the identification, collection and analysis of the evidence from the storage media. File systems or file management systems is a part of operating system which organize and locate sectors for file storage [3,4].

1. Basic Steps in Storage Media Investigation

1) Replication of forensic image: Nonintrusive acquisition of a replicated image of data extracted from the questioned device.

2) For integrity perform Hash value calculation.

3) Conducting a file-fragment recovery procedure to recover files and folders to a new location.

4) Examine all files especially deleted files.

5) Reviewing typical evidentiary objects such as:

a) Analyse free spaces, slack spaces and bad sectors.

b) Application software filec) Digital camera, printer and ancillary devices.

d) E-mails, Games & Graphics images.

e) Internet chat logs & Network activity logs.

f) Recycle folders.

g) System and file date/time objects.

h) User-created directories, folders, and files.

i) Latent data extraction from page, temp, and registry space.

6) Copy the content of the evidentiary object into text files.

7) Searching for key-term strings.

8) Reviewing file notations.

9) Scrutinize applications or indications of as file eradications, file encryption, file compressors or file hiding utilities.

10) Preparing evidence summaries, exhibits, reports, and expert findings based on evidentiary extracts and investigative analysis.

Hidden Evidence Analysis in the File System

Suspects can hide their sensitive data in various areas of the file system such as Volume slack; file slack, bad clusters, deleted file spaces [5].

1) Hard Disk: The maintenance track/Protected Area on ATA disks are used to hide information. The evidence collection tools can copy the above contents.
2) File System Tables: A file allocation table in FAT and Master File Table (MFT) in NTFS are used to keep track of files. Figure 2 shows MFT structure. MFT entries are manipulated to hide vital and sensitive information [5].
3) File Deletion: When a file is deleted, the record of the file is removed from the table, thereby making it appear that it does not exist anymore. The clusters used by the deleted file are marked as being free and can now be used to store other data. However, although the record is gone, the data may still reside in the clusters of the hard disk. That data we can recover by calculate starting and end of the file in Hex format and copy it into a text file and save with corresponding extension.

Recover a JPEG file

a) Open file in the hex format.
b) Check the file signature.
c) Copy From starting signature upto ending signature.
d) For example (JPEG/JPG/JPE/JFIF file starting signature is FF D8 FF E1 XX XX 45 78 69 66 00 (EXIF in ascii Exchangeable image file format trailer is FF D9).

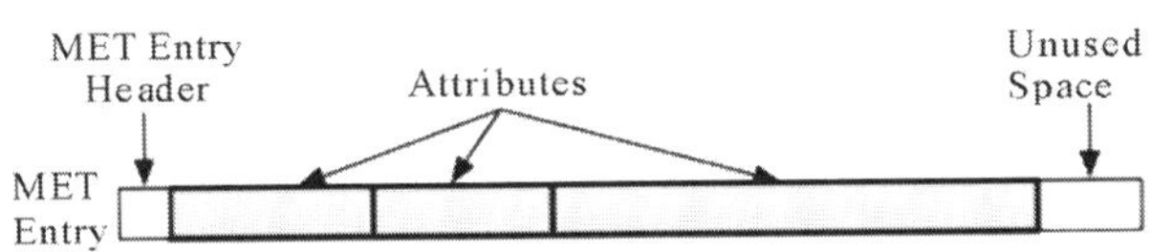

Figure 2. MFT structure [5].

e) Open the file with corresponding application.

4) Partition Tables: Information about how partitions are set up on a machine is stored in a partition table, which is a part of the Master Boot Record (MBR). When the computer is booted, the partition table allows the computer to understand how the hard disk is organized and then passes this information to the operating system. When a partition is deleted, the entry in the partition table is removed, making the data inaccessible. However, even though the partition entry has been removed, the data still resides on the hard disk.

5) Slack Space: A file system may not use an entire partition. The space after the end of the volume called volume slack that can be used to hide data. The space between Partitions is also vulnerable for hiding data, file slack space is another hidden storage. Figure 3 shows slack spaces in a Disk. When a file does not end on a sector boundary, operating systems prior to Windows 95 a fill the rest of the sector with data from RAM, giving it the name RAM slack. When a file is deleted, its entry in the file system is updated to indicate its deleted status and the clusters that were previously allocated to storing are unallocated and can be reused to store a new file. However, the data are left on the disk and it is often possible to retrieve a file immediately after it has been deleted. The data will remain on the disk until a new file overwrites them however, if the new file does not take up the entire cluster, a portion of the old file might remain in the slack space. In this case, a portion of a file can be retrieved long after it has been deleted and partially overwritten.

6) Free Space: However, when a file is moved from one hard disk or partition to another, it is actually a multistep process of copying and deleting the file. First, a new copy of the file is created on the target partition. After the file has been copied, the original file is then deleted. This process also requires some housekeeping in the FAT or MFT tables. A new entry is created in the table on the partition where it has been copied, whereas the record for the deleted file is removed from the table on its partition. When a file get deleted, that space considered as free space, there also criminal can hide sensitive information [6].

7) Faked Bad Clusters: Clusters marked as bad may be used to hide data. In NFTS, bad clusters are marked in metadata file called $BadClus, which is in MFT entry 8.

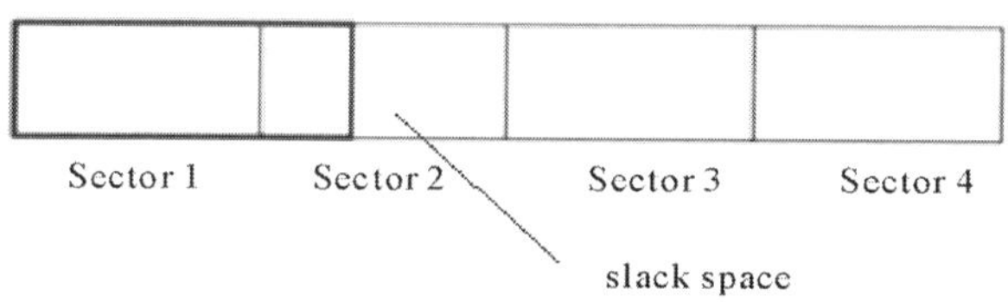

Figure 3. File slack [5].

Originally, $BadClus is a sparse file which file size is set to the size of entire file system. When bad clusters are detected, they will be allocated to this file. The size of data that can be hidden with this technique is unlimited. Suspects can simply allocate more clusters [6].

Network Forensic Analysis

Network forensics is capturing, recording and analysis of network events in order to discover the source of cyber attacks. In network forensics there are two major types of investigation [7,8] i.e. Network Traffic Analysis & Log Files Analysis.

Network Traffic Analysis

Network traffic analysis can be used to reconstruct and analyse network-based attacks, inappropriate network usage. The content of communications carried over networks, such as e-mail, chat etc can also support of an investigation. A Packet Sniffer tool is used for capturing network traffic. The header information encapsulated in the captured packet can be analysed by the forensic analyst [8,9]. This is very important when an investigation conducting on active network intrusions or attacks. Some cases evidences are available only in running processes or RAM.

Procedure for Network Live Acquisition

1) Create a bootable forensic CD.
2) Perform Remote access to the suspected machine or insert bootable CD in suspects machine directly.
3) Record or keep a log of all the actions of forensic investigator.
4) If need to take out away the evidence then use USB.
5) Next, Take a copy of the physical memory using a forensic tool example memfetch.
6) Create an image of the drive.
7) For Intrusion first check Root kit is installed or not, for that root kit revealers are available.
8) Perform hash value of the created image for integrity checking.

Network Investigation Tools

There is a powerful windows tools available at Sysinternals:

- Filemon shows file system activity.
- RegMon shows all Registry data in real time.
- Process Explorer shows what files, registry keys and dynamic link libraries (DLLs) are loaded at a specific time.
- Pstools is a suite created by SysInternals that includes the following tools.
- PsExec—Run processes remotely.
- PsGetSid—Displays the security identifier of a computer.
- PsKill—Kills processes by name or processes ID.
- PsList—Lists detailed information about processes.
- PsLoggedOn—Displays who's logged on locally.
- PsPassword—Allows user to change account passwords.
- PsService—Enables to view and control services.

- PsShutDown—Shut down and optionally restarts a computer.
- PsSuspend—Allows to suspend processes.
- Tcpdump and Ethereal—Packet sniffers.

Log Files Analysis

During investigation to recognize malicious activities by mining user log files. Access logs can contain vast amount of data regarding each user activities [10].

Analysis steps:

1) Input a server log file;
2) Identify each sessions;
3) Log file parser converts dump file into formatted order;
4) Using a Search function find the required data. Or Data mining algorithms give relations or sequential patterns.

DATA MINING FOR DIGITAL FORENSICS

Cyber Crime Data mining is the extraction of Computer crime related data to determine crime patterns. With the growing sizes of databases, law enforcement and intelligence agencies face the challenge of analysing large volumes of data involved in criminal and terrorist activities. Thus, a suitable scientific method for digital forensics is data mining. Crime data mining is classified as follows [11,12].

1) Entity extraction has been used to automatically identify person, login ID, Password, ID no, IP of the system, and personal properties from reports or logs.
2) Clustering techniques such as "concept space" have been used to automatically associate different objects (such as persons, organizations, hardware systems) in crime records [12].
3) Deviation detection has been applied in fraud detection, network intrusion detection, and other crime analyses that involve tracing abnormal activities [12].
4) Association rule has been applied to finding aassociations and sequential patterns between web transactions are based on the Apriori Algorithm. Mining results shows motive, pattern and counts of similar types of attacks happened during a period.

Crime Data Mining Algorithm

1) Identify variables/itemsets from a case report (our proposed system stores these variables as attributes of tables, filesystem table, network table).
2) Item sets I = {I1, I2, I3 ··· Im}.
3) Set of actions D = {t1, t2, t3 ··· tn}.
4) Find frequent item sets by using Apriori algorithm.

Employs an iterative level to find set of frequent item sets.

E.g. if an attacker attacked database, login attempt results a data loss/Data tampering and case report show actions like Data deleted, Login attempt, attack type = SQL injection, If these item sets are frequent then we can set a rule " motive of attack is Data theft".

5) Make Association Rules i.e. It is a rule in the form X → Y showing an association between X and Y that if X occurs then Y will occur.

If the attacker accessed operating system files then we can say motive of attack is system Crash.

If the attacker attacked Database login and Password steel then we can say criminal motive for data theft/data change.

This maximum frequent item sets also shows attack patterns.

Finding other signs of evidence Correlation, contingences

(Consider these values while making rule sets).

6) Set SQL queries according to the rules.

7) Retrieve data.

Proposed Digital Forensic Tool

Our proposed model is the combination of digital forensics and data mining. Our proposed system helps to in

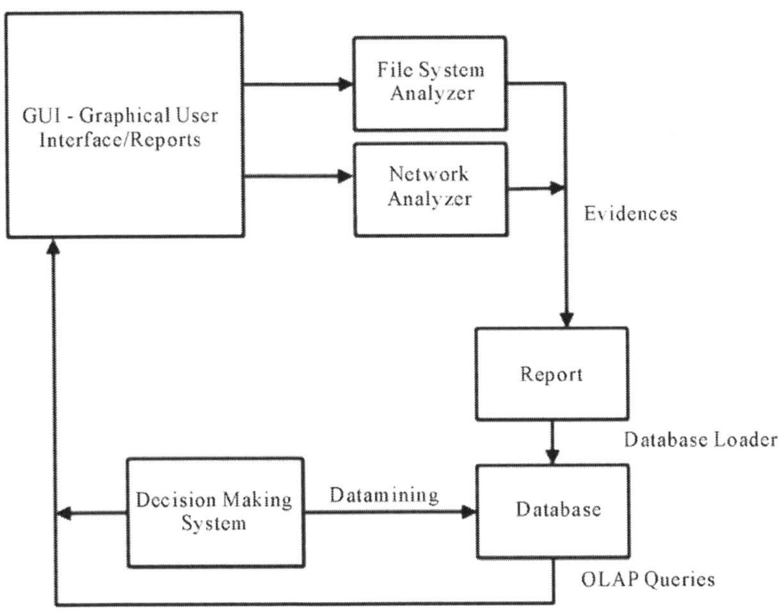

Figure 4. Block diagram of proposed system.

crease the security of the organization. When an incident reported, it investigates and report is saved in the database. Using crime data mining tool the nature of the attack is identified and alert administrator about similar attacks in future. Proactive measures can be initiated to prevent future cyber attacks. Figure 4 shows the Block diagram of our proposed tool.

Block Diagram of the Proposed System

Graphical User Interface: It is used by the forensic investigator to enter case details and apply tools (File system, Network) to collect evidences. Investigators can input their queries in the system. This also displays the result of the query in the form of Bar chart or report. It is the presentation layer of our three tier architecture.

File System Analyser: This tool Collects evidence from the file system, it recovers all files, searches data in the free space, slack spaces and deleted spaces. Network Analyser: This tool collects data from the network traffics and server log files.

Database: Database loader collects evidences from the above tools and loader loads into the database as attributes of the tables. OLTP (Online Transaction Processing): Set relations between the tables of the detected crime attributes. This applies data mining and extracts of required data. OLAP (Online Analytical processing) apply analytical queries and retrieves the output/decisions. Database server helps to store and retrieve crime attributes and results.

Decision Making System: This module applies data mining algorithm and also SQL queries into the database and generates reports. Log file analyser module parses the web server logs,

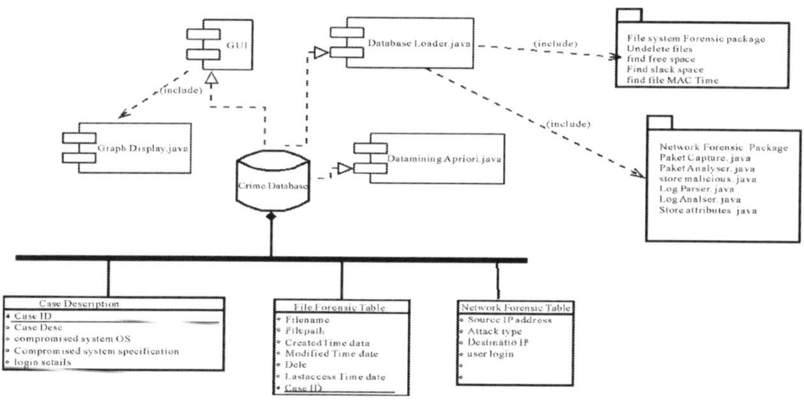

Figure 5. Software architecture of proposed tool.

syslogs and searches required keywords and patterns, which helps investigator to detect attacks like SQL injection, Brute Force attack for the login attempt.

Software Design of the System

Network forensic module is equipped with a traffic monitoring tool for data/evidence collection. A packet analyzer provides live forensic information about an attack. Java has API Jpcap captures information from the live network. The Network Analysis module analyse different types of packets ICMP, TCP, UDP. File system analyzer module finding the evidence from the deleted files, free spaces (File slack, Volume slack). The above modules give the output to flat file or CSV file. A Java program module (File converter/Database Loader) converts as Table format and loads into the database. Apply an Association mining (Apriori Algorithm) finding relation between these item sets of Crime Data and generate a prediction. Graphical visualization module generates the required results in the form of Bar Charts or Graphs. Figure 5 shows the Software Architecture of the proposed System

Conclusion

This paper explains the hidden evidence acquisition from file system. Second section explains investigation on the Network. There are two types of investigation in network, live data acquisition (Packet capturing and analysis) and log file analysis. Third section explains crime data mining. On the basis we propose a new system with Digital forensic tool for decision making in the computer security domain.

REFERENCES

1. K. Kent, S. Chevaller, T. Grance and H. Dang, "Guide to Integrating Forensic Techniques into Incident Response," NIST SP800-86 Notes, 2006.
2. S. K. Brannon and T. Song, "Computer Forensics: Digital Forensic Analysis Methodology," Computer Forensics Journal, Vol. 56, No. 1, 2008, pp. 1-8.
3. D. Klieiman, K. Timothy and M. Cross, "The Official CHFI Study Guide for Forensic Investigators," 2007.
4. B. Carrier, "File System Forensic Analysis," Addison Wesley Professional, 2005.
5. C. Kaiwee, "Analysis of Hidden Data in NTFS File System," Whitepaper.
6. M. Alazab, S. Venktraman and P. Watters, "Effective Digital Forensic Analysis of the NTFS Disk Image," Ubiquitous Computing and Communication Journal, Vol. 4, No. 3, 2009, pp. 551-558.
7. N. Meghanathan, S. R. Allam and L. A. Moore, "Tools and Techniques for Network Forensics," International Journal of Network Security & Its Applications, Vol. 1, No. 1, 2009, pp. 14-25.
8. E. Casey, "Network Traffic as a Source of Evidence: Tool Strengths, Weaknesses, and Future Needs," Journal of Digital Investigation, Vol. 1, No. 1, 2004, pp. 28-43.
9. H. Achi, A. Hellany and M. Nagrial, "Network Security Approach for Digital Forensics Analysis," International

10. Conference on Computer Engineering & Systems, 25-27 November 2008, pp. 263-267.

11. R. Arasteh, M. Debbabi, A. Sakha and M. Saleh, "Analyzing Multiple Logs for Forensic Evidence," Digital Investigation, Vol. 4S, 2007, pp. S82-S91. doi:10.1016/j.diin.2007.06.013

12. H. Chen, W. Chung, Y. Qin, M. Chau, J. J. Xu, G. Wang, R. Zheng and H. Atabakhsh, "Crime Data Mining: An Overview and Case Studies," Proceeding of ACM International Conference, Vol. 130, 2003, pp. 1-5.

13. V. Justickis, "Criminal Datamining," Security Handbook of Electronic Security and Digital Forensics, 2010.

2
CHAPTER

TIMEPRINTS FOR IDENTIFYING SOCIAL MEDIA USERS WITH MULTIPLE ALIASES

Fredrik Johansson, Lisa Kaati, and Amendra Shrestha

Keywords: Alias detection, Time profile, Machine learning, Social media

INTRODUCTION

An increasing amount of many people's life is spent online. People are using Internet and social media in order to communicate, express their opinions and beliefs, discuss topics of interest to them, etc. While much of the information is expressed publicly, there is also more sensitive information available in web forums and other social media services that potentially could be harmful to the author if it became widely known who the physical person behind the user that is posting information is in reality. There are many examples from the Security Informatics research community related to the analysis of terrorist activities on the Web (see e.g., [1–3]), such as the spreading of extremism propaganda and discussions on how to make improvised explosive devices. In such settings, it can be of fundamental importance to intelligence analysts to find out what a person writes and who the physical person behind some pieces of texts really is. Similarly, it can be highly relevant for the police to find out who the author behind anonymous posts in a cybercrime investigation really is by linking the anonymized social media account to non-anonymized postings or accounts. This is the main motivation and driving factor for the research presented in this article. However, the Web is, fortunately, not only used for activities related to terrorism or crime. Ordinary citizens may also want to preserve their anonymity when discussing private issues such as religion, sexual preferences, political ideas, diseases, etc. in public. Obviously, what

Citation: Fredrik Johansson, Lisa Kaati and Amendra Shrestha, Timeprints for identifying social media users with multiple aliases, DOI 10.1186/s13388-015-0022-z

is considered as private and sensitive information varies from country to country and individual to individual. Many people would like to be able to freely express their ideas and beliefs, while at the same time avoid revealing their true identity to e.g., friends, employers, commercial companies, police, or intelligence services. A quite common approach to reach some kind of anonymity when discussing sensitive issues online is to make use of "anonymous" or "alter ego" social media accounts when posting user generated content of private nature, while using other accounts for non-sensitive postings. A rather obvious problem with such an approach is that the Internet service provider and social media service can log the IP-address and help identifying the user from this information, unless the providers can be fully trusted by the user or if extra counter-measures are applied, such as logging in from various Internet cafes or making use of tools such as Tor1 [4]. There are, however, also less obvious problems with such an approach. It has for a long time been known that stylometric techniques can be used to identify an author among a small set of candidate authors given a large enough data material, but more recent research experiments presented in [5] suggest that this can be accomplished with reasonable accuracy also on large-scale datasets. A user who is aware of such techniques can in theory obfuscate their writing style intentionally, e.g., by using methods similar to those suggested in [6–8], but this is probably quite unusual. In our previous work [9], we implemented a subset of the features suggested in [5] and used them for alias matching (i.e., the problem of identifying multiple aliases belonging to the same individual in an unsupervised fashion). In addition to the use of stylometric features we also used time as a feature to increase the possibility to detect users with multiple aliases. As the use of stylometric features sometimes is referred to as a user's "writeprint" in the sense that it can be compared to a fingerprint when it comes to identifying a person, we are here using the term "timeprint" when referring to how various time features can be used to identify a person. A timeprint can be seen as a property that reflect something about the characteristics of an individual's activity and her habits. In our previous work the timeprints were based on the publishing times when a user post messages, capturing the distribution of messages over the hour-of-the-day. By using timeprints in combination with stylometry, the detection rate of finding multiple aliases has been shown to increase significantly [9]. In this article, we are exploring various time features in more depth in order to increase the quality of timeprints and in order to find out how successfully they can be used for author identification and alias matching. One of the reasons why we are investigating to what extent timeprints can be used to identify a user is due to the fact that in some cases the publishing time is the only thing that is present, in particular in cases where users post images or videos with illegal content such as child pornography. Another reason is that a person's timeprint can be expected to be quite uncorrelated to her writeprint, making it possible to combine the two into a more powerful feature set. We explore time features by explorative studies and experiments using the ICWSM forum dataset, containing data from an Irish forum site.2 We show that a set of time features can be powerful for unmasking an author's identity in both a supervised (author identification) and an unsupervised (alias matching or similarity detection) setting. Additionally, we make experiments to find out which impact the amount of available posts and the way we split the posts into sub-users have on the resulting accuracy. The rest of this article is structured as follows: in "Author identification and alias matching", we define the problems of author identification and alias matching, and present related work. In "Timeprints and activity profiles", we present various time features which potentially can be useful components of a timeprint, and show how the time features are varying among different users and over time for the Irish forum data. Moreover, we explain the concept of "circadian topology" or "chronotype" as a motivation for why people can be expected to have timeprints which are different from other individuals' timeprints. Next, we describe the experimental setup that has been used in our experiments on synthetically generated data in "Experimental setup". This section is followed up with the actual machine learning experiments, presented in "Experiments on author identification". In these experiments, we evaluate how well a classifier can learn to predict the correct author or user among a larger set of potential candidates by using time features. Hence, this is an example of how the classic problem of author identification can be tackled using non-textual features only. In "Experiment on alias matching", the usefulness of using timeprints for alias matching is evaluated and compared to stylometric-based features. In the case of alias matching we compare each user identity to all other identities and group together users (aliases) which are more similar than a certain threshold. In "Discussion", we briefly discuss under which circumstances the obtained results can be expected to hold in "the wild" and which implications our experimental results are likely to have. Finally, we present some conclusions and directions for future work in "Conclusions and future work"

AUTHOR IDENTIFICATION AND ALIAS MATCHING

Author identification, also known as authorship attribution, can be defined as the problem of assigning a text of unknown authorship to one candidate author, given a set of candidate authors for whom texts of undisputed authorship are available [10]. Authorship identification is a fairly well-studied problem, where algorithms and various features have been extensively described in, e.g., [5, 11–13]. However, existing approaches rely on linguistic/stylometric features (lexical, syntactic, idiosyncratic, etc.), while we in this article mainly study the usefulness of time features based on when texts have been written or published. To the best of our knowledge, time features have not previously been used for author identification purposes except for in [14], which the work presented in this article is an extension of. Clearly, information about time is not always available, but when analyzing posts from social media (e.g., Twitter, web forums, etc.), such information can often be extracted. In the author identification problem we compare each anonymous user to a fixed set of pre-defined known entities. In this way, we assume that the anonymous user is one of the exhaustive list of candidate authors present in the training set. This kind of problem setting can for example be of interest in a criminal investigation in which threatening messages have been received from a specific computer or IP-address to which only a limited number of suspects have access. Now, given that we can retreive the publishing times of the threatening messages, we can construct timeprints and writeprints from the threatening messages and compare them to timeprints and writeprints extracted from blog posts, tweets, forum posts, etc. written in user-generated content on social media using the suspects' known social media accounts. In an alias matching setting (described in more detail in [9]), we cannot assume that we have knowledge of all potential authors. The (intra-platform) alias matching problem is instead to compare each anonymous identity to all other identities and group together users (aliases) which are more similar than a certain threshold. Hence, while author identification can be seen as a supervised machine learning problem, alias matching is an unsupervised problem where the same supervised algorithms cannot be used. Instead, we are for the alias matching problem making use of a vector space-representation for the various aliases, where each feature corresponds to a single dimension in the vector space. Next, we make use of a distance function (in our case cosine similarity, although other alternatives such as Manhattan distance could be used) to calculate the similarity among the various aliases. In addition to publishing time, i.e., timeprints, there are also other kinds of features which can be used for alias matching. One obvious candidate is the use of stylometric features. In this work we compare the usefulness of stylometric features and timeprints, as well as their combination. Usernames is another feature that can be considered when linking multiple aliases to each other. In [15] an attempt to link user accounts across different social media services is presented. The authors show empirically that in almost 60 % of the cases, people use the same username in all social media platforms they are part of. A more sophisticated study is presented by Perito et al. [16]. They also consider usernames for linking user accounts but have instead developed a model for estimating that two usernames from two separate social media services belong to the same individual. In their approach a Markov chain model trained on approximately 10 million usernames gathered from Google and eBay is used to estimate a probability of how common tho usernames are. Although both these studies are very interesting, usernames would hardly be as useful for situations where people actively would try to hide who they are when making sensitive postings, which is the main reason for not including them in this study. In [17], a supervised method for finding mappings among identities of individuals across social media sites is introduced. While the methods suggested in [15, 16] make use of only one and two features, respectively, extracted from the usernames, the MOBIUS approach in [17] builds upon a large set of features extracted from the usernames (including the ones suggested in [15, 16]). Many classification techniques are evaluated in their experiments, but a logistic regression classifier is shown to perform best (with an accuracy of 93.8 %). This classifier performs much better than the methods suggested in [15, 16] as well as a number of baselines (such as exact username matching and substring matching). Overall, the most important features in MOBIUS are the standard deviations of the normalized edit distance and normalized longest common substring between the candidate username and prior usernames, and the username observation likelihood, but in total more than 400 features extracted from the candidate usernames, observed prior usernames, and relations between the candidate username and the prior usernames are used by the classifier. The results are impressive, but are not likely to work well in situations where people actively are trying to avoid their usernames being linked to their physical identity. Another type of approach to detect "split identities" of web authors is presented in [18]. They argue that feature extraction and machine learning on Web scale is very costly and does not scale well, since pages or postings written by the same author can be similar in many different ways (demanding large feature sets). Instead, they suggest using (open source) compression software for extracting the compression distance for pairs of web pages, hypothesizing "that every author has a unique compression signature that is similar across all the pages of the same author". Technically speaking, they make use of a two-sided normalized compressor distance (NCD) which measures how much the compression of each of two pairs of web pages is improved by using information in the other web page. The resulting distances are then used to cluster web pages, where the aim is to group all pages written by the same author in a common cluster. As shown in our experiments, our method can be applied to datasets containing quite a large number of users (although it obviously is a difference between a few thousand users and "Web scale"). Another approach to identify users with multiple aliases on social media services that has been suggested in existing literature is to make use of social network analysis (SNA). In [19], a social network based on aliases (email addresses collocated on the same web pages) is constructed. Depending on the number of web pages that the aliases are co-occurring on, the network is weighted and the the geodesic distance is computed. Social networks can potentially be used in other ways for linking multiple aliases as well, for example to construct a social network based on communication patterns or what topics an alias is writing about, as suggested in [9, 20]. In [21], the framework HYDRA is proposed for enabling large-scale social identity linkage across social media platforms. According to the authors, such linkage would allow for more complete and consistent user information when profiling users. HYDRA consists of two main components: one for measuring the heterogeneous behavior similarity between users and one for leveraging users' core social network structures. These components are combined using multiobjective optimization. In the behavior similarity calculation, many features are taken into account including a comparison of user profile images, various textual attributes from the users' profiles, and a rudimentary modeling of writing style (based on extraction of the most unique words of each user). The authors have been able to verify their suggested method on impressively large datasets (several million Chinese users with accounts on several social networks obtained from a third-party data provider). The results show that HYDRA outperforms the other approaches, which is unsurprisingly since the other approaches take fewer sets of features (mostly usernames) into account. Although there are many different approaches to author identification and social media linkage suggested in existing research literature, there are to the best of our knowledge no previous attempts to make use of publishing times, except for our previous papers [9, 14], which this article is an extension of.

TIMEPRINTS AND ACTIVITY PROFILES

A chronotype or a circadian typology is an individual difference in personality, which is believed to be the cause of why some individuals prefer to work and exercise in the morning hours while others prefer evening hours. In 1976, Horne and Östberg published a 19-item morningness-eveningness questionnaire [22] that was used to measure if a person was a morning or evening person. The questionnaire has been validated in many countries with regards to local cultures and ages. Apart from the morningness-eveningness questionnaire, circadian typology has been described and measured using different questionnaires in many studies and several countries [23]. Circadian preferences are based on genetic influence. The circadian typology classifies individuals according to three different types: morning-type, evening-type, and neither-type. Most people are neither-types and are positioned somewhere between evening or morning types while half of the population are either morning-types or evening-types. It has been noted that people who have the same chronotype have similar activity pattern timing: they prefer to sleep, eat and exercise during more or less the same hours. The circadian typology seems to have an impact on the behavior of an individual and various studies have for example suggested that evening types spend more time in front of the screen [24] or that evening types have a higher tendency for cigarette craving and alcohol usage [25]. When a person is active or not on social media services may also be correlated to the person's chronotype. In a discussion forum such as boards.ie, it is possible that a morning-type individual post most of her messages during the morning hours, while an evening-type prefers posting messages during the evening. In addition to chronotypes, there are other aspects that affects when a user is active on social media. These factors are related to the living situation of a person, for example factors such as during what hours a person is at work, what time zone the person lives in, when a person has vacation and what kind of occupation the person has all matter when it comes to usage of social media. Altogether there are several distinguished features that are characteristic for a user's social media usage. To obtain an understanding on how users behave, and investigate if there are some features that seem to be more characteristic than others when it comes to activity of a user, we studied the time-based activity patterns of a set of randomly selected users that were active in the discussion board. Figure 1 shows a randomly selected user's distribution of posts throughout a day. As can be noted in the figure, it seems to be the case that this user has a quite similar behavior of when he/she is active and not throughout all 5 years that are compared. When analyzing users' activity during various time intervals we noted that the activity pattern or time profile of a user seemed to be quite specific for each of the selected users. We also noted that the activity of a user seemed to be consistent over time (using data from different years). This might have to do with the fact most people are creature of habit and unconsciously prefer to do the same things during the same hours and periods. Some of the features that we considered in our manual analysis were:

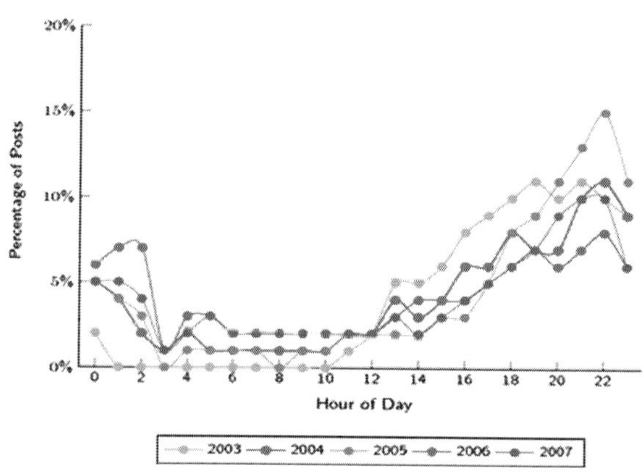

Figure. 1 Distribution of messages for a single user throughout the day during 5 years.

- Activity during each month
- Activity during each hour of the day
- Activity during each day of week
- Activity during weekdays and weekends
- Activity during 4-h intervals (early morning, morning, midday, evening, night, midnight).

Figure 2 shows the distribution of messages (posts in the discussion board) in 4-h intervals for a single user in the boards.ie dataset. Each number on the x-axis represents a 4 h interval where 1, 00.00–03.59; 2, 04.00–07.59; and so on. The same user has been active during 2003– 2007, and the distribution of messages is shown for each year. As can be noted in the figure, this user seems to have a consistent behavior when it comes to distribution of messages over the years. The fact that the behavior seems to be consistent over the years and that the pattern for each user seems to be somewhat unique is something that has been noted previously. How the behaviors and patterns can be used for author identification and alias matching is studied in more detail in later sections, but let us first see how such activity patterns have been utilized in related literature. In [26], a temporal analysis of the blogosphere was done. The assumption was that each blogger has a different preference for posting. A dataset consisting of nearly 700,000 blog articles was analyzed according to two factors: (1) day of the week and (2) time of the day. One of the conclusions in the paper is that each blogger has a different temporal preference for posting which supports our thoughts that different discussion board users have different preferences for posting, and therefore will have timeprints that differ from each other. In

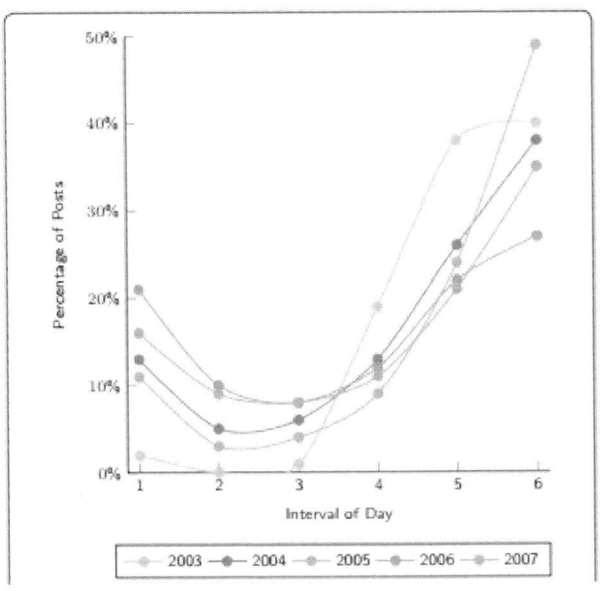

Figure. 2 Distribution of messages for a single user in 4 h intervals.

[27], a double-chain hidden Markov model is used to characterize individuals' behavior in e-mail communication. The results show that users fall into two wellseparated clusters: "day laborers" and "e-mailaholics". Given these clusters it is shown that a vast majority of the users retain their routines over an extended period of time. The above studies indicate that timeprints may be useful for separating users to some degree, but the experiments presented in the following sections investigate this possibility much more thoroughly

Experimental setup

We have conducted a number of different experiment to understand how well timeprints perform on the two problems of author identification and alias matching. In our experiments we have made use of the following sets of features when constructing our timeprints:

- Hour of Day Hour1, Hour2, ..., Hour24
- Period of Day MidNight, EarlyMorning, Morning, MidDay, Evening, Night
- Month Jan, Feb, ..., Dec
- Day Sunday, Monday, ..., Saturday
- Type of Day WeekDay, WeekEnd.

In the construction phase we go through each post made by an alias/user. We count the number of occurrences of each attribute and then express the values as relative frequencies, so that the values of each set of attributes sums to 1 (e.g., WeekDay = 0.65 and WeekEnd = 0.35). The relative frequencies obtained from individual posts are then averaged into a single timeprint for each alias. In some of our experiments we also combine our timeprint with stylometric features which are calculated in the same way. The stylometic features that we use are summarized in Table 1 and consist of various features which are supposed to be able to help distinguishing between various users without being sensitive to the actual topic of the text. We have in our stylometric implementation included a subset of the features used in the article by Narayanan et al. [5] plus an extra feature: the relative frequency of various smileys. As for the timeprints, the values for each set of stylometric features sum to 1. A lot of other features could have been used, including lexical features such as vocabulary richness [e.g., using frequency of hapax legomena (once-occuring words) or Yule's K measure], syntactic features such as part-of-speech tag n-grams, and idiosyncratic features such as misspelled words. We are not arguing that we have used the richest set of features possible, but rather that we have incorporated a lot of useful features that reasonably fast can be extracted from forum posts. The present features can be extended in the future to allow for even better stylometric "writeprints". While we ultimately would have preferred to run our experiments on real-world data in which a subset of the users were known to make use of multiple aliases, such data is very hard to get hold of for research purposes and also raise ethical concerns. Instead, we have synthetically created data based on posts extracted from the ICWSM boards.ie forum dataset. First of all, we have identified and extracted the posts for the 4000 users who have posted most posts in the forum during year 2007. The reason for choosing those users is that we wanted to have as large data material as possible, since a reasonable assumption is that the amount of data will have an impact on the achieved results. This assumption is tested further in one of our experiments described below.

Table 1 The stylometric features

Category	Description	Count
Word length	Relative frequency of words with 1–20 characters	20
Letters	Relative frequency of *a–z* (ignoring case)	26
Digits	Relative frequency of 0–9	10
Punctuation	Relative frequency of characters . ? ! , ; : ( ) " - '	11
Function words	Relative frequency of various function words	293
Smileys	Relative frequency of various smileys :') :-) ;-) :P :D :X <3 :) ;) :@ :* :| :$ %)	14

In our alias matching experiment we have from the set of top-posters first selected a smaller set of users (n = 500) (where the selection is based on the descending order of the users' amount of posts). Each of these users have been split into two separate users u_{ia} and u_{ib}, where $1 \leq i \leq 500$ and posts are assigned randomly among user u_{ia} and user u_{ib}. The intention of this split is to simulate a user who make use of two separate aliases, without assuming too much about the patterns in which the user will switch among the two aliases. Now, each user in the set {u1a, u2a, u3a, ... , u_{na}} is compared, one at a time, with all the users in the set B = $\{u_{1b}, u_{2b}, u_{3b}, \ldots, u_{nb}\}$. Based on the results from the time-based matching we rank the members of set B according to how similar they are to the selected user (where the similarity among two vectors is calculated using cosine distance). The most similar member of the set B is ranked as number one, the next most similar as number two and so on. The reported accuracy is calculated as the fraction of times the index of the selected alias is found within the top-N rankings (where the results for N = 1 and N = 3 are reported). This kind of experiment has then been conducted for increasing values of the number of users n, where we have varied n from 500 to 4000 in steps of 500. In the author identification experiments, we have only made use of the top-1000 users, since a larger set of potential classes would have been hard to cope with for the more complex classifiers that have been used. Each user u_i has been split into five "sub-users" $u_{i1}, u_{i2}, \ldots, u_{i5}$. The posts are in most of our experiments divided randomly among the sub-users, but we have also made a separate experiment on how the results differ if the posts are divided sequentially rather than randomly (i.e., where the user's first post has been assigned to ui1, the second post to ui2, etc.). The reason for using five sub-users is that we in this way construct several training instances for each user in order to facilitate the learning phase in our supervised learning experiments. Based on the extracted posts, timeprint vectors have been constructed (one for each sub-user). In the author identification experiments we incorporate the UserID ui as the target class. Hence, we have five (different) data instances for each UserID. In our supervised learning experiments we compare the accuracy for two popular supervised learning algorithms: a Naive Bayes (NB) classifier and a support vector machine (SVM) classifier [28]. For the author identification experiments we have made use of the Waikato Environment for Knowledge Analysis (WEKA) [29]. For the SVM classifier, we have used the nu-SVC classifier from the libsvm package in WEKA. We have used a linear kernel with default parameter settings since this was shown to give better results than a radial basis function in our initial experiments. In each step we have performed tenfold cross validation and the results from the ten folds have been averaged into a single accuracy value which is reported.

Experiments

As explained in the previous section, we have conducted a number of different experiments to understand to what extent timeprints can be used for author identification and for alias matching. In this section we describe the individual experiments in further detail and present the obtained results.

Experiments on author identification

In our first experiment, we have varied the number of potential authors from 200 to 1000 in steps of 200 as explained above. First, we have randomly divided a user's posts among its five sub-users. After this, we have used tenfold cross validation in which a Naive Bayes and a support vector machine have been trained and evaluated. We have then compared the obtained accuracies for the Naive Bayes and support vector machine classifiers. The results from the experiment are reported in Fig. 3 using the labels NBRand and SVMRand. Next, we have repeated the same experiment again, but this time we have distributed the posts sequentially among the five sub-users, rather than to distribute them randomly. These results are reported in Fig. 3 using the labels NBSeq and SVMSeq. Now, what is the reason for studying the effect of the way the sub-users are selected on the obtained results? The explanation to this is that it is hard to know exactly how someone would make use of several aliases.

Would they first make a post using one of their aliases, then switch to a second, and so on? Would they first write a large number of posts using one account, then switch to the next, and so on? The answer is probably neither, and the exact behaviour is probably very different for different individuals and different purposes for why multiple aliases are used in the first place. For this reason, the sequential and random splits of posts are intended to be seen as two extreme points, where the sequential way of dividing the posts into sub-users is intended to give an upper bound on the classification accuracy that can be expected when using timeprints, while the random way of dividing posts is more challenging for the classifier and can be seen as a lower bound on what classification accuracy that can be obtained.

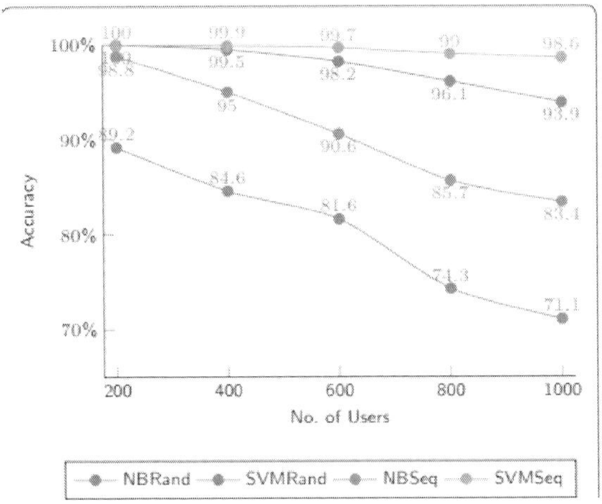

Figure. 3 Accuracy results from classification with a NB classifier and a SVM classifier. Experiments conducted on the 1000 users that made most posts in year 2007. Timeprints have been created by random and sequential division of users into sub-users

In reality, we would expect the accuracy to be somewhere between these upper and lower bounds, depending on the individual and what she is using the multiple aliases for. As can be seen when studying the results in Fig. 3, both classifiers perform well on the classification task, especially the SVM classifier. For 200 users the SVM classifier is achieving 100 % accuracy on the sequentially generated data and the NB classifier is not far away from this result either. On larger problem instances, the SVM classifier is consistently outperforming the NB classifier with approximately 5–20% higher accuracy, but this comes with a price. The training and evaluation phase of the NB classifier took a few minutes while the last steps took days to perform for the SVM classifier on the standard computer we used for the experiments, due to the large number of classes. As expected, higher accuracies are achieved when distributing posts sequentially rather than randomly among sub-users. This is expected since features such as Month will have very similar relative frequencies among subusers corresponding to the same user when dividing the posts sequentially. In a setting where people make use of several accounts sequentially (such as when having a "discussion" between two or more alter egos) the sequential approach make sense, while it probably is less realistic for more normal use of multiple aliases. For this reason we are in the rest of the experiments distributing posts among the sub-users in a random fashion, although this probably is closer to a lower bound on the accuracy. In this experiment, the correct user is in more than nine out of ten cases selected when using the SVM, both when using the random and sequential approach to creating the timeprints. As can be seen, the accuracy is still over 90 % for the SVM classifier when increasing the number of users to 1000. The results are somewhat worse for the NB classifier, but are still impressive given the simple nature of the classifier. The achieved results imply that time features can be very useful for author identification when having access to large amounts of data material. Those results are significantly higher than those obtained for author identification with textual (stylometric) features on a forum dataset reported in [11]. It should however be noted that it is not the same forum datasets that have been used in those experiments, making it hard to make a fair comparison between the results. In order to find out which of the time-based features that are most important for the achieved classification performance, we have applied information gain, which is an entropy-based feature selection method [30]. The results vary somewhat depending on which number of users the measure is applied to, but in general we can see that attributes related to Period of Day (such as Night and Morning) receive highest average ranks, followed by the Type of Day (i.e., weekend or weekday). After this follows Months and Days, while the set of attributes which seem to be least useful is the Hour of Day. An important part of the explanation to the decrease in accuracy when the number of potential authors is increased is obviously that there are more candidates to chose among for the classifiers, but a contributing factor may also be that there is less data material for the users further down in the list (since they are ordered based on their number of posts). To get a better understanding of what impact the amount of posts has on the results, we have in a second experiment modified the original dataset so that we start out with randomly selecting only 100 posts for each of the top-200 users. Since each user is decomposed into five sub-users, this means that the timeprint vectors are built from 20 posts each only. The number of users is kept fixed to 200 while we are increasing the number of randomly selected posts in steps of 100, until reaching 1400 posts (since the 200th user has written a total of 1484 posts). In effect, this experiment simulates a setting where only a restricted amount of data material is available for creating the timeprints. When adjusting the experiment in this manner, the results shown in Fig. 4 were obtained. As can be seen in this figure the accuracy increases for both classifiers when the numbers of posts are increased and the SVM classifier consistently performs better than the NB classifier. When only 100 posts are randomly selected for 200 users, the accuracy is below 20 % for both classifiers. When the number of posts are increased to 500, the SVM classifier has an accuracy over 80 % while the NB classifier is just above 55 %. The SVM classifier reaches over 95 % accuracy when the number of posts is around 800 and slowly continues to increase. The figure gives a good idea of what amount of data that is needed to reach a specific accuracy level for the classifiers, but please note that the although the shape of the curves is similar also for other number of users, the exact values will differ.

Experiment on alias matching In our alias matching experiment, we have selected the top-4000 users from year 2007 and randomly splitted a user's post into two equally sized users as explained in "Experimental setup". Now, we have for each sub-user created three sets of feature vectors from its posts: (1) a timeprint vector, (2) a stylometric-based vector, and (3) a combination of the timeprint feature vector and the stylometric-based feature vector. The results from this experiment are summarized in Fig. 5. As can be seen, both time-based and stylometric-based features work very well for a limited number of users, but as the number of users is increased the decrease in performance is less steep for the timeprints compared to the stylometricbased features.

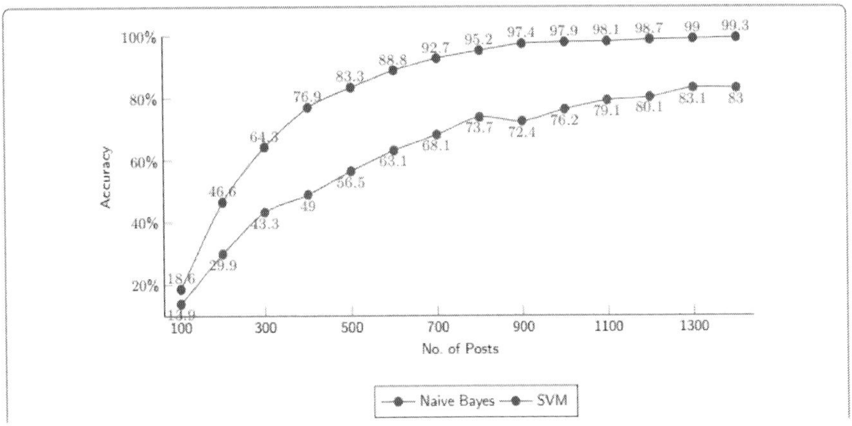

Figure. 4 Accuracy result for classification with a NB classifier and a SVM classifer. Experiments conducted with 200 users for varying number of posts on data from year 2007. The posts have been selected randomly.

Looking at the top-1 rankings (with top-3 ranking within parantheses), time alone yields 100 % (100 %) for 500 users, 89.6 % (94.4 %) for 2000 users, and 70.6 % (79.0 %) for 4000 users. The corresponding results for stylometric features are 98.2 % (99.2 %) for 500 users, 71.4 % (78.5 %) for 2000 users, and 44.6 % (51.7 %) for 4000 users. To combine both time-based and stylometric-based features seem to give better performance than using the individual time-based or stylometric-based features on their own, and this effect seems to increase as the number of users is increased. More specifically, the corresponding results for the combination of time-based and stylometric-based features yield 100 % (100 %) for 500 users, 93.0 % (96.6 %) for 2000 users, and 75.4 % (82.8 %) for 4000 users. Based on these results we can conclude that time-based features are vey powerful on their own for alias matching and that combining time-based features with stylometric-based features allow for even (statistically significantly) better results.

Discussion

The experimental results presented in the previous section indicate that timeprints can be very useful for both author identification and alias matching. However, it should be noted that the results have been obtained in quite well-controlled experimental settings which does not necessarily hold true in a real-world environment.

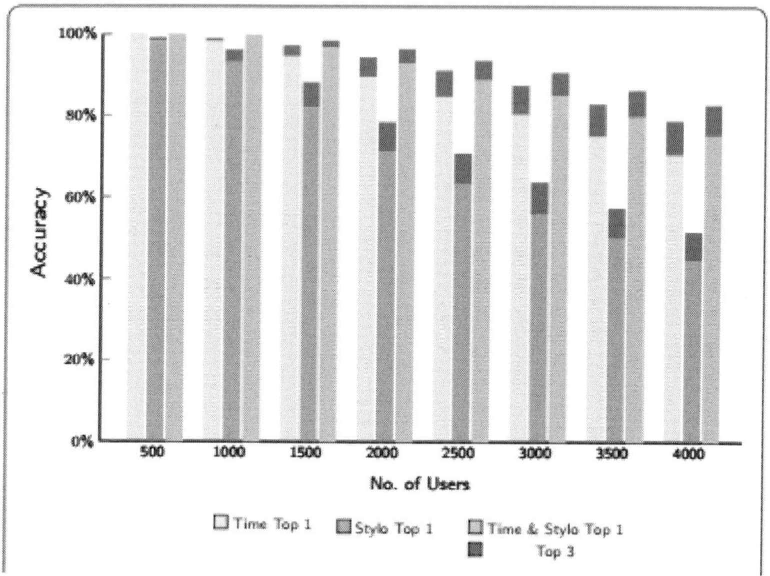

Figure. 5 Top-1 and Top-3 accuracy results for the alias matching experiment involving time-based features, stylometric-based features, and a combination of both

As have been shown in our experiment where we have used various ways to split users into sub-users (using random and sequential splits), the effect on the results can be quite large. The effect of splitting users into sub-users has been discussed before in existing literature on stylometric-based author identification [31, 32] but we are not aware of any previous studies on the effect on time-based author identification or alias matching. In our alias matching experiments, we have been able to control so that posts have been evenly distributed among sets A and B. In a realistic setting, posts from two aliases belonging to the same individual could potentially be more unevenly distributed, so that the posts for one alias could have been created during a completely other time period than the posts for the first alias. If this would be the case, this would have a negative impact on the obtained accuracy. Similarly, it can be expected that lower accuracy would be obtained for the author identification problem if the classifiers were applied on timeprints based on posts from a different time period than they were trained on. Furthermore, it is expected that timeprints from the same individual obtained from various social media platforms would look quite different from each other, even though they most likely would be correlated. For these reasons, the obvious next step is to attempt to evaluate the suggested algorithms on realworld data obtained from various social media platforms. Although it is not straightforward how to do this, there are various ways in which evaluation on real datasets could be made. One such way would be to make intraplatform experiments in which we attempt to find user accounts which are very similar to each other in terms of stylometric and time-based profiles and manually assess the matches to be either true or false positives, i.e., similar to the approach used in [33]. A drawback with such an evaluation is that only precision can be calculated, not recall. Another approach would be to try to get hold of a ground truth dataset based on uniquely identifying information such as e-mail addresses from a number of user accounts and use this as ground truth for whether two accounts should be matched. This would, however, only work for linking aliases across different social media services and would not be as suitable for evaluating how well we can detect users who actively try to remain anonymous. In addition to the question of in which real-world settings the suggested approach is expected to work well from a technical perspective, a very related question is in which situations it would be ethically acceptable to make use of alias matching and author identification techniques? We have no definitive answer to this, but as future (and already ongoing) work we intend to discuss this issue with a combination of law enforcement agencies, ethical philosophers, and IT law scholars. From our point of view, it would make sense from an ethical perspective to use this kind of techniques for author recognition purposes in a cyber crime investigation involving a few suspects, while it would be much more questionable to use it on large scale in an inter-platform setting which would allow for general dredging of possible matches. With this said, development of better and more exact guidelines for when this kind of techniques can and should be applied are left as future work. For the author identification problem, we have split the available posts for a user into five separate training samples. This has proved to work quite well, but the number of training samples per user has been quite arbitrarily selected. The optimal value of training samples is probably dependent upon the number of potential authors as well as how much posts we have available for each user, but finding such an optimal value has been outside the scope of this article. However, as a rule of thumb, the more posts we have for a certain user, the more highquality training samples we can create. One positive interpretation of results that have been obtained (if transferable to the real-world) is that police and intelligence services around the world can become more effective in finding the author of large quantities of terrorist propaganda and other crime- or terrorism-related content. A more negative interpretation is that the online anonymity of ordinary citizens in worst case may be weakened if this kind of techniques would be used by, e.g., commercial companies or repressive regimes. This raises the question of whether the use of time-based features can be defended against by an individual who wants to preserve his or her anonymity. A potential solution could be to use software which does not publish posts directly as they are written, but rather delay the creation time of new posts randomly. However, it is unlikely that many people would make use of such techniques, which in practice will add the use of timeprints (combined with stylometric features) as a potential attack vector on online anonymity.

CONCLUSIONS AND FUTURE WORK

In this article, we have presented the idea that a user's timeprint (which can be extracted from the publishing times of a large number of social media services) can be useful for identifying users who make use of multiple aliases. This idea has been motivated by arguments such as the existence of individual differences in personality preferences related to time (morning-type, evening-type, neither-type) and the fact that people have different working hours and sleeping hours. By selecting a few users and looking at their behavior over time we have noted that many users seem to have a quite stable activity behavior over time. Our initial manual analysis has indicated that there might be a possibility to tell individuals apart based on their timeprints. However, by just looking at a set of users' behavior over time we cannot say much about how unique a timeprint is. To get a better understanding of the uniqueness of individuals' timeprints, we have made supervised machine learning experiments where we have attempted to learn classifiers to tell users apart based on various time features. This can be thought of as author identification based on activity rather than textual style. The results suggest that high accuracy can be obtained also for large number of potential authors (over 90 % up to 1000 users), but that the accuracy is highly dependent upon the number of posts from which the timeprints are created. In a second set of experiments, we have tested the usefulness of time features for the unsupervised alias matching problem. We show that good performance can be achieved and that even better results are achieved when combining the time-based features with stylometricbased features. The results in the article are encouraging from an intelligence and security perspective, but they might pose a threat towards privacy and online anonymity. If this kind of techniques can be used to reveal the true identity of a potential terrorist, there is a risk that the same techniques can be used also for other purposes, even though the usefulness of the technique decline as the number of users is increased. One way to defend against the use of "timeprint attacks" could be to use tools that automate the process of publishing. A more drastic defense could be that some individuals choose to stop posting sensitive information at all, but this would obviously have potentially severe consequences for democracy and individuals' right to freedom.

Future work

In this article we have only considered users in a discussion forum, but it is likely that the results can be transferred to other social media services as well. As future work we plan to test the usefulness of the developed timeprints on other social media services such as Twitter. We also aim at cross-platform experiments, in which correlations among discussion forums and other social media services can be explored. Moreoever, we would like to carry out large-scale experiments like those in [5], where the full set of their stylometric features are combined with the timeprint features developed in this article. Another direction for future work is to move on and make real-world experiments using the proposed algorithms. Before this is done, it is however important to find out during which circumstances it is ethically acceptable to use alias matching and author identification on real data, both for research purposes and for use by police and security agencies. For this reason, we are currently undertaking a project in which law enforcement agencies, ethical philosophers, and IT law scholars are involved. The results from this work will influence how and if the proposed methods will be evaluated on realworld data.

REFERENCES

1. Abbasi A, Chen H (2007) Affect intensity analysis of dark web forums. In: Proceedings of the 5th IEEE international conference on intelligence and security informatics

2. Brynielsson J, Horndahl A, Johansson F, Kaati L, Måartenson C, Svenson P (2012) Analysis of weak signals for detecting lone wolf terrorists. In: Proceedings of the 2012 European intelligence and security informatics conference, pp 197–204
3. Brynielsson J, Horndahl A, Johansson F, Kaati L, Måartenson C, Svenson P (2013) Harvesting and analysis of weak signals for detecting lone wolf terrorists. Secur Inform 2(11):1–15
4. Goldschlag D, Reed M, Syverson P (1999) Onion routing. Commun ACM 42(2):39–41
5. Narayanan A, Paskov H, Gong NZ, Bethencourt J, Stefanov E, Shin ECR, Song D (2012) On the feasibility of internet-scale author identification. In: 2012 IEEE symposium on security and privacy (SP), pp 300–314
6. Brennan M, Afroz S, Greenstadt R (2012) Adversarial stylometry: circumventing authorship recognition to preserve privacy and anonymity. ACM Trans Inf Syst Secur 15(3):12:1–12:22
7. Kacmarcik G, Gamon M (2006) Obfuscating document stylometry to preserve author anonymity. In: Proceedings of the 2006 COLING/ACL
8. Almishari M, Oguz E, Tsudik G (2014) Fighting authorship linkability with crowdsourcing. In: Proceedings of the second ACM conference on online social networks (COSN'14). ACM, New York, pp 69–82. doi:10.1145/2660460.2660486
9. Johansson F, Kaati L, Shrestha A (2013) Detecting multiple aliases in social media. In: Proceedings of the 2012 international conference on advances in social networks analysis and mining (ASONAM'13), pp 1004–1011
10. Stamatatos E (2009) A survey of modern authorship attribution methods. J Am Soc Inf Sci Technol 60(3):538–556
11. Abbasi A, Chen H (2008) Writeprints: a stylometric approach to identitylevel identification and similarity detection in cyberspace. ACM Trans Inf Syst 26(2):7–1729
12. Zheng R, Li J, Chen H, Huang Z (2006) A framework for authorship identification of online messages: writing-style features and classification techniques. J Am Soc Inf Sci Technol 57(3):378–393
13. Juola P (2006) Authorship attribution. Found Trends Inf Retr 1(3):233–334
14. Johansson F, Kaati L, Shrestha A (2014) Time profiles for identifying users in online environments. In: Proceedings of the 2014 IEEE joint intelligence and security informatics conference (JISIC'14), pp 83–90
15. Zafarani R, Liu H (2009) Connecting corresponding identities across communities. In: Adar E, Hurst M, Finin T, Glance NS, Nicolov N, Tseng BL (eds) Proceedings of the third international conference on weblogs and social media
16. Perito D, Castelluccia C, Kaafar M, Manils P (2011) How unique and traceable are usernames? In: Fischer-Hübner S, Hopper N (eds) Privacy Enhancing Technologies. Lecture Notes in Computer Science, vol 6794. Springer, Berlin, Heidelberg, pp 1–17 (2011)
17. Zafarani R, Liu H (2013) Connecting users across social media sites: a behavioral-

modeling approach. In: Proceedings of the 19th ACM SIGKDD international conference on knowledge discovery and data mining, pp 41–49

18. Amitay E, Yogev S, Yom-Tov E (2007) Serial sharers: detecting split identities of web authors. In: ACM SIGIR 2007 workshop on plagiarism analysis, authorship identification, and near-duplicate detection. ACM, New York
19. Hölzer R, Malin B, Sweeney L (2005) Email alias detection using social network analysis. In: Proceedings of the 3rd international workshop on link discovery (LinkKDD'05). ACM, New York, pp 52–57
20. Dahlin J, Johansson F, Kaati L, Måartenson C, Svenson P (2012) Combining entity matching techniques for detecting extremist behavior on discussion boards. In: Proceedings of the 2012 international conference on advances in social networks analysis and mining (ASONAM'12), pp 850–857
21. Liu S, Wang S, Zhu F, Zhang J, Krishnan R (2014) Hydra: large-scale social identity linkage via heterogeneous behavior modeling. In: Proceedings of the 2014 ACM SIGMOD international conference on management of data (SIGMOD'14), pp 51–62
22. Horne JA, Östberg O (1976) A self-assessment questionnaire to determine morningness-eveningness in human circadian rhythms. Int J Chronobiol 4(2):97–110
23. Adan A, Archer SN, Hidalgo MP, Di Milia L, Natale V, Randler C (2012) Circadian typology: a comprehensive review. Chronobiol Int 29(9):1153–1175
24. Urban R, Magyarodi T, Riga A (2011) Morningness-eveningness, chronotypes and health-impairing behaviors in adolescents. Chronobiol Int 28:238–247
25. Adan A (1994) Chronotype and personality factors in the daily consumption of alcohol and psychostimulants. Addiction 89:455–462
26. Lee B (2012) A temporal analysis of posting behavior in social media streams. In: International AAAI conference on weblogs and social media
27. Malmgren RD, Hofman JM, Amaral LAN, Watts DJ (2009) Characterizing individual communication patterns. In: Proceedings of the 15th ACM SIGKDD international conference on knowledge discovery and data mining, pp 607–616
28. Vapnik VN (1995) The nature of statistical learning theory. Springer, New York
29. Hall M, Frank E, Holmes G, Pfahringer B, Reutemann P, Witten IH (2009) The weka data mining software: an update. SIGKDD Explor Newsl 11(1):10–18. doi:10.1145/1656274.1656278
30. Lee C, Lee GG (2006) Information gain and divergence-based feature selection for machine learning-based text categorization. Form Methods Inf Retr 42:155–165
31. Layton R, Watters P, Dazeley R (2010) Authorship attribution for twitter in 140 characters or less. In: Proceedings of the second cybercrime and trustworthy computing workshop
32. Zechner N (2014) Effects of division of data in author identification. In: Proceedings of the fifth Swedish language technology conference

33. Novak J, Raghavan P, Tomkins A (2004) Anti-aliasing on the web. In: Proceedings of the 13th international conference on world wide web. ACM, New York, pp 30–39

3
CHAPTER

A FRAMEWORK OF IDENTITY RESOLUTION: EVALUATING IDENTITY ATTRIBUTES AND MATCHING ALGORITHMS

Jiexun Li and Alan G. Wang

Keywords: Identity resolution, Social behavior, Social relationship, Collective clustering

INTRODUCTION

The world is moving away from paper-based documents to electronic records. Due to the ease of generating identity records and lack of sufficient verification or validation during data entry processes, duplicate and false identity records become quite common in electronic systems. In many practices of identity management, especially those that require integrating multiple data sources, it is often inevitable and tedious to deal with the problem of identity duplication. Particularly, finding an effective solution to this problem is extremely critical in fighting crime and terrorism to enforce national security. Criminals and terrorists often assume fake identities using either fraudulent or legitimate means so as to hide their true identity. In a number of cases documented by government reports, terrorists in different countries are known to commit identity crimes, such as falsifying passports and baptismal certificates, to facilitate their financial operations and execution of attacks, either in the real world or in the cyber space [1, 2]. The problem of an individual having multiple identities can easily mislead intelligence and law enforcement investigators [3]. Therefore, to determine whether an individual is who they claim to be is essential in the mission of counterterrorism to identify potential terrorists and prevent terrorism acts from occurring [4]. Identity resolution is a process of semantic reconciliation that determines whether a single identity is the same when

Citation: Jiexun Li and Alan G. Wang, A framework of identity resolution: evaluating identity attributes and matching algorithms, DOI: 10.1186/s13388-015-0021-0

being described differently [5]. The goal of resolution is to detect duplicate identity records that refer to the same individual in the real world. Over the years, researchers in the areas of database and statistics have proposed many different techniques to tackle this problem. Traditional resolution techniques rely on key attributes such as identification numbers, names and date-of-birth to detect matches. These attributes are commonly used for they are simple describers of an individual and often available in most record management systems [6, 7]. However, such personal identity attributes also vary in terms of availability and reliability across different systems. These attributes are not always accurate due to various reasons such as unintentional entry errors and intentional deception [6]. In the context of cybersecruity, it is much easier and more common for criminals to fake identities to cover their traces. In order to improve resolution accuracy, several recently proposed resolution techniques have taken into account social contextual information, in addition to traditionally used descriptive identity attributes, as new evidence for identity matching [5, 8, 9]. Social contextual information, such as employment history, credit history and friendship networks, has shown to be effective in identity resolution because it is very difficult to be manipulated [10].

A review of related work leads us to believe that, although a variety of identity resolution techniques have been developed, there is not a comprehensive framework that covers various types of identity attributes and matching algorithms. This leads to the main goal of our study. In this paper, we provide an overview of various identity attributes that are useful to computational identity resolution. We develop an identity resolution framework that comprehensively considers both profile-based personal identity attributes and social identity attributes, especially with a focus on the latter. Our framework also considers different computational algorithms for matching identities, ranging from simple pairwise matching to collective clustering. Compared to existing identity resolution research, our proposed framework has the following advantages. First, the framework is generic and applicable to most record management system without introducing an overhaul in the database schema. Second, the integration of both personal and social attributes provides complementary and convincing evidence for identity resolution. Third, the collective resolution technique makes joint decisions on matching identities and therefore leads to more accurate results.

The remainder of the paper is organized as follows. We first review identity theories and existing resolution techniques. Next, we introduce our proposed identity resolution framework including several matching techniques based on various attributes and algorithms. We report a comparative study of several resolution techniques in the framework using a synthetic dataset and a real-world dataset. Finally, we conclude the paper with a summary and a discussion on future research directions.

LITERATURE REVIEW

In this section, we review existing identity resolution approaches, with a focus on the identity attributes and matching techniques adopted.

Entity Resolution and Identity Resolution

Identity resolution is a special type of entity resolution that specializes in identity management. Entity resolution is also known as record linkage and deduplication in the areas of statistics and database management. Record linkage, originated in the statistics community, is used to identify those records in one or multiple datasets that refer to the same real-world entity [11]. The very same task is often called and studied as record deduplication in database and artificial intelligence communities [12, 13, 14]. Given a number of records that are comprised of multiple fields, these techniques determine whether two records match by comparing the values in corresponding fields. A good survey on individual field matching models for record deduplication can be found in [15].

Entity resolution techniques can be extended to different contexts, e.g., identity resolution in identity management. However, as a special type of entity resolution, identity resolution can be very complex due to the special data characteristics of identity records. First, identity resolution, especially in the intelligence and law enforcement communities, often suffers greatly from the missing data problem [7]. Missing values, if present in many fields of a record, can present a big challenge for identity resolution techniques. Second, identity resolution needs to handle not only duplicates caused by entry errors or data ambiguities but also intentional identity fraud and deception, which tend to be hidden and concealed. Third, identity resolution techniques may need to be adjustable to different evaluation criteria. For instance, false positives may be less tolerable than false negatives for identity authentication that grants access to a critical facility. In contrast, a high false positive rate may not be a big concern when a detective searches for records related to a crime suspect with limited information. Therefore, accurate identity resolution requires a careful design that considers the special characteristics of identity records.

Identity Attributes

Based on the identity theories from the social science literature, an individual's identity is considered to have two basic components, namely a personal identity and a social identity. A personal identity is one's self-perception as an individual, whereas a social identity is one's biographical history that builds up over time [16]. In particular, one's personal identity may include personal information given at birth (e.g., name, date and place of birth), personal identifiers (e.g., social security number), physical descriptions (e.g., height, weight), and biometric information (e.g., fingerprint, DNA). In contrast, a social identity is concerned with one's existence in a social context. Social identity theories consist of psychological and sociological views. The psychological view defines a social identity as one's self-perception as a member of certain social groups such as nation, culture, gender identification, and employment [17, 18]. The sociological view focuses on "the relationships between social actors who perform mutually complementary roles (e.g., employer-employee, doctor-patient)" [19]. While psychological view deals with large-scale groups, the sociological view emphasizes the role-based interpersonal relationships among people [20]. These two views combined together provide a more complete concept for understanding a social identity at levels of social context. Traditional identity resolution methods primarily rely on personal identity attributes such as name, gender, date of birth, and identification numbers mostly because they are commonly available as identifiers in record management systems. These attributes, however, may suffer from data quality problems such as unintentional errors [21], intentional deception [6], and missing data [7]. Biometric features such as fingerprints and DNA also belong to the category of personal attributes. Although they are considered as more reliable, they are not available or accessible due to issues such as high costs and confidentiality in most systems. A study conducted by the United Kingdom Home office [22] suggests that identity crimes usually involve the illegal use or alteration of those personal identity components. The low data quality in fact-based personal attributes can severely jeopardize the performance of identity resolution [7].

Individuals are not isolated but interconnected to each another in a society. The social context associated with an individual can be clues that reveal his or her undeniable identity. Recognizing the limitations of personal attributes, many recent studies have started exploiting social context information such as social behaviors and relationships for identity resolution. For example, Ananthakrishna et al. [23] introduced a method that eliminates duplicates in data warehouses using a dimensional hierarchy (e.g., city-state-country) over the link relations. This method scales up the ability of the matching technique by only comparing attribute values that have the same foreign key dependency. For example, the similarity of two identity records will be computed only when they both live in the same city. Kalashnikov et al. [24] incorporated co-affiliation and co-authorship relationships into an resolution model for reference disambiguation. Köpcke and Rahm [25] categorized entity resolution approaches into attribute value matchers and context matchers. While value matchers solely rely on descriptive attributes, context matchers consider information inferred from social interactions represented as linkages in a graph.

Resolution Techniques

We can categorize existing resolution techniques into rule-based and machine learning approaches. There have been several rule-based identity resolution approaches based on matching rules encoded by domain experts. For instance, to integrate cross-jurisdictional criminal records, a simple rule can be: two identity records match only if their first name, last name, and date-of-birth (DOB) values are all identical [26]. Such exact-match heuristics tend to have high specificity but low sensitivity in detecting true matches, especially when data quality problems such as missing values, entry errors and deceptions are present. Hence, a good resolution technique must support partial-match as well to reduce false negatives. IBM's InfoSphere Identity Insight is a leading commercial software platform for entity resolution and analysis. It provides an identity analytics solution with a set of rules predefined by human experts as well as sophisticated algorithms. For example, given two identity records with identical dates of birth and last names, the system will resolve them into one if the matching score of their first names is above a threshold. The most critical asset and the biggest challenge of a rule-based system is the creation of the rule set. Creating a compressive rule sets can be highly time-consuming and expensive. Furthermore, rules could be domain-dependent and not portable across different contexts. As an alternative to manual rule coding, machine learning can automatically extract patterns from annotated training data with annotated matching pairs and build resolution models for new identity records. Given a pair of identity records, distance/similarity measures are defined for different descriptive attributes and then combined into an overall score. If the overall distance (or similarity) score is below (or above) a pre-defined threshold, then the pair should be regarded as a match. Brown and Hagen [27] proposed a data association method for linking criminal records that possibly refer to the same suspect. This method compares two records and calculates a total similarity measure as a weighted-sum of the similarity measures of all corresponding feature values. Similarly, Wang et al. [6] proposed a record linkage algorithm for detecting deceptive identities by comparing four personal attributes (name, DOB, social security number, and address) and combining them into an overall similarity score. A supervised learning process determines a threshold for match decisions using a set of identity pairs labeled by an expert. However, these methods based on a limited number of descriptive attributes tend to fail if one or more of these attributes contains missing values [7]. Rather than simply labeling an identity pair as match or non-match, probabilistic methods for identity resolution root in the seminal work of [11]. By posing record linkage as a probabilistic classification problem, they propose a formal framework to predict the likelihood of matching identity pairs based on the agreement among attributes. Assuming conditional independence among features given the match class, the framework estimates the probabilistic parameters of the record linkage model in an unsupervised fashion. Built upon this work, many later studies follow and extend this framework by enriching the probabilistic model [7, 28, 29, 30]. These studies have shown that the probabilistic models achieve good performance for identity matching. However, the parameters of the probabilistic models may not be accurately estimated in the absence of sufficient training data [31].

More machine learning based techniques have been proposed for the more general problem of entity resolution. Culotta and McCallum [32] constructed a conditional random field model (CRF) for record deduplication that captures inter-dependencies between different types of entities. This method, however, fails to model the explicit links among the same type of entities. Pasula et al. [9] proposed a citation matching approach based on probabilistic relational model (PRM), which is built upon dependences among entities in a relational database schema through foreign key relationships. Li et al. [3] developed a systematic approach to deriving social behavior and social relationship features for identity matching based on a database schema and PRMs. This approach can be used as a plug-and-play solution for most relational database-based record management systems. For less structured collections of record data (e.g., criminal reports, news articles), a lot of efforts for information extraction and transformation will be needed. Bhattacharya and Getoor [33] proposed a graph-based method for entity resolution. It defines a similarity measure that combines corresponding attribute similarities with graph-based relational similarity between each entity reference pair. Furthermore, Bhattacharya and Getoor [8] extended their relational resolution approach and introduced a collective entity resolution algorithm. Rather than simply making pair-wise entity comparisons, their method can derive new social information from decisions already made and incorporate it into further resolution process iteratively. More recently, in order to tackle the problem of one individual having several profiles on different social media platforms (e.g., Facebook and Twitter), researchers have developed techniques for matching user profiles. Bartunov et al. [34] developed a CRF-based approach that combines two user graphs using both user profile attributes and social linkages. All these studies have demonstrated that social information, when incorporated in matching algorithms, can improve the performance for identity resolution.

Research Gap

According to our literature review, many researchers have recognized the limitations of traditional identity resolution techniques that solely rely on personal identity attributes such as name and DOB. Although these profile-based identity attributes are available in most record management systems, they are subject to data entry errors, deception, and fraud [6]. Hence, techniques based on such attributes would fail drastically in recognizing the unconventional truth like the synonym between Osama bin Laden and The Prince [35]. Several recent studies have demonstrated the benefits of utilizing social contextual information in identity resolution [3, 36]. However, most studies lack the guidance of identity theories to construct and examine different types of social attributes for identity resolution. Identity theories suggest that personal and social identity may complement each other for the purpose of identity resolution. The social aspect of identity reflects one's psychological and sociological perception of his/her own identity. Social identity attributes might be more reliable than personal profiles in that they cannot be easily altered or falsified by an individual. Furthermore, existing resolution techniques mainly employ pair-wise comparison [6, 27, 37, 38] when finding matching identity records. Entity resolution studies have shown that resolution accuracy can improve significantly if matching of related identity references are performed in a collective fashion [8]. The effectiveness of a collective approach in the context of identity resolution is yet to be examined. Built upon our previous work in [39], this study is to develop a comprehensive identity resolution framework by examining a variety of identity attributes and evaluating different matching strategies.

A framework of identity resolution

In this study, we aim to contribute to the field of identity resolution from the following three aspects:

- Developing a comprehensive framework of identity resolution that covers both the usage of identity attributes and matching algorithms;
- Examining the predictive powers of personal identity attributes and social identity features for resolution; and
- Evaluating different matching algorithms for identity resolution.

Problem Definition

We define the identity resolution problem as follows. Given a set of identity references, $R=\{r_i\}$, where each reference r is described by a set of attributes $r.A_1, r.A_2, \ldots, r.A_l$

. These references correspond to a set of unknown individual $E=\{e_i\}$. Due to certain reasons (e.g., entry errors, duplicates or deceptions), multiple references may be co-referent to the same underlying individual e. We use r.E to refer to the individual to which reference r refers to. Each reference r may have participated in some incident(s) (e.g., a financial transaction, a criminal misconduct, a terrorist attack) and each incident may involve one or multiple references. We use a set of hyper-edges $H=\{h_i\}$ to represent all incidents. Each incident is a hyper-edge that connects multiple references. Each hyper-edge h can also be described by a set of attributes $h.B_1$, $h.B_2$, …, $h.B_m$. We use h.R to denote the set of references involved in h. We use r.H to denote the set of hyper-edges in which r participates. In addition, the participation of r in h can be described by a set of attributes $r.h.C_1$, $r.h.C_2$, …, $r.h.C_n$. The objective is to uncover the hidden set of individuals $E=\{e_i\}$ and the entity labels r.E for all references given the observations of the references and their involved hyper-edges.

Figure 1 illustrates the problem of identity resolution in a graph of five reference nodes connected by three hyper-edges. In this graph, two nodes (references) r_1 and r_2 are in fact co-referent to the same person; r_4 and r_5 are co-referent to another person. Our goal is to uncover the underlying matches from the graph. In addition to simply comparing the node-level attributes of references, we should also consider the attributes related to their involved incidents, represented by hyper-edges. For example, if h_1 and h_2 share some similar patterns (e.g., incident type, time of day), or if r_1 and r_2 have similar patterns (e.g., role, activeness) in their participation in h_1 and $h_2$respectively, these should be considered as supporting evidence for r_1 and r_2 being co-referent to the same individual. Furthermore, Moreover, the common neighbor r_3 shared by r_1 and r_2 can also indicate potential linkage between the pair. Furthermore, once r_1 and r_2 are determined to be co-referent, the joining of these two can bring in new contextual information for inferring the matching relationship between other identity references (e.g., r_4 andr $_5$). We will discuss how to mathematically represent and compute such evidence in the rest of Section "A framework of identity resolution".

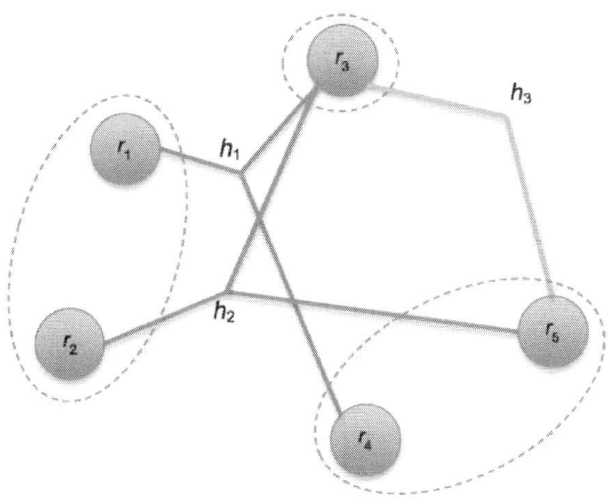

Figure. 1 A graphic view of the identity resolution problem.

To solve this problem, we develop a framework of identity resolution by considering two aspects: identity attributes and matching algorithms. Identity attributes are features that can be used to describe certain distinctive characteristics of identity references. A matching algorithm defines the computational procedure of recovering the matching entities from the given set of references. In this section we first define various types of identity attributes that can be used in identity resolution. We also discuss how we calculate the similarity for each type of identity attributes. Lastly, we introduce several matching algorithms that match identity references based on attribute similarities.

Identity Attributes

To determine whether two references are co-referent, we need to compare their common attributes and calculate corresponding similarity scores for these attributes. Given our problem definition, we divide all identity attributes into three categories and describe their similarity measures as follows.

Personal Identity Attributes

Personal identity attributes are identifiers that are commonly used in record management systems to distinguish one person from others. In our problem definition, each reference r is represented by a node in the graph. Personal identity attributes are the node-level attributes, $r.A_1$, $r.A_2$, …, $r.A_l$, Examples include but not limited to name, date of birth, social security number, and passport number. For an attribute in text format, the similarity between two attribute values can be calculated by edit distance measures such as the Levenstein Distance [40]. For an attribute in number or date format, absolute difference or percentage difference can be used as similarity measure. We usep to refer to resolution approaches based on personal identity attributes alone:

$$sim_p(r_i, r_j) = \frac{1}{l}\sum_{k=1}^{l} sim(r_i.A_k, r_j.A_k). \quad (1)$$

If the similarity score $sim_p(r_i, r_j)$ is above a threshold, references r_i and r_j are considered to be co-referent. These approaches tend to perform well for references with duplicates and typos, but are likely to have low recall for cases involving intentional deceptions.

Social behavior attributes

Based on social identity theories, we consider an individual's behaviors in the society as reflections of his/her underlying identity. Social behavior attributes represent the common characteristics of the social group(s) that one belongs to. They reflect the psychological view of personal identity. Most identity management systems contains information about incidents (e.g., credit card transactions, crime misconducts) related to each individuals. In our problem definition, each incident is denoted by a hyper-edge in the graph. Therefore, we use incident-based behavioral patterns to describe the characteristics of an individual. Each hyper-edge h is associated with a set of attributes $h.B_1$, $h.B_2$, …, $h.B_m$ (e.g., transaction day/time/amount, crime type). In addition, the participation of r in hhas a set of attributes $r.h.C_1$, $r.h.C_2$, …, $r.h.C_n$ (e.g., role, start/end time). Such attributes, capturing information about how individual behave in certain incidents, should also be considered as social behavior attributes for identity resolution. It is worth noting that this type of participating attributes was not considered in previous work [8, 39], adding these attributes has enriched the social behavior attributes and made this a more comprehensive framework of identity resolution. We denote the set of hyper-edges involving reference r as r.H. Then, each hyper-edge r_i.hinvolving r_i is compared with each hyper-edge r_j.h› of r_j based on attributes $\{B_k\}$ and $\{C_k\}$. The overall behavior similarity between r_i and r_j, $sim_b(r_i, r_j)$, is the average of similarity scores between each hyper-edge pairs:

$$sim_b(r_i, r_j) = sim_b(r_i.H, r_j.H) = \frac{1}{|r_i.H| \times |r_j.H|} \sum_{h \in r_i.H, h' \in r_j.H} sim_b(r_i.h, r_j.h'),$$

where |r.H| denotes the number of hyper-edges involving r, and $sim_b(r_i.h, r_j.h')$ is defined as the average similarity score for each attribute of $h.B_k$ and $r.h.C_k$:

$$sim_b(r_i.h, r_j.h') = \frac{1}{2mn}\left(n\sum_{k=1}^{m} sim(h.B_k, h'.B_k) + m\sum_{k=1}^{n} sim(r_i.h.C_k, r_j.h'.C_k)\right).$$

Social relationship attributes

The sociological view is the other level of a social identity that concerns with social relationships of an individual. We can define social relationship attributes to capture this aspect of social identities. If two references r_i and r_j are both related to the same reference r_k (e.g., r_i and r_j co-occur with r_k in different hyper-edges), this can be regarded as evidence that these two references are co-referent. We denote the neighborhood of a reference r as Nbr(r). Then, the neighborhood similarity between two references r_i and r_j, $sim_n(r_i, r_j)$, can be defined as:

$$sim_n(r_i, r_j) = sim_n(Nbr(r_i), Nbr(r_j)) = sim_n(r_i.H, r_j.H).$$

To compute the neighborhood similarity between references r_i and r_j, we define hyper-edge neighborhood similarity $sim_n(h_i, h_j)$ between two hyper-edges h_i and h_j as a pair-wise match between their references.

Here, the relational similarity between two hyper-edges h_i and h_j is computed as the maximum of the similarity score between a reference $r \in h_i.R$ and a reference $r› \in h_j.R$:

$$sim_n(h_i, h_j) = \max_{r \in h_i.R, r' \in h_j.R}(sim_p(r, r')).$$

Furthermore, the neighborhood similarity between two references r_i and r_j is defined as:

$$sim_n(r_i, r_j) = \frac{1}{|r_i.H| \times |r_j.H|} \sum_{h \in r_i.H, h' \in r_j.H} sim_n(r_i.h, r_j.h'),$$

where |r.H| still denotes the number of hyper-edges involving r. It is worth noting that the neighborhood of referencer contains r. Thus, if two references r_i and r_j do not share any common neighbor, their neighborhood similarity $sim_n(r_i, r_j)$ is equal to their personal identity attribute similarity $sim_p(r_i, r_j)$. In other words, two references having the same/similar neighbors can be regarded as evidence to support that they are more likely to be co-referent, whereas two references not sharing a common neighbor will not be treated as evidence of them not being co-referent.

Besides, we can define a negative constraint based on social relationship, i.e., two references that co-occur in the same hyper-edge cannot refer to the same individual. It is unlikely that one real-world individual can assume two different identities in one unique incident.

Aggregated similarity score

For a pair of references r_i and r_j, we have defined three scores that measure their similarity based on personal identity, social behavior and social relationship attributes. In order to take into account different attributes for identity resolution, we need to aggregate these similarity scores to an overall score.

Here we use a weighted average method to computing the overall similarity. It is worth noting that, before being combined, similarity scores should be normalized to the same scale, e.g., in the range of [0, 1]. Thus, the overall similarity score between two references r_i and r_j is a weighted average of all similarity scores: i.e., personal identity similarity, social behavior similarity, and social neighborhood similarity:

$$AVG(r_i, r_j) = \alpha \times sim_p(r_i, r_j) + \beta \times sim_b(r_i, r_j) + (1 - \alpha - \beta) \times sim_n(r_i, r_j)$$

where weights $0 \leq \alpha, \beta \leq \alpha + \beta \leq 1$ and they can be adjusted to control the importance of the three similarity scores.

If $\alpha - 1$, then only personal identity similarity is considered and $AVG(r_i, r_j)$ is simply $sim_a(r_i, r_j)$. We represent this as $sim_A(r_i, r_j)$.

If $\alpha, \beta > 0$ and $\alpha + \beta = 1$, then $AVG(r_i, r_j)$ is the average of personal identity similarity and social behavior similarity whereas social neighborhood similarity is not considered. We represent this as $sim_B(r_i, r_j)$. If $0 < \alpha, \beta \leq \alpha + \beta < 1$, then all three similarity scores are considered in the average score. We represent this as $sim_R(r_i, r_j)$.

Matching algorithms

Given a collection of references and similarity measures defined above, we still design an algorithmic process to traverse and compare all identity pairs and eventually reveal all underlying individuals. Here, we describe three matching algorithms in existing resolution techniques, namely pairwise comparison, transitive closure, and collective clustering.

Pairwise comparison

Pair-wise comparison is a basic and simple procedure for entity resolution. For each pair of references r_i and r_j, we can compute the similarity score using one of the aforementioned functions. If the similarity score $sim(r_i, r_j)$ is greater than a predefined threshold θ, we conclude that r_i and r_j are co-referent. Figure 2 shows the pseudo-code of this algorithm:

```
For each pair of two different references (r_i, r_j) in R×R
    Compute their similarity sim(r_i, r_j)
    If sim(r_i, r_j) is greater than threshold
        Predict the pair (r_i, r_j) as a match
```

Figure. 2 Pseudo-code of pairwise comparison.

Transitive closure

The outcome of pairwise comparison only tells whether each reference pair matches or not. Technically, this still has not yet uncovered the underlying individuals in the reference collection. Consider a simple example where references r_i and r_j are a match, r_j and r_k are also a match, while r_i and r_k are determined to be a non-match. In this case, the pair-wise comparison may produce conflicting resolution outcomes. Hence, to uncover the underlying individuals, an extra step is to use transitive closure and merge all related matching results. In the previous example, even though r_i and r_k are not sufficiently similar, we still consider them as a co-referent pair because r_i matches r_j and r_j matches r_k. This process should be performed iteratively until all transitive closures are reached. Finally, each transitive closure is considered as a distinct individual. Given the output from pairwise comparison, computing transitive closures is straightforward and efficient. However, it is worth noting that such a merging process lowers the threshold of the matching criteria. As a result, it tends to reduce false negatives but introduce more false positives. Figure 3 shows the pseudo-code of this algorithm. Specifically, at Step 4, the results of pairwise comparison in 3.3.1 is used to judge if two references r and r› match. This process does require recalculating any similarity scores. The minimum distance between references from two clusters is simply considered as the distance between the two clusters. In this sense, this algorithm is a single-linkage or nearest neighbor clustering method.

1.	**Initialize each reference as a cluster**
2.	**For each cluster c_i**
3.	**For each cluster c_j**
4.	**If $\exists$ $r \in c_i$ and $r' \in c_j$ s.t. r matches r'**
5.	**Merge c_i and c_j**

Figure. 3 Pseudo-code of transitive closure

Collective clustering

Collective clustering is a different matching technique for identity resolution [8]. It adopts a greedy agglomerative clustering algorithm to find the most similar references (or clusters) and merge them. There are some fundamental differences between this algorithm with the two introduced above.

Collective clustering does requires defining a similarity function on clusters of references. Each cluster formed is considered the same real-world individual. Unlike transitive closure that uses single-linkage clustering, collective clustering uses an average linkage approach instead. It defines the similarity between two clusters c_i and c_j as the average similarity between each reference in c_i and each reference in c_j:

$$sim(c_i, c_j) = \frac{1}{|c_i.R| \times |c_j.R|} \sum_{r \in c_j.R, r' \in c_j.R} sim(c_j.r, c_j.r'),$$

where |c.R| represents the number of references in cluster c.

Figure 4 shows the pseudo-code of this algorithm. Like transitive closure, collective clustering begins with assigning each reference to a different cluster. Iteratively, this algorithm computes the between-cluster similarity and merges the most similar pair of clusters until the similarity drops below the predefined threshold. As clusters merge, one cluster can contain multiple references that are determined to be co-referent. A critical step in this algorithm is that, every time two clusters are merged, all similarity scores that involve references from the merged clusters must be recomputed. Specifically, the merging of two clusters c_i and c_j into one, which could change the linkage structures in the graph, should be regarded as new evidence for computing the similarity between other references that co-occur with those in c_i and c_j. Such an iterative computational procedure, which takes into account resolution decisions on all nodes in the graph jointly, makes this clustering algorithm collective and distinguishes it with the other pairwise comparison based algorithms.

```
1.  Initialize each reference as a cluster
2.  Compute the similarity between each cluster pair
3.  Find the cluster pair with the maximal sim*(c_i, c_j)
4.  If sim*(c_i, c_j) greater than threshold
5.      Merge c_i and c_j
6.      Go to Step 2
```

Figure. 4 Pseudo-code of collective clustering.

Complexity analysis

For a collection of n references, a complete pairwise comparison approach considers all possible reference pairs as potential candidates for merging. Such a process has a complexity of $O(n^2)$. The collective clustering algorithm involves an iterative procedure of recalculating cluster similarities and therefore requires even more computation. Apart from the scaling issue, in reality most pairs will be rejected while often times only less than 1 % of pairs are real matches. Hence, certain blocking steps should be incorporated and performed before matching so as to screen out highly unlikely candidate pairs for matching. There are various blocking techniques but they often employ one simple and computationally cheap function to group references into a number of buckets. Buckets can overlap so one reference can belong to multiple buckets. Only reference pairs within the same bucket should be considered candidate pairs for comparing and merging, whereas a pair of references from two different buckets is not considered as candidate for further comparison. For collective clustering, two clusters must have all of their references belonging to the same bucket to make them a candidate pair to be compared and possibly merged. Furthermore, in the agglomerative clustering process, it is not necessary to recalculate the similarity scores for every cluster pair. Only those involving references from the merged clusters need to be recomputed. We have implemented these aforementioned strategies for reducing complexity in our evaluation. More strategies for reducing the complexity of collective clustering can be found in [8].

COMPARATIVE EVALUATION

In this study, we conducted a comparative evaluation of identity resolution techniques based on different identity attributes and matching algorithms. We describe our experiments and discuss our findings in this section.

Datasets

Our evaluation used both a computer-generated synthetic dataset and a real-world dataset. The synthetic dataset was used to conduct a more comprehensive empirical evaluation on the proposed framework. The real-world dataset was used to test the usefulness and reliability of the proposed framework in a real setting.

A synthetic dataset

Synthetic data allows us to embed ground truth in the data generated for algorithm testing. Here, we adopted a two-staged data generation method, as described in Fig. 5.

```
Creation Stage
1.  Repeat N times
2.    Create entity e
3.    Create attribute x to represent e's node attribute
4.    Create attribute y to represent e's hyper-edge attribute
5.    Create attribute z to represent e's participating attribute
6.  Repeat M times
7.    Choose entities e_i and e_j with P_b(e_i, e_j)
8.    Set e_i = Nbr(e_j) and e_j = Nbr(e_i)

Generation Stage
1.  Repeat L times
2.    Randomly choose entity e
3.    With P_a, select reference r for e or generate r using N(e.x, 1)
4.    Initialize hyper-edge h = <r>
5.    Repeat with probability P_c
6.      Randomly choose e_j from Nbr(e) without replacement
7.      With P_a, select reference r_j for e_j or generate r_j using N(e_j.x,1)
8.      Add r_j to hyper-edge h
9.  Assign hyper-edge h's attribute: h.y = average(h.r.e.y)
10. For each r in h
11.   Assign r's attribute in h: r.h.z = (r.e.z+h.y)/2
```

Figure. 5 Pseudo-code of synthetic data generation.

In the creation stage the algorithm first creates N entities with a node attribute x, a hyper-edge attribute y, and a participating attribute z. We differentiate these three attributes because personal identity attributes (x) can be easily modified or falsified whereas social behavior attributes (y and z) tend to be more consistent and less likely to change significantly over time. Next, we create M linkages among these N entities to represent their underlying social relationships. When we create these links, two entities with similar social behavior attribute y, are more likely to be connected to each other with a probability of $P_b(e_i, e_j) = P_b^{|e_i.y - e_j.y|}$, i.e., i.e., two individuals with similar interests or behavioral patterns are more likely to be related. In the generation stage, we created R hyper-edges that included a set of related entities. An entity may join a hyper-edge of its neighbor with a probability of P_c. Whenever an entity is to join a hyper-edge, we either choose an existing reference of this entity with a probability P_a or create a new reference with its attribute x value following a Gaussian distribution of N(e.x, 1). Each reference rjoins at least one hyper-edge. Each hyper-edge is also assigned an attribute y, which is equal to the average of all participating entities' behavior attribute y. This is to assure the hyper-edge's attribute value not quite distant from the participating entities'. Similarly, for each participating reference r in h, we assign its participating attribute as the average of the underlying entity's attribute r.e.z and the hyper-edge's attribute h.y.

It is worth noting that this synthetic data generator is based on a method used in [8] but has two major differences. First, for each entity, we define a separate attribute y to represent one's behavior characteristics that can be reflected and observed in its involved hyper-edges. Second, our synthetic data allow a reference to join more than one hyper-edge, while in [8] each reference only joins a single hyper-edge. This is more realistic in real-world identity management scenarios and requires more cost in computing similarities between references.

In our experiments, we chose the following parameter values for generating the synthetic data: N=50, M=100, L=200, P_a =0.8, P_b =0.9, P_c =0.6, and the value ranges of attributes x, y and z were set to [0, 100). With such parameter settings, we generated 50 sets of synthetic data and compared different resolution approaches. Since we limit the attribute values to be a number between 0 and 100 instead of actual identity attribute values (e.g., DOB, name), we simplified the similarity calculation introduced in Section "Identity attributes" as follows:

The similarity between two hyper-edges is defined as:

$$sim(h_i, h_j) = \frac{|h_i.y - h_j.y|}{range(y)}$$

The similarity between two participations of references in hyper-edges is defined as:

$$sim(r_i.h, r_j.h') = \frac{|r_i.h.z - r_j.h'.z|}{range(z)}$$

A real dataset

Ideally, to empirically evaluate and compare these identity resolution techniques, we need a real-world dataset in which duplicate identity records exist. In previous literature of entity resolution, many researchers have used citation data as test bed [8]. In order to better differentiate the three types of identity attributes, in this study we chose to use a dataset manually extracted from a set of public web pages and news stories related to terrorism and subjectively linked entities mentioned in the articles. These pages and articles were mostly hosted by web sites of governments and news organizations. This data set was originally collected and annotated by Kubica et al. [41]. It has been used in several studies for testing link analysis and alias detection [35, 42]. In total, this dataset consists of 4088 entity names. Among them, there are 164 names of terrorists. These 164 names have been manually reviewed and recognized as co-references of 20 unique individuals including well-known names such as Osama Bin Laden andAbdel Muaz.

For instance, there are 12 different names and references for Osama Bin Laden. In addition, this dataset also consists of 5581 links among these 4088 names, representing their co-occurrence relationships in articles.

The terrorist names are only a small subset of the entire set of 4088 names. For each terrorist name, we regard all its associated non-terrorist names as its social behavior attributes and all its linked terrorist names as its social relationship attributes.

Experimental design

n the experiments, we compared different identity resolution techniques in our framework. For identity attributes, we considered the following three sets, which cumulatively added one type of attributes on top of existing ones:

- personal identity attributes alone;
- personal identity + social behavior attributes; and
- personal identity + social behavior + social relationship attributes

For each attribute set, we conducted identity resolution using one of the three matching algorithms: pair-wise comparison, transitive closure, and collective clustering. Since the collective clustering algorithm involves social linkages between individuals, our implementation of this algorithm captures all three types of attributes. Table 1 lists seven combinations of identity attributes and matching algorithms that correspond to seven identity resolution approaches we tested in our comparative experiments. Each technique is given an acronym as shown.

Table 1 Experiment design: identity attributes vs. matching algorithms

Attributes			
Algorithms	**Personal Identity**	**Personal Identity + Social Behavior**	**Personal Identity + Social Behavior + Social Relationship**
Pair-wise Comparison	A	B	R
Transitive Closure	A*	B*	R*
Collective Resolution	--	--	CR

We evaluated the performance of each identity resolution approach by checking the correctness of the matching decisions for each reference pair. We followed most identity resolution studies and chose precision, recall and F-measure as our evaluation metrics [8]. As illustrated in Table 2, each matching decision on a pair of references is either a “match” (positive) or a “non-match” (negative). A decision can be either true or false.

Table 2 Possible outcomes of matching decisions

	Decision	
Reality	**Match**	**Non-match**
Match	True positive (TP)	False negative (FN)
Non-match	False positive (FP)	True negative (TN)

Based on the decision outcomes, precision, recall, and F-measure are defined as follows:

$$precision = \frac{TP}{TP+FP}$$

$$recall = \frac{TP}{TP+FN}$$

$$F-measure = \frac{2\times precision\times recall}{precision+recall}$$

RESULTS AND DISCUSSION

Results for synthetic data

In our experiment on the synthetic dataset, we used the weighted average approach to aggregate all similarity scores. We experimented with different parameter settings so as to have a more comprehensive comparison of different identity resolution techniques. We also experimented with different weight parameter values for α (0.0~1.0) and β (0.0~0.5). Table 3 summarizes the best performance for each of the seven resolution techniques. Solely using personal identity attributes (represented by x in our synthetic data), method A tends to have high recall (92.62 %) but very low precision (9.43 %). If two identity references have very similar personal identity attributes, A tends to consider them co-referent. Method B takes into account social behavior attributes represented by y and zin our synthetic data. It achieved significantly higher precision (85.66 %) at the cost of lower recall (37.71 %) but higher F-measure (44.37 %) than A. Furthermore, method R added social relationship attributes and achieved better performance than B in terms of recall (37.87 %) and F-measure (50.41 %). The three methods using transitive closures (A*, B*, R*) did not seem to give significantly better results than their corresponding pairwise comparison methods. Notably, the collective resolution algorithm CR achieved the highest precision (87.95 %) and the highest F-measure (58.17 %), which were both significantly higher than those of the other six methods. Therefore, our experiments on the synthetic data demonstrated that, by considering all three types of identity attributes and matching references in a collective and iterative manner, CR is a more effective method for identity resolution.

Table 3 Peformance of identity resolution for synthetic data

Method	*α*	*β*	1-*α*-*β*	Precision	Recall	F-measure
A	1.0	0.0	0.0	9.43 %	92.62 %	16.97 %
A*	1.0	0.0	0.0	7.72 %	94.27 %	14.16 %
B	0.7	0.3	0.0	85.66 %	30.71 %	44.37 %
B*	0.7	0.3	0.0	85.02 %	31.21 %	44.71 %
R	0.5	0.25	0.25	79.22 %	37.87 %	50.41 %
R*	0.5	0.25	0.25	77.11 %	38.64 %	50.44 %
CR	0.5	0.25	0.25	87.95 %	44.15 %	58.17 %

Results for real-world data

In the empirical evaluation on the real-world dataset, we also experimented with aggregated similarity scores under different parameter settings so as to have a more comprehensive comparison of the identity resolution techniques. Specifically, we compared different weight values for α (0.0~1.0) and β (0.0~0.5). Table 4 shows the best performance of the identity resolution techniques achieved and their corresponding parameter settings.

Table 4 Peformance of identity resolution for real-world data

Method	*α*	*β*	1-*α*-*β*	Precision	Recall	F-measure
A	1.0	0.0	0.0	48.59 %	18.50 %	26.79 %
A*	1.0	0.0	0.0	48.59 %	18.50 %	26.79 %
B	0.9	0.1	0.0	57.98 %	16.47 %	25.65 %
B*	0.9	0.1	0.0	57.98 %	16.47 %	25.65 %
R	0.1	0.0	0.9	97.29 %	38.54 %	55.21 %
R*	0.1	0.0	0.9	97.29 %	38.54 %	55.21 %
CR	0.6	0.0	0.4	99.34 %	54.30 %	70.22 %

Table 4 summaries the performance of identity resolution methods using weighted average scores. When α=0.6, β=0.0 and 1-α-β=0.4, the collective clustering resolution (CR) achieved the highest precision (99.34 %), recall (54.30 %), and F-measures (70.22 %).

Discussion

Our experiment results for the synthetic data show that, with the same matching algorithm, using personal identity attributes alone may achieve higher recall but at the cost of low precision and F-measure. As social behavior attributes being taken into account, we observed a significant boost in both precision and F-measure. This shows that social behavior attributes do contribute to the performance improvement of identity resolution by reducing false positives. Furthermore, when social relationship attributes were also considered, there were some minor drops in precision but with generally higher F-measure. As confirmed by results for both synthetic and real data, the approaches using all three types of identity attributes (R, R* and CR) outperformed its baselines in terms of F-measure. In particular, the collective clustering algorithm (CR), which not only considers all types of personal and social attributes but makes matching decisions on identities in a collective fashion, was demonstrated to be the optimal methods that outperform all others.

Notably, the optimal parameter values (i.e., α and β) varied in our experiments across the two datasets and different algorithms. In general, α was greater than β, indicating personal identity attributes being more important than social relationship attributes. Particularly for the real-world dataset, β values were very small for algorithms B and B* and zero for R, R*, and CR. The results show that social behavior attributes did not help much in finding matching terrorists. In our study, we considered a terrorist's associated non-terrorist names as his/her social behavior attributes. The low β values may be caused by the nature of terrorist incidents, which each time involve different non-terrorist people such as victims. The weight for social relationship attributes, $1-\alpha-\beta$, was high in R, R*, and CR, which showed the important of social relationship attributes in finding matching terrorists.

CONCLUSIONS AND FUTURE DIRECTIONS

In this paper we introduced a framework of identity resolution techniques that utilizes different identity attributes and matching algorithms. Guided by existing identity theories, we defined and examined three types of identity cues, namely personal identity attributes, social behavior attributes, and social relationship attributes, for identity resolution. We also evaluated three matching algorithms: pair-wise comparison, transitive closure, and collective clustering. Our experimental results showed that both social behavior and relationship attributes improved the performance of identity resolution as compared to using personal identity attributes alone. In particular, the collective identity resolution algorithm, which considers all three types of identity attributes in a collective clustering process, was shown to achieve the best performance among all approaches.

Since this study mainly focuses on comparing the three types of identity attributes with three identity resolution algorithms. These three algorithms are all similarity-based unsupervised learning methods. In our future research, we plan to compare them with other existing identity resolution algorithms (e.g., supervised learning algorithms). Another limitation of this study is the type and size of datasets employed in experiments. To validate, improve, and operationalize these identity resolution techniques, we plan to test them on real-world identity datasets with larger scales and more attributes. Furthermore, another direction of our future research is to further optimize the complexity of identity matching algorithms for more efficient processing.

DECLARATIONS

Competing interests

The authors declare that they have no competing interests.

Authors' contributions

JL conceived of the study, carried out the research design, conducted the experiments and drafted the manuscript. AGW co-designed the proposed approach, participated in the experimental study and drafted the manuscript. Both authors read and approved the final manuscript.

Authors' information

JL is an Assistant Professor in Business Information Systems, College of Business, at Oregon State University. He earned his Ph.D. in Management Information Systems from the University of Arizona. His research interests include data mining, business analytics, social media analytics, and health informatics. He has published in Journal of Management Information Systems, Decision Support Systems, IEEE Transactions, Journal of the American Society for Information Science and Technology, Journal of the Association for Information Systems, Bioinformatics, Communications of the ACM, Expert Systems with Applications, and Information Systems Frontiers.

GAW is an Associate Professor in the Department of Business Information Technology, Pamplin College of Business, at Virginia Tech. He received his Ph.D. in Management Information Systems from the University of Arizona. His research interests include heterogeneous data management, data cleansing, data mining and knowledge discovery, and decision support systems. He has published in Production and Operations Management, Communications of the ACM, IEEE Transactions of Systems, Man and Cybernetics (Part A), IEEE Computer, Group Decision and Negotiation, and Journal of the American Society for Information Science and Technology. Dr. Wang is a member of the Association for Information Systems (AIS), the Decision Sciences Institute (DSI), and the Institute of Electrical and Electronics Engineers (IEEE).

REFERENCES

1. TH Kean, CA Kojm, P Zelikow, JR Thompson, S Gorton, TJ Roemer, JS Gorelick, JF Lehman, FF Fielding, B Kerrey, The 9/11 Commission Report. 2004. URL: http://govinfo.library.unt.edu/911/report/index.htm
2. U.S. Department of State: Country Reports on Terrorism 2006. 2007. URL: http://www.state.gov/j/ct/rls/crt/2006/
3. J Li, GA Wang, H Chen, Identity matching using personal and social identity features. Inf. Syst. Front. **13**, 101–113 (2010)
4. JS Pistole, Fraudulent Identification Documents and the Implications for Homeland Security. Statement Rec Before House Sel Comm Homel Secur. 2003.

URL: https://www.fbi.gov/news/testimony/fraudulent-identification-documents-and-the-implications-for-homeland-security

5. J Jonas, Identity resolution: 23 years of practical experience and observations at scale, in Proc 2006 ACM SIGMOD Int Conf Manag data - SIGMOD'06 (ACM Press, New York, NY, USA, 2006), p. 718 [SIGMOD'06]
6. GA Wang, H Chen, H Atabakhsh, Automatically detecting deceptive criminal identities. Commun. ACM **47**, 70–76 (2004)
7. GA Wang, HC Chen, JJ Xu, H Atabakhsh, Automatically detecting criminal identity deception: an adaptive detection algorithm. IEEE Trans. Syst. Man. Cybern. Part a-Systems Humans **36**, 988–999 (2006)
8. I Bhattacharya, L Getoor, Collective entity resolution in relational data. ACM Trans. Knowl. Discov. from Data **1**, 5 (2007)
9. H Pasula, B Marthi, B Milch, S Russell, I Shpitser, Identity uncertainty and citation matching. Adv Neural Inf Process Syst 2003:1425–1432.
10. T Donaldson, A position paper on collaborative deceit, in AAAI-94 Work Plan Interagent Commun, 1994
11. IP Fellegi, AB Sunter, A theory for record linkage. J. Am. Stat. Assoc. **64**, 1183–1210 (1969)
12. M Bilenko, R Mooney, W Cohen, P Ravikumar, S Fienberg, Adaptive name matching in information integration. IEEE Intell. Syst. **18**, 16–23 (2003)
13. Hernandez MA, Stolfo SJ: The Merge/purge Problem for Large Databases. In Proc 1995 ACM SIGMOD Int Conf Manag data (SIGMOD '95) Edited by Carey MJ, Schneider DA. San Jose, CA; 1995:127–138
14. AE Monge, Matching algorithms within a duplicate detection system. IEEE. Data Eng. Bull **23**, 14–20 (2000)
15. AK Elmagarmid, PG Ipeirotis, VS Verykios, Duplicate record detection: a survey. IEEE Trans. Knowl. Data Eng. **19**, 1–16 (2007)
16. JM Cheek, SR Briggs, Self-consciousness and aspects of identity. J. Res. Pers. **16**, 401–408 (1982)
17. H Tajfel, JC Turner, The Social Identity Theory of Inter-Group Behavior (Nelson-Hall, Chicago, 1986)
18. JC Turner, Some Current Issues in Research on Social Identity and Self-Categorization Theories (Blackwell, Oxford, 1999)
19. K Deaux, D Martin, Interpersonal networks and social categories: specifying levels of context in identity processes. Soc. Psychol. Q. **66**, 101–117 (2003)
20. S Stryker, RT Serpe, Commitment, Identity Salience, and Role Behavior: Theory and Research Example (Springer-Verlap, New York, 1982)
21. TC Redman, The impact of poor data quality on the typical enterprises. Commun. ACM **41**, 79–82 (1998)
22. United Kingdom Home Office: Identity Fraud: A Study. 2002. URL: http://www.homeoffice.gov.uk/cpd/id_fraud-report.pdf

23. R Ananthakrishna, S Chaudhuri, V Ganti, Eliminating Fuzzy Duplicates in Data Warehouses. In Proc 28th Int Conf Very Large Data Bases. Hong Kong, China; 2002:586–597.

24. D V Kalashnikov, S Mehrotra, Z Chen, Exploiting relationships for domain-independent data cleaning. In Proc 2005 SIAM Int Conf Data Min. Newport Beach, CA; 2005:262-273

25. H Köpcke, E Rahm, Frameworks for entity matching: a comparison. Data Knowl. Eng. **69**, 197–210 (2010)

26. B Marshall, S Kaza, J Xu, H Atabakhsh, T Petersen, C Violette, H Chen, Cross-Jurisdictional Criminal Activity Networks to Support Border and Transportation Security. In Proceedings 7th Int IEEE Conf Intell Transp Syst. Washington, D.C.; 2004:100–105.

27. DE Brown, SC Hagen, Data association methods with applications to law enforcement. Decis. Support Syst. **34**, 369–378 (2003)

28. D Dey, S Sarkar, P De, A distance-based approach to entity reconciliation in heterogeneous databases. IEEE Trans. Knowl. Data. Eng. **14**, 567–582 (2002)

29. P Ravikumar, WW Cohen, A Hierarchical Graphical Model for Record Linkage, in Proceeding 20th Conf Uncertain Artif Intell(AUAI Press, Arlington, VA, 2004)

30. W. E. Winkler. Methods for record linkage and Bayesian networks. Technical Report, Statistical Research Division, U.S. Census Bureau, Washington, DC, 2002.

31. K Nigam, AK McCallum, S Thrun, T Mitchell, Text Classification from Labeled and Unlabeled Documents using EM. Mach. Learn **39**, 103–134 (2000)

32. A Culotta, A McCallum, Joint deduplication of multiple record types in relational data, in Proc 14th ACM Int Conf Inf Knowl Manag (ACM, Bremen, Germany, 2005), pp. 257–258

33. I Bhattacharya, L Getoor, Entity resolution in graphs, in Min graph data (Wiley-Blackwell, Hoboken, 2006), p. 311

34. S Bartunov, A Korshunov, S Park, W Ryu, H Lee, Joint Link-Attribute User Identity Resolution in Online Social Networks. InProc 6th Work Soc Netw Min Anal (SNA-KDD '12). Beijing, China; 2012

35. P Hsiung, A Moore, D Neill, J Schneider, Alias detection in link data sets. In Proc Int Conf Intell Anal. McLean, VA; 2005.

36. J Xu, GA Wang, J Li, M Chau, Complex problem solving: identity matching based on social contextual information. J. Assoc. Inf. Syst. **8**, 525–545 (2007)

37. MA Jaro, UNIMATCH: A Record Linkage System: User's Manual. Washington: The Bureau, 1978

38. HB Newcombe, JM Kennendy, SJ Axford, AP James, Automatic linkage of vital records. Science **130**, 954–959 (1959)

39. J Li, GA Wang, Criminal identity resolution using social behavior and relationship attributes. In Proc 2011 IEEE Int Conf Intell Secur Informatics, ISI 2011;

2011:173–175.

40. VI Levenshtein, Binary codes capable of correcting deletions, insertions, and reversals. Soviet Physics Doklady **10**, 707–710 (1966)

41. J Kubica, A Moore, D Cohn, J Schneider, Finding underlying connections: a fast graph-based method for link analysis and collaboration queries. Proc. Int. Conf. Mach. Learn. **20**, 392–399 (2003)

42. J Kubica, AW Moore, D Cohn, J Schneider, cGraph: A fast graph-based method for link analysis and queries. In Proc 2003 IJCAI Text-Mining Link-Analysis Work; 2003:22–31

4

CHAPTER

NETWORK INTRUSION DETECTION AND VISUALIZATION USING AGGREGATIONS IN A CYBER SECURITY DATA WAREHOUSE

Bogdan Denny Czejdo, Erik M. Ferragut, John R. Goodall, Jason Laska

Keywords: Cyber Security, Network Intrusion, Anomaly Detection, Data Warehouses, Aggregation, Personalization, Situational Understanding

INTRODUCTION

The concept of anomaly is ubiquitous in the cyber security area. Generally, the term anomaly is defined as a departure from typical values, forms, or rules. The process of anomaly detection should, therefore, detect data that do not conform to established typical behavior [1-4]. Such data are often referred to as outliers. In the case of anomaly detection in network traffic data, anomalous activities are often not individual rare objects, but unexpected bursts in events. Thus anomaly detection requires not only a statistical definition of atypical objects, but also appropriate aggregations of network data. These aggregations enable analysis at multiple scales. More than 25 years ago, Denning [5] employed anomaly detection for cyber security data. In [5], anomaly detection was accomplished with thresholds and statistics. The limitation of simple threshold and statistics were well documented in the more recent literature [3]. One of the directions for improvement discussed in [6] was to include additional information such as classifying objects participating in network traffic, such as users, computers, and programs. Initially, this classification was supported by statistical analysis [6]. Later, there were some proposed solutions based on soft computing [7]. One extension of the research was based on a statistical time series approach. There are many parametric and non-parametric tests to find outliers in time series. One simple way to detect anomalies in time series was described in [8] where a non-parametric method called Washer was introduced. The need to simultaneously consider multiple anomaly

Citation: Bogdan Denny Czejdo, Erik M. Ferragut, John R. Goodall, Jason Laska, Network Intrusion Detection and Visualization Using Aggregations in a Cyber Security Data Warehouse* http://dx.doi.org/10.4236/ijcns.2012.529069

detectors was discussed in [9]. In spite of many successes, rapidly discovering novel and sophisticated cyber attacks from masses of heterogeneous data and providing situational understanding to cyber security analysts is an ongoing problem in cyber defense. In this paper, we describe a part of a comprehensive system to perform knowledge discovery and extraction from security events in large data sets through the integration of various anomaly detectors, real-time cyber security data visualization, and a learning feedback loop between users and algorithms. The requirements for the system are to maintain scalability to voluminous streaming data, and to minimize the time from observation to discovery. The main emphasis of this paper is on specifying the graph of aggregations including probabilistic models for anomaly detection. We propose techniques to generate a variety of models representing typical behavior at multiple scales enabling the comparison of network traffic based on learnt models. The models associated with the graph of aggregations allow for natural graphical representations and address important challenges of knowledge discovery for cyber defense. Cyber security experts can use their domain knowledge to systematically traverse the aggregation graph. Scalability is assured by working with a proper proportion of materialized (precomputed) and virtual nodes in the aggregation matrix. Timeliness of discovery is assured since most of the cyber security data are preprocessed, and analysts can have instantaneous access to anomalousness information using a graphical interface. Uncovering relevant cyber security information is needed for a rapid and accurate decision-making process, which can be significantly improved when an information system allows for a convenient traversal of multilevel anomalousness data by a human user or a software agent. The traditional data warehouse architecture [10-12] can be expanded to provide important functions, such as a drill-down operator for cyber security analysts. Drilldown operators usually are somehow restrictive, limiting the possibilities of different views. The effective use of such an operator can be improved if flexible options are available to the user and information about these options is clearly presented to the user [13]. In this paper, we discuss the theoretical and practical aspects of cyber-security event aggregations in a cybersecurity data warehouse. The event aggregation graph includes the fact table (cyber-security raw data streams) and the set of related summary tables containing information about various event aggregations. The main event aggregation graph includes only summary tables (in addition to the fact table) containing information for simple aggregations that were based directly on key attributes. The main event aggregation graph has a number of levels corresponding to the number of key attributes in the fact table. The aggregations may involve complex aggregation formulas. We will refer to the resulting tables as complex summary tables. In this paper we will discuss aggregations related to sliding windows. The complex summary tables can create their own hierarchies in the form of additional layers of the aggregation graph. The links can connect the complex summary tables with main summary tables. The event aggregation graph with all its components: main summary tables and complex summary tables, can be a good foundation to provide the most noteworthy data for a cyber-security analyst. Using the graph, the interaction between analyst and data warehouse operations can be defined to assist in browsing through the past data and comparing it with the current data stream. By automatically identifying the most noteworthy events and aggregations, a reduced graph can be created for cyber security analyst to show aggregations that are most relevant to anomalies and situational understanding. The event aggregation graph can be also used to dynamically address security problems by restricting some network traffic identified as most risky and when the threat level is very high. That restriction could practically be implemented temporarily until cyber security analyst makes an appropriate decision. The timely response of cyber security analysts requires a timely response of the system which in turn requires appropriate model for optimization of table implementation. The summary tables can be either virtual or materialized. The performance of a data warehouse depends on the proper choice of summary table materialization. In order to build the proper implementation model there is a need to understand computational dependency between tables. It can be represented as a computational dependency graph showing all possible computation paths to create each aggregation table. This paper is organized as follows. In Section 2, we describe anomalies and anomaly detectors for cyber security data using firewall events as an example. In Section 3, a star schema for the example cyber security data is presented. In Section 4, creation of simple summary tables and a main aggregation graph is discussed. In Section 5, the main aggregation graph is extended to include complex summary tables. In Section 6, using aggregation graph for situational understanding of cyber security system is discussed. Section 7 presents architecture of a data warehouse system for cyber security data.

ANOMALIES AND ANOMALY DETECTORS

Cyber security data can come in many forms. There is some structural commonality, though, and alignment points for possible data integration. Most of the data set can be viewed as conveying information about who did, what, to whom, and when they did it, which we refer to as a "Who-What-toWhom-When" structure. A firewall log is a good example of cyber security data. Each record of the log will be referred to as a microevent or simply event. Each event describes the activity taken by the firewall and includes: source IP address and source port that represent "Who"; destination IP address and destination port that represent "to Whom". For each event there are firewall event codes including action (e.g. Build) and the protocol (e.g. TCP) that together identify "What". Time, as usual, is also included and it uniquely represents "When". An example of a sequence of firewall events is shown in Figure 1. The IP addresses are represented graphically as stars, and ports are represented as rectangles. Each event is represented graphically as a directional link. Time is graphically represented as a pentagon attached to the directional link and firewall event codes are represented as rounded rectangles also attached to the directional link. The analysis can be based on the individual events or on the aggregations of events. In the example, there is an event that uses the TCP protocol and destination port 6667, which could be rare since IRC chat services might be prohibited. Another example of an anomalous event would be traffic terminating at a non-DNS server on destination port 53. An example of anomalies for aggregations of events is presented in Figure 1. The occurrence of multiple "Build" events coming from the same "Who" and going to the same "to Whom" in very close time is anomalous with respect to expected network traffic flow. This case shows that in addition to analyzing individual events there is a necessity to analyze aggregations of the events. There are challenges with choosing the proper aggregations in cyber security data.

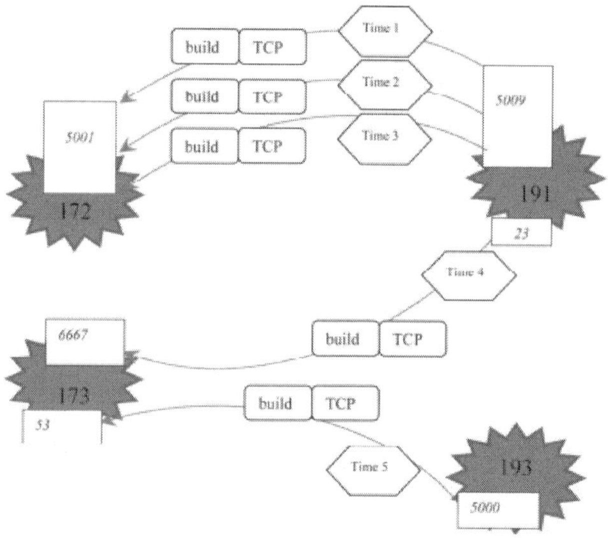

Figure 1. Graphical representation of an example sequence of firewall events.

The groups of events corresponding to aggregations should have appropriate size to differentiate between "typical" and "anomalous" temporal aberrations, e.g. different load for different days of the week vs. malicious events identified from the noteworthy events. With small groups, the sparsity of micro-events may be insufficiently to provide a reliable probabilistic analysis. With the larger group the probabilistic analysis will be more reliable. At the same time if the group is too large it might not properly reflect the typical temporal aberrations. As we move out to wider groups, these more local effects will have reduced impact on the averages. Domain knowledge will guide the choices of the types of aggregations sought after to indicate possible known attacks. Indeed, it is easy to see that the aggregations used to find a Distributed Denial of Service attacks and a Social Engineering Phishing attacks can be at differing scales. Hence, there is a tradeoff between sparsity and specificity. Various aggregations can be used to identify anomalousness of a group of events through probabilistic computations. An aggregation is a way of collecting events into a macro-event and typically assigning some aggregate value to that macro-event, such as count. Many possible ways to aggregate events can be considered. The typical aggregations are by some attribute value, e.g. aggregating events by the same event code and source IP. Since cyber security data analysis should be very sensitive to the temporal aberrations, the time limits are typically imposed on at least some aggregations e.g. by a fixed time window or by a fixed number of events. The goal is to create a model to provide various probabilistic measures for cyber security analyst to assist him/her with maliciousness detection through various anomaly indicators as shown in Figures 2(a) and (b). One model of determining anomalousness is based on simple probabilities of occurrence of a micro- or macroevent. Unfortunately, a basic probability threshold is a poor proxy for anomalousness. We can see it clearly by considering a property with a very big domain of N values (where values have approximately the same probability and no value is ever practically repeated) and a property with a small domain with only two values (where only two values occur but one with the probability 1/N). We would expect the occurrence of any value for the first property to be much less anomalous than the rare value for the second property, even though both would have a probability of about 1/N. The choice of a probability threshold is directly dependent on the underlying probability distribution describing the data. There are different approaches that satisfy the general requirements for understanding of anomalousness. In our system we use the following definition to identify exceptionally rare events:

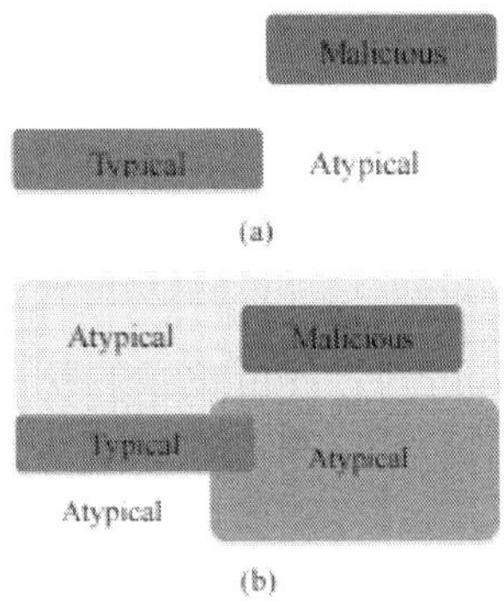

Figure 2. (a) Relationships between Typical, Atypical and Malicious for a simple anomaly analysis; (b) Relationships between Typical, Atypical and Malicious for different anomaly specifications.

$$A(g) = -\log\left(P\left(P(G) <= P(g)\right)\right) \quad (1)$$

where G is a random variable distributed according to the counts and g is one value it can take. The outer probability on the right-hand side is random with respect to G. The computation of this anomalousness is as follows. First, we compute the counts of appropriate groups of events, and then we compute probability distribution for each group P(g). Then we can compute the tail probabilities to find the anomaly for each group g. A similar approach can be used to identify exceptionally frequent events.

CYBER SECURITY DATA WAREHOUSE

A cyber security data warehouse can be built from various network data. Specifically, it can be built from the firewall data log that was described in the previous section. The data warehouse star schema for the firewall data log can be designed as shown in Figure 3. The model includes the four main components of the "WhoWhat-toWhom-When" structure as dimension tables: Source Machine, Request, Destination Machine and Time. The fact table, in our case, contains information about firewall events. The firewall events can be referred to shortly as events. The role of each table is as follows. The Source Machine dimension contains the information for a specific machine initiating the event i.e. IP address and port used by the machine, and other attributes e.g. Machine Class. The key identifier for each object in the Source Machine dimension is the composite attribute {Source IP, Source Port}. The Request dimension contains the information about the firewall event codes that include Action (e.g. "Build") and the Protocol (e.g. "TCP"), and other descriptions and classifications. The key identifier for each object in the Request dimension is the composite attribute {Action, Protocol}. The Destination Machine dimension has a similar structure to Source Machine and contains IP address, port used by the machine, and other attributes e.g. Machine Class. The key identifier for each object in the Destination Machine dimension is the composite attribute {Destination IP, Destination Port}. Each event has a time stamp represented by the Time dimension that can also contain some time classification e.g. part of day. The key identifier for each object in the Time dimension is the attribute {Time} which is actually a composite attribute equivalent to pair of attributes Day and Hour. The fact table, also referred as event table or simply T01, contains the log of all firewall events made from one machine to another machine at a specific time. The fact table has seven attributes: Time, Source IP, Source Port, Protocol, Action, Destination IP, and Destination Port. These attributes are foreign keys and allow to access and group events based on dimension table values. We will refer to all foreign keys as index attributes, and underline their name since other attributes can also be present in the fact table. Since each event has a time stamp, the Time attribute is actually a primary key attribute of the fact table, but the implication of this for our approach is minimal as it is discussed later.

MAIN SUMMARIZATION HIERARCHY FOR A CYBER SECURITY DATA WAREHOUSE

One of the fundamental operations for a data warehouse is the processing of the fact table in an anticipation of user queries. The new tables can be obtained by aggregation of events in the fact table and summarizing information (creating information summary) for each aggregation. These new tables are, referred to as summary tables. Summary tables in a cyber security warehouse can also contain information about event anomalies. It is important, therefore, to develop a systematic method for the design of the hierarchy of summary tables, which results in a systematic method to access anomaly information. In general, the hierarchy of summary tables can be modeled as a directed acyclic graph (DAG). Let us look at an example of hierarchy T11, T21, ···, T71 of summary tables obtained from our fact table (T01) containing as shown in Figure 4. Level zero is for the fact table which describes all events. The first level consists of summary tables containing information about aggregations obtained from the fact table by reducing it by a single index attribute, e.g. the summary table T11 is obtained by summarizing information about all T01 events that came from the same Source Machine, had the same Request, and were directed to the same Destination Machine but happened any Time.

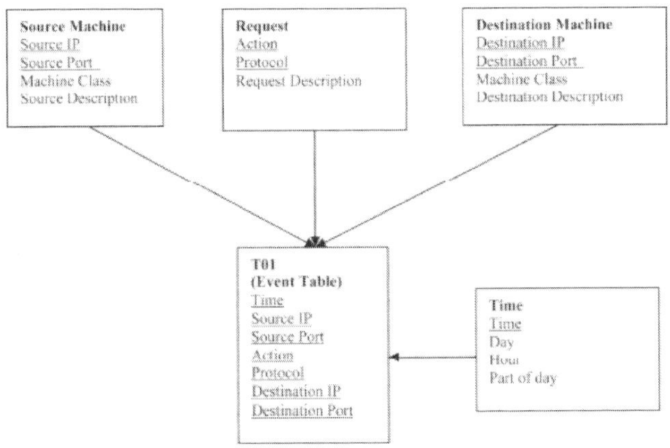

Figure 3. The initial star schema for the cyber security data warehouse.

We can consider the second level as the one consisting of summary tables containing information about aggregations obtained from the first level by reducing it by an additional index attribute. For example, the summary table T21 could be obtained by summarizing information taken from T11 for each group that came from the same Source Machine, had the same Request, and were directed to the same IP address as shown in Figure 4. We could also interpret the third level as the one consisting of summary tables containing information about aggregations obtained from the fact table by reducing it by two index attributes. In this paper, however, we concentrate on investigating the relationships between summary tables in the same or in an adjacent level. The reduce operator, referred to as R, is used to indicate what type of the grouping will be used for summarization. The R operator can be represented graphically as a label on the link between the tables e.g. from table T01 to T11. The first argument for the R operator is an index attribute, e.g. Time. It determines what index attribute will be dropped in the newly created summary table. The second argument for the R operator is the grouping method. For the main summary graph only the simple grouping method based on removing one index attribute will be allowed. This simple grouping method is denoted as "index based". In general, the number of summarization levels in the summarization graph is equal to the number of index attributes and the number of summary tables on each level can be computed based on all possible combinations for the corresponding subset of index attributes. In our case, we have 7 levels and on the highest level there is single table T71 that contains the maximum summarization—the summarization on the highest abstract level. The directed links are showing possible transformations from one table to another. The levels of the summarization graph correspond to various granularities for grouping. The first summarization level corresponds to the least coarse (finest) grouping, the next (second) summarization level corresponds to coarser grouping, etc. There are seven levels of granularity for our data warehouse. At level 0 (lowest level), the granularity is the finest and the records of actual events are stored. When these records are summarized, the level of granularity is coarser. For example T11, a time independent summary table, has the coarser granularity. Furthermore, T21, T31, etc. are even coarser. In general, coarser levels of granularity provide fewer details but require smaller records to be stored. In practice, some nodes in the graph are of a lesser importance. Since the Time attribute is a primary key attribute for the fact table T01, the first summarization level practically has only one meaningful table T11. Applying the R operator with any argument other than Time argument would not perform grouping, but rather it

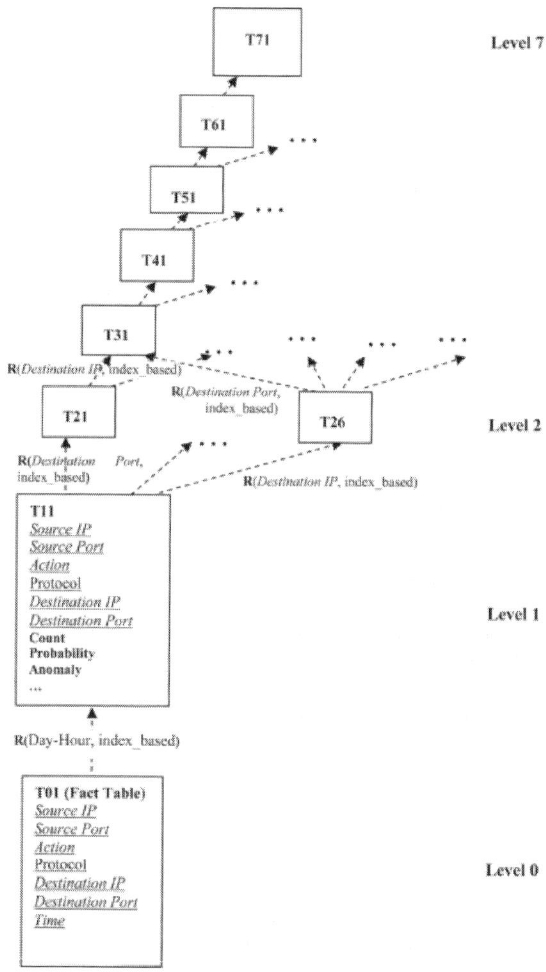

Figure 4. The main summarization hierarchy for the cyber security data warehouse.

would project one of the attributes from the T01 table. The steps described above can also result in new attributes for each table. These attributes describe the properties of newly created groups. Each group can have various properties assigned to it, e.g. Count property can store the number of events. In our example of the summary table T11, the Count property is computed by simply counting the number of events in each group. Let us describe summary tables and their attributes more formally. Each summary table contains a set of groupings G g , , g , , g = { 1i n L L } where each group gi needs to have some properties computed and stored as table attributes. The number of groups is determined by possible values of the summary table index attributes. The R operator specifies how each grouping gi is created. The computation of the property is determined by a computation method. The "Count" computation method allows to compute values of the Count property by simply count ing the number of events in each group gi. The "Sum" computation method allows to compute values of the CountAll attribute by adding count property for each group gi. This is equivalent to counting all events in the fact table. It is important to notice that the summary table does store the actual sequence of events (or sequence of sequences of events, etc.) but rather it stores an information summary for an implicit group of events (identified by its index attributes). This information summary is stored in the form of each group's properties. There are other computation methods, e.g. based on attribute values of the same table. The Probability is a good example of such property. The unconditional probability pi can be computed for each group gi and stored as its non-index attribute probability. For the cyber security applications it is also important to compute various conditional probabilities (if summarization level allows for that) for each aggregation gi and stored as its non-index attributes probabilityC1, probabilityC2, etc. The Anomaly attributes can be computed based on the formula discussed in Section 2. In a typical situation the computation of anomaly is based on attribute values of the same table. The anomaly is computed for each group gi based on distribution of the values of the attribute probability. Actually, the anomalies for low and high values can be computed and stored as its non-key attribute as anomalyLow and anomalyHigh. Additionally, the anomalies for low and high values can be computed for each aggregation gi based on conditional probability distributions and stored as its non-key attribute anomalyC1, anomalyC2, ... To simplify our presentation we will assume that all these anomalies are represented by a single anomaly property. The different tables have different anomaly indicators. The granularity of the tables corresponds to the granularity of anomalies. Since the anomalies of networking events are related to some aggregation of events the granularity of anomaly on the zero level is often considered to be too fine. When anomalies are computed on summarized data the results are more likely to point to noteworthy aggregations. For example T41, a time independent summary table, can show a significant atypical behavior.

COMPLEX AGGREGATION TABLES FOR EVENT WINDOWS

So far we have discussed the main hierarchy graph with its main summary tables using nodes and simple reductions (by one index attribute) as directed links. In the case of network traffic data, anomalies are often not rare objects, but unexpected bursts in events. Thus anomaly requires not only a probabilistic definition of atypical objects, but also appropriate probabilistic computations for aggregations of network events. In this section we present data models for bursts of the events and techniques to identify anomalies in the bursts of the events. Generally the aggregation method to model bursts of events can be window based or event proximity based. In this paper, we address only window based aggregation. Here, we have different types of windows with two most obvious: fixed-time window and fixed-number-of-events window. Let us concentrate on fixed-number-of-events window. We can model a sliding fixed-number-of-events window by proper aggregation of event (fact) table T01. The previously discussed R operator needs to be extended to denote this aggregation properly. The extension is based on an observation that a simple index based aggregation would not suffice here, but more complex aggregation of events should be here performed, i.e., aggregation of all events within the window. Additionally, each window needs to be uniquely identified since we want to perform various window based computations. The beginning or ending time of window can be used for that purpose. We will denote the operator to perform window based aggregation as R({}, fixed-number-of-events-window). There is an empty set as a first argument of R since the Time index is kept even though it needs different interpretation. The second argument fixed-number-of-eventswindow indicates the type of complex aggregation. Other types of aggregation can also be used, e.g. fixed-timewindow. Deciding about the overlap of sliding windows requires some attention since it will affect the number of aggregations. The extreme case of associating a window with each event is not practical because of the large amount of computations and data (no data reduction), while single events would not affect the total count that much. Another extreme case of making window disjoint is not sufficient since the burst of events divided into two windows might not trigger the anomaly detector. Practically, some overlapping factor needs to be selected, e.g. 50%. As a result the data contain many redundancies since the same event will be present in many groupings. For the window overlapping factor of 50%, the replication factor will be close to 2. The information about window based aggregations can be stored in a summary table, e.g. the new table T01A1. This new table does not belong to main summarization hierarchy since complex aggregation was used. It will be placed in the new layer of the node T01 since it uses the same index attributes. In general, any newly introduced complex aggregation will result in the creation of the new table and new layer of the summarization hierarchy. The new table is placed in that layer in the same node as the main summary table with the same index attributes. The new table, in our case was named T01A1 since "A1" will stand for additional layer number one related to the additional complex aggregation. The newly created table can be a starting node of a new hierarchy placed in the new layer. Other tables of the new hierarchy would also correspond to main summary tables that have the same index attributes. For example, data in table T00A1 can be summarized into another table T11A1 by the R operator with the simple aggregation i.e. R(Time, index-based). The table T21A1 will also belong to the same layer since the simple aggregation was used. In general, any new table constructed by a simple aggregation will belong to a layer of the initial table. The relationships between tables in the different layers of the same node can be identified. For example the table T11A1 can be very similar to T11 after adjusting for event redundancies by, e.g., dividing count by 2 when windows are overlapping by 50%. The summarization hierarchy will, therefore, consists of a main layer, called also layer number zero or main hierarchy and additional layers corresponding to other aggregation methods or derived hierarchies. The aggregations' properties can be computed using different computation methods as before. Let $G = \{g_1, \cdots, g_i, \cdots, g_n\}$ be a set of aggregations (groups) stored in table T00A1 where each aggregation gi consists of network events in a fixed size window. We will use again our basic probabilistic model for computing anomalies: count of events of the same type in each window (counti), compute the probabilities for each aggregation (events of the same type), and then compute the anomalies for each aggregation based on the probability distribution of P(G).

USING SUMMARIZATION HIERARCHY FOR SITUATIONAL UNDERSTANDING OF CYBER SECURITY SYSTEM

We implemented our cyber-security data warehouse model on the IEEE Vast 2012 Situational Understanding and Cyber-forensics data [14]. The summarization hierarchy graph was created based on the previously defined index attributes: Time, Source IP, Source Port, Action, Protocol, Destination IP, and Destination Port. We used mostly the layer of the summarization hierarchy corresponding to window based aggregations. These aggregations were constructed for non-overlapping windows with the five minutes window duration. First, the anomalous behavior with respect to the volume of all traffic was detected based on the appropriate table on the sixth level of aggregation (called table T62A4) with the single index attribute Time indicating the beginning of the window, and non-index attribute Count describing the traffic volume. Using this grouping, we were able to determine that the network traffic was

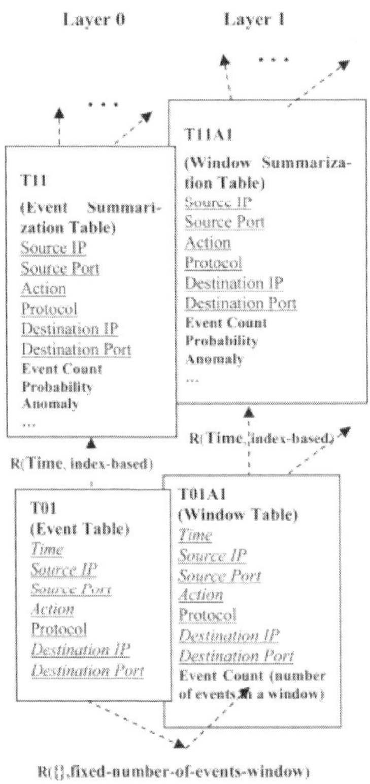

Figure 5. The additional layer of complex summary tables for the window based aggregations.

anomalous (drastically lower) for many windows. More specifically we could identify a four-hour period of anomalous traffic. This anomaly was a starting point of a down traversal (drill-down operation) of the summarization graph. We looked at the lower level (level 5) aggregation described by a table (called table T52A4) with two index attributes Time and Action, and non-index attribute Count describing the traffic volume. We observed an anomalous high percentage of traffic through the firewall that was related to the value "system log entry" of the attribute Action. The discovery of these anomalous events was very important. The system log entries indicated that the connections were made to the firewall itself and that changes were made to the firewall settings. It looked like dangerous tampering to firewall information that may have contributed to other traffic deviations around the same time. Another anomaly was discovered by traversing the part of the summarization graph containing tables on the fourth and lower aggregation level with at least three index attributes Time (indicating the beginning of the window), Source IP and Destination IP. This traversal resulted in the observation that exactly one source IP was responsible for all traffic from workstations to websites for some specific window sequences. This strongly indicated a possible misdirection or man-in-the-middle attack where all traffic is routed through an intermediate contact.

Yet another anomaly was discovered by applying complex aggregation to the attributes Machine Class for both source machine and destination machine. The aggregation resulted in the summary table (called table T62A5) with the original index attribute Time uniquely identifying each window and three new attributes Source Computer Class, Destination Computer Class, and Count. Indeed, by considering the collection of events partitioned by computer class, we observed the deviation from the typical traffic pattern originating from the DNS server and ending at DNS servers. Actually, for the IEEE Vast 2012 data, the anomalous behavior was observed after the first 20 hours. Departure from this baseline indicated a misdirection of routing, possibly involving serious exfiltration of protected data.

SYSTEM ARCHITECTURE

The conceptual system architecture is shown in Figure 6. It is built based on typical data warehouse architecture and contains two main components: Cyber Security Data Warehouse and Cyber Security Event Database. Both components use the aggregation hierarchy graph as a model for the data storage. The Update Data Warehouse processor updates Cyber Security Data Warehouse periodically (e.g. daily) with recorded events that occurred after the last update from the Cyber Security Event Database. In addition, there are Anomaly Global Patterns, and Anomaly Occurrence databases. Anomaly Global Patterns are updated periodically at the same time the data warehouse is updated. Anomaly Global Patterns are computed based on values of the anomaly attributes in the aggregation hierarchy graph. The simple interpretation of the content of Anomaly Global Patterns is that patterns contain all historical event probability distributions (Layer 0, 1). The simple interpretation of the Cyber Security Event Database is that it contains the current events in the form of the most recent window (Layer 1). The Identify Anomaly processor is a crucial component of the system and works on-line to compute anomalies in the current event table T11 and in the tables above based on historical event table T11 practically updating the Anomaly Occurrences database (actually a part of Cyber Security Event Database). There are two main tasks for Anomaly Integration and Visualization processor. First, it combines the anomalies into a single measure and displays the result as a warning meter. Second, it displays the individual anomalies for the cyber security analyst.

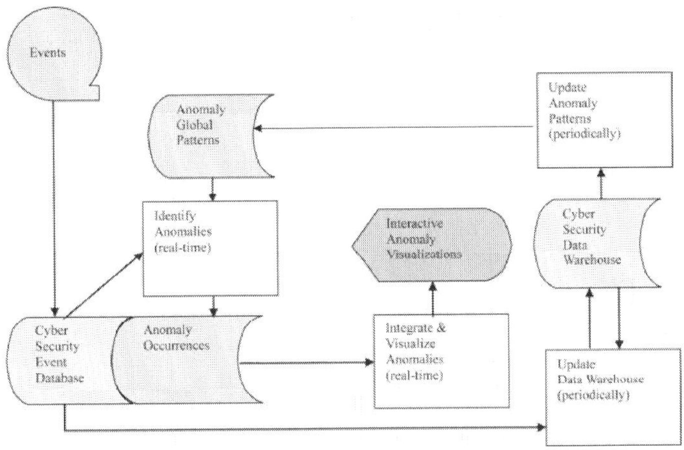

Figure 6. System architecture.

The cyber security analyst can specify globally and for each node the threshold for anomalies to be displayed. The cyber security analyst can also define new nodes in the graph by associating the new aggregation with it.

CONCLUSION

In this paper, we introduced the generalization of aggregation operation as applied to a cyber security system. We discussed the concept of an event aggregation graph that contains not only information about various aggregations but also anomalies related with each aggregation level. The aggregation graph once implemented can be explored to enhance the cyber security analyst's situational understanding. When the graph is presented to the cyber security analyst, only the relevant nodes are included, allowing him/her to focus on most probable threats of network intrusion.

REFERENCES

1. H. Kriegel, P. Kröger and A. Zimek, "Outlier Detection Techniques," Proceedings of 13th Pacific-Asia Conference on Knowledge Discovery and Data Mining (PAKDD 2009), Bangkok, Thailand, 2009. http://www.dbs.ifi.lmu.de/Publikationen/Papers
2. V. Chandola, A. Banerjee and V. Kumar, "Anomaly Detection: A Survey," ACM Computing Surveys, Vol. 41, No. 3, 2009, Article 15.

3. S. Axelsson, “The Base-Rate Fallacy and the Difficulty of Intrusion Detection,” ACM Transactions on Information and System Security (TISSEC), Vol. 3, No. 3, 2000, pp. 186-205. doi:10.1145/357830.357849
4. H. Teng, K. Chen and S. Lu, “Adaptive Real-Time Anomaly Detection Using Inductively Generated Sequential Patterns,” Proceedings of IEEE Symposium on Security and Privacy, Marlboro, 7-9 May 1990, pp. 278-284. doi:10.1109/RISP.1990.63857
5. D. Denning, “An Intrusion Detection Model,” Proceedings of the Seventh IEEE Symposium on Security and Privacy, 7-9 May 1986, pp. 119-131.
6. Jones and R. Sielken, “Computer System Intrusion Detection: A Survey,” Technical Report, Department of Computer Science, University of Virginia, Charlottesville, 1999.
7. S. Cho, “Incorporating Soft Computing Techniques into a Probabilistic Intrusion Detection System,” IEEE Transactions on Systems, Man, and Cybernetics, Vol. 32, No. 2, 2002, pp. 154-160.
8. Venturini, “Time Series Outlier Detection: A New Non Parametric Methodology (Washer),” Statistica—Università di Bologna, Vol. 71, 2011, pp. 329-344.
9. E. M. Ferragut, D. M. Darmon, C. A. Shue and S. Kelley, “Automatic Construction of Anomaly Detectors from Graphical Models,” Proceedings of IEEE Symposium on Computational Intelligence in Cyber Security (CICS), Oak Ridge, 11-15 April 2011, pp. 9-16. doi:10.1109/CICYBS.2011.5949386
10. Gupta, V. Harinarayan and D. Quass, “AggregateQuery Processing in Data Warehousing Environments,” Proceedings of the VLDB, Zurich, 11-15 September 1995.
11. J. Bischoff and T. Alexander, “Data Warehouse: Practical Advice from the Experts,” Prentice-Hall, Upper Saddle River, 1997.
12. J. Widom, “Research Problems in Data Warehousing,” Proceedings of the 4th International Conference on Information and Knowledge Management, Baltimore, 28 November-2 December 1995.
13. B. Czejdo, M. Taylor and C. Putonti, “Summary Tables in Data Warehouses,” Proceedings of ADVIS’2000, Turkey, 25-27 October 2000.
14. http://www.vacommunity.org/VAST+Challenge+2012

SECTION II: CYBER SECURITY IN DIFFERENT SOCIETY SEGMENTS

5

CHAPTER

CYBER-PHYSICAL-SOCIAL BASED SECURITY ARCHITECTURE

Huansheng Ning, Hong Liu

Keywords: Internet of Things, Physical, Social, Cyber, Security, Architecture

INTRODUCTION

The Internet of Things (IoT) becomes an attractive research topic, in which the real entity in physical world becomes virtual entity in cyber world, and both physical and digital entities are enhanced with sensing, processing, and selfadapting capabilities to perform interaction through special addressing scheme [1]. Along with the combination of Internet and modern sensor technologies such as Radio Frequency Identification (RFID), Near Field Communication (NFC), and Wireless Sensor and Actuator Networks (WSAN), IoT itself is suffering from more rigorous security challenges. Several issues in terms of system architecture, standard, and human involvement are subsequently raised. The following security problems seem to be intense speculations, such as how to design appropriate security framework for things' intelligent applications? What is advanced security technology applied into mass data processing? How to maintain a balance between things' high security requirements and supporting infrastructures' hardware limitation? And how human society securely participates in both cyber and physical worlds with interconnection? Such significant obstacles influence the development of the future IoT, along with the exposure of mass data which causes various potential vulnerabilities from robust adversaries. Besides, resource restrictions including heterogeneous networks and sensor nodes, communication channels/ interfaces, bandwidth, storage, and energy, may also induce unique model design. Towards the general IoT, studies on its architecture model, standard, communication

Citation: Huansheng Ning, Hong Liu, Cyber-Physical-Social Based Security Architecture, dx.doi.org/10.4236/ait.2012.21001.

protocol, and network management have been researched [2-5]. Towards the particular IoT security, there are several open issues such as cryptographic algorithms, authentication protocols, access control, trust/privacy, and governance frameworks [6]. Several researches mainly focus on specific communication techniques (e.g., WLAN, RFID) [7,8], detailed cryptographic mechanisms (e.g., key management) [9], and practical applications (e.g., supply chain management, multimedia traffic) [10,11]. Meanwhile, the security frameworks in traditional networks can also provide merits for IoT security protection. However, security issue towards the future IoT is not a simple technically tough problem, but a multidimensional topic which combines the information security, network security, infrastructure security, and management security. Most existent schemes provide solutions for special communication techniques or applications, which may lack universality for the complicated system. Thus, we will establish an integrated security architecture to promote universal security consideration for the future IoT. In the paper, we focus on a typical future IoT architecture (short for U2IoT) which comprises two subsystems that Unit IoT and Ubiquitous IoT [12]. In the U2IoT model, conceptions of mankind neural system and social organization framework are introduced for the future IoT. Thereafter, we propose a systematic security architecture (named IPM) by integrating the awareness and interacttivity of cyber world, physical world, and human social into the U2IoT model. Meanwhile, the proposed IPM is presented with embedded interactions among information, physical, and management. Specifically, 1) information security model with the considerations for basic and advanced security requirements that are mapped into the security layer to deal with sensing, networking, application, and social attribution; 2) physical security including external context and inherent infrastructure are inspired by artificial immune, and it ensures that the things should be adaptable to dynamic semantic contexts with innate and adaptive immunities against malicious attacks; 3) management security provides recommended strategies for hierarchical classified scenes with rationality and compatibility. IPM realizes the unison of cyber world, physical world and human social to guarantee security and privacy for U2IoT. The remainder of the paper is organized as follows. In Section 2, we illustrate the existent U2IoT model, and propose the security architecture (IPM). The main features of IPM referring to information security, physical security, and management security are given in Section 3. Finally, Section 4 draws a conclusion.

PROPOSED SECURITY ARCHITECTURE FOR U2IOT

The U2IoT model is shown in Figure 1(a), which is essentially a heterogeneous system including Unit IoT and Ubiquitous IoT. Thereinto, Unit IoT resembling human neural network, refers to the basic cell providing solutions for special applications. Ubiquitous IoT includes the industrial IoT, local IoT, national IoT, and global IoT which is integration of multiple Unit IoTs with ubiquitous features, and it is similar to the social organization framework. Concretely, Unit IoT comprises IoT networks and sensors, distributed control nodes, and management and centralized data center (M&DC), and Ubiquitous IoT respectively includes iM&DC, lM&DC, and nM&DC, for the industry, local, and national IoTs. Figure 1(b) illustrates the proposed security architecture (IPM) that addresses U2IoT security in three perspectives.

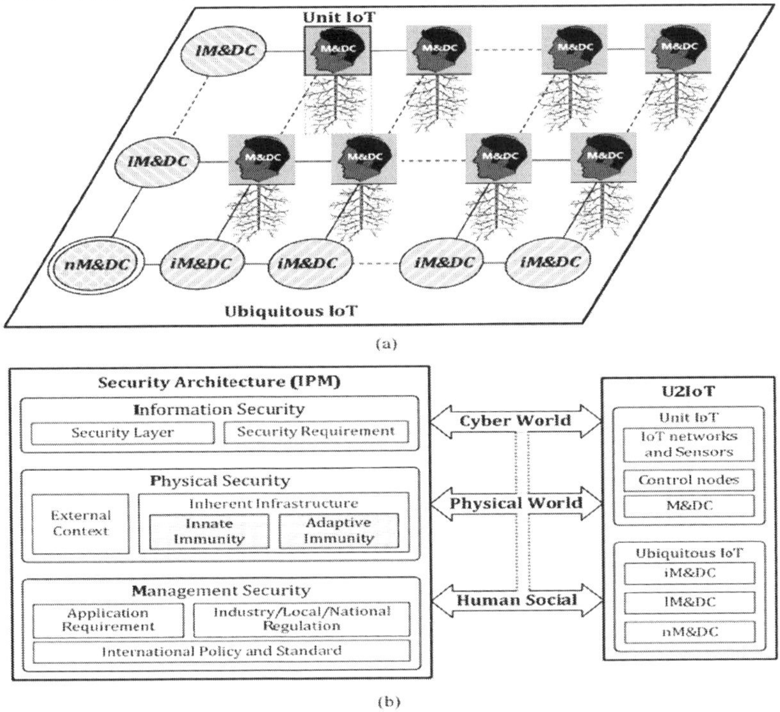

Figure 1. U2IoT model and its security architecture (IPM). (a) The U2IoT (Unit IoT and Ubiquitous IoT) model; (b) The proposed security architecture (IPM) based on U2IoT.

- Information security includes two perspectives (i.e., security layer and security requirement). Awareness of information data is captured, interpreted, and represented by things' capability, along with aggregation algorithms, protocols, and functions are included for intelligent information interactions.
- Physical security relates to environmental monitoring, motion detection, localization, tracking, perimeter control, and consumption supervision. The concept of artificial immunity is applied to detect passive and active defenses for maintaining homeostasis.
- Management security provides the recommended application requirement, industry/local/national regulation, and international policy and standard to guide activities and events in the human social. In IPM, human social activities occurring in physical world are identified and mapped into the unique cyber world, which realizes harmonious unification of human, network and things. Such triple relationships of entity in

U2IoT, makes entity identification and service discovery are effectively performed in current cyber-physical world, and are easily to extend to human social and its social networks. The security aspects underline main characteristics of U2IoT entities, as shown in Table 1.

PROPOSED SECURITY ARCHITECTURE: IPM

Information Security

Information security protects both raw data and contextualized information, and an information security model that comprises U2IoT, security layer, and security requirement is established in Figure 2.

1) Considering Social Factor for Security Layer: U2IoT is generally divided into four layers as follows.

- Sensor layer: it comprises generalized sensors and gateways to perform entity identification and service discovery. The function of sensor layer is to perceive the entities, to extract information, and to realize semantic resource discovery. The sensor techniques are applied to realize effective integration and interaction adaptation of the collected uncertain information.
- Network layer: it includes network interfaces, communication channels, network management, information maintenance, and intelligent processing. The centralized, distributed, and hybrid network topologies are involved to assist monitoring and maintaining the real-time network configuration. The network layer ensures reliable information transmission by adopting data coding, extraction, fusion, restructuring, mining, and aggregation algorithms. The main function is to transfer and process the information obtained by sensor layer, and to realize data exchange among largescale heterogeneous networks.
- Application layer: it exports functionalities for specific applications, and provides embedded interfaces for

Table 1. The main characteristics of U2IoT entities.

Characteristics	Descriptions
Cyber, Physical, Social Co-existence	Any entity exists in the physical world, along with its existence in the cyber world in the virtual form via specific communication and network technologies; and the entity also has its social identity and attribution which not isolated from cyber and physical attribution.
Connectivity, and Interactivity	Any entity can interoperate and collaborate with other heterogeneous entities within its access domain, and the entities are interrelated and interact on each other.
Space-time Consistency	Any entity can dynamically interact with other entities at any time, any place, and in any mode; the entity can freely enter/leave the networks without influencing the ongoing communications; and synchronization is needed during heterogeneous network accessing.
Multi-identity Status	Any entity has multi-identity statuses that include a unique core identity, and other temporary identities according to its underlying applications.

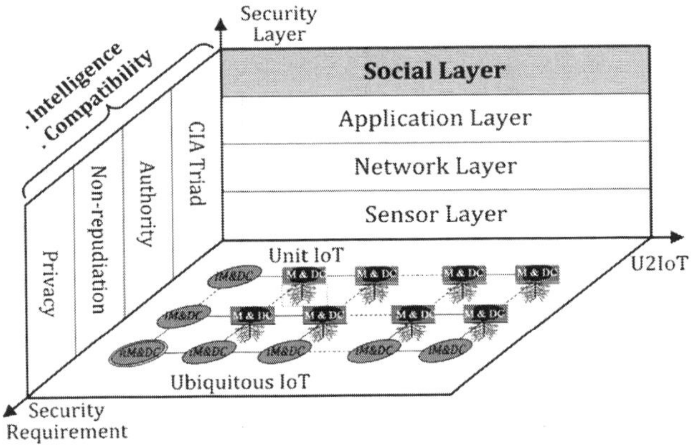

Figure 2. Security layer and security requirement.

infrastructures to perform testing, monitoring, or auditing applications. The standard protocols and service composition technologies are applied to realize the integration between heterogeneous distributed networks and its applications, such as logistics monitoring, smart grid scheduling, intelligent search, and cloud computing. Such applications should adapt in dynamic environments. Particularly, an additional social layer on the top of the architecture considers the social attribution in U2IoT. The social layer is mainly devoted to communicate among objects and other supporting networks to perform correlation between the cyber individual and the corresponding profile in social networks. Correlative social attributions are granted to each entity, and hierarchical management and data centers operate overall security considerations. In social layer, diverse interfaces are accessed by a real entity which acts on its corresponding cyber entity to control its behaviors. Meanwhile, other social compositions are also considered, such as ownership control management, social relationship modeling, and entity behavior formalization. In the perspective of information security, the sensor and network layers specify multiple networks and sensor nodes, which are used to capture data streams, to detect activities and events with identification algorithms, and to realize specific application functions. Core of data acquiring is sensor technology (e.g., RFID, WSN, femtocell) and Global Sensor Network (GSN) middleware, whose security is challenged by constrained resources. Note that distributed control nodes provide the capabilities to survive under formidable conditions, and by information security controls such as error detection and correction, random access control, and fault tolerance are recommended.

2) Adding Intelligence and Compatibility for Security Requirement: Elements of security requirements include CIA Triad, authority, non-repudiation, and privacy. Additional requirements that intelligence and compatibility are added into advanced security considerations, which provide reliable security and privacy protection. Table 2 presents the comparison of security requirements among the traditional network, general IoT, and U2IoT. Intelligence represents that an entity should own abstract capabilities including self-learning, self-adapting, and self-reasoning to adapt itself to dynamic semantic environments. In non-deterministic channels and open interfaces, virtual intelligent entities should be autonomously interconnected in U2IoT. The embedded intelligence makes the entity have strong efficacies to adapt dynamic information that is the mapping of environment interactions, social connections, and human behaviors.

Table 2. Comparision of security requirements.

Requirement	Traditional network [13]	General IoT [14,15]	Additional Requirements in U2IoT
CIA Triad	a) Data Confidentiality: Protect data from unauthorized disclosure; b) Data Integrity: Ensure correctness or accuracy of data; c) Data Availability: Ensure that there is no denial of authorized access to network elements, information flows, services and applications.	Bottom-up cryptographic algorithms should be recommended for heterogeneous network infrastructure: - Key management infrastructures; - Block/Stream ciphers algorithms; - Digital signatures; - Hash function; - Pseudo-random number generators.	a) Ubiquitous forward, backward, and ongoing security: Ensure ubiquitous unlinkability among the prior, later, and the current interrogations, which cannot be correlated. b) Dynamic session freshness: Ensure session freshness check into the integrity check mechanism. c) Self/Non-self identification: Ensure only authorized self entity can access the network resources and services, and eliminate any non-self entity.
Authority	a) Authentication: Ensure that only legal entities can access network resources to exclude any illegal entity from the networks; b) Authorization: Realize different access control among legal entities.	Advanced authentication and authorization mechanisms: a) Assignment of users contributions to a single contributor; b) Upgrading users trust status without revealing identities to service provider.	a) Intelligent access control: Use heterogeneous authentication and identification for semantic access control on legal information interoperation; b) Compatible certificate authority: Authenticate entity and grant authority to access system resources; c) Hierarchical authentication: Establish hierarchical mutual authentication: individual/group authentication, and source/terminal authentication.
Non-repudiation	a) Providing available proofs to prevent any entity from denying having performed a particular behavior related to the exchanged messages; b) Ensuring the availability of evidence that can be presented by a trusted third party, and proving that an entity's behavior has occurred before.		Social attribution: Assign social attribution to an entity's cyber behaviors, which are applied for compatible social computing and behavior supervision.
Privacy	Any sensitive information is protected, that may be derived from the observation of network activities.	Dynamic Consent Tool: Permit certain services or applications to access as little or as much of that the data as desired.	a) Transparency: Let user know which entity contains its related data, when and where the entity has used the data, and how the entity realizes the specific function. b) Traceability: Let the entity know the network and service information that it has even connected.

Compatibility requires that an entity has appropriate interconnection and interoperability to adjust to heterogeneous data formats, interfaces, channels, and networks in U2IoT model. The supplemental requirements address advanced criterions for information interaction. Meanwhile, compatibility can be promoted to scalability, expansibility and modularity among heterogeneous entities and the multi-context environments. The both requirements operate together to promote the security and privacy preservation: 1) ensure diverse entities own artificial intelligence and autonomous security control against the strong attackers; 2) ensure heterogeneous entities, networks and applications establishing reliable interconnection without compromising any communication data and individual privacy.

Physical Security

Physical security is denoted in external context and inherent infrastructure, in which human-like security immune safeguard is achieved.

1) External Context: Simple context and complex context are specified in [16], in which the former determines the basic identity, location, and entity status by a single parameter; the latter refers to geographical structures, traceability information, and real world conditions. Above both contexts are refined to support creating, debugging and integrating applications of Ubiquitous IoT, and provide interface interconnection and restriction for Unit IoTs. In U2IoT model, the borders of each entity's external context merge even vanish, and the obscure contexts spanning from an individual, an object, or an environment to social relationships, should support the hierarchical IoT subsystem. Particularly, intrusion detection algorithm is significant to acquire context information for monitoring sensors behavior, discover control node breaches, and other potential vulnerabilities.
2) Inherent Infrastructure: Artificial immune security system as computational intelligence is applied to analyze inherent infrastructure, which belongs sensorial system inspired by principles and processes of the natural immune system. Typical algorithms (e.g., clonal selection, negative selection, and immune network) exploit the immune system's features of detection, learning and memory to constitute innate immunity and adaptive immunity. Physical security issues such as intrusion detection, adaptive disposition, context-driven feedback, and error recovery can be addressed as follows.
   - Innate immunity: It provides basic barriers against foreign invasions in real-time environment, and it is triggered upon sensors identifying abnormal or malevolent attacks by the intelligent pattern recognition mechanisms. Co-stimulation signals are transmitted to distributed control nodes via Unit IoT networks, and then rejection reactions are performed by management centers. During defense operations, activation thresholds are defined to ensure the detection optimization, and fuzzy diagnosis can also applied for imperfect detection. Note that the innate immune defense is nonspecific, meaning that U2IoT model responds to the various attacks in a general scheme. Such system cannot afford long-lasting immunity against a certain attack. The innate immune system is dominant to confront the dynamic contexts and continuously refreshing threats.
   - Adaptive immunity: It refers to acquired resistance, where an attack is marked as a specific signature. Selective response requires recognizing non-self element during attack prototype presentation. If U2IoT has been infected by the same or similar invasion, specific memory module would be aroused to eliminate damaging effects by generating improved response to return the system into secure state. Adaptive immunity executes fuzzy diagnosis to variations of the same former attack, and optimal stimulation such as subsidiary vaccination is available by updating M&DCs' profile databases.

According to both innate and adaptive immunities [17], three main features should be achieved in U2IoT model.

Multithreaded and Hybrid Configuration: The U2IoT model may apply multithreaded security algorithms for the massively parallel network architecture that comprises a diverse set of components. The components are organized in hybrid mode, in which both centralized and distributed configurations are included. Towards Unit IoT, the allocation of the sensing and query processing is performed by the central M&DC. Towards Ubiquitous IoT, the industry IoTs and local IoTs are relatively independent, which commonly construct national IoT. In U2IoT model, such multithreaded and hybrid configuration are throughout all the networks, sensor and control nodes, and management and data centers.

Multilayered and Autonomous Organization: There is no single security mechanism that offers complete immunity. Therefore, multilayered protection should independently operate for all-round safeguards. During the layered organization, U2IoT model autonomously makes its decisions by detecting potential attacks and proposing feasible solutions based on artificial immune algorithms

Heterogeneity: U2IoT model should be accessible by a large number of heterogeneous communication technologies with different networks, channels, interfaces, and hardware/software capabilities. Such heterogeneity of entities adds complexity to its security situations, which makes that a certain attack may simultaneously act on multiple entities in different IoTs, but the attack cannot act on all the involved IoTs. The immune protection ensures that the entire heterogeneous components cannot be corrupted due to the same attacker.

Management Security

Towards the future IoT, it is scarcely possible to establish a uniform security protocol as Internet, just like different nations and/or regions cannot adopt an identical safety precaution. Hence, distinctive management mechanisms are significant for both security and interconnecttion requirements. Due to the limitations of technological approaches, appropriate management should couple with the implementation of information security and physical security. Security strategies working on human behaviors should be considered to ensure that virtual cyber data is adapted to the real physical contexts.

Application requirement for distributed sensor and control nodes provides generic/specific protection. IPM is of benefit to practical application security, such as historical query, project management, risk assessment, software design, and system certification. For a specific scenario, customized requirements are assigned to describe the authorized/-unauthorized usage in a particular organization or individual. Additionally, application requirement should also be consistent with privacy prevention which realizes that the sensitive data is exchanged, stored, and shared without revealing any user privacy.

Industry/Local/National regulation mainly serves for iM&DC/lM&DC/nM&DC to provide rules and guidance for U2IoT. It takes legal or disciplinary actions to resist the offensive individuals or institutions which do not comply with the regulations. Thereinto, industry regulation describes approaches to achieve high-level security objective for a special industrial authority organization, such as agriculture, energy, and military. For instance, in the chemical hazards medical management, the regulations require certain parameters (e.g., temperature, vibrations, and relative proximity), caution the users for violation thresholds, and guarantee system security by warning abnormal implement and configuration. Thereinto, local regulation should coincide with local customs and practices to adopt humanistic perspectives for designing, implementing, and maintaining the local IoTs. National regulation governs guidelines to realize nation-to-nation compatibility, and formal memorandum of agreements needs to be shared across national boundaries. Additionally, customized roles and responsibilities can be codified among different nations.

International policy considers the global IoT consociation during connectivity and consistency of nM&DC and global IoT. Moreover, international standards should be addressed by governments to promote security confidence and ensure interoperability. It indicates that a general international governance framework with reasonable enforcement policies will provide permanent mechanism towards security protection.

Conclusion

In this paper, a security architecture IPM is proposed for U2IoT model. The main purpose is to establish an integrated security architecture with considerations on cyberphysical-social world. The proposed IPM comprises three essential security perspectives (i.e., information, physical, and management), in which three-dimensional information security model introduces social layer, and intelligence and compatibility for security consideration; artificial immunity is applied to describe physical security; and a series of social strategies are recommended to achieve management security.

ACKNOWLEDGEMENTS

This work is jointly funded by National Natural Science Foundation of China (NSFC) and Civil Aviation Administration of China (CAAC) (61079019), and is also supported by the Fundamental Research Funds for the Central Universities (YWF-11-02-264).

REFERENCES

1. H. Ning, "RFID Major Projects and State Internet of Things (Second Edition)," China Machine Press, Beijing, 2010.
2. J. Ma, J. Wen, R. Huang and B. Huang, "Cyber-Individual Meets Brain Informatics," IEEE Intelligent Systems, Vol. 26, No. 5, 2011, pp. 30-37. doi:10.1109/MIS.2011.55
3. L. Atzori, A. Iera and G. Morabito, "The Internet of Things: A Survey," Computer Networks, Vol. 54, No. 15, 2010, pp. 2787-2805. doi:10.1016/j.comnet.2010.05.010
4. D. Bandyopadhyay and J. Sen, "Internet of Things: Applications and Challenges in Technology and Standardization," Wireless Personal Communications, Vol. 58, No. 1, 2011, pp. 49-69. doi:10.1007/s11277-011-0288-5
5. H. Ning, N. Ning, S. Qu, Y. Zhang and H. Yang, "Layered Structure and Management in Internet of Things," Proceedings of Future Generation Communication and Networking (FGCN 2007), Jeju, 6-8 December 2007, pp. 386-389.
6. R. Roman, P. Najera and J. Lopez, "Securing the Internet of Things," Computer, Vol. 44, No. 9, 2011, pp. 51-58. doi:10.1109/MC.2011.291

7. R. Kaur, "Advances in Intrusion Detection System for WLAN," Advances in Internet of Things, Vol. 1, No. 3, 2011, pp. 51-54. doi:10.4236/ait.2011.13007
8. G. P. Hancke, K. Markantonakis and K. E. Mayes, "Security Challenges for User-Oriented RFID Applications within the 'Internet of Things'," Journal of Internet Technology, Vol. 11, No. 3, 2010, pp. 307-313.
9. R. Roman, C. Alcaraz, J. Lopez and N. Sklavos, "Key Management Systems for Sensor Networks in the Context of the Internet of Things," Computers & Electrical Engineering, Vol. 37, No. 2, 2011, pp. 147-159. doi:10.1016/j.compeleceng.2011.01.009
10. L. D. Xu, "Information Architecture for Supply Chain Quality Management," International Journal of Production Research, Vol. 49, No. 1, 2011, pp. 183-198. doi:10.1080/00207543.2010.508944
11. L. Zhou and H. C. Chao, "Multimedia Traffic Security Architecture for the Internet of Things," IEEE Network, Vol. 25, No. 3, 2011, pp. 35-40. doi:10.1109/MNET.2011.5772059
12. H. Ning and Z. Wang, "Future Internet of Things Architecture: Like Mankind Neural System or Social Organization Framework?" IEEE Communications Letters, Vol. 15, No. 4, 2011, pp. 461-463. doi:10.1109/LCOMM.2011.022411.110120
13. Draft ITU-T Recommendation X.805 (Formerly X.css), Security Architecture for Systems Providing End-to-End communications, 2003.
14. D. Havlik, S. Schade, Z. A. Sabeur , P. Mazzetti, K. Watson, A. J. Berre and J. L. Mon, "From Sensor to Observation Web with Environmental Enablers in the Future Internet," Sensors, Vol. 11, No. 4, 2011, pp. 3874-3907. doi:10.3390/s110403874
15. L. Atzori, A. Iera and G. Morabito, "The Internet of Things: A Survey," Computer Networks, Vol. 54, No. 15, 2010, pp. 2787-2805. doi:10.1016/j.comnet.2010.05.010
16. N. Koshizuka and K. Sakamura, "Ubiquitous ID: Standards for Ubiquitous Computing and the Internet of Things," IEEE Pervasive Computing, Vol. 9, No. 4, 2010, pp. 98-101. doi:10.1109/MPRV.2010.87
17. P. K. Harmer, P. D. Williams, G. H. Gunsch, G. B. Lamont, "An Artificial Immune System Architecture for Computer Security Applications," IEEE Transactions on Evolutionary Computation, Vol. 6, No. 3, 2002, pp. 252-280. doi:10.1109/TEVC.2002.1011540

6
CHAPTER

EMERGING ISSUES FOR EDUCATION IN E-DISCOVERY

Shuai Yuan, Raghav H Rao and Shambhu Upadhyaya

Keywords: Electronic Health Record, E-discovery, Security and Privacy

INTRODUCTION

Electronic Health Record (EHR) systems are the aggregate electronic record of health-related information on individuals "created and gathered cumulatively across more than one health care organization and managed and consulted by licensed clinicians and staff involved in the individual's health and care" (National Alliance for Health Information Technology (NAHIT[a]) [1]. EHR has been strongly recommended for adoption in the healthcare industry in the U.S. The increased use of EHR systems has assisted health care professionals in medical practices by storing patients' medical and diagnosis information, exchanging laboratory reports and radiologic images, and also providing decision support tools for the physicians and communication methods with patients [2,3]. The American Recovery and Reinvestment Act of 2009 (ARRA)'s goal was to computerize all Americans health records by 2014 by dedicating nineteen billion dollars to the promotion of health information technology [4,5]. However, EHR systems also bring new liability and litigation risks such as the inappropriate use of the systems, privacy breaches, and inadvertent data disclosures, which in turn may impose heavy costs in terms of preservation of electronic information and potential litigation issues [6].

E-discovery refers to discovery of information, often for civil litigations, that is stored in electronic format, known as Electronically Stored Information (ESI). In 2006, amendments were made to federal rules to facilitate ESI discovery. This resulted in

---

Citation: Shuai Yuan, Raghav H Rao and Shambhu Upadhyaya, Emerging issues for education in E-discovery, doi:10.1186/s13388-015-0017-9.

changes to traditional e-discovery rules [7]. To comply with the new rules, healthcare providers are required to establish and update policies and procedures in terms of information governance and EHR systems along with advanced technologies that may also be needed to be developed to facilitate e-discovery.

EHR adoption will require significant efforts with regard to workforce since it is a complex and large initiative in healthcare industry. This calls for expansion of today's education system to cover topics of security, security technology and policy, and privacy issues. The primary purpose of this study is to lay a foundation for topics in both security issues and e-discovery challenges involving EHR system use. To achieve this purpose, we categorize the emerging issues based on in-depth literature review, into three categories: Development in EHR, E-discovery policy and strategy, and Security and privacy in EHR. We also discuss some key issues related to e-discovery raised from the new technologies of cloud computing and big data contexts. A major contribution of this paper is the development of a framework for education. The outcome of this study can be used to design short courses on security and e-discovery regarding EHR systems in the healthcare domain.

The rest of the paper is organized as follows. Section 2 provides discusses three categories- Development in EHR, E-discovery policy and strategy, and Security and privacy in EHR. Section 3 studies new and emerging issues associated with e-discovery when cloud computing and big data are becoming prevalent. Section 4 concludes with a discussion on the course-design framework for faculty members.

LITERATURE REVIEW OF E-DISCOVERY IN EHR

Developments in EHR

EHR systems that contain patients' medical data and information, have not only been used in healthcare delivery, but are relevant to litigation and are subject to ESI discovery due to amendments that were passed in 2006. As the adoption of EHR systems in hospitals and other healthcare sectors is increasing, providers and legal counsel must be aware of the advances in EHR technology, get a better understanding of the information they can acquire and retrieve from EHR systems, and prepare e-discovery provisioning requirements [8]. The development of techniques in EHR systems would facilitate e-discovery. In addition, healthcare providers naturally have a wide choice as to how engaged their medical practice will be with EHR technology and which EHR system will be used [8]. With national benchmarks to measure EHR systems in terms of certification and meaningful use, the quality of the system outcomes as well as the functionalities associated with e-discovery request need to be guaranteed. Furthermore, particular EHR technologies, for instance, metadata search algorithms, are necessary to facilitate the review process for e-discovery use. Healthcare providers and legal counsel might not be technology experts in EHR development, however, the knowledge of where relevant ESI exists and how to preserve such information to satisfy e-discovery obligations is a necessary requirement.

Techniques in EHR systems to facilitate e-discovery

Advanced techniques in EHR systems to facilitate e-discovery process are needed, otherwise e-discovery will be inefficient and costly, leading to heavy burden to stakeholders involved. For instance, the 2006 amendments have expanded the use of a "legal hold" for preservation of paper documents as well as ESI document. Healthcare organizations should suspend routine document retention and destruction policy to ensure the preservation of all forms of relevant information avoiding sanctions for ESI spoilage, at the time when the organization receives a notice of litigation [9]. There is a documented lack of efficient technology in EHR systems to establish a legal hold on patients' records and it is costly to put a legal hold on one particular patient in EHR systems [10]. Further, sometimes legal counsels do not have sufficient knowledge in techniques to acquire valuable data from EHR systems. This calls for education about functions of EHR systems.

Information sharing and data interoperability

There is an increasing need to build a national health information infrastructure (NHII) to connect users and manage knowledge of healthcare so that provides functions for information sharing among different EHR systems. There are three main reasons why the NHII is required [11]: First, professionals and researchers face substantial growth and much more complex health data about patients as they encounter more types of illnesses and simultaneously improving diagnostic capabilities; Second, data standardization fulfilled by NHII will facilitate data manipulation so that costs and turnaround times are reduced and last but not least, a platform is needed to assure the benefits of cutting edge technology and method diffuse to different stakeholders in healthcare domain. For instance, large datasets are needed to acquire the knowledge regarding the molecular underpinning of disease through intensive computing capabilities. Such data sets can be one feature of the NHII. In order to achieve the goal to build a NHII connected participants in healthcare, series of agreements on standardization of technology, data, processes and rules need to be reached as well. The quantity and quality of data to support decision-makings in health care delivery are important for implementation of a complete NHII [8]. Each of these issues is critical for system related education.

Data interoperability is a key ability in NHII implementation that two or more EHR systems can exchange and share information. This feature has also been indicated in "meaningful use" stage 1 requirements such that key patient data can be exported to a common format. Currently two formats have been developed: Continuity of Care Records (CCR) and Continuity of Care Documents (CCD) but neither of them has been used to export entire patient's EHR records, since abbreviations and terminology vary among practice [12]. In order to facilitate e-discovery, first, the format used by the export feature must be able to provide a complete record of a patient for production during discovery. In addition, the EHR data should be viewable by a lawyer in a similar layout as viewed by medical professionals since, "A party must produce documents as they are kept in the usual course of business..." Finally, it is necessary for the feature to be able to export specific data required for production such that the lawyer is capable to produce only relevant data for discovery purposes [12].

Metrics for EHR systems quality control

Without appropriate mechanisms and metrics to control the quality of diverse EHR systems in the market, healthcare organizations are at risk of investing large amounts on poorly designed systems which may not improve the outcomes. Therefore, developing national benchmarks to measure not only the technology but systems in terms of certification, meaningful use, and implementation specification, etc. are mandatory [13,14].

Here, it is also worth noticing the difference between certification and meaningful use on EHR systems [15]. Certification of EHR systems ensures that the particular system meets functionality standards. In June 2010, the Office of the National Coordinator for Health Information Technology (ONC) defined the temporary criteria for testing and certifying EHRS functionality [16]. Subsequently in January 2011, ONC issued the final rule on a Permanent Certification Program for Health Information Technology, for functional testing requirement, cases and tools. Meaningful use implies "providers need to show they're using certified EHR technology in ways that can be measured significantly in quality and in quantity", corresponding to quality of the adoption of EHR systems [17]. Identification of these issues is important for educational programs.

Clinical practice guidelines to optimize EHR system use

Clinical practice guidelines (CPG)s assist in decisions about special circumstances in healthcare. CPGs in terms of diagnostic and treatment practices have been developed by professional societies over a long time period. The standard of care is a key to successful defense in medical malpractice litigation since it reveals whether the defendant "proceed [ed] with the reasonable caution that a prudent man would have exercised under such circumstances" [13]. Compliance with well-established CPGs, similar to expert testimony, can be utilized as proof that the defendant met the standard of care, "at least as evidence of a practice that is accepted by a respectable minority". However, at the early age of EHR system development and adoption, few authoritative CPGs exist regarding the design and use of EHR systems, and even less in the litigation context [13]. Any educational program related to e-discovery in health needs to include such CPGs.

Audit trails/ metadata search techniques

Audit trails are the records about "who did what and when" in order to meet requirements on "system integrity, recoverability, auditing, and requirements". Effective audit trails on EHR systems should keep all relevant system input and output not only for the purpose of system validation and problem diagnosis, but also to understand how EHR systems are operating. The audit trails can then serve as unbiased evidence of medical practice for potential litigation use [13].

A key component of the functioning of audit trails is Metadata - which is generated to track how an electronic document has been manipulated. Metadata has been viewed as non-hearsay evidence by the courts because it can be considered to have integrity - it is automatically generated without human intervention [10]. Metadata can also be used as a tool to reveal what documents have been actually created, reviewed, modified and deleted. Federal courts have held that when an electronic document is discoverable, it is to be produced "in native format...with their metadata intact" [10]. E-discovery with metadata would generate a huge amount of ESI. This calls for effective search techniques and strategies to facilitate the review process [13]. Therefore, search techniques for metadata and an understanding of metadata need to be covered in e-discovery courses.

Advances in health 2.0

Health 2.0. has been defined as the phenomenon in which Web 2.0 Technologies provide members of the health community–health professionals, health consumers, and health science students–with new and innovative ways to create, disseminate, and share information both individually and collaboratively. It is a new concept of health care that employs social software and other Web-based tools to promote collaboration between patients, their caregivers, medical professionals, and other stakeholders in health care to create a better, more knowledgeable and cost effective environment for better well-being [18]. Health 2.0 is the use of a set of Web tools (blogs, Podcasts, wikis, etc.) in health care by doctors, patients, and scientists. For example, websites like PatientsLikeMe [19] use knowledge from users the network from social media to personalize health care and promote health education [20].

One key difference between traditional models of medicine and Health 2.0 is the knowledge of patient records and related control. In traditional models, patients' records could only be kept and accessed by medical professionals; while in newer models patients obtain more control and deeper insight into their own information. Web 2.0/technology, patients, professionals, social networking, health information/content, collaboration, and change of health care are the topics closely related to the definition of Health 2.0 [18].

Therefore, any curriculum for Health 2.0 should also include, for instance: 1) the stakeholders involved, e.g. patients/consumers, professionals/caregivers, and biomedical researchers, 2) the emerging methods and technology, e.g. web 2.0 and virtual-reality tools, 3) the change of relationship between stakeholders, such as the improved collaboration and communication between professionals and patients, and 4) the impact on the development of health care system like improvement on safety, efficiency and quality of old system. In addition, inaccurate online information is another concern in Health 2.0. Although research has found that online information is often accurate or can be corrected rapidly, many practitioners believe "the consequences could be disastrous for any inexperienced trainee following the advice" [21]. The use of Health 2.0 raises a challenge for healthcare organizations to serve e-discovery requests. Since the information in Health 2.0 associated with privacy, ethical, and ownership issues is in the scope of discovery as well, failing to preserve relevant information due to un-updated usage and electronic data management policy and techniques could lead to potential sanctions. It is important that students are exposed to each one of these, since these could drive e-discovery lawsuits.

E-discovery policy and strategy

Policies and processes for electronic records management

Electronic health records are composed of types of information within the boundary of the health organization, e.g. email, text messages, and even legacy information systems [22]. Health Information Management and IT professionals need to work together to fulfill the tasks of determining organizational document storage, retention, and destruction schedules as well as for digital information to avoid potential sanctions resulting from failure to preserve relevant documents in e-discovery cases.

For instance, the updated policies and processes should indicate where and in what type of format the electronic health records should be stored, how often to maintain such records, and when to destroy them. Updated policies and processes for electronic medical records are required for healthcare organizations to comply with federal, state requirements to facilitate e-discovery.

Economics of cost

Recently, courts have started to limit ESI discovery based on cost-benefit analysis. Under the Discovery Scope and Limits in Rule 26 of The Federal Rules of Civil Procedure, ESI discovery could be limited if "the burden or expense of the proposed discovery outweighs its likely benefit, considering the needs of the case, the amount in controversy, the parties' resources, the importance of the issue at stake in the litigation, and the importance of the proposed discovery in resolving the issues". For example, in Lorranie v. Markel American Insurance Co., Judge Grimm denied the parties' competing motions for summary judgment by opining that "it makes little sense to go to all the bother and expense to get electronic information only to have it excluded from evidence or rejected from consideration during summary judgment because the proponent cannot lay a sufficient foundation to get it admitted [23]". Therefore, it is important for students to understand how organizations should establish a means for determining the actual costs for production of ESI, and for detecting if this production would be over burdensome in which case such ESI would be out of the scope of discovery [10].

Legal hold policies to handle preservation of relevant documents

Legal hold indicates that a party "must suspend its routine document retention/destruction policy" for the purpose of making sure the preservation of relevant document including ESI, once the party receives a notice of litigation [24]. In order to comply with the preservation obligation, in addition to appropriate techniques, healthcare organizations need to understand the legal hold policy to handle this process, e.g. the instructions and corresponding workflow so that the regular automatic retention/destruction policy would not execute automatically. These issues would fit into an understanding of both law and workflow systems.

Security and privacy issues

Information privacy and data confidentiality

For an information system in any area and domain, security is of crucial concern. Further, information privacy is one key issue that has serious influence on the adoption of EHR systems since all the patients' healthcare information are stored, shared and communicated among different EHR systems and healthcare sectors. Any privacy breach and abuse of data may prohibit the intention to use EHR systems in spite of numerous benefits. Privacy issues have not been addressed sufficiently at either technical or business process level, e.g., in a nationwide survey conducted in February 2005 by Harris Interactive of Rochester, N.Y., 70 percent of people were somewhat or very concerned that personal medical information would be leaked due to weak data security [25].

Data is the primary resource in EHR systems thus its confidentiality is significant for information privacy. Personal information obtained in physician-patient relationship should not be revealed to others unless the patient understands and consents to disclosure [26]. The trend of data sharing among EHR systems and healthcare organizations is inevitable, as a result, innovative management techniques and policies on data confidentiality should be taught to keep in step.

Access controls and policies for EHR

While maintaining information privacy matters, obtaining patients' healthcare information on demand from EHR systems for caregivers like hospitals and doctors is critical as well. There is a trade-off between accessibility to patients' information and privacy concerns, especially when some EHR systems are based on web services which make the information more easily to access while at the same time give rise to potential privacy issues. Therefore, a challenge raised is to develop access control policies that can provide required protection on privacy while keeping flexibility to accommodate authorized users so that only a set of users can access certain level of patient information [27], e.g. which portions of a patient's record can access by whom for a specific period of time. In general, attribute-based access control (ABAC) and role-based access control (RBAC) are the two main approaches to control access to EHR systems [28,29]. ABAC divides the system into subcomponents and for each subcomponent, access policy has been stored as an attribute of the data, while RBAC constructs a hierarchy of roles that can be assigned to each user, through which to authorize privileges to each role instead of each user. Both approaches have their own benefits and shortcomings. Thus understanding existing access control method and policy to ensure both flexibility and security is urgent for any student of e-discovery.

Management of patient consent

As we mentioned earlier, without patient's awareness and consents to disclosure, private information in EHR systems should not be revealed to others, thus consent of patient plays a vital role. Individual patients should know and understand the contents of records in terms of effective notification and truly informed consent for disclosure, which also implies that the particular patient is fully informed of his/her medical status and gives voluntary agreement to permit access to their healthcare information [26]. Failure to truly inform patient's awareness of disclosure, e.g. using implied consent, would lead to unethical issues.

Patients either implicitly or explicitly consent to information disclosure according to different consent models. For example, two types of consent models are considered: General Consent with Specific Denials and General Denial with Specific Consent [30]. Obviously the latter can maintain information at a high level of confidentiality while at the same time, it might hinder the workflow of healthcare providers. Therefore, an understanding of effective consent and control mechanisms are needed that can give patients control for their own healthcare information as well as not impede regular healthcare delivery process.

HITECH and HIPAA privacy and security rules

Significant modifications have been made to Health Information Technology for Economic and Clinical Health Act (HITECH) and Health Insurance Portability and Accountability Act (HIPAA) Privacy and Security Rules. For instance, substantial incentives and grants are provided in the HITECH Act for the adoption of EHR systems and information exchange to improve both quality and efficiency of healthcare. On the other hand, for the HIPAA Privacy and Security Rules, mandatory federal security breach reporting requirements, criminal and civil penalties for noncompliance are established [31,32]. These extensions and enforcements are aimed at continually improving the effect of HITECH and HIPAA rules – clearly an important area of knowledge for the student.

ISSUES ON E-DISCOVERY IN CLOUD AND BIG DATA

The cloud is the place where various users including patients and physicians on EHR systems have started to share resources [33]. E-discovery becomes more complex in the context of the cloud environment. First, the data are preserved by a cloud service provider, which may lead to the consequence that some ESI might be outside the scope of discovery, or alternately, some data may fall under e-discovery but may not be controlled by firms facing a discovery request. The other reason is, since data from various users is intermingled in the cloud controlled only by the service provider, retrieving and placing a hold on one user's information for anticipated litigation request may affect other users who are not involved [34]. Therefore, some unique issues are needed to be understood in the context of e-discovery in cloud as well.

Cloud services support the basic infrastructure and platform for EHR systems, and would be instrumental in the harvesting of big data. Organizations are experiencing exponential growth in the amounts of data they create, capture, and retain within their in-house facilities, as well as that are maintained in the cloud in the current big data world, thus call for advanced analytics techniques dealing with them [35]. E-discovery also relies on high performance analysis tools to reduce the time and cost, but due to the nature of big data more powerful tools will be needed to identify, organize, and analyze big data. In addition to the technical tools, comprehensive policy and strategy according to e-discovery are also required to accommodate the "big" world. Developing guidelines, procedures, and workflows for the creation, storage and destruction of ESI with potential big data involved in litigation procedures for compliance with federal and state regulations has been considered urgent and necessary as well as a big challenge [36].

In addition, cloud computing service and big data interact with each other. Therefore, they have in common some critical issues, e.g. data preservation and analytics techniques in e-discovery, as well as usage policies and "thresholds" of relevancy for evidence to be admissible.

Data analytics

The volume of data, velocity with which data is generated and variety of data-pictures, messages, audio files, text files, in e-discovery procedures, makes it nearly impossible to review them by humans. Data mining along with predictive analytics plays an important role in e-discovery for legal purposes. For instance, text mining, as well as image mining can discover hidden patterns and relationship between people and events that can be used as evidence in litigations [37].

Predictive coding as the service that can rank and code relevant documents might be used in an anticipated litigation through machine learning algorithms and pattern recognition methods built-in. It is increasingly recognized as a field of inquiry and capability development and could reduce the extent of human involvement in the e-discovery process [38]. A hybrid method combining both predictive coding and data mining techniques with extra attention by human review on the most important ESI would help best practice results in e-discovery. Such skills are important for an e-discovery scholar.

Data preservation and control policies

Data in the cloud provides additional difficulties in data preservation since ESI from one particular user can be stored across multiple physical storage locations due to the nature of cloud. Thus, in order to implement preservation, specific cloud resources need to be isolated [34,39]. Data in the cloud are under custody and control by the cloud service provider which means users may not have actual powerful control over them that can serve as key evidence in litigation [34]. When litigation is anticipated, it is required to put a legal hold on relevant ESI as well in the cloud. Failing to maintain relevant ESI, e.g. deletion by routine operation policy, would result in potential spoliation claims.

Further, the users of EHR data have access and control of their accounts and the information. However, it is possible they may delete some information without realizing that such information could be relevant to anticipated legal issues and should be preserved. Under this circumstance, it is necessary to determine whether the users have a duty to preserve the information and whether it is reasonable to foresee that the information is in the scope of discovery [40].

These issues regarding data preservation in cloud environment by the third party service provider and data control are not taught in many universities as of yet and we suggest that they should be required.

Thresholds of relevancy for evidence to be admissible

Courts are determining on a case-by-case basis whether a person's claim of privacy is reasonable [33]. Courts have continued to be opposed to the notion that any protectable privacy interest exists in material posted on social network websites related to health record, for example, in Fawcett v. Altieri, the court reasoned that, "if you post a tweet, [it is] just like you scream it out the window, [and] there is no reasonable expectation of privacy." Effective and efficient approaches to determine a "threshold" showing of relevancy for evidence to be admissible are required when concerned about the impact of privacy interests.

REVIEW AND CONCLUSIONS

This review indicates that there are some "common" issues shared with e-discovery in EHR systems, cloud computing and big data, particularly the attention and emphasis on the needs for organizational policy updates for integrating e-discovery requirements into regular operations and workflows while advances on technical and information privacy are the other two sides. Information is the core in any discovery-related procedure, thus information governance composed of technical and managerial issues would be important for students to understand. We summarize the above discussion in a framework (See Table 1). The framework can be used for potential short course-design on e-discovery and security in the healthcare domain.

This study provides a broad view and better understanding of the critical and urgent issues on e-discovery and security focusing on EHR systems. The list of issues can also help healthcare industry for better training of personnel.

It is important to mention that this study was not intended to capture "all of the issues" within given contexts. Nevertheless, it offers an opportunity to build consensus on what is significant and what is urgent in this field. Furthermore, this study would also contribute to developing guidelines for design of courses on e-discovery in the healthcare domain. In the long term with the increasing rate of EHR adoption and EHR meaningful use achievement, new issues and challenges would emerge. Experts from healthcare organizations, legal institutes, and IT professions as well as privacy and data management communities should work closely to draw a detailed education map for this field by sharing different ideas from various orientations.

Table 1 Framework of key issues for e-discovery in EHR

Domains		Key issues
EHR Systems	Development in EHR	Techniques in EHR systems to facilitate e-discovery
		Information sharing and data interoperability
		Metrics for EHR systems quality control
		Clinical practice guidelines (CPGs) to optimize EHR system use
		Audit trails/metadata search techniques
		Advances in Health 2.0
	E-Discovery policy and strategy	Policies and processes for electronic records management
		Economics of cost
		Legal hold policies to handle preservation of relevant documents
	Security and privacy	Information privacy and data confidentiality
		Access controls and policies for EHR
		Management of patient consent
		HITECH and HIPAA privacy and security rules
Cloud Computing and big data		Data analytics
Data preservation and control policies		
Thresholds of relevancy for evidence to be admissible		

Endnotes

[a]NAHIT ceased operations in 2009, but it concluded several major US health related initiatives before it ceased. (http://www.healthcareitnews.com/news/nahit-no-more).

DECLARATIONS

Acknowledgements

The authors thank the guest editors and reviewers for critical comments that have improved the paper. This research was supported in part by the National Science Foundation under grant # DUE-1241709. The usual disclaimer applies.

Competing interests

The authors declare that they have no competing interests.

Authors' contributions

Author SY carried out the review under the guidance of HRR and SU. All authors participated in the writing of the paper. All authors read and approved the final manuscript.

REFERENCES

1. Gensinger Jr RA, Introduction to healthcare information enabling technologies. Chicago: Healthcare Information and Management Systems Society (HIMSS); (2010)
2. C Chen, T Garrido, D Chock, G Okawa, L Liang, The kaiser Permanente electronic health record: transforming and streamlining modalities of care. Health. Aff. **28**, 323–333 (2009)
3. JA Handler, CF Feied, K Coonan, J Vozenilek, M Gillam, PR Peacock, R Sinert, MS Smith, Computerized physician order entry and online decision support. Acad. Emerg. Med. **11**, 1135–1141 (2004)
4. D Blumenthal, Stimulating the adoption of health information technology. N. Engl. J. Med. **360**, 1477–1479 (2009)
5. Strobel CD, American recovery and reinvestment act of 2009 (ARRA09). J Corp Account Finance 20(5):83-85 (2009) (111th US Congress)
6. R Kaushal, AK Jha, C Franz, J Glaser, KD Shetty, T Jaggi, B Middleton, GJ Kuperman, R Khorasani, M Tanasijevic, Return on investment for a computerized physician order entry system. J. Am. Med. Inform. Assoc. **13**, 261–266 (2006)
7. G Paul and B Nearon, The Discovery Revolution: e-Discovery Amendments to the Federal Rules of Civil Procedure, American Bar Association, Chicago, Illinois (2006)
8. Fulton-Cavett AM, Electronic Health Records: Federal E-Discovery Rules and Case Law Are Guides for State Litigation. The Brief, 40 (2011)
9. KB-S Reich, E-discovery in healthcare: 2010 and beyond. Annals. Health. L. **19**, 173 (2009)
10. TR McLean, EMR metadata uses and E-discovery. Annals. Health. L. **18**, 75 (2009)
11. DE Detmer, Building the national health information infrastructure for personal health, health care services, public health, and research. BMC. Med. Informatics. Decision. Making. **3**, 1 (2003)
12. JL Masor, Electronic medical records and E-discovery: with New technology come New challenges. Hastings. Sci. Tech. LJ.**5**, 245 (2013)
13. S Hoffman, A Podgurski, E-Health hazards: provider liability and electronic

health record systems. Berkeley. Tech. LJ. **24**, 1523 (2009)

14. S Hoffman, A Podgurski, Meaningful use and certification of health information technology: what about safety? J. Law. Med. Ethics. **39**, 77–80 (2011)
15. R Drummond, EHR certification: getting comfortable with the concept. Health. Manag. Technol. **32**, 26 (2011)
16. Certification Process for EHR Technologies. [http://www.healthit.gov/providers-professionals/certification-process-ehr-technologies]
17. Meaningful Use Definition & Objectives. [http://www.healthit.gov/providers-professionals/meaningful-use-definition-objectives]
18. Van De Belt TH, Engelen LJ, Berben SA, Schoonhoven L: Definition of Health 2.0 and Medicine 2.0: a systematic review. J. Med. Internet. Res.**12**, 2 (2010)
19. Patientslikeme [http://www.patientslikeme.com/]
20. Health 2.0 in Wikipedia. [http://en.wikipedia.org/wiki/Health_2.0]
21. Hughes B, Joshi I, Wareham J: Health 2.0 and Medicine 2.0: tensions and controversies in the field. J. Med. Internet. Res. 2008, **10**, 3 (2008)
22. C Dimick, E-discovery: preparing for the coming rise in electronic discovery requests. J. AHIMA. **78**, 24 (2007)
23. Lorraine v. Markel American Insurance Company, 241 F.R.D 534 (D.Md. May 4, 2007)
24. RC Goss, Hot issues in electronic discovery: information retention programs and preservation. Tort. Trial. Ins. Prac. LJ. **42**, 797 (2006)
25. Ray P, Wimalasiri J: The need for technical solutions for maintaining the privacy of EHR. In Engineering in Medicine and Biology Society, 2006 EMBS'06 28th Annual International Conference of the IEEE; New York City. IEEE. 4686–4689 (2006)
26. KT Win, A review of security of electronic health records. Health. Information. Manag. **34**, 13–18 (2005)
27. Norman C: Advances and Challenges in Secure EHR Access. CEISARE's Information Assurance Program 2012, (2012)
28. Yuan E, Tong J: Attributed based access control (ABAC) for web services. In Web Services, 2005 ICWS 2005 Proceedings 2005 IEEE International Conference on IEEE; Los Alamitos. IEEE. (2005)
29. Ferraiolo D, Cugini J, Kuhn DR: Role-based access control (RBAC): Features and motivations. In Proceedings of 11th annual computer security application conference. IEEE Computer Society Press; Los Alamitos. IEEE. 241-248 (1995)
30. E Coiera, R Clarke, e-Consent: The design and implementation of consumer consent mechanisms in an electronic environment. J. Am. Med. Inform. Assoc. **11**, 129–140 (2004)
31. MM Richards, Electronic medical records: confidentiality issues in the time of HIPAA. Professional. Psychol. Res. Practice.**40**, 550 (2009)
32. PLC CGSB, Client Alert: HITECH Act Expands HIPAA Privacy and Security

Rules. In Book Client Alert: HITECH Act Expands HIPAA Privacy and Security Rules. Coppersmith Gordon Schermer & Brockelman PLC; Phoenix (2009)

33. Ashish S. Prasad, Cloud computing and social media: Electronic discovery considerations and best practices. Metropolitan. Corporate. Counsel. 26–27 (2012)
34. Alberto G. Araiza, Electronic Discovery in the Cloud, 10 Duke Law & Technology Review 1–19 (2011)
35. Singh S, Singh N: Big Data analytics. In Communication, Information & Computing Technology (ICCICT), 2012 International Conference on; 19–20 Oct. 2012. IEEE; Mumbai. IEEE. 1–4 (2012)
36. Ingram B: Controlling E-discovery costs in a big data world. Peer Peer.http://www.lexisnexis.com/pdf/Litigation/ArticleILTAPeer2Peer-ControllingEDSCCostsinaBigDataWorld-Ingram032013.pdf(2013)
37. JG Browning, Digging for the digital dirt: discovery and use of evidence from social media sites. SMU. Sci. Tech. L. Rev. **14**, 465 (2010)
38. A Sanfilippo, N Gilbert, M Greaves, Technosocial predictive analytics for security informatics. Security. Informatics. **1**, 1–3 (2012)
39. C Pham, E-discovery in the cloud Era: what's a litigant to do. Hastings. Sci. Tech. LJ. **5**, 139 (2013)
40. 2013 Year-End Electronic Discovery and Information Law Update. [http://www.gibsondunn.com/publications/pages/2013-Year-End-Electronic-Discovery-InformationLaw-Update.aspx]

7
CHAPTER

ANALYSIS OF CAUSES AND ACTUAL EVENTS ON ELECTRIC POWER INFRASTRUCTURE IMPACTED BY CYBER ATTACK

Hongxu Yin, Rui Xiao, Fenfei Lv

Keywords: Cyber Attack, Electric Power Infrastructure, Information Infrastructure, Dependence

INTRODUCTION

Electric power infrastructure provides public power supply services for social production and household use. Recently, with the development of computer and communication technology, information and communication systems become an essential part to support the normal operation of electric power infrastructure. According to the relevant standards set by International Electro-technical Commission (IEC), the future development of power system will be the common construction and management of electric power infrastructure and information infrastructure [1]. Cyber-attack takes advantage of network vulnerability and security flaw to attack on system and resources [2]. For power system, monitoring and communication equipment of electric power infrastructure are the direct target of cyber-attack. But because of the electric power infrastructure's dependency on information infrastructure, cyber-attack will affect the safe and and stable operation of power system [3] [4]. In view of the importance of electric power infrastructure and cyber attack's characteristics of low cost, wide range and hidden action [5], cyber-attack will become a potential threat that we may not neglect [4] [6]-[8]. Currently, many countries, mainly the U.S., have raised the impact of cyber-attack on electric power infrastructure to nation-state level. The Homeland Security Department (DHS) has organized three cyber storm exercises since 2006 to 2010, and electric power infrastructure are significant imaginary target [9]. An

Citation: Hongxu Yin, Rui Xiao, Fenfei Lv, Analysis of Causes and Actual Events on Electric Power Infrastructure Impacted by Cyber Attack, of Power and Energy Engineering, http://dx.doi.org/10.4236/jpee.2015.34012.

Israeli-US strike on Iranian nuclear plants [10] becomes the focus of the international concern in 2011. According to this development trend, cyber-attack on electric power infrastructure will be an important means of network information war [11], which needs to be paid high attention and intensive study. This paper is organized focusing on the impact on power infrastructure caused by cyber-attack. And the background and current situation of the problem are discussed to draw attention of national related departments, enterprises and research institutes. This paper analyses main reasons of the impact on power infrastructure caused by cyber-attack, and summarizes characteristics of existing cyber-attack. Furthermore, the impact of recently published actual events of cyber-attacks on electric power infrastructure is analyzed.

MAIN REASONS OF THE IMPACT ON POWER INFRASTRUCTURE CAUSED BY CYBER ATTACK

The Dependence of Electric Power Infrastructure on Information Infrastructure

According to the IEC standards above, the power system can be divided into two parts, electric power infrastructure and information infrastructure. Electric power infrastructure, often called power primary system, is composed of power generation, transmission, transformation and distribution equipment, and its function is to lower the voltage of electrical energy generated step by step by transmission and transformation equipment and then transfer the electrical energy to distribution system. At last the electrical energy is supplied to customers through distribution line. Information infrastructure, usually called power secondary system, is composed of power monitoring system, power telecommunication, data network, etc. Power monitoring system are the business processing systems and smart devices based on computer and network technology, whose function is to monitor and control the production and operation process of the power grid and power plants [12]. The construction and development of information infrastructure are natural products of the development of communications and information technology, and also the objective requirements of the development of power system to a certain degree, aiming to improve the safety and economy of power system operation. Interdependence of infrastructures is the interrelation or influence of the unions of 2 infrastructures. Generally, this dependence can be divided into 4 types [13]. The first type is physical dependence, which refers to the physical dependence existed between the unions of 2 infrastructures in the form of material flow. The second one is information dependence, which refers to the information dependence existed between the unions of 2 infrastructures in the form of information flow. The third one is geographical dependence, which means that the unions of 2 infrastructures are adjacent geographically and the incident in this site may affect both of the infrastructures. The last one is logic dependence, which means that the dependence exists between the unions of 2 infrastructures, but it can't be attributed to any of interdependence relationships discussed above. Cyber security is the negative factors existed in information infrastructure, and severity of its influence on electric power infrastructure depends on the electric power infrastructure's dependence on information infrastructure. Generally, the units of electricity power infrastructure can be divided into three classes, namely plants, substations, and lines, which constitute the entire electricity network. Information infrastructure, as it provides service to electric power infrastructure, exists in power plant monitoring system and substation automatic system corresponding to the units above. These systems mainly satisfy the units' own needs with a relatively small service scope, and they can realize local automation function, such as protection and operation and control functions based on station control level. From a global perspective, the operating state of power system is adjusted based on the variation of load. So it is necessary to acquire global monitoring information and adjust generator's output power reasonably according to the variation of load to ensure safety and economic operation of the system. These functions are based on local function, and realized by supervisory control and data acquisition/energy management system (SCADA/ EMS). The growth of load and scale expansion of power grid proposes a higher request of safety, promoting the development of wide area measurement and protection control system. The realization of wide area measurement and protection control system is also based on the collection, analysis and control of global information. Compared with SCADA/EMS, this requires more information and higher real-time character [14]-[16]. To satisfy the demand for uninterrupted power supply, it is essential to ensure the safety operation or instant recovery of information infrastructure when suffering internal fault or external attack [17]. The impact of information infrastructure on electric power infrastructure will be negative if the monitoring can't be conducted real-time or being taken advantage of. In summary, information infrastructure serves electric power infrastructure in power system. In turn, electric power infrastructure depends on information infrastructure. The dependence's working point is substation automatic system or power plant monitoring system, but is amplified through the function of SCADA/EMS and wide area measurement and protection control system.

The Concept of Cyber Attack and Motivation Analysis

The Concept of Cyber Attack

According to the concept in the field of information security, cyber-attack takes advantage of loophole and security vulnerabilities existing in the network to attack on system and resources. Information infrastructure serving the power system to a great extent belongs to typical industrial control system. Cyber-attack specified to those systems is generally defined as attack on the behavior of computer-based industrial control system without permission, aiming at destroying or lowering the function of industrial control system [18]. According to the physical security and network security guidelines of substation established by IEEE, cyber-attack specified to substation refers to invading substation through possible network and operating or interfering with electronic equipment [19]. Equipment operated or interfed with include digital relay protection devices, fault recorder, automatics, and substation-control level computer, PLC and communication interfaces [6].

The Benefit of Cyber Attack

Motivation of cyber-attack derives from the aggressor's increasing economic or political interests. Compared with the traditional physical attack, cyber-attack features with hidden action, low cost and wide range [5]. Cyber-attack can implement aggressive behavior from any access network point of information infrastructure without approaching physical device. An attacker needs only relevant knowledge of the network and not special funding. Once an attack on electric power monitoring equipment implemented, some primary system equipment operate, possibly resulting in power system cascading failure and has larger influence sphere.

Threat Sources of Cyber Attack

Combined IEC 62351 standard [20] and reported domestic and international cyber-attack, threat sources of cyber-attack includes the following types.

1) Industrial espionage Industrial espionage is becoming a major threat in higher power system marketization countries. Competition between enterprises increases motivation of illegal acquisition of information. And it is possible to interfere the operation of the competitors' equipment and improve their earnings.
2) Cyber hackers Hackers usually take the Internet as a major gateway to attack, and gain profit by destroying cyber security. The profit may be monetary, industrial, political, social or the curiosity that whether the challenge of intrusion network will be successful [21].
3) Viruses Similar to hackers, viruses and worms are typical attack taking advantage of the Internet. However, some viruses and worms may spread to Internet-isolated system by embedding into software or removable storage device. These viruses include middle attacks viruses, spyware gaining power system data and other trojan horse.
4) Larceny Larceny has the most immediate purpose, namely attacker taking something (such as equipment, data or knowledge) away without permission. Generally speaking, the main motivation is to obtain economic benefits. Under the smart grid environment, the interaction of grid operators and user is emphasized. To tamper energy metering data through cyber-attack is likely to develop into a new way of stealing electric power [22].
5) Terrorism Terrorism is a threat which has minimum probability of occurrence. But it may bring serious consequences due to the purpose of maximizing the physical, financial, social and political damage.
6) Military action Due to its specificity, electric power infrastructure is always taken as a priority target for military action. For example, US Army used graphite bombs to destroy the power system in Gulf War and the Kosovo War [23]. In recent years, with the mode and destructiveness of cyber-attack increasing, physical attack gradually fades out of sight. And electric power infrastructure has become a potential target of cyber-attacks, drawing military's attention [11].

CYBER ATTACKS AGAINST ELECTRIC POWER INFRASTRUCTURE

Classified by the Location of Attack

Depending on different location of cyber attack, attack can be classified as local attack, remote attack and pseudo remote attack. Local attack occurs in the LAN, and remote attack occurs outside the location of the network the target belongs to. Pseudo remote attack is an attack that internal personnel covering up the identity of their attacker gain necessary information about the target from local and attack from the external, causing external invasion phenomenon [24]. Local attack needs to be physically close to the target. But local electric power monitoring system (e.g. Substation Automation System) usually adopt perfect physical isolation means, so it is difficult for attacker to reach the target, let alone attack. Remote attack can invade computers in control center and other critical equipment through any network connected to the power of information and communication network, utilizing the system vulnerabilities and unsound security and confidentiality mechanisms. In comparison, remote attack is most likely to occur [25]. Pseudo remote attack needs spies in Power Company, so it is less likely to occur.

Classified by Attack Mechanism

According to the mechanism, attack can be classified as denial service attack, replay attack, middle attack and reprograming the device [26].

1) Denial service attack (Dos) Denial service attack occurs when excessive communication resources are occupied by an attacker so that the resource is temporarily unavailable when user needs to access, effecting the availability of information. In attacks against electric power infrastructure, attacker keeps sending forged packets in the communication channel, making the normal communication between the control center and RTU unavailable. The control center can't receive the power terminal information transmitted by RTU, meanwhile the control information issued by the control center can't be delivered. If the grid is in a state of emergency at the moment, the consequences would be unimaginable.
2) Replay attack For replay attack, it is necessary to monitor network information flow first, and identify information representing key actions. The information is sent back into the network at specific times to re-simulate the previous occurrence. In electric power infrastructure, attacker can identify and intercept breaker tripping control instruction by network monitoring and replaying this instruction when necessary, resulting in breaker malfunction.
3) Middle attack Attacker' action is imposed between two communicating nodes, and it deceives the sender that it is a true recipients or the recipients that it is the real sender. In this way, the attacker can tamper, delete or insert arbitrary information between two communicating nodes. In electric power infrastructure, attacker can be a middleman between RTU and control center, which intercept emergency fault information sent by RTU and replace with normal or alarm information, so that system does not take action in case of failure. Besides, it

intercept control instruction from control center and delete, modify or insert the instruction. After such an attack, the confidentiality and integrity of information is completely lost. If the attacker is well aware of the power system operating state, then this attack would be devastating.

4) Reprograming the device If RTU, IED and other equipment are reprogrammed, the attacker can easily implant malicious Trojans, disrupting the normal operation of equipment. This kind of attack is not common at present. The reasons mainly lie in two aspects: a) Remote programming of equipment is not allowed in the design of system generally, and local invasion programming needs approaching the equipment. But if the equipment is available, direct physical damage will be easier than reprogrammed and the destruction is more severe; b) As the equipment is numerous and geographically distributed, reprogramming attack is not suitable to launch a massive attack, and the requirement of programming capabilities of attacker is higher. With the development of technology, the likelihood of such an attack still exists. For example, IEC 61850 standard proposes that IED equipment can be remotely configured [27]. Under the background of digital substation widely used and open of remote configuration interface in the future, such an attack would be more practical.

CASE STUDY OF CYBER ATTACK AGAINST ELECTRIC POWER INFRASTRUCTURE

Cyber Attack Instance

In recent years, cyber attacks on the Internet have been very serious, but reports about cyber attacks against electric power infrastructure are relatively few. Overall, the power monitoring system suffering from cyber attacks are on the rise. Some studies suggest that the current reported cyber-attacks are likely just the tip of the iceberg. Due to fear of responsibility and corporate image damage, as well as commercial competition and other issues, most companies are reluctant to report such incidents [28]. Some examples of cyber-attacks against electric power infrastructure are summarized as follows.

1) In the 8 - 14 blackout in USA and Canada in 2003, worm hindered the recovery from power blackout in Ontario in Canada to normal power supply [29].

2) In March 2007, U.S. Department of Defense and Department of Homeland Security (DHS) conducted a cyber-attack experiment, causing generator self-destruction. The experiment was undertaken by the Idaho National Laboratory (INL) of energy, and it simulated a cyber-attack against the copy of Aurora plant's control system. The attack invaded SCADA system and changed the generator's operation trajectory. Then the generator was out of control and galloping, final smoking and damaged. DHS believes that this type of cyber-attack, if taking large-scale coordinated control, can damage electric power infrastructure for months. And DHS is reluctant to disclose specific details of the simulation action [30] [31].

3) On October 16, 2007, cyber security expert Ira-Winkler published a paper on

the Internet Evolution site entitled "How to take down the power grid". This paper points out that it is not difficult to conduct cyber-attack against power information control system, and he entered into American power control system as early as ten years ago. Ira-Winkler and his team have been hired by a power company, conducting test and evaluation of the vulnerability of computer systems for power grid. They can damage the browser, intrude into the control network of the power plant and monitor the power production and distribution, thus simulating the effects on the normal operation of the electric power infrastructure. Ira-Winkler noted that they can not only enter into SCADA system, but also download the file record CIO and CEO via cyber-attack [4].

4) U.S. Central Intelligence Agency (CAI) pointed out that the blackout, which occurred in 2005 and 2007 in Brazil, was due to hacker's cyber-attack against the power control system [32].
5) In an on-line special report of U.S. Public Broadcasting Company (PBS), an interviewee signatured hacker claimed that he could make the grid collapsed by clicking on some buttons. It is important that hackers, vandals and terrorist attackers think it is possible, not the truth of this sentence. And this report reflects that they have targeting the power grid to attack [33].
6) In April 2009, Wall Street Journal quoted the saying of an unnamed national security official. He said that cyber spies in some countries had came into contact with U.S. power grid and installed malicious software tool used to shut down certain services. They also expressed the concern that a malicious hacker may attack during a crisis or war in the future [33], although this intrusion hadn't disrupt the normal operation of the power grid.
7) The Bushehr nuclear power plant in Iran was attacked by the computer worm Stuxnet on October 26, 2010. This worm invaded into the internal of the nuclear plant via USB device and destroyed the centrifuge in nuclear facilities. Meanwhile, the worm used fake data to deceive the operator through replay mode. Thus the virus invasion was undetectable to the operators. The virus is specific to Simatic WinCC SCADA system produced by Siemens company, which is used as industrial control systems in many critical infrastructures in China. Due to the powerful function of Stuxnet virus, the team behind this virus must have superb professional technical staff and strong financial backing. The United States and Israel admitted that they developed the virus jointly soon [34]. A brief analysis of the actual events of cyber-attacks mentioned above in respect of threat sources, vulnerabilities and assaulting modes is available according to the reports, though the relevant information is limited.

Threat Sources Analysis

From the perspective of threat source, the instances above can be analyzed as follows. Threat of instance 1 is derived from the worm. Instance 2 and 6 are associated with military action. Instance 3, 4 and 5 are typical hacker attack. Instance 7 is relatively complex. Due to its powerful destructive capability, stuxnet is not simple computer viruses and closely related to the national military behavior. Instances show that among the threat sources of cyber-attacks, hacker, viruses and military action are the most typical. For in-depth analysis, there are many inherent relationships between these three threat sources. And these relations can't be clearly grasped from the current public information.

Assaulting Mode Analysis

After the text edit has been completed, the paper is ready for the template. Duplicate the template file by using the Save As command, and use the naming convention prescribed by your journal for the name of your paper. In this newly created file, highlight all of the contents and import your prepared text file. You are now ready to style your paper. From the perspective of assaulting mode, instance 2, 5 and 7 are more likely replay attack. And instance 2 and 5 are possibly middle attack. Instance 1 and 6 are typically denial service attacks. The assaulting mode of instance 3 and 4 are not clear, and there exist multifold possibility. According to the occurrence mechanism of the attacks, combined with instance analysis, qualitative comparisons are done according to the implementation difficulty and the severity of consequences (shown in Figure 1).

1) Denial service attack is easy to conduct as its various means and no need for the attacker having a deep understanding of the power system. Judging from the consequences, the influence of denial service attack is relatively small because it can't directly operate key equipments despite its huge influence on monitoring process.

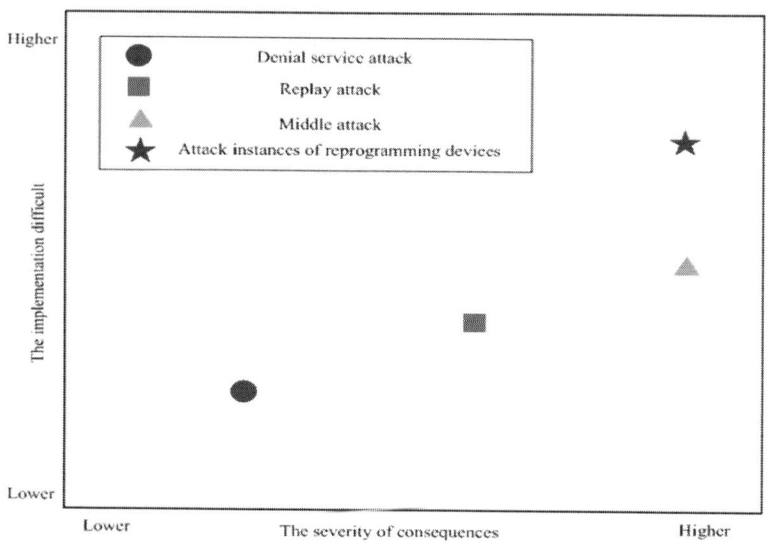

Figure 1. The comparison of impact and difficulty among the four cyber-attack ways.

2) Replay attack and middle attack have much in common. And their essence is to achieve the purpose of maliciously operating critical equipment through attacker deceiving the recipient of information by certain means. But the difference

between the two is that the replay attack has simpler means, and the goals able to achieve is less.

3) Attack instances of reprogramming devices haven't been found by far. But the occurrence of this kind of attack is possible in the future. Once succeed, the impact will be huge.

CONCLUSION

In summary, main reasons of the impact on power infrastructure caused by cyber-attack are analyzed in respect of consequences and threats in this paper. The dependence of electric power infrastructure on information infrastructure determines the seriousness of the consequences of cyber-attack. The main threats are diverse. The seriousness of the consequences improves the profit of cyber-attacks, enhancing the motivation of attacks. Combined with the main assaulting mode of cyber-attacks and currently reported attacks events, the impact of cyber-attack on electric power infrastructure will gradually increase from the number and extent.

REFERENCES

1. Cleveland, F. (2006) IEC TC57 Security Standards for the power system's Information Infrastructure—Beyond Simple Encryption. IEEE PES TD 2005/2006, 21-24 May 2006, 1079-1087.
2. Lin, C., Wang, Y. and Li, Q.L. (2005) Stochastic Modeling and Evaluation for Network Security. Chinese Journal of Computers, 28, 1943-1956.
3. Niu, P.C., Kang, J.T., Li, A.W. and Li, L. (2010) New Operation Form of Power Network Started by Smart Grid. Power System Protection and Control, 38, 240-244.
4. Li, W.W., You, W.X. and Wang, X.P. (2011) Survey of Cyber Security Research in Power System. Power System Protection and Control, 39, 140-147.
5. Watts, D. (2003) Security & Vulnerability in Electric Power Systems. IEEE 35th North American Power Symposium Conference, Rolla Missouri USA, 20-21-19 October 2003, 559-566.
6. Lewis, J.A. (2011) The Electrical Grid as a Target for Cyber Attack. http://csis.org/files/publication/100322_ElectricalGridAsATargetforCyberAttack.pdf
7. Kelic, A., Warren, D.E. and Philips, L.R. (2011) Cyber and Physical Infrastructure Interdependence. http://prod.sandia.gov/techlib/access-control.cgi/2008/086192.pdf
8. Anderson, R.S. (2011) Cyber Security and Resilient Systems. http://www.inl.gov/technicalpublications/Documents/4311316.pdf
9. Department of Homeland Security Office of Cyber Security and Communications National Cyber Security Division (2011) National Cyber Exercise: Cyber Storm. http://cryptome.org/cyberstorm.pdf
10. China News Network (2011) Iranian Officials Have Accused the USA and Israel Manufacture of Computer Viruses Destroy Iranian Nuclear Facilities. http://

www.chinanews.com/gj/2011/04-17/2977981.shtml

11. Headquarters Department of the Army Washington, DC (2011) Infrastructure Risk Management (Army). http://www.apd.army.mil/pdffiles/r525_26.pdf
12. State Electricity Regulatory Commission (2004) Power Monitoring System Security Requirements. Beijing.
13. Rinaldi, S.M., Peerenboom, J.P. and Kelly, T.K. (2001) Identifying, Understanding, and Analyzing Critical Infrastructure Interdependencies. IEEE Control Systems, 21, 11-25. http://dx.doi.org/10.1109/37.969131
14. Liu, J.F., Chen, C.P. and Luo, J. (2004) Design and Application of Information's Security and Protection in Power Supervision and Control Automatic System. Relay, 32, 33-35.
15. Wu, G.W. (2007) Information Disposal and Network Security Analysis in Digital Substation. Relay, 35, 18-22.
16. Du, G.H. and Wang, Z.F. (2010) Design and Research on Power Network Dispatching Integration of Smart Grid. Power System Protection and Control, 38, 127-131.
17. Stamp, J. and Mcintyre, A. (2009) Reliability Impacts from Cyber Attack on Electric Power Systems. The 2009 Power Systems Conference and Exposition, Seattle, 15-18 March 2009, 1-8.
18. Tatum, M. (2011) What Is a Cyber attack? http://www.wisegeek.com/what-is-a-cyberattack.htm
19. Substations Committee of the IEEE Power Engineering Society (2008) IEEE Guide for Electric Power Substation Physical and Electronic Security, IEEE Std 1402-2000(R2008). USA.
20. IEC TS 62351-1 (2007) Power Systems Management and Associated Information Exchange—Data and Communications Security Part I: Communication Network and System Security—Introduction to Security Issues. Geneva.
21. Li, J. (2011) Academician Disclose the Cyber Attack Is Very Serious in China. http://society.people.com.cn/GB/1062/9343749.html
22. Mu, L.H., Zhu, G.F. and Zhu, J.R. (2010) Design of Intelligent Terminal Based on Smart Grid. Power System Protection and Control, 38, 53-56.
23. Han, Y.J., Zhao, N.Q. and Liu, Y.C. (2005) Destructive Mechanism of Blackout Bomb and Its Defending Measures Ordnance Material Science and Engineering, 28, 57-60.
24. Zhang, Y.Q. (2011) Network Attack and Defense Technology. Tsinghua University Press, Beijing, 59-65.
25. Baigent, D., Adamiak, M. and Mackiewicz, R. (2011) IEC61850 Communication Networks and Systems in Substations: An Overview for Users. http://www.sisconet.com
26. Negrete-Pincetic, M., Yoshida, F. and Gross, G. (2009) Towards Quantifying the Impacts of Cyber Attacks in the Competitive Electricity Market Environment.

Bucharest Power Tech Conference, Romania, 28 June-2 July 2009, 105- 111.

27. Liu, N., Zhang, J.H. and Duan, B. (2009) Design of Security Mechanism for Substation Remote Configuration Based on XML Security. Electric Power Automation Equipment, 29, 113-117.

28. Taylor, C., Krings, A. and Foss, J.A. (2011) Risk Analysis and Probabilistic Survivability Assessment (RAPSA): An Assessment Approach for Power Substation Hardening. http://citeseerx.ist.psu.edu/viewdoc/download?doi=10.1.1.80.8323&rep=rep1&type=pdf

29. Hu, Y., Xie, X.R., Han, Y.D., et al. (2005) A Survey to Design Method of Security Architecture for Power Information Systems. Power System Technology, 29, 35-39.

30. Greenberg, A. (2011) Congress Alarmed at Cyber-Vulnerability of Power Grid. http://www.forbes.com/2008/05/22/cyberwar-breach-government- tech-security_cx_ag_0521cyber.html

31. Meserve, J. (2011) Staged Cyber Attack Reveals Vulnerability in Power Grid. http://articles.cnn.com/2007-09-26/us/power.at.risk_1_generator-cyber-attack-electric-infrastructure?_s=PM:US

32. Poulsen, K. (2011) Report: Cyber Attacks Caused Power Outages in Brazil. http://www.wired.com/threatlevel/2009/11/brazil/

33. Oman, P., Schweitzer, E. and Roberts, J. (2011) Protecting the Grid from Cyber Attack Part I: Recognizing Our Vulnerabilities. http://www.elp.com/index/display/article-display/130136/articles/utility-automation-engineering-td/volume-6/issue-7/f eatures/protecting-the-grid-from-cyber-attack-part-i-recognizing-our-vulnerabilities.html

34. Wikipedia (2011) Stuxnet. http://en.wikipedia.org/wiki/Stuxnet

8
CHAPTER

SCADA FRAMEWORK INCORPORATING MANET AND IDP FOR CYBER SECURITY

Goutham K. Chalamasetty, Paras Mandal, Tzu-Liang (Bill) Tseng

Keywords: ACT, Black Hole Attack, Cyber Security, MANET, Residential Microgrid, SCADA

INTRODUCTION

The electric power grid is going through major changes worldwide in order to become smarter, resilient, sustainable, and more reliable [1] . Power utilities are facing a major challenge in maintaining the desired reliability and security while integrating increasing loads and distributed energy resources (DER), primarily wind and solar energy. Furthermore, smart grid and/or microgrid are primary targets of cyber-attacks due to advancement in their communication networks and technologies [2] [3] . Figure 1 shows an example of a multi-microgrid and its energy management system, termed as multi-microgrid energy management system (MMEMS), which comprises of residential, industrial, and commercial microgrids. Such microgrids can operate in connected or islanded mode with the main grid. The MMEMS is controlled by supervisory control and data acquisition (SCADA) system, which is the combination of telemetry and data acquisition [4] . SCADA plays a crucial role in controlling and ensuring a reliable and secure operation of MMEMS. Thus, it is very essential to have a SCADA system, which is persistent and also has the ability to monitor and control the system in real time to enhance the efficient operation and cyber security of the system [5] . SCADA comprises of several components such as 1) SCADA-master that sends the control commands, 2) regional terminal units (RTU), programmable logic controllers (PLC), and intelligent electronic devices (IED) that receive commands from SCADA-master,

Citation: Goutham K. Chalamasetty, Paras Mandal, Tzu-Liang (Bill) Tseng (Bill) Tseng, (2016) SCADA Framework Incorporating MANET and IDP for Cyber Security, doi: 10.4236/sgre.2016.73007.

3) human machine interface (HMI), which provides a graphical user interaction to the operator at control center, and 4) communication networks, which connect all the above mentioned components [4] - [7] . The components and sources of the MMEMS are depicted in Figure 1 where we can observe that MCC is a major control center, which is responsible for the reliable and secure operation of MMEMS. Microgrid control centers (MGCC) are the sub control centers for individual monitoring of residential, industrial, and commercial microgrids. Moreover, each MGCC communicates with MCC to provide the entire system's state of operation. MCC also comprises of the SCADA-master that sends control commands to MGCC, and each MGCC has a sub-SCADA-master to control RTU, PLC, and IED in remote stations.

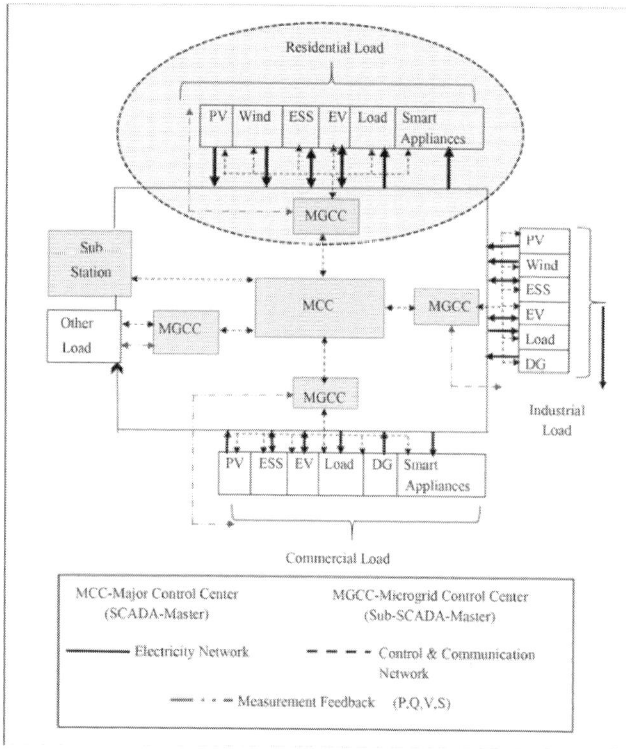

Figure 1. Architecture of MMEMS.

In general, the operation of MMEMS consists of various technologies of DER, wind, photovoltaic (PV), energy storage system (ESS), electric vehicles (EVs), loads and smart appliances (Figure 1). However, MMEMS can have issues, such as handling the variable output power of wind/PV, security and load sharing [8] . In addition, there are several vulnerabilities, which are discussed in detail in Section 2, in the existing SCADA system that lead to physical and cyber-attacks on the control and communication network. Hence, there is a great need to develop a reliable and secure SCADA control and communication network to enhance MMEMS operations by adopting advanced communication technologies (ACT) and providing cyber security.

This paper presents cyber security issues with focus on communication in residential microgrid, which is a part of MMEMS of Figure 1. The major contributions of this paper are: 1) we recommend to integrate ACT into existing SCADA system, 2) we propose to use mobile ad hoc networks (MANET) for residential microgrid where MANET is required to collect the information of power consumption as well as to connect with the mobile system operators, and 3) we propose an intrusion detection and prevention (IDP) technology for preventing cyber-attacks in MANET used in residential microgrid. It is emphasized that to the best knowledge of authors, this paper is the first attempt to use MANET for communication in residential microgrid.

VULNERABILITIES IN EXISTING SCADA SYSTEM

There are numerous developments made to the SCADA system after four major blackouts in the year 2003 through United States, Canada, and Europe [9] . However, there are still many vulnerabilities such as unpatched operating systems, unencrypted data, network design vulnerabilities, lack of proper firewalls used for respective network protocols, and network configuration vulnerabilities, which lead to physical system attacks and communication system attacks [9] - [14] . The recent attack on pacific gas and electric (PG&E) substation in California in April 2013 raised questions on the vulnerabilities in the existing physical systems [15] . Study done by Federal Energy Regulatory Commission (FERC) shows that the attack on 9 substations out of 55,000 transmission substations will take down the transmission grid of the entire U.S. [16] . The attacks on communication system include extracting information from power line carrier communication (PLCC) by tapping high frequency waves with a portable current transformer, and attackers use in-band jamming and out-of-band jamming technologies to corrupt the information in optical fiber cables [14] . The present communication infrastructure used for phasor measurement units (PMU) communication is not authenticated which leads to compromise the data integrity [17] . The vulnerabilities in wireless communication technologies lead to cyber-attacks such as eavesdropping, man-in-the-middle attack, data modification, denial of service (DoS) attacks, phishing attacks, and domain name system (DNS) spoofing. In addition to these vulnerabilities, there could be an emergency situation, e.g., natural disaster, which can destroy the SCADA control and communication infrastructure, and it may result into the operators' losing their control on the system.

Furthermore, for the architecture of MMEMS (Figure 1), the vulnerabilities in the existing SCADA system may cause potential threats to the operation of MMEMS by performing physical attack on substation or power generating sources such as PV stations and wind farms. These vulnerabilities also benefit the cyber attackers to intrude into the system's control and communication network, which will lead to the damage of the entire system. Highly motivated by the aforementioned vulnerabilities and threats, this paper contributes to develop a reliable SCADA communication network with an application of IDP technology in order to provide cyber security for residential microgrid.

PROPOSED WORK

SCADA Control and Communication Network with ACT

The advancement in technology provides many wireless communication technologies such as wireless sensor networks (WSN), MANET, and Internet that can be used in SCADA system. A recommendation is provided to incorporate the above-mentioned technologies into the present SCADA system that will help progress the smart grid by improving the system parameters such as availability, reliability, and security [18] - [20] . Integration of these ACT into the existing SCADA control and communication network have following advantages: 1) more automation into the system, which minimizes the human workers, 2) bringing mobility into the system, which will allow the operators to move from control station without losing control over the system, 3) ability for the system operator to access and control the system wherever they are in the world by using internet SCADA or web SCADA, 4) provide collaboration with other operators, and 5) enhancement in security by an integration of ACT. WSN and MANET continuously monitor and collect the information of current, voltage, and frequency profiles, trip coil status, and battery level of ESS. Finally, this collected information will be sent periodically to the system operators through internet [21] . Integration of ACT into SCADA further provides control to the operators even in emergency situations like natural disasters. Besides the aforementioned advantages by using ACT, there are also some disadvantages in the form of cyber-attacks. Some good examples of papers that discuss about cyber security to ACT are available in [22] - [26] .

The major contribution of this paper that makes it different and novel from the existing papers is that we propose to use MANET to residential microgrid as shown in Figure 2. In our paper, we propose to use MANETs into the SCADA for an efficient and secure communication network in residential micro grid as shown in Figure 2. Note that Figure 2 is a residential microgrid, which is extracted from Figure 1. Implementing a communication network by using MANET is cost effective and it brings more flexibility and redundancy into the network. In the proposed network (Figure 2), MANET is used to acquire the power consumption information of residential houses and EVs from smart meters. Smart meters are the smart grid primary resource for providing a smart interface with consumers [27] . The power consumption pattern of EVs with respect to speed and distance is used to compare the performance of different EVs, and this data is beneficial to analyze and develop the technologies used in EVs. In our proposed residential microgrid communication network, MANET also connects mobile system operators to the network, which helps provide immediate mitigation during emergency situations such as short circuits and power outages in residential areas. Furthermore, by understanding the dynamic nature of MANET and their exposure to cyber-attacks, we propose an IDP technology, which prevents cyber-attacks.

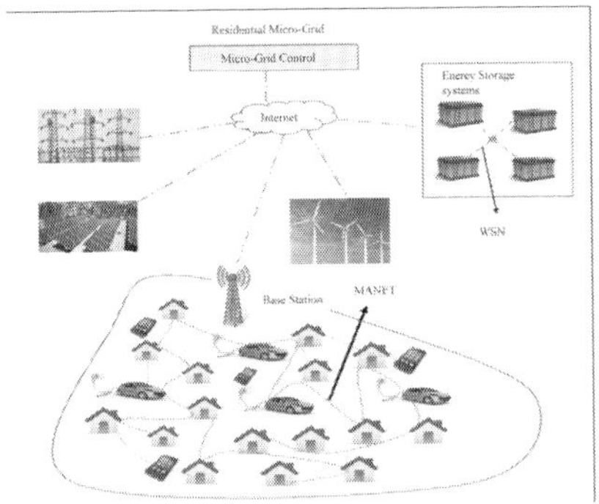

Figure 2. Architecture of SCADA control and communication network with ACT in residential microgrid.

Problem Solution for Identifying and Preventing Cyber-Attacks

By considering the benefits of identifying both known and unknown attacks discussed in [28] , this paper proposes an IDP technology to prevent black hole attacks and other anomaly attacks. The information flow from source to destination node under the propose IDP technology is shown inFigure 3.

Black hole attack gives false information during the route discovery process while sending data from source to destination. This paper uses ad hoc on-demand distance vector algorithm (AODV) as a routing protocol in the MANET network. The routing protocol of AODV is such that when source node sends route request (RREQ) message to all the neighboring nodes, the black hole attacked node immediately sends route reply (RREP) with false information and makes the source node trust that this is an optimal route for sending data packets to destination node, and it then proceeds accordingly for data transmission. During this data transfer process, black hole node absorbs all the data packets, which result into the loss of information. To prevent these black hole attacks on MANET in our proposed network (Figure 2), we applied a secure knowledge algorithm [29] , which is a simple and effective method to prevent black hole attacked nodes in the network. In this algorithm every node in the network monitors the neighboring nodes. Each node also consists of data table that provides information of 1) recent packet forwarded and 2) neighboring node related to the recently forwarded packet. The secure knowledge algorithm compares these two information—if they are same, there is no black hole attack; otherwise, the network is under attack. In addition to the secure knowledge algorithm, we include anomaly detection to prevent unknown attacks after the secure and optimal path is selected. In our proposed IDP technology, we considered the known attack as black hole that will be identified by using secure knowledge algorithm and unknown attacks are considered as misbehaving nodes that drop data packets during data transmission from source to destination even after the secure knowledge algorithm is applied. The anomaly attacks are reported by neighboring nodes, as every node monitors its neighbor node activities.

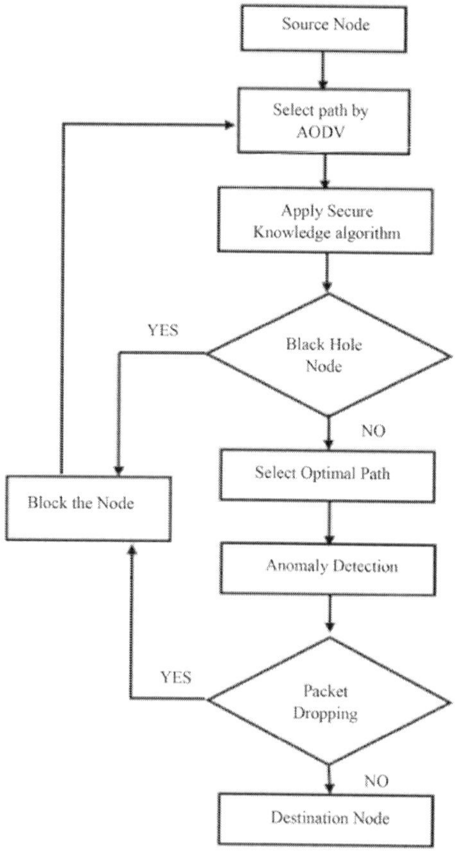

Figure 3. Data flow from source to destination.

SIMULATION AND RESULTS

We developed a communication network with MANET using Network Simulator version 2 (NS-2) as shown in Figure 4 for our proposed residential microgrid (Figure 2). The parameters of the developed communication network are shown in Table 1. The developed network simulation is shown in Figure 4, which is a screen shot taken during the simulation process. The base station, which collects information from all the nodes is represented with big red circle as seen at the top right corner. The remaining nodes include residential houses, EVs, and mobile system operators.

In order to evaluate the effectiveness of the proposed IDP technology, the black hole attacked nodes and misbehaving nodes are added into the MANET network. We then applied secure knowledge algorithm as well as anomaly detection as presented in flowchart in Figure 3. Major network parameters such as network throughput, packet delivery ratio (PDR), and delay in the network are graphically represented in Figures 5-7.

Network throughput is the rate of data successfully delivered, PDR is defined as the ratio of number of packets delivered to the number of packets sent, and delay is total time taken to send the packets from source node to destination node. The proposed IDP technology is applied to the network, where black hole attacked nodes and misbehaving nodes are added to the developed network in NS2 simulator. From Figures 5-7, we can observe that network throughput and PDR are increased (Figure 5 and Figure 6), and delay is decreased (see Figure 7), when the number of nodes in the network increased from 10 nodes to 50 nodes. Test results demonstrate that our proposed IDP technology is very efficient when there are more than 40 nodes in the network, for identifying

SIMULATION AND RESULTS

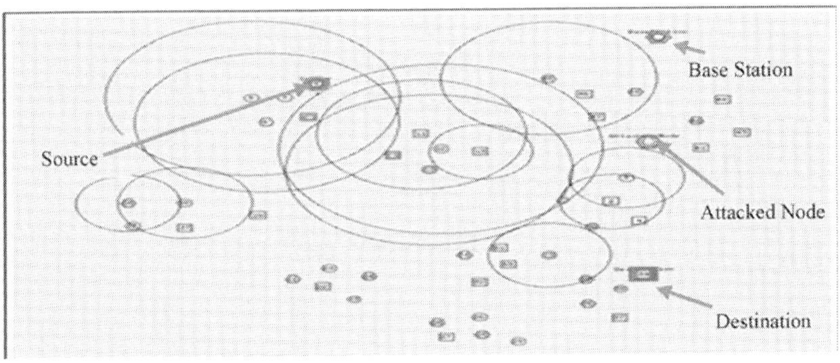

Figure 4. MANET simulation using NS-2.

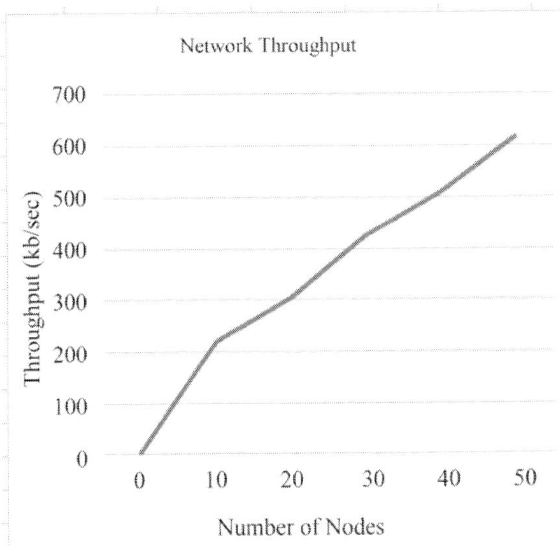

Figure 5. Network throughput vs. number of nodes.

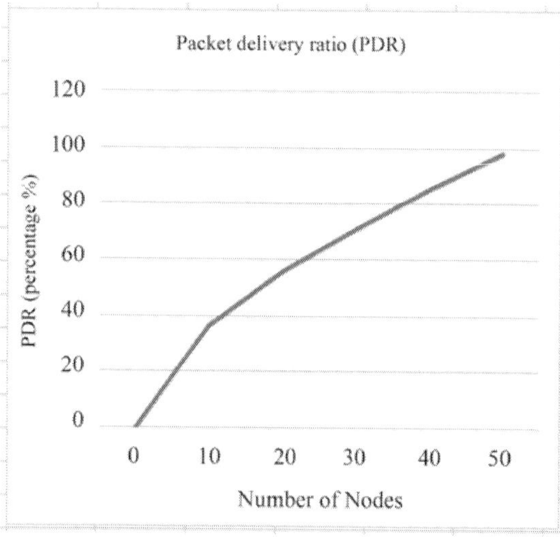

Figure 6. Packet delivery ratio vs. number of nodes.

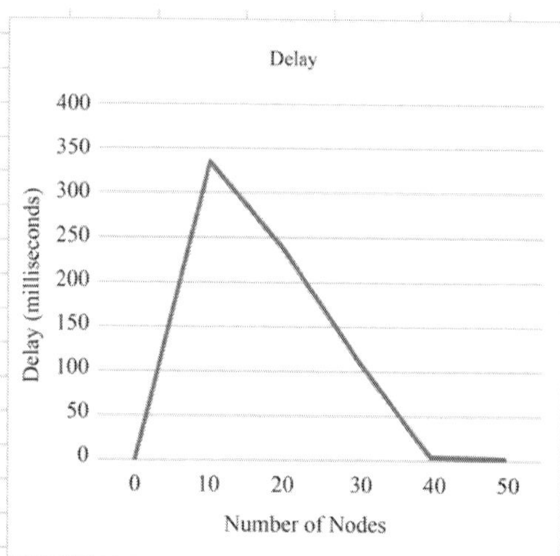

Figure 7. Delay in the network vs. number of nodes.

Table 1. Network simulation parameters.

Simulator	Network Simulator version 2
Simulation of Nodes	50
Interface Type	Phy/WirelessPhy

Channel	Wireless channel
MAC Type	Mac/802_11
Queue Type	Queue/DropTail/PriQueue
Queue Length	201 packets
Antenna Type	Omni antenna
Propagation Type	Two-ray ground
Size Of Packet	Five hundred and twelve
Routing Algorithm	AODV (ad hoc on demand distance vector algorithm)
Traffic	TCP
Simulation Time	7 minutes
Nodes Clustering	K-means algorithm

and preventing black hole attacks and other anomaly attacks that result in packet dropping. When there are only 10 nodes in the network the possibility to find a new route without attacked nodes is difficult, and when the total number of nodes increased in the network it is easy to find the new route which is optimal and secured. This will certainly enhance the cyber security for the proposed residential microgrid communication network.

CONCLUSION

This paper presented a SCADA communication network with ACT in the residential microgrid. Furthermore, IDP technology was applied to the proposed network using MANET, which collect the information of power consumption of residential areas and EVs, and also connect the network with mobile system operators. The major finding of this paper is that our proposed IDP technology, equipped with a secure knowledge algorithm and anomaly detection, was highly efficient in detecting cyber-attacks such as black hole attack and some unknown attacks, which led to create a misbehaving node that resulted into packet dropping. The future work would be interesting to examine the efficiency of multiple communication technologies when they are combined to control and operate MMEMS, and to develop viable IDP technologies that prevent cyber-attacks on the SCADA system.

ACKNOWLEDGEMENTS

This work was supported by the National Science Foundation (DUE-TUES-1246050). The authors would like to express sincere gratitude to National Science Foundation for providing financial support.

REFERENCES

1. Shafiullah, G., Oo, A., Ali, A. and Wolfs, P. (2013) Smart Grid for a Sustainable Future. Smart Grid and Renewable Energy, 4, 23-34. http://dx.doi.org/10.4236/

sgre.2013.41004

2. Heydt, G.T., Liu, C.C., Phadke, A.G. and Vittal, V. (2001) Solution for the Crisis in Electric Power Supply. Computer Applications in Power, 14, 22-30.

3. Zhong, X., Yu, L., Brooks, R. and Venayagamoorthy, G.K. (2015) Cyber Security in Smart DC Microgrid Operations. IEEE 1st International Conference on DC Microgrids (ICDCM), Atlanta, 7 June 2015, 86-91.

4. Sridevi, S.K. and Mohammed, A.A.K. (2015) Preventing Black Hole Attacks in MANETs Using Secure Knowledge Algorithm. International Conference on SPACES, India, 2 January 2015, 421-425.

5. Tesfahun, and Bhaskari, D.L. (2015) Effective Hybrid Intrusion Detection System: A Layered Approach. International Journal of Computer Network and Information Security (IJCNIS), 7, 35. http://dx.doi.org/10.5815/ijcnis.2015.03.05

6. Khanna, A. (2012) Smart Grid, Smart Controllers and Home Energy Automation—Creating the Infrastructure for Future. Smart Grid and Renewable Energy, 3,165-174. http://dx.doi.org/10.4236/sgre.2012.33024

7. Sule, R., Katti, R.S. and Kavasseri, R.G. (2012) A Variable Length Fast Message Authentication Code for Secure Communication in Smart Grids. Power and Energy Society General Meeting, San Diego, 22-26 July 2012, 1-6. http://dx.doi.org/10.1109/pesgm.2012.6345622

8. Chakrabarti, A. and Manimaran, G. (2002) Internet Infrastructure Security: A Taxonomy. Network, 16, 13-21.

9. Gao, J., Xiao, Y., Liu, J., Liang, W. and Chen, C.P. (2012) A Survey of Communication/Networking in Smart Grids. Future Generation Computer Systems, 28, 391-404. http://dx.doi.org/10.1016/j.future.2011.04.014

10. Baayer, A., Enneya, N. and Elkoutbi, M. (2012) Enhanced Timestamp Discrepancy to Limit Impact of Replay Attacks in MANETs. Journal of Information Security, 3, 224-230. http://dx.doi.org/10.4236/jis.2012.33028

11. Parik, P.P., Kanabar, M.G. and Sidhu, T.S. (2010) Opportunities and Challenges of Wireless Communication Technologies for Smart grid Applications. Power and Energy Society General Meeting, Minneapolis, 25-29 July 2010, 1-7. http://dx.doi.org/10.1109/pes.2010.5589988

12. Grilo, A.M., Chen, J.J., Diaz, M., Garrido, D. and Casaca, A. (2014) An Integrated WSAN and SCADA System for Monitoring a Critical Infrastructure. IEEE Transactions on Industrial Informatics, 10, 1755-1764. http://dx.doi.org/10.1109/TII.2014.2322818

13. Alcaraz, C., Lopez, J., Zhou, J. and Roman, R. (2011) Secure SCADA Framework for the Protection of Energy Control Systems. Concurrency and Computation: Practice and Experience, 23, 1431-1442. http://dx.doi.org/10.1002/cpe.1679

14. Kumar, N.R., Mohanapriya, P. and Kalaiselvi, M. (2014) Development of an Attack-Resistant and Secure SCADA System Using WSN, MANET, and Internet. International Journal of Advanced Computer Research, 4, 627.

15. Medida, S., Sreekumar, N. and Prasad, K.V. (1998) SCADA-EMS on the Internet.

Proc. International Conference on Energy Management and Power Delivery (EMPD), 2, 656-660. http://dx.doi.org/10.1109/empd.1998.702766

16. Rihan, M., Ahmad, M. and Beg, M. (2013) Vulnerability Analysis of Wide Area Measurement System in the Smart Grid. Smart Grid and Renewable Energy, 4, 1-7. http://dx.doi.org/10.4236/sgre.2013.46A001
17. Tweed, K. (2014) Attack on Nine Substations Could Take Down U.S. Grid. IEEE Spectrum. http://spectrum.ieee.org/energywise/energy/the-smarter-grid/attack-on-nine-substations-could-take-down-us-grid
18. Tweed, K. (2014) Attack on California Substation Fuels Grid Security Debate. IEEE Spectrum. http://spectrum.ieee.org/energywise/energy/the-smarter-grid/attack-on-california-substation-fuels-grid-security-debate
19. Mahmud, R., Vallakati, R., Mukherjee, A., Ranganathan, P. and Nejadpak, A. (2015) A Survey on Smart Grid Metering Infrastructures: Threats and Solutions. International Conference on Electro/Information Technology (EIT), DeKalb, 21 May 2015, 386-391.
20. Rudrapattana, S. (2013) Cyber-Security Analysis in Smart Grid SCADA Systems: A Game Theoretic Approach. PhD Diss., Texas Tech University.
21. Fovino, I.N., Guidi, L., Masera, M. and Stefanini, A. (2011) Cyber Security Assessment of a Power Plant. Electric Power Systems Research, 81, 518-526. http://dx.doi.org/10.1016/j.epsr.2010.10.012
22. Wei, M. and Chen, Z. (2012) Reliability Analysis of Cyber Security in an Electrical Power System Associated WAN. Power and Energy Society General Meeting, San Diego, 22-26 July 2012, 1-6. http://dx.doi.org/10.1109/pesgm.2012.6345533
23. Ten, C.W., Liu, C.C. and Manimaran, G. (2008) Vulnerability Assessment of Cyber Security for SCADA Systems. IEEE Transactions on Power Systems, 23, 1836-1846.
24. Fernandez, J.D. and Fernandez, A.E. (2005) SCADA Systems: Vulnerabilities and Remediation. Journal of Computing Sciences in Colleges, 20, 160-168.
25. Safdar, S., Hamdaoui, B., Cotilla-Sanchez, E. and Guizani, M. (2013) A Survey on Communication Infrastructure for Micro-Grids. Proc. 9th International Wireless Communications and Mobile Computing Conference (IWCMC), Sardinia, 1-5 July 2013, 545-550. http://dx.doi.org/10.1109/iwcmc.2013.6583616
26. Chalamasetty, G.K., Mandal, P. and Tseng, B. (2015) Cyber Security Model for Power System Based on Game Theory. Proc. 5th Southwest Energy Science and Engineering Symposium, El Paso, 4 April 2015.
27. Sridharan, V. (2012) Cyber Security in Power Systems. Thesis Diss., Georgia Institute of Technology.
28. Daoud, M. and Fernando, X. (2011) On the Communication Requirements for the Smart Grid. Energy and Power Engineering, 3, 53-60. http://dx.doi.org/10.4236/epe.2011.31008
29. Kim, T.H. (2010) SCADA Architecture with Mobile Remote Components. WSEAS Transactions on Systems and Control, 5, 611-622.

SECTION III: CYBER LAWS

9
CHAPTER

DEVELOPING REGIMES AND MOBILE TELECOMS REGULATION IN THE TWENTY-FIRST CENTURY

Bruce Wardhaugh

Keywords: Telecommunications, Competition, Development, Sector Regulation, Competition Agency Design

INTRODUCTION

In this article I examine issues for competition regulation in the twenty-first century. My concern is with the lessons which developed regimes can provide for developing regimes. Though I speak of competition regulation generally, my emphasis is on the mobile telecommunications market and its separate need for regulation.

This emphasis is due to the importance which mobile telecommunications has in facilitating the economic growth. Not only is it is an inexpensive means of communication, but mobile telephony can also be used as an alternative financial system: facilitating the transmission of payments and remittances. Yet the mobile telecoms market is also a market prone to abuse. Typically, mobile networks are established on the backbone of the infrastructure of a former state monopoly. The firm which took over that monopoly during a liberalization process will retain the significant incumbent advantages of the former monopoly. While telecommunications markets can be liberalized, the liberalization of these markets can bring a host of other regulatory issues into play. In addition to more general concerns of (near) monopolies from an incumbent effect, issues of access to essential facilities and margin squeeze also arise.

But also of significance is the degree of independence which a regulatory authority is given. Independence is a broad concept, extending beyond freedom from political interference to freedom from capture, and a sufficient degree of independence to be free

Citation: Bruce Wardhaugh, Developing regimes and mobile telecoms regulation in the twenty-first century, file:///E:/MY%20DATA/Anu/Project%20m3/Feb/Role%20of%20Information%20Technology%20in%20Front%20Office/Input/man/SSRN-id2708078.pdf.

from being 'hamstrung' by other legal measures exogenous to the competition regime. This latter loss of independence can be fatal to effective regulation, as we will see in this article.

This article is organized as follows: the next part examines the use of mobile telephony in developing economies. This part shows that given its use to facilitate inter alia market transactions, careful regulation is needed to nurture this industry in a developing economy, so that the gains which it might provide are actually realized by the population as a whole. These gains can be achieved through market liberalization, provided that the liberalized market is a competitive market. Facilitating competition in markets is the task of a well-structured competition regime, which has both legal content and an administrative and/or judicial structure. Getting both content and structure 'correct' is essential for a competition regime to function effectively.

Part three considers lessons which can be learned from established regimes. In it, I examine both the content of the legal rules and the nature of the agencies which enforce these rules. I show that while there may be a common content which condemns collusive activity, when anti-competitive activities outside this core are considered, the content of rules varies significantly. This can have an impact on the efficacy of a competition regime. This is very apparent with the key anti-monopoly rules that are used to regulate the telecoms market. Further, I consider the nature of the agencies regulating the market. While the focus of most of the literature has been on the relative merits of specialized and generalist agencies, I indicate that agency independence is central, and that a loss of independence can result not only from political interference or capture, but also can arise from legal considerations exogenous to the competition regime.

Part four is a point of illustration. It considers the Mexican telecommunications sector to show how things can go wrong if this market is ineffectively regulated. Rather than serving as a means of economic development and permitting the Mexican public from sharing in the gains from trade, ineffective telecommunications regulation permitted the private appropriation of a substantial portion of these gains, robbing the country of close to 2% of its GDP on an annual basis. The difficulty with the Mexican attempt to regulate the telecoms market was not just in political interference which manifested itself in the attractive packaging of the former governmental monopoly in the privatization process; but also in the peculiarities of Mexican administrative law, which had the consequence of hamstringing effective regulation of the liberalized market.

The article concludes with some remarks regarding the appropriate bodies for competition law regulation in the twenty-first century and concludes that the key determinant of a regime's efficacy is the regulator's independence. However, in reaching this conclusion, this article raises a number of points, which may not have unique solutions, but the adequate resolution of which is essential for any competition regime in the twenty-first century.

MOBILE TELEPHONY, DEVELOPMENT AND COMPETITION

Background: Development and Mobile Telephony

On a casual examination of the World Bank's (2015) development indicators, it is easy to notice that in spite of the fact that many developing countries have low levels of developed infrastructure (in terms of measures such as percentage of paved road, percentage of the population with access to electricity and improved sanitation facilities), they have is a relatively high rate of penetration in the mobile telephone market. These statistics (World Bank 2015) show that, for example, in Kenya, 7% of the roads are paved, 19.2% of the population have access to electricity and 30% of the population have access to sanitary facilities. Nevertheless, there are 71 mobile subscriptions (both pre- and post-paid) per 100 people. In Guinea-Bissau (which is among those countries recognized by UNCTAD as a least developed country), no data exists for the percentage of paved roads or access to electricity, only 20% of the population have access to improved sanitation, yet there are 74 mobile subscriptions per 100 people. In contrast, both Kenya and Guinea-Bissau have less than 1 landline per 100 people. It is fairly easy to see why mobile telephony has leapfrogged fixed-line telephony outside of the so-called first world: relying on radio waves, mobile communication does not require the extensive and expensive infrastructure of physical connections between every receiver and central exchanges, which would be impossible to install in areas where there is no access to electricity to run that portion of the network. Further the use of pre-pay subscriptions eliminates the problems of assessing creditworthiness and the costs of writing-off accounts that are uncollectible.

This market penetration of mobile telephony can be used to enhance a country's ability to gain through trade, and thus increase its level of development, according to any measure which uses an increase in GDP as a criterion for developmental status (see Sen, 1999: 5). This can be illustrated by Aker and Mbiti's study (2010: 213 - 214) of sub-Sahara Africa which identifies five mechanisms by which mobile telephony enhances development. To paraphrase these authors' conclusions:

1. mobile phones improve access to and use of information, reducing search costs, improve coordination among agents, hence increasing market efficiency;
2. increased communication improves firms' productive efficiency through better supply chain management;
3. mobile phones create employment due to demand for mobile-related services;
4. mobile phones facilitate communication among social networks in response to shocks, thereby reducing households' exposure to risk; and,
5. 'mobile phone-based applications and development projects-sometimes known as 'm-development'-have the potential to facilitate the delivery of financial, agricultural, health, and educational services'. (Aker and Mbiti, 2010: 214)

Point 5 is significant, as will be discussed below, as mobile telephones can be used as a form of a basic banking and money transfer service.

Expanding on the above, we note that points (1) and (2) relate directly to the use of mobile telephony to obtain the information required for arbitrage and arbitrage-like opportunities, including the ability to buy and sell goods or services on the most profitable markets. Mobile phones permit the real-time transmission of market data. It is possession and use of information (in particular on prices) which will give market participants the ability to maximise their position and thus ensure a more efficient use and distribution of resources.

We note for instance, Abraham's 2006 study of the Indian fishing industry which shows the effects mobile telephones had in transforming that industry to the economic betterment of the fishers.

That industry is characterised by its highly perishable product, making arbitrage between markets difficult once fish are landed. Abraham (2006: 51) notes:

Another feature of the market before the introduction of mobile phones were occasions on which there would be a glut of fish in some markets while other markets experienced acute scarcity. This meant that prices would be unnaturally low in some markets and unnaturally high in others due to the mismatch between supply and demand. When they were asked whether the introduction of mobile phones had lowered the possibility of this mismatch occurring, close to three-quarters of the respondents replied in the affirmative ...

In addition to these demand-side advantages provided by information communicated by mobile telephone, there are also supply-side advantages. Abraham continues (52):

Sizable numbers of fishermen and owners agreed that the search costs involved in looking for fish had come down since the advent of mobile phones. This reduced wastage of resources in two ways:

- By reducing the time spent out at sea searching for fish. Other boats in the fishing unit would send out alerts on the mobile phones if large shoals were found. Over 94 percent of owners and fishermen had used mobile phones to alert other boats to the presence of shoals of fish at some time or the other.

- By reducing the number of fishermen who had to spend time idling on shore. News of large shoals could be easily communicated and the idle resources put to use at once. The reduced wastage has an immediate impact in terms of fuel costs. Most people in the community point to rapidly increasing fuel costs as one of the main reasons why the sector is seen to be increasingly unprofitable. Additionally, and not to be lightly discounted, is the enhanced security while at sea which a mobile phone provides (Abraham 2006: 54). Risk, whether market or personal, is a quality which can be reduced through the use of mobile phones.

Following on point 5 above, mobile banking services can be used domestically or, more significantly, internationally, to send and receive remittances. Describing one such service, the Kenyan M-Pesa, Aker and Mbiti (2010: 221) note that money transfer by this sort of ebanking is 60 - 80% less expensive than its next cheapest competitors. The relationship between access to banking services and development potential is well explored elsewhere (see e.g. Burgess and Pande, 2005). In addition to the e-finance uses to which mobile telephony can be put, it has also been rolled-out as part of a public health strategy. In a study in Kenya (Lester et al, 2010), HIV positive patients undergoing antiretroviral treatment (ART) were randomly placed into two groups, one group receiving weekly SMS messages to prompt them to take ART (and provide other support), the other group received standard (unprompted) treatment. Not surprisingly, those patients who were SMS-prompted were not only more likely to selfreport increased compliance with ART, but also 'were more likely to have their viral load suppressed below detection levels than patients who received the standard care alone' (1842). In an earlier reflective piece, Lester and Karonja (2008: 738) note that the implications of this extend beyond treatment for HIV to include other chronic conditions such as tuberculosis, and short term conditions like malaria. They observe: The key advantage to using mobile phones to track patients is that they offer a low-cost, instantaneous, and increasingly ubiquitous communications medium, and are unrestricted to location. The goal is to improve effectiveness and efficiency of health service delivery with the farthest possible reach. (739)

In addition to the obvious economic advantages which this sort of support in treatment provides (as the costs of early intervention are less than the costs of subsequent treatment of a serious or terminal condition), successful public health uses of mobile telephony increase other metrics of development (World Bank 2015), most notably those surrounding life expectancy.

Mobile Telephones, Transaction Costs and Anti-Competitive Appropriation

Mobile phone use, while facilitating information acquisition which leads to Pareto-superior market outcomes, nevertheless imposes a transaction cost. Since Coase (1960) it has been recognised that in the absence of transaction costs, irrespective of the initial assignment or entitlement, resources will flow to their most valued use. However, the presence of transaction costs has the ability to impede an otherwise utility maximising exchange. Indeed, if the transaction costs exceed the gain from the envisaged transaction, the parties will not consummate the exchange. In a competitive market, to the extent that those services the provision of which involves imposing transactions costs are needed (e.g. solicitors' costs in conveyancing), such services will be provided at the marginal cost of their provision. In a competitive market, a party which attempts to obtain a super-competitive return (i.e. above the marginal cost of the provision) for their services will soon be out-competed by an entrant. However, should entry be impossible (or difficult) due to entry barriers, the provider of these services will be in a better position to realise a super-competitive return (economic rent). This has three consequences. First, a profit-maximising firm, when it has a dominant position on a non-competitive market, will attempt to maximise its revenue on the (goods or) services it provides, by increasing the price. Second, if entry barriers to a market are sufficient to permit a situation where artificially high transaction costs are created, these costs represent a direct transfer of wealth from the parties to the transaction to those imposing the transaction costs. Third, to the extent that artificially high transaction costs impede transactions, they cause a deadweight loss to the economy. These are simple propositions of microeconomics (see e.g. Motta 2004: 40 - 48). The implications of these consequences for telecommunications (and to a significant degree, banking and finance) are profound. First, to the extent that entry to the market is difficult, the opportunities for entrants to compete away rents will be reduced. Second, to the extent that there is a sole or few provider(s) in the market, collective activity which facilitates pricing at super-competitive levels is made easier. This activity can take the form of outright collision (cartel activity) or collective dominance, where firms 'aware of common interests, consider it possible, economically rational, and hence preferable to adopt on a lasting basis a common policy of selling at above competitive prices, without having to enter into an agreement …' (Schwalbe and Zimmer, 2009: 222). Of course, if there is only one provider in the market, in the absence of effective entry, the monopolist has every incentive to maximize revenue through super-competitive pricing.

Barriers to entry into the mobile telecommunications market include the network itself.

While the construction of a mobile network is significantly cheaper than a land-line network, there are costs incurred with matters such as erecting and maintaining mobile towers, the supply of energy required for their operation, and the switching of calls through the network. Even if it is economically feasible to construct a second, competing, network, the value of this second network is limited unless that network can be integrated with the existing mobile network, and other outside (including international) networks. Finally, as mobile telephony operates on the radio spectrum, allocation (licencing) of the spectrum has access implications. This set of concerns raises the competition issues surrounding essential facilities, and illustrate how a difference in their legal resolution can affect the competitive environment in the mobile telecommunications market. A broad (akin to the EU) standard which determines what constitutes essential facilities is more likely to permit greater access to networks than what would be mandated under an American-influenced rule. This will be illustrated in Part Three.

Outside of access to the network, other significant competition problems arise. Even in wealthy jurisdictions, it is rare for more than two or three parallel but interlinked, physical networks to exist (Li and Lyons 2011). Added competition can be provided by 'virtual' mobile telecoms networks, which buy wholesale quantities of mobile time from vertically integrated physical networks (which also operate on the retail market) and then retail these minutes under their own 'label.' The temptation for the wholesaler is to engage in a 'margin squeeze,' charging a sufficiently high wholesale price that their competition cannot make an adequate return. Again, the difference in chosen rule can make a significant difference. To the extent that a positive obligation is imposed to avoid this practice, and virtual networks are not squeezed out of existence, these networks can provide added competition to physical networks, and thus facilitate downward pricing in the telecoms market.

The competition consequences for the mobile market are clear. Aker and Mbiti (2010: 227 - 228) conclude:

There is a strong correlation between mobile phone coverage, the types of services offered, the price of such services, and the telecommunications market structure for a particular country. In markets with limited competition, we would expect profit-maximizing firms to offer more limited services at higher prices. … [And] on average, prices decreased and services increased following market liberalization; average call prices fell by a minimum of 31 percent with partial liberalization and by up to 90 percent following full liberalization. Liberalization was also associated with an increase in international traffic volumes and improved call quality. Overall, these patterns suggest that more competitive telecommunications environments can be beneficial for poor consumers. Although the precise correlation between mobile telephone penetration and economic growth is unclear [2] for our purposes we need only point out that there is such a correlation. This link adds further justification for the need to regulate the telecoms market with care. In addition to the standard, consumer surplus protecting justification for regulation of the market, these developmental concerns add a further, pressing reason for the need of such regulation, and that this regulation be done appropriately.

SOME LESSONS LEARNED

If we look at existing competition regimes we can learn some lessons from two features present in them: (1) the type of body tasked with rule formulation and/or adjudication; and (2) the content of these rules. Both of these features shows particular lessons for those who may wish to adopt these characteristics into a new regime, with the idea of facilitating competition to improve a country's growth.

The Type of Body Tasked With Rule Formulation And/Or Adjudication

The main focus of the literature on this point to date has been to determine the relative efficacy of specialised bodies versus generalist bodies (e.g. Crane 2011; Wright and Diveley 2013; Ginsberg and Wright 2013). Both have their relative merits. Specialized bodies typically possess the technical expertise required to appropriately evaluate the industry-specific elements of the dispute. As Wright and Diveley note, 'There is no debate that theoretical potential for superior agency performance lies in its ability to harness its expertise' (2013: 84). In competition matters this includes the ability to understand, critically assess and apply economic evidence regarding the relevant markets in dispute. There are at least two obvious advantages of this. The first is cost efficiencies in the evidence gathering and hearing process (such evidence can be presented without the need for it to be 'translated' by expert witnesses into laymen's' terms). The second is a reduction in error rate in the decisions. Given that the adjudicators are fluent with economic analysis, they are less likely to get the answers to the problems 'wrong.'

The difficulty with specialised bodies is their expense and how the expense can be justified.

This is a particular issue for developing regimes and their use not just of a general competition agency (perhaps with a consumer protection co-mandate); but of their use of specialised sectorial regulatory agencies to regulate matters such as infrastructure (air-and seaports), utilities (electricity, water and sewer) and telecommunications. While these sorts of hyper-specialised bodies are less likely to get matters 'wrong,' they require a significant level of expensive expertise to ensure that this is in fact the case. The significance of this is simple: every unit of currency spent in one area means that it cannot be spent in other areas. To enhance economic development, developing nations need infrastructure (to transport goods), education, and public health-to name just a few concerns. A choice therefore must be made among these options. The choice is not binary. And this is a normative political choice: though economics may fill in some of the blanks in hypothetical budget allocation scenarios, ultimately any choice cannot be made by that discipline.

The main merit possessed by generalist bodies is that they are relative inexpensive. The cost of the adjudication of competition law disputes by generalist courts is only the incremental costs of hearing that case (less the costs of not hearing another case, should use of that court not be by right). A generalist competition agency (perhaps with a consumer protection co- mandate) could possibly provide needed generalist expertise (e.g. in cartel, dominance and merger matters) as well as (likely limited) insight into sectorial regulatory issues. Such bodies do require governmental expenditure; however, the precise level of expenditure is-as noted above-a political choice with normative content.

However, what has not been well explored by the literature is the need for independence of the adjudicatory or regulatory bodies. Assuring judicial independence is a problem in developing regimes. In addition to problems with appointment of the judiciary, there may also constitutional issues with regard to the isolation of that branch of government from political pressure from other branches. Likewise, independence requires insulation from lobbying efforts. Judicial independence is one element of the rule of law. There are studies that indicate strong correlation between economic development and an independent judiciary are correlated (these studies are summarized in Dam (2006) and

World Bank (2004)). Other studies also show that effective competition regimes advance economic development (OECD, 2013; Sokol et al, 2013). But these studies do not show causality. While judicial independence and economic development correlate, in what direction does the causal arrow flow, or is it a matter of bootstrapping? This is a point for further research.

With regulatory bodies, there is a second concern, namely that market regulators require highly specific expertise. It is trite to observe that almost by definition as the needed level of technical expertise becomes highly specific, fewer people possess this knowledge. Those possessing this expertise likely work in the regulated industry. Hence, the regulated and the regulator share the same talent pool. Regulatory capture is thus a plausible outcome. This is not just a problem with developing jurisdictions, but also exists in the so-called 'first world' (see e.g. the concerns expressed in e.g. Dnes 1995 and van Koten and Ortmann 2008).

Seeking expertise from outside the industry is likely to require recruitment abroad. In itself, this may not be problematic; after all there is no need to invent the same wheel twice. But to carry the wheel analogy a step further, we may be requiring the import of a Ford wheel when an (also imported) Fiat wheel may be more appropriate. 'Imported' expertise can bring with it imported legal content. The first section of this paper showed that content can make a difference-not just with how cartel behaviour may be regulated, but also in regard to permissible behaviour for a dominant enterprise. American and European views regarding essential facilities, refusal to deal and margin squeeze vary.

These latter three doctrines will be significant to any regulation of many industries, in particular telecommunications.

Further, imported 'expertise' can also be a source of suspicion. The US has been known to suggest providing antitrust advice to developing countries as a means of influencing the development of their regimes (Weiser, 2009). However, such 'donations' of expertise is often viewed with suspicion, as having ulterior motives. In particular there is the view that the underling desire to make markets in developing economies 'more competitive' is so that American firms can enter and 'compete' in them. That American law permits export cartels

(Export Trade Act 1918) only enhances this cynicism. Further, there is the suspicion that the use of criminal sanctions in cartel matters is to ensure that the double criminality aspect of any extradition treaty is satisfied, putting the liberty of local businesspeople in jeopardy. Given the increasing number of non-US citizens extradited to face American criminal antitrust proceedings, this latter point may well be justified.

All of this is in addition to any other underlying concerns about differing cultural attitudes to cooperation, competition and distributive institutions in society which underlie the socionormative foundations of a society's views towards regulation of competition. [3] To the extent that these foundations differ from the American (or any other 'imported') paradigm, then the justification for the use of the imported paradigm loses a significant amount of its force. [4]

A balance needs to be struck between the legitimate provision of advice and assistance to an independent government and the co-option of that government for other purposes.

Likewise, assistance in offsetting the significant costs of staring up (and running) such agencies and assisting in the development of competition law and economics expertise in existing institutions (like the judiciary) if offered as some form of a cash based aid, may appear to be a bribe, and once given may be hard to verify whether it was effectively put to use.

Irrespective of the manner in which this international assistance is implemented, any developing jurisdiction must develop a prioritized agenda for competition regulation and enforcement. The typical development of competition regimes is from cartel control through dominance to merger control, with sector regulation being added along the way. It may well be that a developing regime should follow this pattern, concentrating initially on national or regional cartel activity which is likely to immediately harm consumers. Here price fixing in goods such as food staples (UNCTAD, 2014: 130), fuel, and agricultural inputs can appropriate a significant amount of consumer welfare. Similar harm can be done through abusive practices of dominant firms in these markets.

But beyond this, there is an additional concern, which will be made apparent in our consideration of the Mexican case. This is the independence of the relevant competition body from the interference of legal rules exogenous to the competition regime. In this

Mexican case, these rules included the peculiarities of administrative law which could be exploited by the firm whose conduct is under review, the effect of which was to facilitate the delay in imposition of consumer welfare enhancing remedies. While the Mexican case may be an extreme example of the dysfunctional relationship the administrative and competition law regimes had with each other, its very extreme nature provides a powerful warning of what can go wrong.

The Content of the Rule

It is trite that the content of the rules is very determinative of the efficacy of the regime. For the most part, competition regimes worldwide are in agreement that certain practices are 'bad' and as a consequence, these activities are to be controlled. The means of control (private sanctions, administrative control, criminal penalties) are of course of importance, [5] but what may be more significant is the sort of activity which falls under the prohibition.

Hard core cartel activity with its collusive origin (price fixing, customer allocation, output restrictions) is generally regarded as wrong and condemned. But there is no universal consensus as to the form by which this condemnation takes place (criminal or other means). Although there may be universal agreement as to the core, the further from the core that conduct is, the less agreement there may be. Collusive behaviour among competitors at the horizontal level is bad for the consumer, but the cases of vertical arrangements such as territorial restrictions or resale price maintenance are less clear. There is even less clarity with regards to cooperation agreements in research and development, and joint ventures.

Likewise the content of the antitrust (dominance) rules is important. This is particularly so with the concepts of essential facilities refusal to deal and margin squeeze, both of which are significant to telecommunications regulation. Typically, liberalising a jurisdiction's telecoms market involves wrestling away the dominant grasp that the incumbent player (usually the former government-owned monopoly) has on the market. As seen below, this player not only controls the essential facilities necessary to operate a competing network, but also is likely to be in a position to be the sole (or dominant) wholesale provider of telecoms services, which it in turn sells on to its competitors. As a consequence of this market power, the incumbent may be in a position to charge a wholesale rate which is sufficiently high that the potential competitor cannot realise an adequate return on its investment-in other words, engage in a 'margin squeeze.'

In telecommunications, essential facilities include access to mobile towers, rights of way to erect same, access to the frequency spectrum (often granted to the former national monopoly when mobile service was first introduced), and other structural features (e.g. assignment of telephone numbers, use of switching facilities, integration with foreign telecommunications operators) which give their owner an advantage. It would be either impossible (due to network effects) or economically wasteful to duplicate these facilities. These facilities are almost always owned by the former governmental monopoly, giving it a significant incumbent advantage. Thoughts regarding essential facilities are far from the agreed core of antitrust thought, as a comparison of the US and EU reveals. American doctrines of essential facilities and refusal to deal are primarily creations of the Circuit Courts [6] to limit the conclusion of the Supreme Court's 1919 decision in United States v Colgate in which that Court held (at US 307) at trade may deal with whomever it wishes on whatever terms it pleases. However, recent US Supreme Court decisions, particularly Verizon v Trinko, cast doubt on the extent-or even the existence-of a doctrine of essential facilities in US law.

Recently, in Verizon, the issue was access to local telephone exchanges owned by an incumbent carrier (here Verizon). Under the provisions of theTelecommunications Act of 1996 incumbents were required to share access to the local network with new entrants who could then sell on these services at the retail level. In dismissing the complaint that Verizon denied interconnection services to prevent entry of competitors, the Court held (at US 407 - 8, S Ct 879):

The mere possession of monopoly power, and the concomitant charging of monopoly prices, is not only not unlawful; it is an important element of the free-market system. The opportunity to charge monopoly prices-at least for a short period is what attracts 'business acumen' in the first place; it induces risk taking that produces innovation and economic growth. To safeguard the incentive to innovate, the possession of monopoly power will not be found unlawful unless it is accompanied by an element of anticompetitive conduct.

The American rule makes essential facility and refusal to deal claims difficult to prosecute.

The European doctrine is different. Although the Commission takes the starting point that a trader is free to choose its own trading partners [7] (a starting point is shared with the

American Authorities) the Commission goes a step or two further. It identifies the problems that an unmitigated duty to supply would have (e.g. disincentives in investment encouraged by free riding (Guidance: para 75)) but seeks to balance this against the potential harm to consumers which might occur under a strict regime of freedom of choice of contractual partners. This balance is announced (Guidance: para 81) in its enforcement priorities, which prioritizes enforcement when: all the following circumstances are present:

- the refusal relates to a product or service that is objectively necessary to be able to compete effectively on a downstream market,
- the refusal is likely to lead to the elimination of effective competition on the downstream market, and
- the refusal is likely to lead to consumer harm.

This is broader than the US view.

The importance of this is magnified by the realisation that the telecommunications industry is susceptible to margin squeeze (Geradin and O'Donoghue, 2005; International

Telecommunications Union 2014). In in his study of the EU case law on margin squeeze between January 2003 and March 2012, Veljanovski (2012) noted that in this timeframe, of the 41 European cases (of which 38 were national, and 3 were EU), 29

(71%) of these were in the telecommunications sector, with 3 in the postal sector, 2 cases in the water sector and 1 each in the gas, electricity, aviation, railway, pharmaceutical, entertainment and construction sectors. This is consistent with US experience, where the leading case (Pacific Bell v Linkline) is a telecommunications matter.

Again, antitrust thinking regarding margin squeeze is not part of the agreed core, as US and EU jurisprudence demonstrate. In the US, where there is a duty to deal only in the most extreme of cases, and where predatory pricing requires the proof of recoupment (Brooke Group Ltd v Brown and Williamson Tobacco Corp), the difficulty of establishing a margin squeeze case can be seen from the Supreme Court's conclusion in Pacific Bell v Linkline (at S Ct 1120): Plaintiffs' price-squeeze claim, looking to the relation between retail and wholesale prices, is thus nothing more than an amalgamation of a meritless claim at the retail level and a meritless claim at the wholesale level. If there is no duty to deal at the wholesale level and no predatory pricing at the retail level, then a firm is certainly not required to price both of these services in a manner that preserves its rivals' profit margins.

However, compare the American position to the European rule stated in TeliaSonera, (at para 40): Where an undertaking introduces a pricing policy intended to drive from the market competitors who are perhaps as efficient as that dominant undertaking but who, because of their smaller financial resources, are incapable of withstanding the competition waged against them, that undertaking is, accordingly, abusing its dominant position...

The difference in content is significant. In the mobile telephone market, where towers are essential to the network infrastructure, if the chosen rule precludes an incumbent from being required to grant a potential competitor access to its towers, then the incumbent may have to duplicate the network. This cost would have to be passed onto consumers, and may preclude entry in the first place

Likewise, the content of margin squeeze rules will have significance. In telecommunications cases it is typically the ex-governmental monopoly player that has the advantage. In markets where there is no duty to deal at the wholesale level to potential downstream competitors, foreclosure to potential competitors becomes an increased probability.

These points show that in designing a regime for the twenty-first century there are a number of considerations that must be borne in mind by those designing the system. That there are no unique answers in addressing these concerns is a significant answer in itself: the resolution of many of the issues likely lies in the nature of the market and the social structure of the society in which the market is found, than in the legal regime (and its social structure) from which the rules are borrowed.

LIBERALIZATION OF THE MOBILE TELEPHONE MARKET: THE CASE OF MEXICO

The Mexican liberalisation of the telecommunications market has been selected as a case study for a number of reasons. First, as a part of Mexico's side of the bargain in ratifying the North American Free Trade Agreement, the government of Mexico undertook to develop and implement an effective competition regime, in a jurisdiction which theretofore had no such regime. Its choice was to implement both a generalist competition agency, which soon became (OECD 2004) by global standards an effective competition regime. However, the Mexican government chose to regulate the Telecoms industry by the use of a sectorial regulator, which being hamstrung by procedural hurdles in Mexican administrative law, was of limited efficacy. Second, the liberalisation of the Mexican telecoms market via

privatization was a cornerstone of the Washington consensus (Williamson 2003), a package of reforms promoted by International institutions such as the IMF and World Bank and academic and development economists to enhance the development of Central and South American economies. Third, as a result of the ineffective liberalization of the telecoms market, the Mexican government was the subject of a complaint before the WTO (2004), which one commentator remarked was that organizations first competition complaint (Fox, 2006). As a result of these features which surround Mexican telecom liberalization, the Mexican case has been well researched, thus producing a large and publically available data set.

Mexico's Privitization of the Telecoms Market

As part of a wider drive towards a privatization that began in the mid-1980s, the Mexican Government chose to divest itself of its ownership of Telmex, its telecommunications monopoly. To make this enterprise as attractive as possible for potential investors, Telemex was packaged as a vertically integrated firm, which was granted a national monopoly. This was in spite of the fact that other means of selling this governmental asset were available: regional monopolies, or spinning-off its various services and selling these as distinct entities (Mariscal and Rivera, 2005: 761).

In December 1990, Telmex was auctioned off to a joint venture of Grupo Carso and two foreign telecoms firms. Although the Government imposed a number of service mandates on Telmex, it was granted a six-year monopoly on the long distance market (Solano, del Villar and Garcia-Verdú, 2006: 540). However, it was not until 1996 that the Mexican Government established a specialized Telecommunications regulator, with the Ministry of Telecommunications (SCT) regulating (without a statutory charter or mandate) in the interim (Mariscal and Rivera, 2005: 761 - 762). When long distance competition opened up, as a result of the manner in which the Long Distance Rules were written, Telmex could set the prices for the interconnection rates (Mariscal and Rivera, 2005: 763; Solano, del Villar and Garcia-Verdú, 2006: 541). The rates were set at 5.3 US cents per call in 1997 and 1998. This was over two and a half times the World Bank's suggested weighed average tariff of 1.9 cents (Mariscal and Rivera, 2005: 763). Telmex was able to rapidly leverage its status as the incumbent landline operator to in favor of Telcel, its wholly owned mobile subsidiary. Telcel soon became the dominant mobile operator in Mexico, with a 70% market share (OECD 2012: 23).

The Attempts at Telecoms Market Regulation

In 1996, the Government established the Federal Telecommunications Commission

(Coftel) with a mandate to regulate the industry. It, however, was not given true independence. It makes recommendations to the SCT which then implements the decision (Mariscal and Rivera, 2005: 762). In addition to this sector regulator, the Federal Competition Commission (CFC) has an overarching mandate ensure Mexico's markets are competitive, and as part of this mandate it has the responsibility to perform market studies. The CFC will use these market studies to provide opinions to sector regulators, who in turn will use these opinions as a basis for further regulation (Solano, del Villar and Garcia-Verdú, 2006: 530 - 537). These opinions can include determinations of market dominance.

However, this process is ineffective. The sequencing is strict: the CFC must first form the opinion before the sector regulator can act upon it and regulate. There is no means for the sector regulator to develop its own opinion. Further, the efficacy of the regulatory process is further hindered by peculiarities of Mexican administrative law. Solano, del Villar and Garcia-Verdú (2006: 537) note:

The Mexican judicial system provides a legal recourse, amparo that allows a plaintiff to demand a temporary suspension of regulatory actions when they consider regulatory resolutions to have violated their constitutional rights. Most regulated companies have used this procedure and given that the court system operates slowly, amparos have remained in place for 2-3 years. The result has been a temporary suspension of most regulatory decisions. [8]

The results of this have been catastrophic for consumers. The amparo regime will allow, for instance, the challenge of a determination of a dominant position, once that is reconsidered (several years later) and then any regulations made subsequent to a revised finding of dominance can be challenged. These regulations, in turn, will be effectively stayed by a further use of an amparo for a number of years (Solano, del Villar and Garcia-Verdú, 2006: 538 - 539, 544 - 546; Mariscal and Rivera, 2005: 762). In the meanwhile, the abusive practice will continue at the consumers' expense.

The Failure of Regulation

In its 2012 Review of Mexican Telecommunications Policy, the OECD (2012: 17) described these consequences: The poor development of telecommunication infrastructure in Mexico is due to a large part to lack of effective competition, and the resulting high level of market concentration. In turn, this has implications for consumers, leading to lower levels of consumption as a result of high prices across the range of telecommunication services. This has resulted in a significant welfare loss for users in Mexico. ... Consumer welfare loss in the Mexican telecommunication sector over the period 2005-09 is estimated at USD 129.2 billion, or an average of USD PPP 25.8 billion per year. The latter amount is equivalent to 1.8% of Mexican GDP per year (or USD PPP 240 per capita per year). [9]

In addition to these deadweight and consumer surplus losses, there will be additional losses resulting from the loss of productive efficiency associated with the use this form of communication (to better organize behaviour in the market-e.g. obtain price information, coordinate deliveries, etc.).

The fundamental problems with Mexican Telecoms regulation are that the regulator has been captured, lacks independence, and is subject to the control of a legal system which can be used to frustrate the implementation of welfare enhancing policies. [10] Second-guessing past decisions is always a strategy of dubious worth; however, three decisions made in the privatization process merit a further look.

First, the decision to make the government company as attractive or potential investors is a concern. In circumstances like this, the obvious means to dress-up a company to attract suitors is to sell it as a monopoly. Potential investors thus bid on the present value of a stream of monopoly profits. The successful investor gets an excellent (because supercompetitive) return; and the government gets a good price for its asset. Hence, it is a winwin situation for these parties: but not for the consumer.

Second, in dressing-up Telmex in this way, the firm was sold as a vertically integrated national monopoly. The national scale and integrated nature of its operations provided it with the resources sufficient for it to remain the dominant operator (at every level). Indeed, by permitting it to set the interconnection rates (with weak regulatory oversight), the privatized firm was given a carte blanche to squeeze the margins of its potential competitors.

Third, the decision to permit this incumbent firm to enter into the mobile market allowed it to use this advantage to rapidly achieve dominance in that market. This is to be contrasted with the British decision where BT (the former public monopoly) was not permitted to enter into the mobile market immediately (BT 1998), due to the well-justified concerns that such leveraging would occur.

In addition to these blunders in the privatization of Telmex, there are additional concerns with the regulatory process as a whole. In addition to theamparos regime, which permits significant delays to the implementation of regulation, the delayed (6 years postprivatization) establishment of a sector regulator (and its subsequent capture), lead to questions regarding the efficacy of its sectoral regulator. This is in contrast to Mexico's generalist competition authority, the CFC, which in a 2004 OECD (2004) peer-review was generally well regarded. Competition expertise does not appear to be the issue.

It may well be that due to the manner in which Telmex was packaged to be as attractive to investors as possible, the political will for effective regulation is simply not present. Mariscal and Rivera (2005: 773) conclude:

The significant market power that Telmex enjoys today is a direct consequence of the mode of privatization. The maintenance of a vertically integrated firm introduced consequential costs to regulatory activities; regulating a vertically integrated firm became a difficult task as the regulator lacked comparative information. The delayed creation of governance structures (a telecommunications law and a regulatory agency) and later, the lack of autonomy of the regulatory agency, Cofetel, contributed to increased regulatory uncertainties. In the circumstances, it may not be far from the truth to suggest that this regulation was designed to fail.

CONCLUSION: REGULATING FOR THE TWENTYFIRST CENTURY

The link between competitive markets and individuals' gains is clear. To the extent that developing economies may wish to encourage such gains, they require some means of ensuring that any gains are not 'expropriated' or are otherwise 'privatized' through anticompetitive practices. To the extent that development is facilitated through trade, the need to prevent such extraction of market gains becomes more pressing. A strong competition agency appears to be the most effective means to preserve such gains.

The lesson here is that the rules chosen for the regime should suit the particular circumstances of the market to be regulated and the society in which it is found. The rules, whether American or European, must reflect these conditions, and not the a priori assumptions of international 'advisors' supplying advice.

Further, the regulators must develop priorities. There is no doubt that international cartels will operate in developing countries. This can be a rational strategy for them. A developing regime may lack investigative ability, hence the probability of the cartel's detection is low. In which case, the collusion is rational. Indeed, the profits from this activity can be used to offset the costs incurred if collusion in other markets is detected (Levenstein and Suslow, 2003).

However, it may not be prudent for a developing regime to invest much of its resources in combatting such cartels. The international dimension will make investigation, particularly with regard to the acquisition of evidence, difficult and expensive. It may perhaps be more advisable in terms of maximizing consumer welfare within the jurisdiction relative to the demands and costs imposed on the agency for that agency to liaise with and assist other agencies in these international investigations.

The Mexican case tells us that effective infrastructure regulation is needed. Given the ubiquity and necessity of mobile telecommunications, an ill-regulated market can serve as the vehicle for significant consumer harm and concurrent stunting of trade-related economic growth. The same conclusion can be drawn with internet access. Likewise shipping infrastructure-ports and airports-are susceptible to similar abuse. If unwatched, industries operating with the modes of shipment-ferries, trucks and railways-can cost the economy.

Electrical generation and distribution are also need to make this infrastructure run.

This list is not exhaustive, but it is a suggestion of markets in which where collusive or abusive practices occur, there is a potential for not just loss of consumer surplus but also deadweight loss which would arise through lost trade opportunities as a result of the supernormal prices. Further this list itemizes markets which are somewhat more complex to regulate than, say, a simple (but cartelized) food staples market. To point to a few considerations: mobile telecommunication regulation is characterized by network effects, issues of essential facilities and margin squeeze; electrical regulation is compounded by issues of natural monopoly; and shipping companies may need to coordinate their schedules to operate efficiently.[11]

These factors point to the need for rule formulation and adjudication by specialized agencies. Furthermore, however funded or whatever rules they use, such agencies need to be independent not just from the government which creates them, but also from the industry which they regulate. This specialization has implications for review of their decisions.

Generalist courts are unlikely to have the skill set to critically assess the economic aspects of the decisions. On the other hand, they may be more likely to be able to adequately assess the legal justification provided by such administrative bodies. This points to a great degree of deference in the former case, but less so in the latter.

Key to the success of the regime is political will. This is in many respects a rule of law issue.

Independence demands that such agencies operate without the interference of any other arm of the government. [12] This takes a significant degree of political will, particularly when the regulated industry may be politically well connected or when sold off as part of an economic liberalization program. [13]

The increasing complexity of markets in the twenty-first century shows us that it is likely that the old-style generalist courts are unlikely to be adequate to adjudicate these complex issues. Their days of adjudicating such disputes are over. Rather, given that this century should also see the spread of competition regimes into what are classified as developing

(and least developed) countries, and with the need for such jurisdictions to carefully regulate their markets, not just to protect consumer welfare, but to facilitate other forms of gains through trade, we should see and facilitate the development of specialized agencies.

Yet, the development of these agencies alone will not suffice. They must be developed in conditions where they are independent, in a system where there is the political will to do so.

As the Mexican telecommunications case study shows us, where these agencies are captured, under the control of some political master or hobbled by a dysfunctional legal system, they are unable to make any call at all-never mind the right call. Thus their ability to make the call requires them to be an independent operator.

REFERENCES

1. Abraham, Rueben (2006), "Mobile Phones and Economic Development: Evidence from the Fishing Industry in India" Information and Communications Technologies and Development ICTD DOI 10.1109/ICTD.2006.301837
2. Aker, Jenny C and Mbiti, Isaac M (2010), 'Mobile Phones and Economic Development in Africa', Journal of Economic Perspectives, Vol. 24, No. 3 pp. 207 - 232.
3. Botta, Marco (2009), 'Fostering Competition Culture in the Emerging Economies: The Brazilian Experience', World Competition, Vol. 32, No. 4, pp. 609 - 627.
4. Brisimi, Vasiliki and Ioannidou, Maria (2011), 'Criminalizing Cartels in Greece: A Tale of Hasty Developments and Shaky Grounds', World Competition, Vol. 34,

No. 1, pp. 157 - 176.

5. British Telecom (BT) (1998) Annual Report on Form 20-F 1998 available at: http://www.btplc.com/report/1997-98/annual20fmain.html, accessed 16 November 2015

6. Burgess, Robin and Pande, Rohini (2005), 'Do Rural Banks Matter? Evidence from the Indian Social Banking Experiment', American Economic Review,Vol. 95, No. 3, 780 - 795.

7. Coase, Ronald (1960), 'The Problem of Social Cost' Journal of Law and Economics, Vol 3 No. 1, pp. 1 - 69.

8. Commission (2014), Press Release, 'Antitrust: Commission extends validity of special competition regime for liner shipping consortia until April 2020', 24 June 2014, available at: http://europa.eu/rapid/press-release_IP-14-717_en.htm accessed 30 October 2015.

9. Crane, Daniel A. (2011) The Institutional Structure of Antitrust Enforcement (Oxford: Oxford University Press).

10. Dam, Kenneth W (2006), The Law-Growth Nexus: The Rule of Law and Economic Development (Washington DC: Brookings Institute).

11. Dnes, Antony. (1995), 'Post-Privatization Performance-Regulating Telecommunications in the U.K.: Testing for Regulatory Capture'(Washington DC, World Bank), available at: https://openknowledge.worldbank.com/handle/10986/11647

12. Fox, Eleanor M (2006), 'The WTO's First Antitrust Case-Mexican Telecom: A Sleeping Victory for Trade and Competition' Journal of International Economic Law Vol. 9, No. 2 pp. 271 - 292.

13. Geradin, Damien and O'Donoghue, R (2005), 'The Concurrent Application of Competition Law and Regulation: The Case of Margin Squeeze Abuses in the Telecommunications Sector', Journal of Competition Law and Economics, Vol. 1, No. 2, pp. 355 - 425.

14. Ginsburg, Douglas H and Wright, Joshua D (2013), 'Antitrust Courts: Specialists versus Generalists', Fordham International Law Journal, Vol. 36, No. 4, pp. 788 - 810.

15. GSMA ('Groupe Speciale Mobile') (2006), Gateway Liberalization: Stimulating Economic Growth, available at:http://www.gsma.com/publicpolicy/wpcontent/uploads/2012/03/gatewayliberalisation.pdf accessed 16 November 2015.

16. International Telecommunications Union and World Bank (2000), Regulatory Handbook Module 5: Competition Policy, available at:http://www.itu.int/ITUD/treg/Documentation/Infodev_handbook/5_Competition.pdf accessed 16 November 2015.

17. Lester, Richard T and Karanja, Sarah (2008) 'Mobile Phones: Exceptional Tools for HIV/AIDS, Health, and Crisis Management'www.thelancet.com/infection Vol 8 pp. 738 - 739

18. Lester, Richard T. et al (2010), 'Effects of a Mobile Phone Short Message Service

on Antiretroviral Treatment Adherence in Kenya (WelTel Kenya1): a randomised trial' The Lancet 2010; Vol 376, pp. 1838-45.

19. Levenstein, Margaret and Suslow, Valerie Y (2003), 'Contemporary International Cartels and Developing Countries: Economic Effects and Implications for Competition Policy', Antitrust Law Journal, Vol. 71, No. 3, pp. 801 - 852.

20. Li, Y. and Lyons, B. (2011), 'Three Private Firms and an Independent Regulator are Sufficient for Rapid Mobile Network Penetration', CCP Working Paper 11-1, available at: http://competitionpolicy.ac.uk/documents/8158338/8253131/CCP+WP+11- 1/61c1ecb0-0d83-4e8c-8e8e-b6cad06d2397accessed 16 November 2015.

21. Mariscal, Judith and Rivera, Eugenio (2005), 'New Trends in the Latin American Telecommunications Market: Telefonica and Telmex',Telecommunications Policy, Vol. 29, pp. 757 - 777.

22. Motta, Massimo (2004) Competition Policy (Cambridge: Cambridge University Press).

23. OECD (2013), Competition and Poverty Reduction DAF/COMP/GF(2013)12 (Washington DC: World Bank Group).

24. OECD (2004), Competition Law and Policy in Mexico: An OECD Peer Review (Paris: OECD Publishing).

25. OECD (2012), OECD Review of Telecommunication Policy and Regulation in Mexico (Paris: OECD Publishing).

26. Roller, Lars-Hendrik and Waverman, Leonard (2001), 'Telecommunications Infrastructure and Economic Development: A Simultaneous Approach',American Economic Review, Vol. 91, No. 4, pp. 909 - 923.

27. Rosenzweig, Mark, Waverman, Leonard, Meschi, Meloria and Fuss, Melvyn (2005), 'The Impact of Telecoms on Economic Growth in Developing Countries', Africa: The Impact of Mobile Phones, Vodafone Policy Paper, Vol. 2.

28. Schwalbe, Ulrich and Zimmer, Daniel (2009), Law and Economics in European Merger Control (Oxford: Oxford University Press).

29. Sen, Amartya (1999), Development as Freedom (Oxford: Oxford University Press).

30. Sokol, D Daniel, Cheng, Thomas K and Lianos, Ioannis (eds) (2013), Competition Law and Development (Stanford CA: Stanford University Press).

31. Solano, Oliver, del Villar, Rafael, and Garcia-Verdú, Rodrigo (2006), 'Challenges to the Effective Implementation of Competition Policy in Regulated Sectors: The Case of Telecommunications in Mexico', Northwestern Journal of International Law and Business, Vol. 26, No. 3 pp. 527 - 545.

32. Stryszowska, Marta (2012), 'Estimation of Loss in Consumer Surplus Resulting from Excessive Pricing of Telecommunication Services in Mexico',OECD Digital Economy Papers, No. 191 (Paris: OECD Publishing), available at: http://dx.doi.org/10.1787/5k9gtw51j4vben accessed 16 November 2015.

33. UNCTAD (United Nations Conference on Trade and Development) (2014),

Mexico's Agricultural Development: Perspectives and Outlook (New York and Geneva: UNCTAD). Van Koten, S. and Ortman, A. (2008), 'The Unbundling Regime for Electricity Utilities in the EU: A case of Legislative and Regulatory Capture?'Energy Economics Vol. 30, pp. 3128 - 3140.

34. Veljanovski, Cento (2012), 'Margin Squeeze: An Overview of EU and National Case Law', eCompetitions No. 46442, June 6, 2012, available at:http://papers.ssrn.com/sol3/papers.cfm?abstract_id=2079117, accessed 16 November 2015.

35. Wardhaugh, Bruce (2014), Cartels, Markets and Crime: A Normative Justification for the Criminalisation of Economic Collusion (Cambridge: Cambridge University Press).

36. Weiser, Phil (2009), (Deputy Assistant Attorney General Antitrust Division, US Department of Justice), 'Antitrust Doctrine, Competition Policy, and International Dialogue' Speech at the Fall Forum, Antitrust Section, American Bar Association, Washington, DC, 12 November 2009, available at:http://www.justice.gov/atr/public/speeches/251859.htm accessed 16 November 2015.

37. Williamson, John (2003), 'From Reform Agenda to Damaged Brand', Finance and Development, Vol. 40, No 3, pp. 10 - 13.

38. World Bank (2004), Initiatives in Legal and Judicial Reform (Washington DC: World Bank Group)

10
CHAPTER

THE APPLICATION OF DIRECTIVE 95/46/EC AND THE DATA PROTECTION ACT

Claire Bessant

Keywords: Data protection, personal information, privacy, data protection directive, data protection regulation

INTRODUCTION

It is traditional for schools in the United Kingdom to host an annual Christmas play, at which parents take photographs of their children. In the summer these schools also host sports days, where again, parents are invited to attend, and to take a photographic record of their children's achievements. Schools have, traditionally imposed few restrictions upon such photography; in the era when photographs were printed out and stored in family albums few parents had any issue with the fact that another parent might take a photograph of their child. In the age of digital photography, however, questions are increasingly being raised about whether schools should restrict parental photography, or impose conditions upon the use of such photographs.

Consider the following scenario: A parent takes several photographs of their child and his school friends at sports day and subsequently posts those photographs to their Facebook page and to their personal blog. The parent photographer does not ask the children or their parents whether they consent to their photographs being shared online. Indeed the parent who has posted the images perceives no need to do so. As Bennett (1992, p13) notes 'It is not immediately obvious … what harm results from the computerized collection, use and disclosure of personal data'. The other parents do in fact object to their children's images being posted online, and they ask for the offending photographs to be taken down. They make clear that they are not happy

Citation: Claire Bessant, The application of Directive 95/46/EC and the Data Protection Act, http://nrl.northumbria.ac.uk/24267/.

for their children's pictures to be disseminated online, and state that if such online dissemination is proposed their consent should be sought. It is arguable that in the situation described, the parents are justified in objecting to online dissemination of their children's photographs without their knowledge or consent. The right to data protection is recognised as a fundamental right (Charter of Fundamental Rights of the European Union, Article 8). The online posting of children's images may also raise child protection issues (NSPCC, 2013).

Whilst the Charter does not define data protection, 'data protection is broadly analogous to the concept "information privacy" (Bennett, 1992, p14). It essentially describes "the claim of individuals, groups or institutions to determine for themselves, when, how and to what extent information about them is communicated to others" (Westin, 1967, p7). On that basis, it is the child, or upon their behalf, their parent's right to determine whether the child's image is shared online, not the photographers.

The principal legislative instrument protecting personal information/personal data in Europe is Directive 95/46/EC on the protection of individuals with regard to the processing of personal data and on the free movement of such data ('the Directive'). Whilst the Directive has been described as 'a milestone in the history of data protection,' (European Commission, 2012a, p2) the unfortunate reality is that in 1990 when the Directive was first proposed the Internet did not exist, indeed even when the Directive was adopted in 1995 the internet had barely begun (per Advocate General Jääskinen in C131/12 'Google Spain') and less than 1% of Europeans used the internet (European Commission, 2012b). Few could then have imagined the technological changes that have transformed the way we now disseminate and receive information; online information sharing is part of life for the 250 million individuals across Europe who now use the internet on a daily basis (European Commission, 2012a; European Commission 2012c).

That the internet revolution has brought with it new challenges when it comes to protecting personal information is widely acknowledged. Across Europe, individuals, organisations and data protection authorities alike, seeking to ensure that individuals' personal data are effectively protected, have called for clarification as to how data protection principles apply to new technologies (European Commission, 2010). The Information Commissioner's Office ('the ICO'), charged with implementing data protection rules within the UK, made clear in 2010 that it believed clarification was needed as to how data protection legislation applies when individuals post personal information online (ICO, 2010). A recent survey of UK education authorities provides evidence that professionals who provide advice upon parental photography at school events are similarly unsure how the law applies when individuals take photographs which may subsequently be shared online.

The European Commission has accepted that in the digital age the Directive may no longer be an effective way to ensure the right to personal data protection (European Commission, 2012a). It has accordingly proposed a comprehensive reform of the current data protection rules, with the Directive to be replaced by a new general data protection regulation ('the Regulation'), which will strengthen individuals' rights by enhancing the protection and control they have over their own data (European Commission, 2010b).

The two primary questions that this article seeks to answer, therefore, are: how does data protection legislation currently apply to individuals who share photographs online; and to what extent will the Regulation clarify the position in relation to individuals processing third party personal information online. In order to answer these questions the article explores current domestic and European case law and guidance, seeking to understand how courts and regulators consider the Directive to apply when an individual shares third party personal information, including photographs, online. Drawing upon the author's own research in which freedom of information requests were made to local education authorities seeking information about the guidance that they provide to schools in relation to parental photography, it will consider the difficulties that practitioners apparently face in understanding the application of the Directive. The extent to which the Regulation will clarify the position in relation to individuals processing third party information online will then be reviewed. Whilst a child's right to respect for private life is also undoubtedly affected when a third party disseminates the child's photographs online the protections offered by Article 8 European Convention for the Protection of Human Rights and Fundamental Freedoms ('the European Convention') are not explicitly considered in this article due to word constraints.

THE APPLICATION OF THE DIRECTIVE TO ONLINE DISCLOSURES

The Directive is a general framework legislative provision. It 'seeks to establish an equivalent level of protection for personal data in all Member States' (Carey, 2009, p6), detailing certain conditions under which personal data processing may be lawfully undertaken, the rights of individuals whose personal data is processed and certain standards to which those who process data must adhere. The Directive is not directly effective in the domestic law of EU Member States. Member States must thus instead pass national legislation to give effect to the Directive. The UK government ostensibly fulfilled its obligations under the Directive when it implemented the Data Protection Act 1998 ('the DPA'). It is necessary, therefore, to consider the relevant provisions both of the Directive and the DPA when considering the Directive's application within the UK. Whilst the Directive is not directly enforceable within the UK, and any action for infringement of rights to data protection would be brought in accordance with the provisions of the DPA, the DPA must be interpreted in accordance with the Directive. The recent Court of Appeal decision in Google v Vidal-Hall and others [2014] EWHC 13 confirms, further, that, in interpreting the domestic provisions, consideration should also be given to Article 8 of the Charter of the Fundamental Rights of the European Union, 'which makes specific provision for the protection of the fundamental right to the protection of personal data' (Google v Vidal-Hall, paragraph 78).

The Directive states that it applies 'to the processing of personal data wholly or partly by automatic means, and to the processing otherwise than by automatic means of personal data which form part of a filing system' (Directive Article 3). Where the Directive, and thus in the United Kingdom the DPA applies, certain obligations are imposed upon the data controller; the person who determines the purposes and means of processing of personal data (Directive Article 2; Section 1 DPA). The phrase 'personal data', a phrase which is essential to an understanding of the European data protection regime, means 'any information relating to an identified or identifiable natural person ('data subject'); an identifiable person is one who can be identified, directly or indirectly, in particular by reference to an identification number or to one or more factors specific to his physical, physiological, mental, economic, cultural or social identity' (Directive Article 2(a)). The leading European case of Lindqvist (ECJ C101/01 [27]) confirms that 'the act of referring, on an internet page, to various persons and identifying them by name or by other means,... constitutes the processing of personal data wholly or partly by automatic means within the meaning of Article 3(1) of Directive 95/46.' Accordingly, the European jurisprudence appears to suggest that when a person posts information about another person online, and this action results in the identification of those individuals, that person is processing data. It is certainly arguable that some photographs taken at school events may when uploaded, and depending also upon any accompanying information, result in the identification of a child. If that is indeed the case then, the photographer is to be treated as a data controller and, as such, they must comply with the obligations detailed within the Directive and thus the DPA.

Whilst the position so far seems clear, the difficulty, unfortunately, arises when one recognises that certain exemptions and derogations from the Directive exist. Two potential exemptions or derogations apply when a parent takes and shares a photograph of a school event. If either of these exemptions or derogations apply that parent is not required to comply with the Directive/the DPA.

When the Directive might not apply to an individual who has posted photographs online

The second limb of Article 3(2) of the Directive states that the Directive 'shall not apply to the processing of personal data ... by a natural person in the course of a purely personal or household activity'. This provision is implemented in UK law through Section 36 DPA, which states that 'Personal data processed by an individual only for the purposes of that individual's personal, family or household affairs (including recreational purposes) are exempt from the data protection principles and the provisions of Parts II and III.' We will return shortly to consider the different terminology which appears in the two provisions. The important thing to note here is that if the parent photographer is considered to fall within the personal/household exemption when posting a photograph to Facebook or their personal/family blog (even a photograph which includes images of third parties) then Article 3(2)/s36 will apply. If Article 3(2)/s36 applies, the parent photographer is under no obligation to tell the child whose photograph she has taken that she intends to post those images online, nor is she required to obtain consent to taking/sharing their images.

Even if Article 3(2)/s36 were not considered relevant (perhaps because the parent photographer's blog is used for both commercial and personal purposes) the photographer might argue that their actions, particularly when compiling their blog, are undertaken in the exercise of their right to freedom of expression. Section 32 DPA (implementing Article 9) specifically provides for an exemption from data protection principles 1-6 and 8 and Sections 7, 10, 12, 12A or 14(1)-(3) of the DPA where a data controller processes personal data (for example by sharing photographs online) for journalistic, literary or artistic purposes, and where that data controller reasonably believes that dissemination is in the public interest.

If either Article 3(2)/s36 or Article 9/s32 were considered to apply the parent photographer would effectively be free to disseminate their photographs online (including photographs of friends, family and acquaintances). Many might agree that this is only right and proper, that it is not the state's role to intervene when an individual uses the internet in such circumstances, and indeed that it is impractical for the state to intervene in all such cases. The consequence of such an approach, however, is to leave third parties with no effective remedy under data protection legislation, and if their complaint would not lead to the possibility of an alternative legal claim (for example under the law of libel), there is effectively nothing they can do to prevent that information being disseminated. That individuals should be left with no effective remedy under the very legislation designed to protect their personal information, indeed to protect their privacy, is no small concern, given the extent of data sharing in Europe. 29% of the Europeans interviewed for a Eurobarometer survey published in 2011 use sharing sites for pictures, videos and/or movies, 34% use social networking sites (European Commission, 2011). Europeans regularly disclose personal information online; '[c]ountry-by-country analysis of social networking or sharing sites reveals that photographs are regularly disclosed by social network users (in the United Kingdom (67%), Denmark, Sweden (64%), and Malta (61%)) (European Commission, 2011 p41). A more recent OFCOM survey suggests that within the UK at least internet use continues to grow, with internet take-up increasing 'from 54% of UK households in 2005 to 79% in 2012' (OFCOM 2013, p14). Of particular relevance to this article, in 2013 64% of adult internet users had their own social network profile (OFCOM, 2013), 17% of these social network users confirmed they were sharing video clips and other content online, and between 2 and 3 out of 10 of those adults with a social networking profile admitted to sharing photographs with people potentially unknown to them (OFCOM, 2013).

As internet usage and online information sharing has increased so has the need to clarify how the Directive applies to such activity. Indeed, in 2010 the ICO made clear that:

> 'A better understanding is needed of what comes within the scope of purely personal or household activity. This is becoming an acute practical problem given private individuals' capacity to process personal data on the internet and to make it widely available to other individuals, for example through social networking services. There are also questions about how far the current exemption that relates to journalism or the purposes of literary or artistic expression can be applied to the activities of private individuals on the internet. There are also significant practical consequences for data protection authorities in terms of the extent to which any new legislative framework may require them to regulate private individuals' online behaviour' (ICO, 2010, p5).

As our consideration of the European and UK guidance on the matter will demonstrate, however, domestic and European authorities have interpreted the requirements of Article 3(2) and Article 9 very differently; they have reacted in very different ways to the challenge of achieving a balance between data protection on one hand and freedom of expression and freedom from state interference on the other. As a result practitioners are struggling to understand how the law actually applies.

THE EUROPEAN POSITION

Lindqvist (ECJ C-101/01): the starting point

Lindqvist, a case decided more than 10 years ago, remains the leading European case on the application of Articles 3(2) and 9 when an individual shares other people's information on the internet. This relatively unusual case concerned a Swedish lady who worked on a voluntary basis for the Swedish Protestant Church as a catechist and had created a website to provide parishioners with information. This website, which could be directly accessed by members of the public from a link on the website of the Swedish Protestant Church, included personal information about Ms Lindqvist's colleagues, and it was one of those colleagues who, objected to online dissemination of her personal information. The Swedish Government had initially found Ms Lindqvist liable for breach of the Directive, but doubtful as to its interpretation of the law in this area it referred the case to the European Court of Justice ('the ECJ') for a preliminary ruling. The ECJ agreed with the Swedish authorities; Ms Lindqvist was in breach of the Directive.

The first of Ms Lindqvists's arguments to be considered by the ECJ was that, as a private individual, her activities, not being market-related activities, fell "outside the scope of Community law." Had Ms Lindqvist's argument been accepted she would have been exempted from complying with the Directive by virtue of the first limb of Article 3(2). The ECJ were adamant, however, that the Directive was as applicable to Ms Lindqvist and her personal website as to large corporations. Whilst the ECJ might be criticised for the stance it took, it is arguable that the ECJ's interpretation was a realistic or pragmatic one, 'driven not so much by the text as by the spectre of future litigation' (Bignami, 2008, p232). Any other interpretation would undoubtedly have resulted in arguments about the distinction between market-related and other activities (Bignami, 2008, p232).

It is, however, the ECJ's conclusions in relation to the second limb of Article 3(2) that are most relevant to this article. Importantly, the ECJ determined that Article 3(2)

> 'must ... be interpreted as relating only to activities which are carried out in the course of private or family life of individuals, which is clearly not the case with the processing of personal data consisting in publication on the internet so that those data are made accessible to an indefinite number of people'.

Effectively, therefore, the ECJ closed the door on the use of Article 3(2) when an individual provides unrestricted online access to another person's personal information. If one follows the Lindqvist decision to its logical conclusion, an individual who lives in the UK and who posts photographs of third parties to a blog or website, thus revealing personal information about those individuals, cannot rely upon Article 3(2). They should: register with the ICO; inform those individuals of the purposes of the processing, and to comply with the conditions for processing detailed at Schedule 2 DPA they are likely to need to obtain that individual's consent to processing. Any individual whose information is processed on such a blog will be able to ask the processor what information they are processing and for what purposes (s7 DPA), and if the information being processed causes the individual unwarranted and substantial damage or unwarranted and substantial distress (s10 DPA) require the blogger or website owner to cease processing their information. The individual would potentially have recourse to the court and/or the ICO.

The interpretation of Article 3(2) in Lindqvist, and subsequently

Bignami suggests that whilst the ECJ 'easily found that uploading personal data onto Lindqvist's website constituted "personal data processing" covered by the Directive' it was '[w]ith a bit more difficulty' that 'the Court determined that Lindqvist's website did not qualify for any of the exceptions to the personal data processing covered by the Directive' (Bignami, 2008, p230-1). One of the suggestions that Bignami makes is that in order to reach the conclusion that it did, the ECJ adopted an overly narrow interpretation of the term 'outside the scope of community law,' in doing so departing from the plain meaning of the directive (Bignami, 2008, p231-2). Criticisms might also be made of the narrow interpretation of the personal and household exemption adopted by the ECJ in Lindqvist. It must be recognised, however, that the recent case of Ryneš, appears to offer some support for the ECJ's approach.

In Ryneš the court states explicitly that 'the exception provided for in the second indent of Article 3(2) ... must be narrowly construed' in order to protect the right to privacy, and to ensure respect for the fundamental rights set out in the European Union Charter of Fundamental Rights (Ryneš C-212/13, paragraph 29). The facts of the Ryneš case were very different to those in Lindqvist; Mr Ryneš had installed a camera system on his home to protect his home and family and this camera also monitored the public footpath and entrance to a house opposite. What Ryneš might be considered to signal, however, is that the CJEU is not currently inclined to review the approach to the personal and household exemption that it first adopted in LIndqvist. This is notwithstanding the fact that concerns have been raised about whether, in the digital age, the premises which inform Article 3(2), and its interpretation in Lindqvist 'can be insisted upon ... considering the central role private individuals are assuming in the processing of data' (Warso, 2013, p495).

A key difficulty with Lindqvist, of course, is that it reflects an assumption that 'if something happens online, it is accessed by an unrestricted number of people' (Warso, 2013, p495-6). The CJEU's position therefore is that consequently an online disclosure 'must be "public", and therefore the application of the personal/household exemption is out of question.' At the time of the Lindqvist decision websites such as Twitter, Facebook, Instagram and Flickr had yet to be created; the extent to which individuals would use the internet to share information could not be foreseen. The fact that individuals could choose whether to share information online with a select group, or the public generally, was simply not relevant in Lindqvist. Yet it is now undoubtedly the case that when an individual shares photographs on a social networking or photo sharing site they may, if they know how, take steps to ensure that only 'friends' or 'followers' can view those photos. Indeed across Europe, but particularly in the UK, many individuals do take steps to change their privacy profiles in order to limit access (European Commission, 2011).

The ECJ cannot perhaps be blamed for not anticipating the technological changes that would ensue over the next ten years, and thus for not foreseeing the wider implications of its decision. Indeed, none of the governments submitting remarks, nor the Commission thought that Art 3(2) should apply. The Advocate General, similarly, did not consider that activity with a 'strong social connotation' could be purely personal or household activity, and indeed this was perhaps at the time a logical stance to have taken. The decision, nonetheless, does pose challenges 10 years on. It is presumably for this very reason that the Article 29 Data Protection Working Party ('the Working Party') have offered their opinion on how Article 3(2) should apply in the online context, specifically when individuals share information using social media. In doing so they are undoubtedly proposing a relaxation of the constraints resulting from Lindqvist.

The Working Party pragmatically recognises the need to accept that the personal/household exemption applies to some online activities. Whether or not Article 3(2) does apply to online information sharing, will, however, according to the Working Party be essentially a matter of judgment in each case. Crucially, the Working Party acknowledges that many social network users change their privacy settings to limit access to material posted. The Working Party thus introduces the concept of 'access restriction' (Warso, 2013, p496). Effectively in determining whether Article 3(2) applies it is necessary to consider whether the user took steps to limit accessibility of the information to self-selected contacts or allowed it to be made available either to all members of a social network, or to be publically available and indexable by search engine. It is the Working Party's submission, therefore, that '[a] high number of contacts could be an indication that the household exception does not apply' or, alternatively, that if a user takes an informed decision to extend access beyond self-selected 'friends' they then acquire data controller responsibilities and are subject to the same legal regime as applies to any person who publishes personal data on the web' (Working Party, 2009, p6). Similarly, if a social network user 'acts on behalf of a company or association, or uses the SNS mainly as a platform to advance commercial, political or charitable goals, the exception does not apply' (Working Party, 2009, p6).

There is certainly much to be recommended in the Working Party's opinion, which now answers a key question that Lindqvist failed to, indeed had no need to answer; how does the second limb of Article 3(2) apply when an individual is sharing information online, but only with a limited number of friends or contacts? It still, however, undoubtedly, leaves questions to be answered about how far the 'personal' and 'household' sphere actually extends (Korff, 2010). Furthermore, as Warso notes (2013, p496) the 'approach where the onus is placed on the user to restrict access to their pages to a defined group is based on the dichotomy of "private" and "public".

The criterion used by the [Working Party] may … however, prove incompatible with reality as daily experience shows that the borders of the private and public spheres are often blurry, and that the notions of private and public rather than constituting a binary opposition, form a continuum. Also in the online context, various types of content are positioned at different points within this continuum. At one end are data published seeking broad dissemination, at the other, that, which although in the open and public space of the Internet, are not intended for mass communication (or mass communication in aggregate).'

These are not, however, the only concerns that must be raised about the European interpretation of the personal and household exemption. The Working Party make an interesting comment, in suggesting that an individual who shares information online but cannot rely on Article 3(2) due to the extent of dissemination, may be considered to have 'taken on some of the responsibilities of a data controller'. In reality, however, the outcome of the Lindqvist decision is that the same regulatory scheme applies to all online entities, irrespective of their legal status or the purpose of their posts. Whether this is what the drafters of the Directive would have intended is debatable. Pragmatically, is it feasible for Member States to ensure that every individual who makes third party personal information available online complies with the Directive? An obvious alternative might be to grant a full exemption from data protection requirements to anyone who uploads materials to the Internet as a private individual. The problem with this, however, would be to fundamentally undermine data protection. 'The question - the challenge - is then perhaps whether a middle way be found?' (Korff, 2010, p8)

In France, where the national data protection authority has applied Article 3(2) strictly, and restrictively, 'to really purely personal distribution of personal information only', one possible middle way has already been found. Whilst the French data protection law applies to blogs, bloggers are exempt from notification, a technicality which would otherwise potentially pose a significant administrative burden (Korff, 2010, p9). The Commission clearly recognised the onerous nature of many of the obligations imposed upon data controllers by European data protection legislation, suggesting that under the new regulation where the data controller is a micro, small or medium enterprise some relaxing of the rules may be appropriate (Recital to the Regulation as originally drafted). The Council of Ministers' proposed revisions to Chapter IV of the Regulation and their proposed risk-based approach to data protection regulation, similarly recognises that not all data controllers need necessarily to be subject to the same onerous requirements. There is an argument that if relaxations from obligations are appropriate for SMEs, there is a still greater need to relax the rules which apply to individuals processing personal information, particularly when individuals are disseminating information not to the world at large but only to 'friends'. The idea that the law should take into account apply appropriate legal penalties according not merely to the nature of the information disclosed but also taking account of who has disclosed that information has been suggested elsewhere in the context of the regulation of free speech, with a recommendation made that;

'the casual amateur speaker with limited resources or legal advice should be held to lower standards than professional journalists. ..,any regulations should be suited to the digital context, and the procedure and sanctions should be proportionate not only to the harm, but to the level of responsibility expected from the speaker.' (Rowbottom, 2012)

Whilst Rowbottom's suggestion may make sense also in the data protection context, until or unless 'special rules' are introduced specifically for individuals who share information online, individuals who wish to make third party information (including photographs) widely available online may need to consider an alternative route, Article 9, if they wish to 'escape' the Directive's obligations.

Article 9 and the right to freedom of expression

It is to Lindqvist that we must again turn to understand the European position in relation to Article 9. The Swedish Government, the ECJ and those making submissions to the ECJ were all alive to the possibility that Ms Lindqvist might be said to be exercising her right to freedom of expression. The Swedish Government accepted, for example, that Article 3(2) 'might cover cases in which a natural person publishes personal data on an internet page solely in the exercise of his freedom of expression and without any connection with a professional or commercial activity' (Lindqvist, para 31). The European Commission submitted alternatively 'that an internet page such as that at issue in the main proceedings cannot be considered to fall outside the scope of Directive 95/46 by virtue of Article 3(2) thereof, but constitutes, given the purpose of the internet page at issue in the main proceedings, an artistic and literary creation within the meaning of Article 9 of that Directive' (Lindqvist [33]).

The ECJ ultimately accepted neither of these interpretations, choosing instead to return the question of the application of Article 9 to the national authorities, and stating that it is 'at the stage of the application at national level of the legislation implementing Directive 95/46 in individual cases that a balance must be found between the rights and interests involved' (Lindqvist [85]). Whilst recognising that Ms Lindqvist's situation did highlight tensions between data protection/privacy and freedom of expression the ECJ thus effectively abdicated responsibility to the national authorities to balance these competing rights.

In support of the decision, Bignami comments that in 'sending the fundamental rights question back to the Swedish court, the Court of Justice both avoided a difficult issue and allowed for consideration national discretion. The fundamental-rights balance between privacy and speech is by no means a precise science and by holding the Swedish court responsible for the balancing, the Court acknowledged that the outcome would be distinctive to Swedish law.' Accordingly, in deferring to the Member State to consider the privacy-speech balance the ECJ Court in Luxembourg 'both affirmed a European commitment to privacy and free expression *and* made a room for diverse moral orderings of public life at the national level'. The ECJ's decision can thus be seen as demonstrating tolerance for constitutional diversity (Bignami, 2008, p243-4)

In stark contrast to Bignami's plaudits come criticisms that the judgement leads almost inevitably to a too narrow interpretation of freedom of expression across the Member States. This is particularly the case when one recognises that Article 9 does not recognise the right to freedom of expression per se (as the similar provision in Article 10 of the European Convention does) but provides only for exemptions or derogations 'for journalistic purposes or the purpose of artistic or literary expression,' and then 'only if they are necessary to reconcile the right to privacy with the rules governing freedom of expression.' The CJEU in Tietosuojavaltuutettu v Satakunnan Markkinapörssi Oy and Satamedia Oy CJEU C-73/07 (Satamedia) has recently recognised that the term 'journalistic purposes' is a wide one, that does not necessarily mean activity undertaken by a media organisation. It suggests it is a term which might also encompass the online processing of personal information by an individual, if their object is to disclose information, opinion or ideas to the public. Nonetheless under the Directive individuals are still afforded only a limited right to freedom of expression, and only when those individuals are exercising their right to freedom of expression for specified limited purposes. There has been no sign from the CJEU that it believes that a more expansive interpretation of freedom of expression is appropriate. Indeed the 2014 judgement in Google Spain and Google Inc v Mario Costeja Gonzalez (C-131/12, paragraphs 69 and 85) suggests the contrary.

The second major criticism that can be made of the Lindqvist decision in relation to the Article 9 issue, is that it can arguably be seen as the root cause of an inconsistent approach to the privacy-free speech issue; across Europe marked divergences in approach to the implementation of Article 9 can be seen. Whilst the most liberal states, Denmark and Sweden, have extended the exception related to freedom of expression to everyone, not just journalists, artists and artistic writers, recognising that everyone should be able to effectively exercise their freedom to seek, receive or impart information, at the other extreme one finds Spain, which makes no reference to freedom of expression at all in Spanish law (Korff, 2010). In between numerous countries, including the UK, adhere strictly to the letter of Article 9, with exemptions or exceptions applying only to press, to journalists, or for journalist, artistic or literary purposes. The extent to which an individual who has posted photographs online in the exercise of their right to freedom of expression may rely upon Article 9, and thus receive relief from the Directive's strict obligations is therefore an issue that cannot be established from consideration of European law alone. It is necessary also to consider the applicable domestic law. It is thus that we turn to the UK law, and the guidance issued by the UK regulator to determine how, in practice Article 3(2) and Article 9 are being applied to UK individuals who share images of third parties online.

THE UK POSITION

The UK Information Commissioner is charged both with promoting good practice and ensuring observance of the DPA, in particular through the dissemination of appropriate information and advice (Section 51 Data Protection Act 1998). If ever there were an area in which guidance were needed it would seem to be in relation to the DPA's application in the online sphere. Whilst the Information Commissioner's Office ('the ICO') has undoubtedly recognised this, publishing guidance on the DPA, social networking and online forums (ICO, 2014a) and guidance on data protection and journalism (ICO, 2014b), unfortunately these pieces of guidance do not address all questions which this article has raised. Whilst the guidance relating to Section 32 (which implements Article 9 in UK law) does acknowledge the need to broadly interpret the notion of journalism (as per Satamedia), little consideration is given to how the Section 32 exemption applies to individuals. Of greater concern, the UK/ICO's interpretation of Section 36, the personal/household exemption, seems to be at direct odds with the European approach, an issue which understandably causes problems for practitioners.

Section 36, the personal/household exemption

The first thing to be said about Section 36 is that its wording is noticeably different to that used in Article 3(2). Whilst Article 3(2) refers to processing 'in the course of a purely personal or household activity', section 36 refers instead to processing 'only for the purposes of that individual's personal, family or household affairs (including recreational purposes)'. The potential scope of s36 is therefore significantly wider; the phrase 'recreational' potentially including any activity undertaken for one's own personal enjoyment or relaxation. A key distinction needs also to be made between the word 'activities' (which signifies something that an individual does) with the word 'purposes' (signifying the reason for which something is done). Although these might appear to be only minor differences in wording, the outcome, when one compares the UK interpretation of s36 with the European interpretation of Article 3(2), is a significant divergence in approach.

Whilst Lindqvist focuses upon whether the online processing of personal information might be construed as an action falling within the personal/household sphere (a term which in Lindqvist is narrowly construed), the ICO guidance instead emphasises the '*purposes*' for which information is shared online. The ICO thus suggests that if an individual is sharing information online, in a personal capacity, and *purely* for their own domestic or recreational purposes (ICO, 2014) the exemption *will apply*, irrespective of the nature of the data being shared, what that data reveals, or indeed the number of people to whom that information is revealed. Accordingly the ICO suggests that the s36 exemption applies whenever individuals, post personal data on social networking sites to keep in touch with friends, when they publish blogs or online diaries sharing information about their daily life, and when they use online forums to 'rant' about neighbours or political figures (ICO, 2011). The ICO suggests further that even when a group of friends share information, for example, if a group of friends meet on holiday and subsequently set up a social networking page to share photographs, the online sharing of such photographs will fall within the exemption, because it will be processing undertaken for 'recreational purposes' (ICO, 2014a).

The ICO's 2014 guidance, indicates that it conceives of few, if any situations, when an individual who is posting information online for *purely* personal, family, household or recreational purposes would not be able to rely upon the s36 exemption. It is only when an individual shares information online for non-personal purposes, for example for business or charitable purposes that the ICO consider the exemption would not apply to that individual. Accordingly, the ICO has made clear that it 'will not consider complaints made against individuals who have posted personal data whilst acting in a personal capacity, no matter how unfair, derogatory or distressing the posts may be'

(ICO, 2014a, p15). Firstly, the ICO has made clear that it believes that it is the right of individuals to use the online space to express their own personal views, in accordance with Article 10 of the European Convention, and that the protection afforded by Article 10 is reflected in both s36 and s32 (ICO, 2011; The Law Society and others v Rick Kordowski [2011] EWHC 3185 (QB) [96] ('Kordowski')). This is in stark contrast to the views of the CJEU in Google Spain, in which the court (C-131/12, para 69) emphasised not the right to freedom of expression but the right to respect for private life and right to protection of personal data. Secondly, the ICO has argued that the DPA is simply not equipped to deal with such a situation, and that it is impossible for the ICO to regulate what one individual wishes to say about another when exercising their right to freedom of expression (Kordowski). Whilst the ICO's position is perhaps understandable given the resources available to it, it is undoubtedly problematic, for several reasons.

Whilst the ICO does recognise that individuals often use the internet to make both commercial and personal postings, and makes clear that those posts which are made for commercial purposes would be required to comply with the DPA (ICO, 2014a), the ICO arguably fails to recognise the fact that parents are increasingly making postings which are neither clearly personal nor clearly for business purposes, and where the line between the personal/private and public/business sphere is increasingly blurred. Consider, for example, when parents use blogs both to share the minutiae of their family lives and to publicise well-known brands (see www.tots100.co.uk_for an illustration of the way in which brands work with parent bloggers).

The ICO's interpretation of the personal/household exemption flies in the face of the European jurisprudence and the Working Party opinion. (Whilst neither of these are mentioned in the 2014 guidance, internal guidance (ICO, 2011) makes clear that the ICO is certainly aware of Lindqvist, but simply disagrees with that decision). It should also be noted that the ICO's approach has failed to find favour in the domestic courts. Although expressing sympathy with the practical difficulties that the ICO would undoubtedly face if s36 were not deemed to apply when individuals posted third parties' personal information online, Mr Justice Tugendhat made clear that he did not consider the Information Commissioner's approach to be sustainable. Whilst acknowledging that 'the DPA was not designed to deal with the way in which the internet now works' (Kordowski [97]), Mr Justice Tugendhat made clear that he did believe that

> 'the DPA does envisage that the Information Commissioner should consider what it is acceptable for one individual to say about another, … The fact that a claimant may have claims under common law torts, or under HRA s.6, does not preclude there being a claim under, or other means of enforcement of, the DPA.'

The ICO's refusal to follow the European line undoubtedly poses problems in practice. Most individuals based in the UK who wish to complain about online postings effectively have no remedy. The ICO, to whom a complaint about breach of the DPA would ordinarily lie, has made clear that the ICO is unlikely to take action in response to a complaint that one individual has posted information online about another individual. This is notwithstanding that, under European law the aggrieved individual would have a potential remedy under the Directive, provided at least that the information has been disseminated to an unlimited number of individuals. It is only if an individual were minded to, and had the money to bring a claim before the domestic courts, for example under Section 10 (the right to prevent processing likely to cause damage or distress) or Section 13 (relating to compensation for failure to comply with the DPA) that such an individual might obtain a remedy. It *seems* that before the courts an interpretation more in line with the European position would be likely. Certainly the cases of Hegglin and another v Google inc [2014] EWHC 2808 and Google v Vidal-Hall [2014] EWHC 13 both suggest that the courts may be willing to use the Data Protection Act to afford a claimant a remedy in damages if their personal data is used in such a way that they are caused damage (whether of a pecuniary or non-pecuniary nature) and/or distress. At present, however, the area is a potential minefield for practitioners tasked with advising upon and implementing the DPA.

Section 32

If the ICO interpretation of s36 is problematic, the position in relation to s32 is little better.

In 2011 Mr Justice Tugendhat dealt explicitly with the application of Section 32, and the interaction between Articles 8 and 10, commenting that:

> 'Those who drafted the directive and the DPA omitted to address generally the relationship between the Art 8 rights which the Directive sought to implement, and the Art 10 rights which must also be respected, in accordance with both EU and English law. If there is a provision of the DPA which would give effect to Art 10 rights …, it would be s.32 (journalism, literature and art). Journalism that is protected by s.32 involves communication of information or ideas to the public at large in the public interest. Today anyone with access to the internet can engage in journalism at no cost' (Kordowski [99]).

It is clear, therefore, that, in line with Satamedia, the domestic courts clearly recognise the potential application of s32 to ordinary individuals. The ICO similarly acknowledges in its social networking guidance that s32 might apply to an individual who has posted personal data online if such information has been posted for one of the special purposes of journalism, art and literature, in the reasonable belief both that publication would be in the public interest and that compliance with the DPA would be incompatible with the special purposes (ICO, 2014a). The problem for individuals, unfortunately, is that the ICO has yet to publish guidance which explains clearly when s32 would be considered to apply to an individual. The one brief reference to individuals in the ICO's recent guidance (ICO, 2014a) is not particularly helpful;

> 'We accept that individuals may be able to invoke the journalism exemption if they are posting information or ideas for public consumption online, even if they are not professional journalists and are not paid to do so. … Of course, this doesn't mean that every blog or comment posted online will be journalism. In many cases, people will simply intend to take part in normal social interaction or other recreational internet use.'

What can be gleaned from the guidance that has been issued to the media (ICO, 2014b) however, is that if individuals do wish to rely upon Section 32, they must demonstrate that their actions in making information public are in the '*public interest*'. It is establishing the necessary public interest that many individuals who share information online are likely to struggle with.

Although there is, unfortunately, no definitive public interest test to which an individual can turn, the ICO does provide some 'pointers' for the media, which would appear to be equally relevant to individuals. Crucially, the ICO makes clear that the public interest is not the same as what is interesting to the public. He confirms also that to be in the public interest, any online publication of third party personal information must be in the best interests of society as a whole. These comments might suggest that few, if any, online posts by individuals will be deemed to be in the public interest. It is important to recognise, however, that there is a general public interest in freedom of expression itself, and that the ICO has made clear that it 'will always consider the importance of freedom of expression' in its interpretation of the DPA and when it decides whether to exercise its powers (ICO, 2014b, p19). What this means, therefore, is that, in principle, online postings relating to another individual *might* be deemed to fall within the s32 exemption – although the fact that information has been posted online in the exercise of one's freedom of expression is decidedly not the end of the matter.

The ICO has also made clear that consideration must always still be given to the impact that a publication will have on the individual whose information is disseminated. One should not automatically assume that an individual's private life is the subject of legitimate public interest (ICO, 2014b, p34) and indeed the ICO makes clear that

> 'it cannot be in the public interest to disproportionately or unthinkingly interfere with an individual's fundamental privacy and data protection rights. If … the details … published are particularly intrusive or damaging to an individual a stronger and more case-specific public interest argument will be required to justify [disclosure] over and above the general public interest in freedom of expression.'

It is where a publication is of an intrusive nature that an individual may struggle to demonstrate that their publication is in the public interest. The type of case-specific justification for/public interest in publication that the ICO envisages here, includes for example, a publication that exposes crime or anti-social behaviour, a publication which will prevent people from being misled by a statement made by an individual or organisation, or a publication which serves to disseminate information that will help people understand matters of public importance (ICO, 2014b).

What can, as a minimum, be concluded from the guidance, therefore, is the fact that an amateur blogger is acting in the exercise of their right to freedom of expression, or that they claim their purpose to be journalism (or art or literature), will not always be sufficient justification for interference with another person's privacy. Certainly, whilst online dissemination via a blog might satisfy the general public interest in freedom of expression, the topics covered in personal blogs, websites and on social media posts are rarely of the type to satisfy more specific public interests. For this reason, it is perhaps safest for individuals to assume that their blogs and online comments may not be considered to fall within the 'special purposes'. This certainly seems to be the implication in the ICO's media guidance (referred to above). Given that there appear to be few situations when the ICO would not allow an individual posting information online to rely upon the s36 exemption there is probably little need for an individual to seek recourse to s32 in any event.

THE PARENT PHOTOGRAPHER REVISITED

This article began with an illustration of a specific situation in which a parent takes a photograph at a school event, captures images of her own and other people's children and subsequently shares that photograph online. It has now been established that if such photographs identify the children then, unless the parent photographer can rely upon one of the exceptions to the DPA the parent will be treated as a data controller, and must therefore comply with the obligations detailed within that Act. The primary difficulty, as this article has illustrated, is in establishing whether any exceptions to the DPA apply in this specific situation.

Various articles published in the press between 2009 and 2012 (Appleton (2012); Clark (2009); Shoesmith (2010)) certainly suggest that schools are struggling to understand how the law applies to parent photographers. These articles indicate that many schools have either imposed stringent restrictions on parental photography or banned it entirely because they believe that the law requires such actions to be taken.

In order to determine what advice schools actually receive about parental photography, and the relevant law, in December 2013 Freedom of information requests were sent to all 206 local education authorities in England, Scotland and Wales. Each authority was asked whether it had produced any guidance or policy documents or had provided advice to schools in their area in relation to parental photography at school events. 198 authorities responded; 74 of these authorities did not provide any guidance, 28 stated that they refer schools exclusively to guidance produced by the ICO, 96 provide their own guidance (18 of those providing guidance also refer schools to the ICO guidance).

Reading through the guidance it was clear that there was significant disagreement between authorities as to whether parents should be allowed to take photographs at school events, or alternatively whether parents who take photographs at school events should be permitted to upload those photographs. 36 authorities (37% of the 98 authorities who provide guidance and 18% of the authorities who responded) explicitly state that posting online is not permitted, distinguishing clearly between the situation when parents keep photos for close family and friends to view (when they consider s36 will apply) and the situation when photos are shared online/more widely (when potentially s36 may not apply). Only 6 of these 36 authorities explicitly state, however, that online sharing may contravene the DPA. By contrast, 46 authorities (24% of respondents) explicitly refer schools to guidance published by the ICO, guidance which asserts that *the DPA imposes no restriction on parental photography at school events*. This ICO guidance, which was first published in 2005 and has been regularly republished in a variety of forms since that date (ICO, 2005, 2007, 2010b, 2010c, 2010c, 2012b, 2014c and undated) is premised upon the belief that s36 applies to parents taking photographs at school 'for personal or domestic use'. (No reference is made to the s32 exemption but given the ICO's advice that s32 is unlikely to apply when people are simply taking part in normal social interaction or other recreational internet use (ICO, 2014b) this is understandable).

As discussed above, the ICO has interpreted s36 widely. The ICO has made clear that in most instances, when parents post information online in their personal capacity and either for purely personal or recreational purposes then s36 will apply. Strangely, however, the ICO guidance on parental photography makes no reference to parents taking digital photographs to share photographs online. Although the examples that the ICO includes in his guidance (of parents storing photographs in a family album and taking a video for family viewing) hark back to before the digital era, one cannot imagine that the ICO is not aware that parents might share photographs of school events online. Certainly, many education authorities seem to be aware, not only of the possibility that parents will wish to share photographs online, but also of the risks involved when they do so (disclosure of the whereabouts of vulnerable children whose identity and whereabouts should not be revealed, identification and possible grooming of children, misuse of images, breach of privacy).

In the absence of explicit guidance on how s36 applies to a parent who wishes to post photographs online, it is perhaps inevitable that some confusion about the application of the DPA continues to exist. It may, of course, be the case, that as discussed above, the ICO holds a firm conviction that the s36 exemption will apply when a parent takes a photograph at a school event, whether or not that photograph will subsequently be placed in the family album, stored on a computer or shared online. If this is the case then it would be helpful for the ICO to update its parental photography guidance to clarify this. Even if the ICO were to do so, however, questions must be asked about whether this would in reality resolve the issue once and for all.

The divergence between the ICO's interpretation and the European interpretation are likely to cause continuing confusion for education authorities and thus also for parents. At present, depending upon which school a child attends/which local education authority a child lives in, a parent may, or may not, be permitted to take photographs, and may or may not be told that they must not share those photographs online. Can we expect the position to improve if and when the Directive is replaced by the Regulation?

UPDATING THE LAW TO ENSURE IT REMAINS FIT FOR THE 21ST CENTURY

In a communication to the European Parliament in 2010 the European Commission spelt out clearly its belief that a new data protection framework is needed, both 'to clarify and specify the application of data protection principles to new technologies' (European Commission, 2010a, p3) and to address 'divergences between the national laws implementing the Directive,' divergences which create 'legal uncertainty not only for data controllers but also for data subjects, creating the risk of distorting the equivalent level of protection that the Directive is supposed to achieve and ensure.' (European Commission, 2010a, p10). The Commission's comments certainly seem to be well founded given the differing approaches to Article 9 (the freedom of expression exemption) and to the personal/household exemption highlighted above. Whether the Commission's ambitions are realisable, however, have yet to be seen.

Certainly the ICO has recognised a need for comprehensive updating to address the challenges posed by new technologies, and, given 'the pan-European nature of the problem' accepts the need for either a Regulation or new Directive (ICO, 2012a, p2). It is clear, however, that the ICO is not wholly convinced that the Regulation will achieve all that the Commission suggests. The more detailed, prescriptive approach detailed in the regulation, an approach which the ICO suggests may not necessarily result in better data protection, is questioned (ICO, 2012a). The ICO further queries whether complete harmonisation is possible or even desirable (noting that key concepts in the law such as fairness depend on factors which necessarily vary from one member state to another). Given the current lack of harmony of interpretation both of Article 3(2) and Article 9, the issue of harmonisation is a key issue to be considered in the analysis of the new personal/household provision (Article 2(2)(d)) and the new provision authorising derogations from the directive in the interest of freedom of expression (Article 80).

The revised personal/household exemption

The wording of Article 2(2)(d) (and of the related Recital 15) have proved to be a subject of some contention for those involved in the process of agreeing the new regulation. This is to be expected given current divergences in approach to the personal/household exemption. Article 2(2)(d), as originally drafted by the Commission stated simply that the Regulation 'does not apply to the processing of personal data ... (d) by a natural person without any gainful interest in the course of its own exclusively personal or household activity.' In its earliest iteration Recital 15 stated similarly that the Regulation 'should not apply to processing of personal data by a natural person, which are exclusively personal or domestic, such as correspondence and the holding of addresses, and without any gainful interest and thus without any connection with a professional or commercial activity. The exemption should also not apply to controllers or processors which provide the means for processing personal data for such personal or domestic activities.'

The application of the exemption to the online sphere was thus not explicitly addressed by the Commission in the initial version of the Regulation (at best it is hinted at in the final sentence of the recital). The undoubted problem with this first iteration of the Regulation, therefore, was that it quite simply left wide open the question of whether Article 2(2)(d) never applies within the online sphere (as Lindqvist suggests), instead applies to all individuals processing information online in the course of personal activities (the ICO approach) or alternatively applies only to certain individuals (as the Working Party suggests). Surprisingly, however, it was the phrase 'without any gainful interest', which seemed initially to cause most offence both to the European Parliament (European Parliament, 2012), and to the ICO (ICO, 2012a), both of whom recognised that a natural person who processes personal data for private and household purposes may sometimes have a gainful interest in doing so (e.g. when selling private belongings to other private persons) but that such a person should still fall outside the Regulation provided there is no connection to a professional or commercial activity.

The amended version of Article 2(2) and Recital 15, approved by the European Parliament in March 2014 made no reference to 'gainful interest.' Indeed the European Parliament's version of Article 2(2)(d) revealed little difference to the original Article 3(2). The most important changes, were that the revised draft provision referred to 'processing ... by a natural person in the course of *its own exclusively* personal or household activity' as opposed to processing 'in the course of a *'purely* personal or household activity'. The Parliament also suggested that the exemption should only apply where it could be reasonably expected that the publication of data would only be accessed by a limited number of persons. Importantly, the European Parliament also made significant changes to the Recital to address the vital need to clarify how, and whether the exemption applied to the online sphere (European Parliament, 2012). Taking the Parliament's wording of Article 3(2) and Recital 15 together, therefore, the personal/household exemption, undoubtedly moved much closer to the interpretation of Article 3(2) that is currently found in UK law, which sees s36 being used as a vehicle by which to recognise individuals' rights to freedom of expression. At the same time, however, it sensibly also recognised the logic of the Working Party opinion, the need to recognise that widespread online sharing, by definition, may not always be 'personal'. It thus specifically addressed one of the key concerns raised by the ICO when the Regulation was first published, that the Regulation should *explicitly* consider whether the activities of individuals processing personal data online, about themselves and others, should fall within the personal/household exemption.

What the final version of Article 2(2) and Recital 15 will look like is as yet unclear. The Council of Ministers is in apparent agreement with the European Parliament that the application of the personal and household exemption to the online sphere needed clarifying. The most recent version of the regulation proposed by the Council thus retains the following sentence in Recital 15; 'Personal and household activities include social networking and on-line activity undertaken within the context of such personal and household activities.' The Parliament's wording of Article 2(2) has, however, been changed by the Council of Ministers. The wording of the personal and household exemption proposed by the Ministers now states that 'the Regulation does not apply to the processing of personal data ... by a natural person in the course of a personal or household activity.'

Potentially significant changes have thus been made to the Parliament's version. The Parliament's version of Article 2(2) using the word "*exclusively*" and making specific reference to disclosures being to a "*limited number of persons,*" reinforced the idea that personal data should not be widely distributed. Both of these constraints have been removed. It has been suggested that this implies that 'the Council of Ministers seek a broad "personal use" category involving an unknown (perhaps unlimited) number of persons' (Pounder, 2015). Perhaps more importantly Chris Pounder has suggested that the Council of Ministers' text directly undermines the CJEU's conclusions in Ryneš (Pounder, 2015). In Ryneš the CJEU made clear that the personal and household exemption was 'to be narrowly construed' recognising that Article 3(") refers to processing carried out as a "purely' personal or household activity ... not simply a personal or household activity"' (Ryneš, paragraph 30). The absence of the words 'purely' or 'exclusively' in the Council of Ministers' version of the Regulation text means that the personal and household exemption proposed by the Council of Ministers now does refer simply to 'a personal or household activity'. This is not, however, the only problem that has been identified with the Council's new wording. It has been suggested that;

'[t]here is also an issue with the absence of the word "*limited*" (which appears in the Parliament's text). For instance, FaceBook has a maximum number of 5000 friends; more than 5000 then you have to have a "fan page" (of which I have several anonymous ones). The Council of Ministers' text opens up an argument that a posting to say 500 friends is "personal" (because it is "limited" to well below the 5000 maximum) (Pounder, 2015).

Let us consider again the scenario posed at the beginning of this article, when a parent takes a photograph capturing images of her child and their friends at a school sports day and posts the images to Facebook. It seems relatively easy to see how this could be construed as a "personal activity." If so, the effect of the Council's revisions to Article 2(2) is that the Regulation will do little to protect the children whose images have been shared. This is of concern given that the rights of third parties whose information is processed by individuals subject to the exemption seem to have been largely neglected. The Article 29 Working Party/Working Party on Police and Justice noted in 2009 (p18) that 'thought should be given to the question whether data subjects should be given more means to execute their rights on the internet, including the protection of rights of third parties whose personal data may be object of processing (eg social networks).' If many online activities will fall outside the Regulation, as is proposed, the rights of third parties whose personal data is processed will presumably be commensurately more limited. Despite assertions by the Commission that the Regulation will strengthen individuals' rights (European Commission, 2010b), it is arguable that for third parties whose information is processed online the opposite may be the case. Clarity, harmonisation and a renewed emphasis on individuals' rights to freedom of expression through the personal/household exemption may arguably in future be improved, but this appears to be at the expense of other individuals' right to data protection.

Article 80 of the Regulation

Although Article 2(2)(d) may expand the sphere in which individuals can exercise their rights of freedom of expression to the online world, there is undoubtedly still room for a further derogation or exemption for freedom of expression, one that applies to organisations, the media, and individuals whose activities do not fall wholly within the personal sphere. This is certainly recognised by the Commission in their inclusion of Article 80.

The explanatory memorandum which accompanies the Regulation states simply that 'Article 80 obliges Member States to adopt exemptions and derogations from specific provisions of the Regulation where necessary to reconcile the right to the protection of personal data with the right of freedom of expression. It is based on Article 9 of Directive 95/46/EC, as interpreted by the Court of Justice of the EU' (in Satamedia).

Despite the memorandum's comments, which suggest that Article 80 is little different to Article 9, in its first iteration, as drafted by the Commission, two key differences in wording could be identified. Where Article 9 allows for exemptions or derogations '*only if they are necessary* to reconcile the right to privacy with the rules governing freedom of expression' Article 80, as originally drafted, provided for such derogations '*in order to* reconcile the right to the protection of personal data with the rules governing freedom of expression'. Article 80 thus removed the need for derogations to be 'necessary' replacing it with the weaker wording 'in order to'. A more subtle change to the wording is also introduced in its reference to the balance to be achieved between *data protection* and freedom of expression rather than privacy and freedom of expression (such a reference to data protection in place of privacy is a theme throughout the regulation, perhaps in acknowledgement that the Article 8 of Charter of Fundamental Rights of the European Union and Article 16 of the Treaty on the functioning of the European Union now explicitly recognise a free-standing right to data protection). These changes in wording were, however, only minor when compared with the later changes introduced by the Parliament. The Commission's position was to effectively clarify and reiterate the existing position, as interpreted by the CJEU. The exemption continued to apply only for the limited specific purposes of journalism, literature and art (albeit that journalistic purposes was to be interpreted widely to apply to anyone (Recital 121 to the Regulation).

Interestingly, however, the European Parliament in its review of Recital 121 and Article 80 clearly considered that the Commission had not gone far enough. Article 80, as revised by the Parliament, referred explicitly to Member States providing exemptions or derogations 'whenever this is necessary in order to reconcile the right to the protection of personal data with the rules governing freedom of expression in accordance with the Charter of Fundamental Rights of the European Union.' The Parliament thus took a significant step forward, going beyond the court's interpretation of the directive, an interpretation which had been restricted by the need to pigeonhole data processing activities into journalistic, artistic or literary purposes. If a version of Article 80 akin to that drafted by the Parliament were ultimately accepted, one might anticipate a significantly different approach to the freedom of expression/privacy/data protection balancing act within the UK, adopting a much wider notion of freedom of expression in line with that which is seen in Denmark and Sweden, and which more clearly reflects the approach of the European Court of Human Rights (Warso, 2013). The Council's version of Article 80, however, has much more in common with the Commission's more narrow exemption. Article 80(1) states that '[t]he national law of the Member States shall reconcile the right to the protection of personal data pursuant to this Regulation with the right to freedom of expression and information, including the processing of personal data for journalistic purposes and the purposes of artistic or literary expression.' This might perhaps be interpreted expansively, to allow for the balancing of privacy/data protection and freedom of expression in all cases, including but not limited to situations where personal data is processed for journalistic purposes. Article 80(2) however refers very clearly to member states providing exemptions and derogations '[f]or the processing of personal data carried out for journalistic purposes or the purpose of academic artistic or literary expression.' This suggests that the Council's intention is to maintain the status quo.

CONCLUSION

Warso suggests that the fact that Art 9 is restrictive (far more so than Art 10 ECHR), the fact that the ECJ in Lindqvist has shown a willingness to defer to national authorities to undertake the privacy-free speech balancing exercise, and the fact that the ECJ's chose to interpret Art 3(2) narrowly 'shows that EU law "tilts" towards the protection of privacy ... at the expense of other fundamental rights.' Warso argues further that '[i]n light of the human rights standards established by the ECtHR, this puts into question whether the Directive 95/46/EC fulfils the task of balancing all fundamental values involve. Perhaps, most importantly she contends that 'the standard set by CJEU in Lindqvist, which still constitutes the main point of reference with regard to the application of the personal/household exemption online, fails to keep up with the rapid development of new communication technologies and ignores the complex fabric of the Web' (Warso, 2013, p496)

These criticisms are certainly understandable when one considers the approach that the ECJ/CJEU have taken to the issue of individuals sharing personal information online. The European court's approach currently prevents individuals from sharing personal information online (unless they accept the substantial obligations which lie upon them, as data controllers (and which are likely to continue even once the regulation becomes law, no specific provision being included in the Regulation to relieve an individual of the full burden of data controller obligations). Whilst the Working Party opinion undoubtedly lessens the full effect of the Lindqvist judgment, it remains the case that individuals who do not choose to limit who has access to online postings should only post information online if they are prepared to accept their obligations under the Directive.

Within the UK, however, very different criticisms can be made. With the ICO having effectively chosen to ignore the decision in Lindqvist, it is apparent that UK individuals who share information online, including information and images of third parties, are free to do so, in the exercise of their right to freedom of expression. This is subject only to the proviso that their actions are undertaken for personal, domestic or recreational purposes. The ICO has chosen to define such terms widely, and it is entirely possible that even when a parent receives economic benefits such as free merchandise or free or reduced entrance fees as a result of blogging about the lives, likes and activities of their family and friends they will still benefit from the s36 exemption. Such individuals thus effectively have little or no need to rely upon the s32 exemption introduced into UK law to ensure that in appropriate cases (specifically for the special purposes of journalism, art and literature) individuals' rights to freedom of expression are not entirely disregarded in favour of the right to privacy/data protection. The effect of the ICO position, however, is that individuals whose information is shared online by others have seen an erosion of their rights to privacy and data protection, with no remedy afforded to them under the DPA, and no real ability to prevent online processing of their information by others. The clear divergence between the European and UK problems and the uncertainty that it causes for organisations and individuals can be illustrated by reference to a scenario where a parent takes a photograph at a school event with the intention of posting that photograph online. Whether the parent is allowed to take that photograph and post it online appears to largely depend upon whether the school believes that s36 DPA does or not apply to the parent. If the school accepts the ICO position then no restriction upon parental photography is required (at least for DPA purposes). By contrast if the school adopts the approach advocated in Lindqvist the school is likely, as a minimum, to ask parents not to share photographs online.

If the European Parliament's revisions to the Regulation are accepted it is arguable that the current uncertainties will be removed. Recital 15 to the Regulation goes a long way to clarifying how, throughout the Member States, the personal/household exemption should be applied. In many cases where individuals are sharing information only with a defined number (friends or family only) the Parliament has signalled clearly that it believes that the personal/household exemption should apply. Its revisions to Recital 121 also open the door to individuals being able to rely upon Article 80 as an alternative to Article 2(2)(d) when information is disseminated to the public at large. For individuals who wish to share personal information online, including third party information, the position is therefore improved; it seems clear that in many cases the data protection framework will not apply. For the individuals whose information is being shared by others, however, the position is not so much improved as clarified. It seems likely that their rights to object to the online processing of their information by other individuals are effectively disappearing.

REFERENCES

1. Appleton, Josie, (2012) 'Why do schools really stop parents taking photographs of their children?' The Guardian 23 June 2012 http://www.theguardian.com/lifeandstyle/2012/jun/23/photos-children-school-ban
2. Article 29 Data Protection Working Party (2009), 'Opinion 5/2009 on online social networking' 00189/09/EN WP 163, adopted 12 June 2009
3. Article 29 Working Party/Working Party on Police and Justice (2009) 'The Future of Privacy: Joint contribution to the consultation of the European Commission on the legal framework for the fundamental right to the protection of personal data' 02356/09/EN WP 168, adopted 1 Dec 2009
4. Bennett, Colin (1992) 'Regulating privacy: Data protection and public policy in Europe and the United States' (Ithaca: Cornell University Press)
5. Bignami, Francesca (2008) 'The case for tolerant constitutional patriotism: The right to privacy before the European courts', Cornell International Law Journal 41(2) 230-231
6. Carey, Peter (2009) 'Data Protection: A Practical Guide to UK and EU Law' (Oxford: OUP Oxford) 3rd Edition
7. Clark, Laura (2009) 'Parents banned from taking photos of their own children at school sports day' The Daily Mail, 17 June 2009) http://www.dailymail.co.uk/

news/article-1193697/Parents-banned-taking-photos-children-school-sports-day.html

8. Costa, Luis and Poullet, Yves (2012) 'Privacy and the Regulation of 2012' Computer Law & Security Review 28, 254-262
9. Council of the European Union (2014) Proposal for a Regulation of the European Parliament and of the Council on the protection of individuals with regard to the processing of personal data and on the free movement of such data (General Data Protection Regulation)
10. Data Protection Act 1998
11. Directive 95/46/EC on the protection of individuals with regard to the processing of personal data and on the free movement of such data
12. European Commission (2010a), Communication from the Commission to the European Parliament, the Council, the Economic and social committee and the committee of the regions: A comprehensive approach on personal data protection in the European Union COM (2010) 609 final 4.11.2010
13. European Commission (2010b), Data Protection Reform Frequently Asked Question Memo/10/542 04/11/2010
14. European Commission (2011) Special Eurobarometer 359: Attitudes on Data Protection and Electronic Identity in the European Union
15. European Commission, (2012a) Communication from the Commission to the European Parliament, the Council, the European Economic and Social Committee and the Committee of the Regions: Safeguarding Privacy in a Connected World: A European Data Protection Framework for the 21st Century (COM (2012) 9 Final) 25.12.12
16. European Commission (2012b)– Press Release 'Commission proposes a comprehensive reform of data protection rules to increase users' control of their data and to cut costs for businesses IP/12/46 25/01/12 http://europa.eu/rapid/press-release_IP-12-46_en.htm
17. European Commission (2012c) How does the data protection reform strengthen citizens' rights? http://ec.europa.eu/justice/data-protection/document/index_en.htm
18. European Parliament (2012) Draft report on the proposal for a regulation of the European Parliament and of the Council on the protection of individual with regard to the processing of personal data and on the free movement of such data (General Data Protection Regulation) (COM (2012)0011 – C7-0025/2012 – 2012/0011 (COD))
19. ICO (2005) Data Protection Good Practice Note Taking Photographs in Schools
20. ICO (2007) Data Protection Good Practice Note Taking Photographs in Schools
21. ICO (2010a) The Information Commissioner's response to the Ministry of Justice's call for evidence on the current data protection legislative framework
22. ICO (2010b) Data Protection Good Practice Note Taking Photographs in Schools

23. ICO (2010c) Parents can snap away at this year's sports day
24. ICO (2010d) Parents can snap away this Christmas
25. ICO (2011), Line to take - Dealing with complaints about information published online
26. ICO (2012a) Information Commissioner's Office: initial analysis of the European Commission's proposals a revised data protection legislative framework
27. ICO (2012b) Report on the data protection guidance we gave schools in 2012
28. IC (2013) Proposed new EU general data protection regulation: Article-by-article analysis paper
29. ICO (2014a) Social networking and online forums – when does the DPA apply? V1.1
30. ICO (2014b) Data protection and journalism: a guide for the media
31. ICO 2014c) Data Protection Good Practice Note Taking Photographs in Schools
32. ICO (undated) Does the Data Protection Act stop me taking photos of my children at school?
33. Korff, Douwe (2002) EC study on implementation of data protection directive (Study Contract ETD/2001/B5-3001/A/49) Comparative summary of national laws
34. Korff, Douwe, (2010) Comparative Study on Different Approaches to new privacy challenges, in particular in the light of technological developments. Working paper no 2: Data protection laws in the EU: The difficulties in meeting the challenges posed by global social and technical developments
35. Lindqvist ECJ C-101/01
36. NSPCC (2013) 'Using photographs of children for publication: NSPCC factsheet' http://www.nspcc.org.uk/Inform/research/briefings/Photographing-children_wda96007.html
37. OFCOM (*2013) Adults Media Use and Attitudes Report*
38. Opinion of Advocate General Jääskinen delivered on 25 June 2013 in Case C131/12 Google Spain SL Google Inc. v Agencia Española de Protección de Datos (AEPD) and Mario Costeja González
39. Pounder, Chris (2015) 'Council of Ministers' Regulation text negates ECJ rulings in Linqvist and Ryneš http://amberhawk.typepad.com/amberhawk/2015/07/council-of-ministers-regulation-text-negates-ecj-rulings-in-lindqvist-and-ryne%C5%A1.html
40. Shoesmith, Ian 'When can't you take photos of a nativity play?' BBC News UK, 8 December 2010) http://www.bbc.co.uk/news/uk-11947374
41. The Law Society and others v Rick Kordowski [2011] EWHC 3185 (QB)
42. Tietosuojavaltuutettu v Satakunnan Markkinapörssi Oy and Satamedia Oy CJEU C-73/07
43. Warso, Zuzanna, (2013) 'There's more to it than data protection – Fundamental

rights, privacy and the personal/household exemption in the digital age', Computer Law & Security Review (29) 491-500

44. Westin, A. (1967) Privacy and Freedom (New York: Atheneum)

11
CHAPTER

THE ROLE OF ANONYMIZATION AND PSEUDONYMISATION

Samson Yoseph Esayas

Keywords: Personal data, Anonymisation and pseudonymisation, Encryption, Breach notification requirements, EU data privacy, Security of personal data

INTRODUCTION

Understanding the concept of personal data'is at the center of data privacy discussions. This is so because the processing'of personal data is the main criteria for the applicability of data privacy rules. The main objective of the European Data Protection Directive (hereafter the Directive) is the protection of the fundamental rights and freedoms of natural persons, in particular their right to privacy with respect to the "processing of personal data" (Article 1(1)). It is evident from the article that at least two preconditions must be fulfilled for the Directive to apply: data being processed and this data being personal. According to Article 2(b), the term „processing involves a wide range of activities including the collection, recording, organization, storage, adaptation or alteration, retrieval, consultation, use, disclosure by transmission, dissemination or otherwise making available, alignment or combination, blocking, erasure or destruction.' Further, the Directive is primarily concerned with the processing of personal data wholly or partly by automatic means. The term partly implies that an automated operation that involves some manual use of personal data is within the realm of the Directive. In addition, the Directive is applicable to nonautomated processing which form part of a filing system or are intended to form part of a filing system, such as specially structured paper file (Article 3(1)). Essentially, the Directive applies whenever personal data is processed, either automated or non-automated, barring certain exceptions. The second

Citation: Samson Yoseph Esayas, The role of anonymization and pseudonymisation, http://ejlt.org/article/view/378/568.

precondition is that the data being processed must be personal. The Directive defines personal data as any information relating to an identified or identifiable natural person' (Article 2(a)). Identification involves describe[ing] a person in such a way that he or she is distinguishable from all other persons and recognisable as an individual'(European Union Agency for Fundamental Rights, 2013, p.40). The reference to identification includes both the term identified 'and identifiable'. The former involves a situation where the identity of the person is already distinguished or manifestly clear. Such identification could happen directly from the information being processed, such as the full name of the person, or indirectly from information regarding the physical, physiological, mental, economic, cultural, or social identity of that particular individual (Article 2(a)). This implies that the person need not be identified at the level of his name; this indicates that identifying the individual at the level of, for example, his addresses, health, and financial data would also suffice. This is taken slightly further under the draft data protection Regulation in that the identification at behaviour level is also included. This seems to cover situations where individuals may be tracked and singled out at their behaviour level, for example, for making decisions about them (tailor ads according to their behavior) without their names or identities necessarily being known (Costa and Poullet, 2012, 255). However, for the Directive to apply, it is not required that the person be identified; it is sufficient that the person concerned be identifiable. Identifiability' implies that identification has not happened yet but is possible, for example, by combining the information being processed with other information. This implies that the mere possibility of associating certain information with a particular individual is sufficient. According to Recital 26 of the Directive, identifiability of a person should be assessed taking into account all the means likely reasonably to be used either by the controller or by any other person to identify the said person. The Recital further indicates that the principles of protection shall not apply to data rendered anonymous in such a way that the data subject is no longer identifiable.

Two points within Recital 26 require particular mention, given their importance for the role of anonymisation and pseudonymisation. The first point relates to the term „likely reasonably. The duo introduces two criteria for identifiability: the term likely' referring to probability' of identification and the term reasonably' referring to the difficulty' in identification—for example, in terms of costs, time required for identification, and available technology (Bygrave, 2002, p.44). The second point relates to a situation where certain information is rendered non-personal' through anonymisation in such a manner that the data subject is no longer identifiable. Data being rendered anonymous implies that information that ceases to be personal data 'may be processed without any need of compliance to the requirements in the Directive. The use of anonymisation can have many social and economic benefits. For example, anonymising data can be relevant in publishing data in rich and reusable formats for research and statistical purposes whilst privacy is being protected (ICO, 2012, p.9). However, in practice, it is often difficult to determine whether data has been sufficiently anonymised or is still personal data. This is partially because of the risk-based nature of anonymisation and its dependence on a variety of factors that are difficult to quantify. More particularly, this is related to the difficulty in foreseeing the available technology and information that could be used for re-identification. There are also challenges in articulating the harms on privacy (Oswald, 2014, p.260). Thus, the role of anonymisation and pseudonymisation in data privacy is considered one of the difficult areas of the law (ICO, 2012, p.9). The combination of these factors implies that individual as well as entities tend to downplay risks and simplify technical explanations in an attempt to reassure (Oswald, 2014, p.260). For example, there is a prevalent understanding in certain sections of the business and academic community that key-coded (e.g. encrypted) data may not be considered personal data so far as there are appropriate measures to exclude re-identification (i.e. strong encryption algorithm, strong encryption key, and secure key) (OPTIMIS, 2011, p.8; Hon, Millard, and Walden, 2011, p.216). Similarly, for data subjects, anonymisation gives a false sense of security to individuals, as they find it difficult to fully understand the potential risks of such measures and how such data is used (Ohm, 2009). This notwithstanding, most discussions regarding anonymisation are mainly at a technical level and focus on the risks of re-identification of different techniques (see Ohm, 2009 and Cavoukian, 2013). When legal perspectives are attached, they are only limited to whether a certain technique meets the conditions for providing a safe harbour from the entire application of data privacy rules without going into the other roles of such measures—a reference to the all or nothing' approach. Furthermore, the subject of rendering certain information non-personal' through different mechanisms in data privacy rules raises a number of legal issues. Thus, the main goal of this article is to examine and elaborate the different roles of anonymisation and related legal issues under the EU data privacy rules. To this end, the following section examines whether the process of anonymising data constitutes the processing of personal data under the EU data privacy rules and its implications. This is followed by a discussion on the three major roles of anonymisation under the EU data privacy rules. Section 2 discusses the role of anonymisation as a safe harbour from data privacy rules in its entirety. Section 3 examines the role of anonymisation as a safe harbour from certain data privacy obligations, particularly notification of personal data breaches and further proposals under the ongoing data protection reform. This section also highlights the requirements for notifying personal data breaches under Regulation 611/2013, the eIDAS Regulation, and the proposed General Data Protection Regulation (GDPR). Section 4 analyses the role of anonymisation as a mandated compliance requirement under data privacy rules. The last section concludes the article with some observations.

ANONYMISATION AND PSEUDONYMISATION AS PROCESSING OF PERSONAL DATA?

Generally, the term anonymisation includes a number of techniques that aim at reducing the identifiability of individuals, and pseudonymisation can be considered as one technique of anonymisation. However, given the different legal significance attached to different anonymisation techniques under data privacy rules, in this article, a distinction is made between these two terms. Anonymisation is referred to as a process through which identifying information is manipulated (concealed or deleted) to make it difficult to identify data subjects (Ohm, 2009, p.1707). This definition mainly encompasses techniques used to produce aggregated information without any reference to information regarding a specific individual. Pseudonymisation involves replacing names or other direct identifiers with codes or numbers (Article 29 Working Party, 2007, p.18). The main purpose of such techniques is to enable the data to be associated with a particular individual without the individual being identified (ICO, 2012, p.51). In this context, given that the term processing‘ encompasses a wide range of activities on data under the Directive, a relevant question that comes into play is whether the process of anonymisation (pseudonymisation) in itself would constitute processing‘ under the Directive, thereby implying the need for compliance to perform anonymisation over certain data. This is because to generate anonymised or pseudonymised data, one has to apply a specific anonymisation or pseudonymisation technique to the personal data (Emam and Alvarez, 2014, p.8). According to Article 29 Working Party (2014a, p.3), a group comprising national data protection authorities, anonymisation constitutes a further processing of personal data; as such, it must satisfy the requirement of compatibility by having regard to the legal grounds and circumstances of the further processing.‘ This implies that the process of anonymising data by itself must comply with the test of compatibility with the original purpose. In other words, anonymising personal data for purposes not compatible with the original purpose constitutes a violation of data privacy rules, unless there are other legitimate grounds for the processing. For example, if personal data is collected to provide a certain service to the data subject, anonymising the data in order to use such data for advertising purposes would constitute a violation of data privacy rules unless, there are other legitimate grounds for processing (i.e. anonymising or marketing purposes), such as consent of the data subject. The approach of Working Party in addressing the anonymisation process as compatible or incompatible with the original purpose represents a very narrow view of the role of anonymisation. As briefly noted above, the role of such measures is not limited to providing safe harbour from the entire application of data privacy rules. Rather, they can constitute mandated measures to comply with data privacy rules, such as purpose limitation and data security principles. For example, anonymisation could be used to comply with Article 6(1)(e) of the Directive, which requires that information should not be kept in identifiable form for a period longer than is necessary for the purposes for which the data were originally collected or for which they are further processed. Among others, Article 6(1)(e) would require the deletion of personal data, which can be achieved through anonymisation when the original legal basis is exhausted (Emam and Alvarez, 2014, p.9). Similarly, a data controller might need to anonymise personal data as part of additional security measures, even though such anonymisation does not fulfil the conditions discussed in Section 2. In this sense, anonymisation is something different or something more than a compatible use‘ and might constitute mandated compliance measures (Emam and Alvarez, 2014, p.9). In addition, given that the underlying privacy interests are not threatened by such a process, the stance adopted by the Working Party would discourage the use of anonymisation and pseudonymisation as privacy-enhancing techniques (Hon, Millard, and Walden, 2011, p.214). This is the approach adopted by certain Data Protection Authorities (DPAs) like the UK Information Commissioner‘s Office (ICO). The ICO (2012, p.28) indicated that in the absence of any unwarranted damage or distress resulting from anonymisation, there is no need to justify the process of anonymisation‘ itself. In this respect, a new notion in the Commission draft Regulation states that …processing of data to the extent strictly necessary for the purposes of ensuring network and information security…constitutes a legitimate interest of the concerned data controller.‘ Given that anonymisation and pseudonymisation could be considered as necessary for information security, this might give some leeway to argue that controllers might legalize the anonymisation or pseudonymisation under Article 6(f) of the draft Regulation as necessary for the legitimate interest of the controller‘, provided the controller‘s interests are not overridden by the interests or fundamental rights of the data subject. Similar arguments based on the legitimate interest of the controller‘ can be made under the current Directive Article 7(f) for anonymising personal data, except where such interests are overridden by the fundamental rights and freedoms of the data subject.

ANONYMISATION AND PSEUDONYMISATION AS A SAFE HARBOUR FROM DATA PRIVACY RULES

Anonymisation

According to the opinion of the Working Party, anonymisation for purposes other than the original purpose could still be considered as compatible with the original purpose as long as it fulfils certain conditions. For the anonymisation to be considered as compatible with the original purposes, the anonymisation process should produce reliably‘ anonymised information (Article 29 Working Party, 2014a, p.7). This implies that anonymising personal data for purposes that are incompatible with the original purpose would constitute a violation of the EU data privacy rules if it fails to fulfil the conditions of producing reliable anonymised data as laid down in the Working Party‘s document. The document reiterates the sentiments under Recital 26 of the Directive and indicates that only when data is anonymised to the effect that it is no longer possible to associate to an individual by using all the means likely reasonably to be used‘, either by the controller or a third party, it will not constitute personal data. Data being rendered reliably anonymous implies that such data can be processed without any need of compliance to legal requirements in the Directive. However, such safe harbour would require irreversible anonymisation. In the opinion of the Working Party, the outcome of such kind of anonymisation should be, in the current state of technology, as permanent as erasure, i.e. making it impossible to process personal data‘ (Article 29 Working Party, 2014a, p.6). One consideration in assessing the notion of impossibility is the robustness of the anonymisation technique employed. In assessing the robustness of different techniques of anonymisation, the following questions should be taken into account: (1) Is it still possible to single out an individual, (2) is it still possible to link records relating to an individual, and (3) can information regarding an individual be inferred? Using these three questions, the Working Party identified two major families of anonymisation (randomisation and generalisation) and discussed the strengths and weakness of these different techniques (Article 29 Working Party, 2014a, p.3). Further, the Working Party also underlined the dynamic nature of risks of identification as a result of developments in powerful data analysis techniques and, therefore, organizations are required to revisit the residual risks regularly. As such, even effectively anonymised data should be supported by the following follow-up measures: (1) Identify new risks and re-evaluate the residual risk(s) regularly, (2) assess whether the controls for identified risks suffice and adjust accordingly, and (3) monitor and control the risks (Article 29 Working Party, 2014a, p.24). Thus, if the result of such assessment entails an unacceptable risk of identification of data subjects‘, the processing has to comply with data privacy rules (Article 29 Working Party, 2014a, p.10). However, the Working Party does not specify when the risk of identification is considered to be acceptable at a given time. The lack of an acceptable risk threshold has been subject to criticism on the basis that the Working Party follows an absolute definition of acceptable risk in the form of zero risk‘ (Emam and Alvarez, 2014, p.9). First, the Directive itself does not require a zero risk approach. As noted above, the use of the term likely‘ represents the probability‘ of identification, whereas the term reasonably‘ represents the difficulty‘ in identification (Bygrave, 2002, p.44). Both are terminologies common in the field of risk management reasoning, thereby indicating the potential for a certain level of acceptable risk. Such criticism of the zero risk approach complements the claim that technologists and regulators often misunderstand the term anonymisation‘. As Ohm (2009) puts it, a word that should mean, "try to achieve anonymity" is too often understood,‘ just as the case with the Working Party, to mean achieve anonymity‘. Such an approach will significantly affect the widespread use of anonymisation measures. Some commentators suggest that only where risk of identification is sufficiently realistic (for example, „more likely than not), should information be considered „personal data (Hon, Millard, and Walden 2011, p.226). In other words, where identification risk is remote or highly theoretical, given the time, expense, technology, and labour required to associate the data to a particular individual, then the data should not be considered personal. Such an approach accommodates the existence low risk or very small risk in anonymised data, which might be considered acceptable. Some member states have adopted such a stance. For example, the UK ICO has held that anonymised data is not required to be completely risk free, rather it must be able to mitigate the risk of identification until it is remote (ICO, 2012, p.13). Second, if the acceptable risk threshold is zero for any potential recipient of the data, there is no existing technique that can achieve the required degree of anonymisation. From a technical point of view, achieving full anonymisation of the data that would not allow re-identification is considered very difficult (ENISA, 2012, p.44). This implies that the processing, including the process of anonymising the data, has to be justified under one of the legitimate grounds listed in Article 7 of the Directive. Adopting such an approach represents higher risks, as it encourages the processing of data in identifiable form. Another factor in the assessment is to examine if there is any kind of data either in the hands of the „controller or any other person that could be used to identify the individual. For example, if a data controller keeps the original (identifiable) data and shares part of this dataset by removing or masking the identifiable data to another party, the resulting dataset is still personal data (Article 29 Working Party, 2014a, p.9). This is because there is still data in the hands of the controller that could be used to associate to the individual. However, this overlooks the possibility where the original data might not have any assistance in associating the anonymised data to certain individual. Ultimately, the existence of any data—either in the hands of the controller or any other party—which could be used to associate the anonymised data to a certain individual, implies that the data is not considered to be truly anonymised and has to comply with data protection rules. The challenge with this approach is that it establishes a universal basis for assessing whether there is any other information‘ that could be combined with the anonymised data to identify the individual. According to Ohm (2009, p.1752), there is always some piece of information [...] that could be combined with anonymised data to reveal private information about an individual‘. In addition, determining what —other information is available, who it is available to and whether it is likely to be used in a re-identification process‘ would be an extremely formidable task (ICO, 2012, p.18). A more practical, but still difficult, approach would have been to assess whether it is likely that the receiver of the anonymised data would come into the possession of such information, taking into account whether the information is available on the Internet or available only to certain organizations or public bodies. For example, the UK ICO indicates that the disclosure of anonymised data is not a disclosure of personal data—even where the data controller holds the key to enable re-identification, which is also confirmed by a decision from the UK high court (ICO, 2012, p.13). Such an approach would allow recipients to process anonymised data without the need to comply with data protection rules, despite the controller retaining an identifiable form of the data. Generally, the recent opinion of the Working Party seems to indicate that true anonymisation is unattainable in a world of open‘ datasets, thereby indicating that the current state of technology and given the increase in computational power and tools available, „likely reasonably is easily attainable (Article 29 Working Party, 2014a, p.4). It is true that re-identification has become easy as a result of the technological advancement and the ubiquity of information on the Internet, but the alternative should not be a boundless and overbroad application of the Directive. This approach dislodges the appropriate balance between information flow and privacy, which hinges on restricting the application of data privacy rules to personal data‘ (Ohm, 2009, p.1763). A more practical approach would dictate establishing different layers of risks of harm that takes account the sensitivity of the data and the context of its usage. For example, the following four layers might be envisaged, where (1) the anonymisation is employed to sensitive data and would be publicly available, (2) the anonymisation is applied to sensitive data and would be available with limited access, (3) the anonymisation is applied to non-sensitive data and would be publicly available, and (4) the anonymisation is applied to non-sensitive data and would be available with limited access. At least the fourth layer could be subject to less strict requirements of anonymisation. Overall, anonymised data that irreversibly prevents identification can be processed without the need to adhere to the legal requirements under the Directive. However, it must be noted that the Directive will still be applicable if the anonymisation techniques are engineered inappropriately; thus, any doubt in this regard should be interpreted as involving the processing of personal data.

Similarly, member states might extend the scope of national legislation to areas not included within the scope of the Directive. For example, in France, the reasonableness‘test does not exist, thereby implying that data remains personal data even if it is extremely difficult to re-identify the data subject and unlikely that re-identification will take place (Article 29 Working Party, 2014a, p.6). Furthermore, if a person (natural or legal) is able to associate certain data, for example by accidental matching, from truly anonymised data, that person has to comply with data privacy rules. Although, at the EU level, the responsibility of the controller that released the anonymised data that is subject to re-identification is unclear, the ICO (2012, p.41) recommends that this be treated as a breach of security and that the concerned individuals be notified of the breach. Simultaneously, it is important to acknowledge the difficulties associated with such compliance, because the data might already be exported outside the EEA.

Pseudonymisation

Another method to reduce the likelihood of identifiability of individuals is pseudonymisation. Examples of pseudonymisation techniques include encryption and hash function. Similar arguments were made with regard to pseudonymised data in that so long as it is effective, it should not be considered personal' (OPTIMIS, 2011, p.8). However, the Working Party indicates that equating pseudonymised data to anonymised data is considered as one of the misconceptions among many controllers. This is because pseudonymised data continues to allow an individual data subject to be singled out and linkable across different datasets' and is subject to data protection rules (Article 29 Working Party, 2014a, p.10). On the one hand, individuals continue to be identified by a unique attribute that is the result of the pseudonymisation (the pseudonymised attribute) (Article 29 Working Party, 2014a, p.21). On the other, it is still possible to single-out individuals from pseudonymised data, either because someone is holding the key that could be used to re-identify the individual or the key can be bypassed by brute force attacks, or as a result of a data breach (Article 29 Working Party, 2014a, p.29). This is in line with the Working Party's suggestion that there should not be any kind of data either in the hands of the „controller or any other person that could be used to identify the individual. Although such a stance seems to effectively exclude the use of pseudonymisation as a measure that provides safe harbour from data privacy rules, a combination with some anonymisation techniques such as removing and generalising attributes or deleting the original data could achieve the required level for safe harbour (Article 29 Working Party, 2014a, p.21). Some DPAs like the UK ICO have adopted a different approach. In its guide on anonymisation, the ICO indicated that although pseudonymised data may create a higher risk of re-identification, it does not mean that effective anonymisation through pseudonymisation is impossible (ICO, 2012, p.21).

Encryption

Encryption can serve as a pseudonymisation technique when it is used to conceal directly identifiable information. Encryption is the process of changing a plain text in to unintelligible code; in contrast cryptography, often used interchangeably with encryption, is the related science dealing with the technicalities of creating encrypted information (Perkins, 2005, p.1628). The use of encryption has been tipped as a privacy-enhancing measure, particularly in case of cloud computing services (Kuner, 1996, p.186). As noted above, there are also arguments that as far as the encryption is effective—that is, there is a strong encryption algorithm, strong encryption key, and the key is kept secure—the data may not be considered personal in the hands of a third party that is not in possession of the decryption key and, thus, the Directive is inapplicable (OPTIMIS, 2011, p.8). The underlying rationale behind such suggestions is that the application of data privacy rules should be based on access to „intelligible data (Hon et al. 2014, p.10). However, according to the opinion of the Working Party, given that the security of encryption or the hash function is affected by many technical and organizational measures, the focus on the robustness of the encryption, as such, is misleading. (Article 29 Working Party, 2014a, p.29). In particular, this opinion identifies essential differences in the use of encryption and anonymisation. One major difference pertains to the goal of the techniques. The goal of anonymisation is primarily to eliminate linking attributes and avoid identification of individuals (Article 29 Working Party, 2014a, p.29). With regard to encryption and key-coding, the goal is not making a data subject unidentifiable, since, in the hands of the controller at least, the original data are still available or deducible (Article 29 Working Party, 2014a, p.29). In other words, encryption does not eliminate the identifiability aspect of the information, that is, the relationship of the information to the individual and the possibility of identifying the person from the encrypted information theoretically exists. This is particularly the case in an era where cryptographic attacks are being continuously improved due to increased computing power and the availability of cryptographic key cracking cloud services (Wayne and Grance, 2011, p.12). Therefore, as long as the key or the original data are available, even in the hands of a trusted third party, the possibility of identifying a data subject is intact (Article 29 Working Party, 2014a, p.29). This implies that the use of two-way cryptography algorithms (rendering personal data unintelligible with the possibility of backtracking the individual under predefined circumstances, for example, by entering the correct key/password) is still subject to data privacy rules. In an earlier Opinion, the Working Party suggested that data containing one-way cryptography identifiers (irreversibly encrypted data) would not be personal data' provided that the cryptography is effective (Article 29 Working Party, 2007, p.18; Hon, Millard, and Walden 2011, p.217). In other words, one-way encrypted data or keyed-hash function with deletion of the key can be processed independent of the Directive. Although the latest Opinion does not provide a clear indication to this effect, it acknowledges that when deterministic encryption or keyed-hash function with deletion of the key is used, it becomes computationally hard for an attacker to decrypt or replay the function, as it would imply testing every possible key' (Article 29 Working Party, 2014a, p.21). It is the opinion of this author that such data should benefit from safe harbour. However, the safest approach is that the use of encryption or the hash function does not provide safe harbour for the application of data privacy rules under the EU data privacy framework, unless complemented by anonymisation techniques. This is not to mention that such measures can still be mandated as a compliance requirement, as discussed in Section 4.1. In summary, the recent opinion of the Working Party does not seem encouraging for businesses to use anonymisation and pseudonymisation in processing personal data. Furthermore, the Opinion does not provide any guidance for data controllers or data processors to follow to anonymise their data (Emam and Alvarez, 2014, p.3). One important contribution could be that the Opinion has identified the different risks associated with different techniques. As the Working Party has indicated, different combinations could be used to reach the required level of anonymisation', in which case the Directive does not apply. In certain cases, it is advised to apply a double anonymisation, that is, the application of a second anonymisation on the result of a first anonymisation. However, it might be useful to come up with different layers of risks that take account the kind of data, the anonymisation or pseudonymisation technique employed, the context of their use, and then lay down different conditions accordingly. A further consideration could be to mitigate some obligations with respect to the use of a specific anonymisation technique if certain risks no longer exist. As discussed below, recent developments in the data privacy discourse seem to heed such suggestion by introducing a safe harbour from certain obligations when such measures are implemented.

ANONYMISATION AND PSEUDONYMISATION AS A SAFE HARBOUR FROM CERTAIN DATA PRIVACY OBLIGATIONS

As noted above, the current data privacy framework has been criticized for its all or nothing approach‘ where if there is slight possibility to associate certain information to an individual, the data privacy rules apply entirely regardless of whether the data is anonymised or pseudonymised. However, in the past few years, there have been some developments that exempt controllers from certain obligation if data is anonymised or pseudonymised and fulfil certain conditions. Currently, such initiatives are essentially focused on personal data breach notification requirements. At the EU level, the amendment to the 2002 ePrivacy Directive, through Directive 2009/136/EC, introduces mandatory personal data breach notification obligation under its Article 4(3). However, the inconsistent implementation of the breach notification requirements within the ePrivacy Directive is believed to create significant legal uncertainty, complexity and considerable administrative costs for providers operating crossborder‘ (Recital 4, Regulation 611/2013). Therefore, Regulation 611/2013 is adopted to harmonize the notification of personal data breaches by public electronic communications service providers, which include both traditional telecom providers such as telephony companies and Internet Service Providers (ISPs). Similarly, the Regulation on electronic identification and trust services (eIDAS), which will replace the eSignature Directive 1999/93/EC, introduces personal data breach notification requirement for trust service providers, which could range from telecom service providers to banks and other financial institutions to universities (Regulation No 910/2014). Furthermore, the proposed General Data Protection Regulation (GDPR) contains personal data notification obligations for controllers and, to a certain extent, processors. In the following paragraphs, the personal breach notification requirements under these laws are briefly highlighted, followed by the role of anonymisation and pseudonymisation in providing safe harbour from such obligations.

Notification of Personal Data Breaches under the Eu Legal Framework

It is not the aim of this article to examine the details of personal data breaches under the EU legal framework. Such requirements are only discussed to the extent they are relevant to the discussion on the role of anonymisation and pseudonymisation. In this regard, it is important to note that the breach notification requirements under Regulation 611/2013 are essentially similar to the requirements under the proposed GDPR and the eIDAS Regulation. This is not incidental. It originates from the legislators intent of harmonizing notification requirements regarding personal data across sectors. Thus, unless mentioned otherwise, the discussions regarding Regulation 611/2013 on notification of personal data breaches are generally relevant to the proposed GDPR and the eIDAS Regulation. Under Regulation 611/2013, providers of electronic communication services are required to notify personal data breaches to the relevant authorities within 24 hours after detection of the breach (Article 2(2)). Moreover, Article 3(1) of the Regulation provides that „when the personal data breach is likely to adversely affect the personal data or privacy of a subscriber or individual, the provider shall, in addition to the notification referred to in Article 2, also notify the subscriber or individual of the breach. An important aspect of Regulation 611/2013 is that it covers breaches affecting not only natural persons but also legal persons. Thus, it is important to distinguish between the subscriber' and individual' user because, the subscriber, which can be either a legal person or natural person, may not always be the same person as the user. For example, some parents may subscribe to a service that locates the mobile phone of their children. In such instances, the parents are the subscribers and their children are the individual users. Further, according to Article 3(1) of the Regulation, both the subscriber and the individual user are to be notified when a personal data breach is likely to affect the privacy of the subscriber or the individual. Providers are required to notify the affected individual or subscribers when the breach „is likely to adversely affect their personal data or privacy rights. Article 3(2) of the Regulation lists three elements as essential in determining the adverse effect of a breach. These are (a) the nature and content of data concerned, (b) the likely consequences of a personal data breach for the subscriber or individual concerned, and (c) the circumstances of the personal data breach.' Breaches affecting certain categories of personal data are considered to fulfil such a requirement. Examples are breaches affecting financial information, like credit card data, and special categories of data, e-mail data, location data, internet log files, web browsing histories and itemized [sic] call lists' (Regulation 611/2013, Recital 61). This is because such breaches might lead to identity theft [,] fraud, physical harm,... [significant] humiliation or damage to reputation' (Regulation 611/2013, Art 3(2(b))). This implies that the assessment is not limited only to breaches that result in economic loss, but also breaches that may cause immaterial damages, such as any moral and reputational damages' (EUR. CONSUMER ORG, 2011, p.4). The Working Party also underlines the need to consider secondary effects of the breach such as the time spent in attempts to rectify the breach and the extent of distress suffered (Article 29 Working Party, 2014b, p.13). In addition, the reference to the term likely' implies that the mere likelihood that the breach will adversely affect the individual is sufficient, meaning that an actual adverse effect is not necessary. The notification to the subscriber or individual shall be made without undue delay after the detection of the personal data breach (Regulation 611/2013, Art 3(3)). Furthermore, the notification shall not be dependent on the notification to national authorities (Regulation 611/2013, Art 3(3)). This implies, for example, that an organization should not attempt to prioritize notification to the authorities over the subscribers or individuals. Given that the aim of such notification is to avoid or mitigate the consequences of the breach, the notification should be given immediately or in such time as to enable the subscriber or individual to mitigate the adverse effects of the breach. In light of such rationale, Barcelo and Traung (2010, p.96) argue that the term without undue delay involves a shorter interval than notification to the authority. Similar provisions are to be found in the eIDAS Regulation. Article 19(2) of the Regulation requires trust service providers to notify personal data breaches to the relevant authorities without undue delay but in any event within 24 hours after having become aware of it. Moreover, paragraph 2 of Article 19(2) states that Where the breach of security or loss of integrity is likely to adversely affect a natural or legal person to whom the trusted service has been provided, the trust service provider shall also notify the natural or legal person of the breach of security or loss of integrity without undue delay.This is essentially similar to the requirements under Article 3(1) of Regulation 611/2013.

Furthermore, the different drafts—that is, the initial Commission draft, LIBE draft, and the Council draft of the proposed GDPR—contain provisions for notification of personal data breaches both for the DPAs and individual data subjects. There are slight differences among the three drafts and the main differences with respect to the breach notification will be highlighted when relevant. All the three drafts of the Regulation require notification to the data subjects to happen without undue delay after the controller becomes aware of the breach.

ANONYMISATION OR PSEUDONYMISATION AS A SAFE HARBOUR FROM BREACH NOTIFICATION OBLIGATIONS

According to Article 4(1) of the Regulation 611/2013 notification of a personal data breach to a subscriber or individual concerned shall not be required if the provider has demonstrated to the satisfaction of the competent national authority that it has implemented appropriate technological protection measures, and that those measures were applied to the data concerned by the security breach.' More particularly, the Regulation indicates that individuals or subscribers do not need to be notified when providers manage to demonstrate that the data affected by the breach was rendered unintelligible (Regulation 611/2013, Article 4(1)). According to Article 4(2) of the Regulation, data is considered to be unintelligible where (a) it has been securely encrypted with a standardized algorithm or replaced by its hashed value, calculated with a standardized cryptographic keyed hash function, (b) the key used to decrypt or to hash the data has not been compromised in any security breach, and (c) it has been demonstrated that the key used to decrypt or hash the data cannot be ascertained by available technological means by any person not authorized to access the key. Data can be rendered unintelligible in a number of techniques, but the reference under Article 4(1) to encryption or hashing, in particular, indicates that the provision focuses on pseudonymisation techniques that enable the re-identification of the individual subsequently. However, this does not imply that the use of anonymisation would not exempt the controller from notifying data subjects. As noted above, this flows from the general principle that if data is rendered non-personal' through anonymisation, data protection rules do not apply. In fact, for the exemptions under Article 4(1) to apply, it is not necessary that the outcome of such anonymisation should be as permanent as erasure, thereby making it impossible to process personal data (Article 29 Working Party, 2014a, p.6). For example, as noted above, the Working Party has held that if a data controller keeps the original (identifiable) data and hands over part of this dataset by removing or masking the identifiable data to another party, the resulting dataset is still personal data and has to comply with data protection rules (Article 29 Working Party, 2014a, p.9). However, the controller might still benefit from safe harbour for notifying breaches, even if it keeps the original (identifiable) data, unless the security of the latter is compromised. A number of reasons exist for such a safe harbour. First, if certain data was made initially unintelligible, the residual privacy risks of the breach are considered to be minimal—not likely „to adversely affect the personal data or privacy rights of individuals (Article 29 Working Party, 2014b, p.1). Second, such exemption aims to reduce the regulatory compliance burden on organisations and the negative impact of over-notification, referred to as notification fatigue, for users. Schwartz and Janger (1999, p.916) argue that if consumers are flooded by frequent caution messages with merely putative threats, it is likely that they will fail to act when important warnings finally arrive. Furthermore, it could serve as an incentive for the wider adoption of technological measures. A survey shows that such safe harbour from notifying breaches have increased the use of encryption (Ponemon Institute 2009). Meanwhile, the exception related to technological protection measures under EU rules is not an automatic safe harbour and must be approved by the competent regulatory authority. This is derived from the following statement: the provider has demonstrated to the satisfaction of the competent national authority in Article 4(1). Three approaches to providing safe harbour to such obligation could be identified: an exemption, a rebuttable presumption, and factor-based analysis (Burdon, Reid, and Low, 2010, p.529). The EU legislator seems to prefer the factor-based analysis, where the implementation of such measures is one factor in demonstrating to the regulatory authorities that the rights of the data subject are not affected. In addition, organizations are still required to notify the relevant national regulatory authorities regardless of such measures, thereby implying that the technological measures under Article 4(1) serve as a safe harbour only from the notification to individuals and not from regulatory authorities. In some cases, the organizations might even be required to notify the breach to individuals even if the data is sufficiently encrypted. This is because in the absence of adequate backups, a loss or alteration of encrypted data can still negatively affect data subjects (Article 29 Working Party, 2014b, p.1). This is important because encryptions cannot prevent loss of data. Thus, for the purposes of the exemptions, it is important to make a distinction among the three kinds of personal data breaches: "availability breach" —which refers to the —accidental or unlawful destruction of data[;] "integrity breach"—which refers to — alteration of personal data, and "confidentiality breach"—which relates to — unauthorized disclosure of, or access to, personal data (Article 29 Working Party, 2014b, p.2). This implies that the safe harbour regarding unintelligible data does not prevent availability breach and might not exempt the entity from notifying the individual. Although one could argue that breaches affecting availability might not, in the strict legal sense, affect the privacy rights of individuals, Article 3(1) of the Regulation refers to personal data or privacy of a subscriber or individual.' This implies that breaches affecting availability might still adversely affect the personal data of subscribers or individuals. There are similar provisions for safe harbour to the notification of data subjects under the proposed GDPR. However, unlike Regulation 611/2013 that provides a detailed description regarding the exemptions for notifying individual data subjects, the initial Commission draft and the LIBE draft adopt a very general approach without any reference to specific technological measures in rendering data unintelligible. This might be because of the issues of technology neutrality in making specific reference to encryption or hashing within Regulation 611/2013. However, the Council draft refers to encryption or pseudonymisation as mechanisms that can be employed to render personal data unintelligible. Given that encryption can be considered as one technique of pseudonymisation, the reference to both terms seems to be redundant. Moreover, the Council draft does not employ the term ...has demonstrated to the satisfaction of the competent national authority, thereby implying that the Council prefers an automatic safe harbour (an exemption as opposed to the factor-based analysis under Regulation 611/2013, the Commission draft, and the LIBE draft). However, for this to apply, the encryption or pseudonymisation has to fulfil two conditions that can be derived from the definition of pseudonymous data‘ under Article 4(2a). These are (1) the data cannot be attributed to a specific data subject without the use of additional information, and (2) such additional information is kept separately and subject to technical and organisational measures to ensure non-attribution. However, the reference to encryption specifically might create a misunderstanding that the implementation of such measures can relieve an organization from notifying and overlooks the possibility of breaches affecting the availability of data. Furthermore, one important deviation of the Council draft from the other drafts and Regulation 611/2013 is that the safe harbour also applies to the notification of the regulatory authorities. This implies that when notification to individuals is not required because of technological measures including encryption or pseudonymisation (Article 31(1a)), controllers do not need to notify the DPAs. In addition, the Council draft requires notification to the DPAs only when the breach is likely to affect the rights and freedom of data subjects. This implies that, apart from the safe harbour through encryption or pseudonymisation, if the controller is able to demonstrate to the regulatory authorities that the breach does not affect the rights of the data subjects, it will benefit from a safe harbour. This could be achieved through measures that do not necessarily fall under Article 4(2a). Some scholars argue that the notification of personal data breaches to the DPAs may not be necessary when the rights and freedoms of data subjects are not likely to be affected‘ (Hon et al., 2014). However, the rationale behind the notification to the DPAs goes beyond the protection of rights and freedoms of individuals. On the one hand, such notification enables the authorities to identify patterns of breaches and learn where policy interventions and cooperation might be required. On the other hand, the notification to the authorities enables them to assess whether notification to individuals should take place. This ensures that the assessment of whether the rights of the data subjects are likely to be affected does not solely rest in the hands of the entities. Moreover, such requirement would introduce unjustified discrimination among entities that process personal data in the electronic communications sector that have to notify any breaches to the authorities under Regulation 611/2013 and others that have to notify only data breaches that are likely to severely‘ affect the rights and freedom of data subjects. Thus, the notification to DPAs should not be dependent on the severity‘ of the breach to the rights of data subjects. Overall the approaches for the safe harbour from notifying breaches as a result of the technological measures under the Commission draft and LIBE draft are essentially similar to Regulation 611/2013. However, the Council draft deviates in terms of the following aspects: (1) employs an automatic safe harbour from notifying individuals when personal data is encrypted or pseudonymised, (2) gives safe harbour from notifying the DPAs when personal data is encrypted or pseudonymised, (3) requires notification to the DPAs only where the breach is likely to affect the rights and freedom of data subjects. Quite surprisingly, the eIDAS Regulation does not provide similar safe harbour for notifying breaches to the individuals, as in Regulation 611/2013 and the proposed GDPR. However, this might not necessarily imply that trust providers are not exempted when they have implemented appropriate technological measures. This is because the concept of „adversely affect under Article 19(2) of the Regulation apparently encompasses the exemption of technological measures. As noted above, the main rationale behind such exception is that if certain data was made initially unintelligible, the residual privacy risks of the breach are considered to be negligible (Article 29 Working Party, 2014b, p.1). This implies that the requirement of adverse effect would not be fulfilled and, thus, notification is not required. However, this has to be approved by the competent regulatory authorities. Apart from the data breach notification exemptions, there is a rare case where the European Commission has held, in its Frequently Asked Questions (FAQs), that transfer of key-coded data outside the EU without transferring or revealing the key does not involve transfer of personal data (see in Hon, Millard, and Walden, 2011, p.216). This implies that the use of such measures might exempt controllers from complying with the requirements under Articles 25 and 26 of the Directive. Although, the Commission might have adopted a different stance following the Snowden revelation, such an approach mitigates the application of certain provisions to pseudonymised data. Similarly, Austria's implementation of the Directive recognizes information which is indirectly personal data' if the controller, processor, or recipient cannot identify individuals using legally permissible means (Hon, Millard, and Walden, 2011, p.216). This implies that such data can, for example, be exported without regulatory approval (Hon, Millard, and Walden, 2011, p.216). Furthermore, the ICO (2012, p.12) indicates that the disclosure of anonymised data is subject to fewer legal restrictions. More particularly, if data is anonymised, the Data Protection Act's purpose-limitation rules do not apply to it (ICO, 2012, p.12). This implies that the use of anonymised data for incompatible purposes would not constitute a violation of data privacy rules. Such an approach involves a move from the all or nothing approach' regarding personal data and introduces room for more or less personal' data and accordingly more or less protection' (Robinson et al, 2009, p.26-27). This would encourage the wider use of such techniques.

Other Proposed Safe Harbours

The different drafts for the proposed GDPR contain additional safe harbours from other obligations. One such obligation that could be exempt through the use of pseudonymisation is the prohibition against measures, which are based on profiling by means of automated processing. In this regard, Article 20 of the Commission draft prohibits the use of automatic processing intended to evaluate, analyse, or predict a natural person's performance at work, economic situation, location, health etc. and which can significantly affect this natural person except when carried out in the course of entering or fulfilment of a contract, or when the data subject has given his consent. However, the LIBE draft indicates that profiling based solely on the processing of pseudonymous data should be presumed not to significantly affect the interests, rights, or freedoms of the data subject (Recital 58a). This creates a rebuttable presumption that implies that unless proven otherwise, the controller may use such measures if the data is pseudonymised and does not permit the controller to attribute pseudonymous data to a specific data subject. Furthermore, one of the recommendations of the Committee on the Internal Market and Consumer Protection to the LIBE draft contains an exemption from the obligation to rectify inaccurate or incomplete personal data under Article 16 of the proposed Regulation related to the processing of pseudonymous data.

ANONYMISATION AND PSEUDONYMISATION AS AN INTEGRAL PART OF DATA PRIVACY COMPLIANCE

In this section, the role of anonymisation and pseudonymisation as mandated compliance measures with data privacy rules are examined. More particularly, the role of anonymisation and pseudonymisation as measures to comply with the data security obligation, purpose specification and limitation principle is provided.

Anonymisation and Pseudonymisation for Fulfilling Data Security Obligations

Data security is one of the fundamental principles of data privacy under the EU legal framework. Article 17(1) of the Directive requires the controller to take „appropriate technical and organisational measures to protect personal data against accidental or unlawful destruction or accidental loss, alteration, unauthorised disclosure or access, in particular where the processing involves the transmission of data over a network and against all other unlawful forms of processing. According to Recital 46 of the Directive, the appropriate technical and organizational measures be taken, both at the time of the design of the processing system and at the time of the processing itself.' Article 17(2) of the Directive also requires the controller to choose a processor that has the appropriate technical and organizational measures in place and that ensures its compliance. Furthermore, Article 17(3) the Directive requires data processors to implement appropriate security measures as defined by the law of the Member State in which the processor is established. Similarly, Article 4(1) of the ePrivacy Directive contains provision for protection of personal data stored or transmitted against accidental or unlawful destruction, accidental loss or alteration, and unauthorised or unlawful storage, processing, access or disclosure. Therefore, taking appropriate security measures is an integral part of data privacy compliance. More generally, Article 17(1), in particular, refers to two kinds of data security measures, that is, technical and organization. The Directive does not stipulate which specific technical and organisational measures have to be taken by the controller or processor. In this section, organizational measures are only discussed so far as they are relevant for elaborating the technological measures. Overall, the reference to security includes availability, which includes measures against the accidental or unlawful destruction or loss of data; integrity, which includes measures against alteration of personal data; and „confidentiality', which includes measures against unauthorized disclosure of, or access to, personal data. Technical measures such as anonymisation and pseudonymisation could help to comply with the above obligation, particularly the confidentiality and the integrity aspects. The specific requirements are left to the member states. Studies show that there is a considerable disparity in the security requirements of member states (Hon, Hörnle, & Millard, 2012, p.151). For example, In the UK the requirement is simply to take appropriate technical and organizational measures', whereas Italy has set out in detail what those security measures should be, e.g. for reuse of storage media, access to sensitive passwords, etc.; Denmark requires internet transmissions of personal data to be encrypted, and Austria, as well as defining detailed minimum security measures, requires documentary records of those measures (Hon, Hörnle, & Millard, 2012, p.151). Thus, some member states like Denmark explicitly require the use of encryption. Similarly, the Spanish Royal Decree identifies three levels of security for processing of personal data: basic, medium, and high security levels (Royal Decree, Article 80). Further, in a high-level security environment, which is applicable where sensitive data as defined under Article 8 of the Directive is processed, the transfer of personal data through public or wireless electronic communications networks shall guarantee that the information shall not be intelligible or manipulated by third parties (Royal Decree, Article 104). One way of fulfilling such a requirement is by encrypting communications through such networks. Such a requirement also applies to backup copies. Furthermore, according to Article 93, the data controller has to guarantee the correct identification and authentication of users. When the authentication mechanism is based on the use of passwords, passwords shall be stored in an unintelligible way, for example, in encrypted form. In Italy, the Privacy Code requires the implementation of encryption techniques for specific processing operations with respect to data disclosing health and sex life. The integrity of the backup files should also be ensured, possibly through anonymisation of the data. Referring to the information stored in back-up systems, the Italian Data Protection Authority (2014) specified that it must be protected against unauthorized access by means of suitable encryption techniques or, where necessary, by anonymising the data in question'. In Germany, the obligation for disclosure control aims to ensure that personal data cannot be read, copied, altered, or removed without authorization during electronic transfer or transport or while being recorded onto data storage media (Section 9 and Annex of the Federal Data Protection Act (Bundesdatenschutzgesetz)). This requirement might be fulfilled by encrypting data during transmission or during recording onto data storage media. Moreover, the obligation regarding Data protection by design and by default under the proposed Regulation has similar requirements for the use of technical measures such as anonymisation and pseudonymisation. More particularly, Article 23 of the Council draft stipulates that having regard to available technology, the cost of implementation and risks presented, the controller shall implement technical and organisational measures appropriate to the processing activity being carried on and its objectives, including the use of pseudonymous data, in such a way that the processing will meet the requirements of this Regulation'. Similarly, the Council draft added a specific reference to the use of pseudonymous data into Article 30(1) of the proposed Regulation, which specifies data security obligations for both controllers and processors. This shows that the use of anonymisation and pseudonymisation could constitute an integral part of compliance with data security obligations. However, in the event that the anonymisation or pseudonymisation is reversible, for example, for the purpose of establishing correlations between various data, organisational measures should complement the technical measures, for example, ensuring the confidentiality of the secret key and tracking accesses to such a key.

State of the art and context of the processing

It has to be noted that the mere use of anonymisation and pseudonymisation might not be sufficient for compliance. According to Article 17, the technical and organizational measures should be appropriate. The term appropriate‘ aims at highlighting the impact that different —security related threats and vulnerabilities might have on an organisation‘s data processing‘ (OPTIMIS, 2011, p.28). According to Recital 46, the appropriateness of a security measure should be assessed taking into account the state of the art and the costs of their implementation in relation to the risks inherent in the processing and the nature of the data to be protected. Overall, the Directive requires neither the implementation of the most sophisticated security measures available in the market nor does the use of obsolete security technology meet the requirements of the Directive (OPTIMIS, 2011, p.27). The Directive does not refer to any technology as state of the art‘ and borrows a similar concept from the fields of computer science and information security (OPTIMIS, 2011, p.27). Furthermore, the Directive does not refer to existing standards, thereby enabling more flexibility—both at national and organizational levels—in adopting appropriate measures for compliance with such requirements. However, there are attempts to map existing standards as state of the art‘ technologies. In this regard, Meints (2009) makes a distinction among the different international standards according to their target. Accordingly, international certification standards aiming at best practices‘ are considered as exceeding the state of the art whereas standards aiming at good practice‘ are considered to meet the state of the art requirements. This notwithstanding, member states might have different requirements. For example, where encryption is the appropriate security measure, the French Data Protection Authority (CNIL) recommends the use of state of the art algorithms, such as AES (Advanced Encryption Standard) or triple Data Encryption Standard (Triple-DES) for symmetric encryption and the use of RSA (Rivest, Shamir, and Adelman) or Elliptic Curve Cryptography (ECC) for asymmetric encryption (CNIL, 2010, p.31). In addition, the context or circumstance of the processing should also be taken into account. This involves the type of data under processing (whether it is sensitive personal data or not), and other circumstances like whether they involve a transmission through a public network such as the Internet, and the costs of implementing the measure. This implies that, for examplc, an cncryption technique that might be relevant for protecting certain kind of data may be considered insufficient when employed to secure the integrity of sensitive personal data that involves transmission over, for example, public Wi-Fi. Similarly, whether the encrypted data is stored in another jurisdiction (democratic or non-democratic) also plays a role. This is because most government authorities have sufficient resources to decrypt an encrypted data backed by statutory restrictions on the use of certain encryption methods.

ANONYMISATION AND PSEUDONYMISATION FOR FULFILLING THE PURPOSE SPECIFICATION AND LIMITATION PRINCIPLE

Pursuant to Article 17(1) of the Directive, the technical and organizational measures to be implemented should also protect personal data [...] against all other unlawful forms of processing‘. This aspect attempts to establish compliance with all the principles under the Directive. One such principle, apart from data security, that can be complied with through the use of anonymisation or pseudonymisation is the purpose specification and limitation principle. The purpose specification principle, which is laid down under Article 6(1)(b) of the Directive, sets the boundaries within which personal data may be processed by providing that the controller is only allowed to process the personal data under specific and legitimate purposes and that the data may not be processed further in a manner that is not compatible with those purposes that were originally specified. Hence, it is required to set clear purposes for each processing activity prior to the collection of such data, and not use the collected personal data for other incompatible purposes. Furthermore, Article 6(1) (e) provides that personal data must not be kept in a form that permits identification of data subjects for no longer than is necessary for the purposes for which the data were collected or for which they are further processed.‘ This implies that when the data are no longer necessary for the purposes for which they were originally collected or for which they are further processed, they should be deleted or anonymised. In fact, the Article 29 Working Party underlines that Article 6(1) (e) of the Directive makes a strong point that personal data should be anonymised by default‘ (Article 29 Working Party, 2014a, p.7). Moreover, Article 6(1) of the ePrivacy Directive states that „Traffic data relating to subscribers and users processed and stored by the provider of a public communications network or publicly available electronic communications service must be erased or made anonymous when it is no longer needed for the purpose of the transmission of a communication ... In addition, Article 9(1) of the ePrivacy Directive provides that „where location data other than traffic data, relating to users or subscribers of public communications networks or publicly available electronic communications services, can be processed, such data may only be processed when they are made anonymous, or with the consent of the users or subscribers to the extent and for the duration necessary for the provision of a value added service. Both Articles 6(1) and 9(1) of the ePrivacy Directive require the use of anonymisation. The former is essentially similar to Article 6(1)(e) of the Data Protection Directive in that traffic data must be deleted or made anonymous when such data is no longer necessary for the purpose (i.e. transmission of a communication). On the other hand, the use of anonymisation under Article 9(1) provides a legitimate purpose to process location data. This implies anonymising traffic data provides a legitimate ground for processing such data. For such compliance under Article 6(1)(e) of the Data Protection Directive and Articles 6(1) and 9(1) of the ePrivacy Directive to be achieved, the data should be anonymised in such a way that the data subject is no longer identifiable. As elaborated above, the anonymisation should be used so as to irreversibly prevent identification (Article 29 Working Party, 2014, p.7). In other words, pseudonymisation of data that would enable the re-identification of the person would not be sufficient.

Therefore, deleting the data is a more privacy-friendly solution and preferable, although this may entail a trade-off with the utility of the data (ENISA, 2012, p.44). In this regard, some member states explicitly require the legitimate duration of certain kinds of processing. For example, the French DPA (CNIL) issued a simplified notification norm, which defines the kind of data that can be processed by the employer and the maximum duration of storage, which in general is two months (ENISA, 2012, p.47). This implies that employers have to anonymise or delete the data after the expiration of two months. Similarly, the Italian Data Protection Authority (2012) indicates that data subjects have the right to object, in whole or in part, on legitimate grounds, to the processing of personal data concerning him/her, even though they are relevant to the purpose of the collection. More particularly, in case of a breach of the law, data subjects may have their data blocked, erased, or anonymised. This implies that in Italy, anonymisation could be mandated subsequent to a breach of the data privacy rules. The different drafts for the proposed GDPR contain additional provisions on the role of pseudonymisation as an integral part of compliance with the legitimate purpose' principle. Article 6(2) of the Commission draft permits the processing of personal data, which is necessary for the purposes of historical, statistical, or scientific research subject to the conditions and safeguards referred to in Article 83. Accordingly, Article 83(1) allows such processing only if (a) these purposes cannot be otherwise fulfilled by processing data which does not permit or not any longer permit the identification of the data subject; (b) data enabling the attribution of information to an identified or identifiable data subject is kept separately from other information, as long as these purposes can be fulfilled in this manner. Although Article 83 requires the fulfilment of both conditions in paragraphs a' and b', the latter, in particular, is a reference to the use of pseudonymised data and securely managing the key for such data. There are also some suggestions to enable bodies conducting historical, statistical, or scientific research to publish or otherwise publicly disclose personal data if the personal data is processed for the purpose of generating aggregate data reports, wholly composed of anonymous data, pseudonymous data, or both. Furthermore, the recommendation from the Committee on the Internal Market and Consumer Protection to the LIBE draft proposed the inclusion of a legitimate ground for processing under Article 6 if only pseudonymous data is processed. This implies that processing pseudonymous data as defined in Article 4(2(a)) of the LIBE draft Regulation serves as a legitimate basis for processing personal data.

CONCLUSION

To date, discussions on anonymisation and pseudonymisation have been more focused on the technical aspects of these measures and the associated risks of re-identification. When legal perspectives are attached, they are only limited to whether a certain technique meets the conditions for providing the safe harbour from the entire application of data privacy rules without going to other roles of such measures—a reference to all or nothing'. This article takes the next step and provides an in-depth analysis of the role of anonymisation and pseudonymisation (including encryption) under the current and en route European Data Privacy rules—a reference to the beyond the all or nothing approach'. To this end, the article identifies three major roles of anonymisation and pseudonymisation. First, anonymisation and pseudonymisation can serve as a safe harbour from the application of data privacy rules entirely, provided they are used to irreversibly prevent identification. Second, they can provide a safe harbour from certain data privacy obligations such as the notification of personal data breaches provided they are engineered appropriately and complemented by adequate organizational measures. Third, they can constitute mandated requirements for compliance with data privacy obligations such as the data security and purpose specification and limitation principles. This notwithstanding, it is worth noting that the above three roles are interrelated. This implies that if a data controller is compliant with the data security requirements under data privacy rules and implements all the appropriate measures in advance, it is likely that it will benefit from safe harbour for notifying breaches under the same rules. Similarly, implementation of the appropriate technological protection and organisational measures is relevant in ascertaining whether a personal data breach has taken place and thereby comply with the notification requirements. Furthermore, an anonymisation that aims at compliance with data privacy rules— for example, with the purpose limitation principle—leads to providing the safe harbour from compliance with the rules in entirety so far as it is implemented in a manner that prevents reverse identification.

REFERENCES

1. Article 29 Working Party (2014a), Opinion 05/2014 on Anonymisation Techniques, WP216.
2. Article 29 Working Party (2014b), Opinion 03/2014 on Personal Data Breach Notification, WP213.
3. Article 29 Working Party (2007), Opinion 4/2007 on the Concept of Personal Data, WP136.
4. Barcelo, R, & Traung, P (2010), The Emerging European Union Security Breach Legal Framework: The 2002/58 ePrivacy Directive and Beyond. In S. Gutwirth et al. (eds.), Data Protection in a Profiled World (Springer), pp. 77–104.
5. Burdon, M, Reid, J.F, and Low, R (2010), Encryption safe harbours and data breach notification laws‘, Computer Law and Security Review 26(5).
6. Bygrave, L (2002), Data Protection Law: Approaching Its Rationale, Logic and Limit (The Hague: Kluwer Law International)
7. Cavoukian, A (2013), Looking Forward: De-identification Developments—New Tools, New
8. Challenges (Canada Information & Privacy Commissioner, May 2013)
9. CNIL (2010), Guide: Security of Personal Data, available (link), accessed 28 September 2014
10. Commission, Proposal for a Regulation of the European Parliament and of the Council on the Protection of Individuals with regard to the Processing of Personal Data and on the Free Movement of Such Data (Draft General Data Protection Regulation)‘ Com (2012) 11 final Commission draft)

11. Commission Regulation (EC) 611/2013 of 24 June 2013 on the Measures Applicable to the Notification of Personal Data Breaches under Directive 2002/58/EC of the European Parliament and of the Council on Privacy and Electronic Communications OJ L173/2

12. Council Directive 95/46/EC of 23 November 1995 on the Protection of Individuals with regard to Processing of Personal Data and the Free Movement of such Data OJ L281/31 (Data Protection Directive).

13. Committee on Civil Liberties, Justice and Home Affairs, European Parliament, Report on the proposal for a regulation of the European Parliament and of the Council on the protection of individuals with regard to the processing of personal data and on the free movement of such data' (2013) (COM(2012)0011 – C7-0025/2012 – 2012/0011(COD)) (link) (LIBE draft).

14. Council of the European Union, document 17831/13 on proposal for a regulation of the European Parliament and of the Council on the protection of individuals with regard to the processing of personal data and on the free movement of such data (2013) (link) (Council draft).

15. Costa, L and Poullet, Y (2012), Privacy and the regulation of 2012', Computer Law and Security Review (28) 254-262.

16. Directive 2009/136/EC of the European Parliament and of the Council of 25 November 2009 amending Directive 2002/22/EC on universal service and users' rights relating to electronic communications networks and services, Directive 2002/58/EC concerning the processing of personal data and the protection of privacy in the electronic communications sector, and Regulation (EC) No 2006/2004 on cooperation between national authorities responsible for the enforcement of consumer protection laws [2009] OJ L 337/11.

17. Directive 2002/58/EC of the European Parliament and of the Council of 12 July 2002 concerning the processing of personal data and the protection of privacy in the electronic communications sector OJ201/37 (ePrivacy Directive).

18. ENISA (2012), Study on data collection and storage in the EU (Deliverable: 2012-02-08).

19. Emam, K.E., and Alvarez, C (2014), A Critical Appraisal of the Article 29 Working Party Opinion 05/2014 on Data Anonymisation Techniques, Draft paper for a web conference.

20. Eur. Consumer Org., E-Privacy Directive: Personal Data Breach Notification (2011), available at http://www.beuc.org/publications/2011-09742-01-e.pdf

21. European Union Agency for Fundamental Rights (2013), Handbook on European data protection law (Belgium: Council of Europe) German Federal Data Protection Act (Bundesdatenschutzgesetz).

22. Hon, W.K., Kosta, E., Millard, C., and Stefanatou, D (2014), Cloud Accountability: The Likely Impact of the Proposed EU Data Protection Regulation, Tilburg Law School Legal Studies Research Paper Series No. 07/2014

23. Hon, W.K., Millard, K., and Walden, I (2011), The Problem of —Personal Data in

Cloud Computing—What Information is Regulated? The Cloud of Unknowing‘, International Data Privacy Law 1(4).

24. Hon W. Kuan, Hörnle, J., & Millard, K (2012), Data protection jurisdiction and cloud computing – when are cloud users and providers subject to EU data protection law? The cloud of unknowing‘, International Review of Law, Computers & Technology 26(2-3).
25. House Of Lords, Opinions of the Lords of Appeal for Judgment in the Cause Common Services Agency (Appellants) v Scottish Information Commissioner (Respondent) (Scotland), SESSION 2007–08 [2008] UKHL 47 on appeal from: [2006] SCOTCS CSIH 58
26. ICO (2012), Anonymisation: Managing data protection risk code of practice.
27. Italian Data Protection Authority (2014), Decision Setting forth Measures Google Inc. Is Required to Take to Bring the Processing of Personal Data under Google’s New Privacy Policy into Line with the Italian Data Protection Code, (link)
28. Italian Data Protection Authority (2012), Cloud Computing: How to Protect Your Data Without Falling From A Cloud, (link).
29. Kuner, C (1996), Legal aspects of encryption on the internet‘, International Business Lawyer 24.
30. Meints, M (2009), The Relationship between Data Protection Legislation and Information Security Related Standards‘ In Matyáš, V et al. (ed) The Future of Identity, IFIP AICT 298, IFIP International Federation for Information Processing.
31. Ohm, P (2009), Broken promises of privacy: Responding to the surprising failure of anonymisation‘, UCLA Review 57
32. OPTIMIS Project D7.2.1.2. (2011), Cloud Legal Guidelines: Data Security, Ownership Rights and Domestic Green Legislation (Part II).
33. Oswald, M (2014), Share And Share Alike? An Examination of Trust, Anonymisation and Data Sharing with Particular Reference to an Exploratory Research Project Investigating Attitudes to Sharing Personal Data with the Public Sector‘, SCERIPTed 11(3).
34. Perkins, A (2005), Encryption Use: Law and Anarchy on the Digital Frontier [comments]‘, Houston Law Review 41(5)
35. Ponemon Institute (2009), US Enterprise Encryption Trends Regulation (EU) No 910/2014 of the European Parliament and of the Council of 23 July 2014 on electronic identification and trust services for electronic transactions in the internal market and repealing Directive 1999/93/EC OJ L 257/73.
36. Robinson, N., Graux, H., Botterman, M and Valeri, L (2009), Review of the European Data Protection Directive, RAND Europe Technical Report, (link) accessed 28 August 2014.
37. Royal Decree (REAL DECRETO 1720/2007, de 21 de diciembre, por el que se aprueba el

38. Reglamento de desarrollo de la Ley Orgánica 15/1999, de 13 de diciembre, de protección de datos de carácter personal

39. Wayne, J, and Grance, T (2011), Guidelines on Security and Privacy in Public Cloud Computing (NIST publications)

12
CHAPTER

CYBER WARFARE

Yohannes Eneyew Ayalew

Keywords: Cyber Warfare, Hackers, Civilians, Combatants, Soft Law, International Humanitarian Law

INTRODUCTION

To begin with, the concept of cyber warfare is a new phenomenon under International Humanitarian law (here in after "IHL"). Since the era of science and technology, the means and methods of warfare become more sophisticated and very much complex one interalia, the issue of cyber warfare is one of the current debatable issues as far as IHL is concerned. The information revolution has fundamentally changed the way that wars are fought in the 21st C. Needless to say from actors' point of view, the strategies that parties adopted as well as the spread of technology in to all aspects of warfare is pervasive. By similar fashion, technology now controls our daily lives to an unprecedented level from electricity generation, water supplies, communications and almost every aspect of our globalized world, making it increasingly vulnerable to computer attacks and other cyber operations during armed conflicts. From conceptual point of view, cyber warfare is Internet-based attack involving politically motivated missions on information and information systems. Cyber warfare attacks can disable official websites and networks, disrupt or disable essential services, steal or alter classified data and cripple financial systems…among many other possibilities. On top of that, cyber warfare and its effect began to draw the attention of the international legal community among other things law schools in the late 1990s. Most significantly, in 1999 the United States Naval War College convened the first major legal conference

Citation: Yohannes Eneyew Ayalew, Cyber Warfare, http://dx.doi.org/10.4236/blr.2015.64021.

on the subject. In the aftermath of the attacks of 11th of September, 2001, terrorism and the ensuing armed conflicts diverted the attention of the world community from the topic until the massive cyber operations by "hackers" against Estonia in 2007 and against Georgia during its war with the Russian Federation in 2008, as well as cyber incidents like the targeting of the Iranian nuclear facilities with the Stuxnet worm in 2010. Needless to mention, one of the challenges States face in the cyber environment is that the scope and manner of international law's applicability to cyber operations, whether in offence or defense, have remained unsettled since their advent. After all, at the time the current international legal norms (whether customary or treaty-based) emerged, cyber technology was not on the horizon. Consequently, there is a risk that cyber practice may quickly outdistance agreed understandings as to its governing legal regime. The threshold questions are whether the existing law applies to cyber issues at all, and, if so, then how it could be? Views on the area range from a full application of the law of armed conflict as inferred from the International Court of Justice's 8 pronouncement that it applies to "any use of force, regardless of the weapons employed", to strict application of the Permanent Court of International Justice's pronouncement that acts not forbidden in international law are generally permitted. Of course, the fact that States lack definitive guidance on the subject does not relieve them of their obligation to comply with applicable international law in their cyber operations. Surprisingly, almost all IHL treaties are known by their bad connotation called "one war behind reality" thus, due to that reason there were plenty of sufferings and superfluous injuries occurred in history of mankind. In other words, in the past 150 years all most all IHL treaties were not stipulated in advance before those historically known wars had brought the unforgettable and immeasurable sufferings. Albeit; treaties were so far enacted after the drama of a certain warfare. For instance, The 1929 Convention on the treatment of prisoners of war (POW Convention) was the result First World War (WWI) incident meaning that the POW Convention was enacted after mass killings of prisoners. Surprisingly even the Four Geneva Conventions of 1949 were enacted after the scourges of Second World War (WWII)

On top of that, now a day there is no binding legal framework under international law to govern and deal with cyber warfare. The only authoritative document that may question the above assertion if to be cited is Protocols Additional to The Geneva Conventions relating to the Protection of Victims of International Armed Conflicts (Protocol I) here in after "AP I" have even in this document, one can find only one provision which is phrased with terms of vagueness and more general articulations as it is stated. As a result of this gap, the international community so far witnessed plethora of cyber incidents that could be cited as good indicators of how the issue is becoming a serious concern of the world community coupled with lenient and unregulated law on cyber warfare that is why then this paper intends to critically analyze the impact of this newly emerging threat to the world peace in the absence of organized legal framework under international law even to punish the alleged perpetrators of cyber warfare. Finally, the researcher believes that the international community should attentively follow the impact of cyber warfare on IHL, and tried to delve in to various cross-cutting issues with regard to cyber warfare and pinpoints the nexus between cyber warfare and IHL.

THE NOTION OF CYBER WARFARE

As far as the notion of cyber warfare is concerned, it is worthy to reiterate the remarks of ICRC (International Committee of Red Cross) as a base to define cyber warfare. Richard Clarke, former special advisor to National Security Council on cyber security issues and author of the book Cyber War, describes cyber warfare as "actions by a nation-state to penetrate another nation's computers or networks for the purposes of causing damage or disruption." Cyber warfare refers to politically motivated hacking to conduct sabotage and espionage. As one can infer from the above suggested definitions, there is no agreed definition on the term cyber warfare albeit, various literatures opted to define it differently either directly or indirectly via cyber-attack. Similarly such understandings is reaffirmed in The Tallinn Manual. For instance countries have their own standings towards cyber warfare, The United Kingdom outlined four different methods of cyber-attack in its national cyber strategy. On the other hand, The United States also defines Computer Network Attack (CNA) as "actions taken through the use of computer networks to disrupt, deny, degrade, or destroy information resident in computers and computer networks, or the computers and networks themselves". One can make rehearsal of the following recent historical events as indicators that the world is already on the verge of witnessing this kind of warfare; These examples of cyber-attacks show the legitimate threats that can emanate from this new domain. As the critical infrastructure of nations continually becomes more reliant on networks and cyberspace, the possible targets for cyber-attacks greatly increases. The researcher also observes other forms of cyber incidents yet the above are critical and officially acknowledged. The irony is that those nations like the United States and its NATO Allies that have the capacity to excel in cyber war as an adjunct to military operations and can achieve information dominance over the Battle field are also those most vulnerable to unrestricted cyber wars. There are, however, measures that can be taken to reduce these vulnerabilities. Cyber warfare is not fundamentally different from conventional, physical warfare. When conducted by a nation state, it is integrated into a defined strategy and doctrine, becomes part of military planning and is implemented within specific parameters. Consequently, it is subject to analysis and warning in much the same way as other military operations. Indeed, there are several ways of reducing vulnerability to cyber war. These include anticipation and assessment, preventive or deterrent measures, defensive measures and measures for damage mitigation and reconstitution. Therefore the most sensitive point here is, Cyber warfare took the international spotlight as increasingly more attacks are conducted by countries against one another, whereas there exists no set of international laws of war regulating this new warfare species. Countries are perplexed by the string of questions as to whether this kind of warfare is indeed to be regulated with the established law of armed conflict and, if so, to what extent can these rules—established back in times of considerable old—accommodate this very modern war. These questions remain paramount on the bucket list of the General Assembly. In the handful of times it addressed the aspects of cyber warfare, not once has the General Assembly spoken in unanimity on how to handle cyber warfare via concerted effort and, most especially, united rules of international law. It is hoped that in this 2015 session the Assembly will be able to sufficiently address these persistent challenges and decide on what is best, as well as what is first, to be solved in the context of cyber warfare.

THE NEXUS BETWEEN CYBER WARFARE AND INTERNATIONAL HUMANITARIAN LAW (IHL)

To begin with, the nexus between international humanitarian law and cyber warfare now a day is interwoven and interconnected. As we know, International Humanitarian Law (IHL) deals the rules that militaries must follow when participating in a war. These laws of war describe what actions may or may not be taken against non-combatants, soldiers, and unlawful combatants. A key point of IHL is that civilians and non-combatants may not be killed or treated inhumanely during times of war The International Humanitarian law has banned the use of many weapons, which includes ex-ploding bullets, chemical and biological weapons, blinding laser weapons and anti-personnel mines. The International Criminal Court (ICC), with the objective of repressing inter alia war crimes, was created by the 1998 Rome Statute to try cases relating to IHL. The ongoing 21st century is the Era where several new military warfare concepts have emerged. The concept of Cyber warfare is one of them. Where computer networks are used for cyber-attacks instead of conventional weapons; and satellites are used for providing images far more detailed than human spies and reconnaissance units have ever offered. However, as Cyber technology is the new phenomena in the 21st century, IHL faces the new challenge of addressing ethical standards for war in cyber space. Though the obvious wars on land, sea, and air may be claimed as issues covered by the existing rules and customs of warfare, cyberspace is undefined. While cyberspace itself is non-physical, it is a critical infrastructure that can greatly affect the physical world. Logic bombs and computer viruses can disrupt everything from electric grids and the stock market to nuclear power plants and water treatment facilities. Besides, As far as the nexus between IHL and Cyber warfare is concerned, it is worthy to reiterate the central themes of humanitarian laws; Interalia. Jus in bello, conjointly called the law of war, the law of armed conflict (LoAC) or international humanitarian law (IHL) is the section of law of nations handling the protection of persons who are not any longer collaborating within the hostilities which restricts the means and strategies of warfare. It includes written agreement law and customary law, because the latter has been crystallized through- out history. Treaty law consists primarily of two sets of IHL legal package: that is Hague Conventions and Geneva Conventions. The first one, Hague Conventions deals with sensible military aspects of the conduct of hostilities, consisting of city rules of 1899 and 1907, plus numerous other conventions and agreements prohibiting the employment of sure weapons and military tactics. The second one, Geneva Conventions concentrates on the protection of civilians, prisoners of war, wounded and sick toward land and sea, comprising of the four 1949 Geneva Conventions. Further Protocol III was added in 2005 regarding the Adoption of a further Distinctive Emblem. International law is a body of rules and regulations governing the relation between various states and International Humanitarian law is just a part of it, which applies to armed conflict. It covers two areas:

- The protection of those who are not a part or not a party to conflict.
- Restrictions on the means of warfare—in particular weapons and the methods of warfare, like military tactics. International Humanitarian Law protects those who are not taking part in the fighting, like civilians and medical and religious

military personnel. International Humanitarian Law prohibits all means and methods of warfare which fails to discriminate between those taking part in the fighting and those, such as civilians, the purpose being protecting the civilian population, individual civilians and civilian property;

- Cause injury which results into unnecessary sufferings and;
- Cause severe and permanent damage to the environment.

Cyber warfare has been explained as any hostile measure taken against an enemy designed "to discover, destroy, disrupt, alter, destroy, disrupt or transfer data kept in a computer, which is manipulated through a computer or transmitted through a computer network". Simply it is an attack based on networks which is adopted by many countries to reduce their frustration and also to avoid the real war situation. Chinese attack on US, Chinese attack on Google, attack by Ghost net spyware network upon confidential information of more than 100 countries are the examples which introduces the concepts of cyber warfare. Facebook has taught us that some-one is always watching our activities, but it is always acceptable when it is not a big boss. Contemporary armed conflicts are to be controlled by a body of law by which came in to existence as binding and relatively comprehensive document in the second half of the 20th century and which have not yet become adaptable to contemporary legal as well as practical challenges introduced by new technologies of warfare interalia cyber warfare. Some scholars like Cordula Droege, a legal expert of International committee of Red Cross (ICRC), explain that the existing legal framework is applicable and must be respected even in the cyber realm. The researcher on the other hand argues it is very difficult to apply the existing IHL legal regime to cyber realm because the technicality of the subject matter results in non-compliance. The following is an overview of weapons that are regulated by IHL treaties.

Weapon	Treaty
Explosive projectiles weighing less than 400 grams	Declaration of Saint Petersburg (1868)
Bullets that expand or flatten in the human body	Hague Declaration (1899)
Poison and poisoned weapons	Hague Regulations (1907)
Chemical weapons	Geneva Protocol (1925)
	Convention on the Prohibition of Chemical Weapons (1993)
Biological weapons	Geneva Protocol (1925)
	Convention on the Prohibition of Biological Weapons (1972)
Weapons that injure by fragments which, in the human body, escape detection by X-rays	Protocol I (1980) to the Convention on Certain Conventional Weapons
Incendiary weapons	Protocol III (1980) to the Convention on Certain Conventional Weapons
Blinding laser weapons	Protocol IV (1995) to the Convention on Certain Conventional Weapons
Mines, booby traps and "other devices"	Protocol II, as amended (1996), to the Convention on Certain Conventional Weapons
Anti-personnel mines	Convention on the Prohibstion of Anti-Personnel Mines (Ottawa Treaty) (1997)
Explosive remnants of war	Protocol V (2003) to the Convention on Certain Conventional Weapons
Cluster munitions	Convention on Cluster Munitions (2008)

Even though IHL doesn't specifically mention cyber warfare, the Martens clause, that is associated with accepted principle of IHL, says that whenever a state of affairs isn't coated by a global agreement, "civilians and combatants stay below the protection and authority of the principles of jurisprudence derived from established custom, from the principles of humanity, and from the dictates of public conscience". In fact, it is the role of ICRC to look into the valid developments that need to be incorporated in IHL. Generally speaking, it shall be taken for granted that new scenarios of warfare are not far-flung from IHL regulation. However it also regulates, through its general rules, the legitimacy of all means and strategies of warfare, as well as the employment of all weapons. specifically, Article 36 of I protocol to the Geneva Conventions provides that, "in the study, development, acquisition or adoption of a brand new weapon, means that or methodology of warfare, a High contracting Party is below associate obligation to see whether or not its employment would, in some or all circumstances, be prohibited by this Protocol or by the other rule of jurisprudence applicable to the High Contracting Party." On the far side the precise obligation it imposes on States parties, this rule shows that general IHL rules apply to new technology. Unless IHL addresses specific guidelines for warring nations to follow in cyberspace, civilians and non-combatants could be seriously endangered in the event of cyber-war. However, there are still arguments' inclining to the position that IHL provisions do not specifically mention cyber operations. Because of this, and because the exploitation of cyber technology is relatively new and sometimes appears to introduce a complete qualitative change in the means and methods of warfare, it has occasionally been argued that IHL is ill adapted to the cyber realm and cannot be applied to cyber warfare. But one has to note that, the absence in IHL of specific references to cyber operations does not mean that such operations are not subject to the rules of IHL. New technologies of all kinds are being developed all the time and IHL is sufficiently broad to accommodate these developments.

IHL prohibits or limits the use of certain weapons specifically (for instance, chemical or biological weapons, or anti-personnel mines). Beyond the specific obligation it imposes on states party to Additional Protocol I, this rule shows that IHL rules apply to new technology. Now the researcher raises the issue that should International Humanitarian Law in black and white applies to Cyber warfare or not? At this juncture it is worthy to reiterate the notion that IHL is only applicable if cyber operations are conducted in the context of and related to an armed conflict. Thus, there is a fast and hard rule that when cyber operations are conducted in the context of an ongoing armed conflict they are governed by the same IHL rules as that conflict: for instance, if in parallel or in addition to a bomb, Airplane or missile attack, a party to the conflict also launches a cyber-attack on the computer systems of its adversary. However, a number of operations referred to as cyber warfare may not be carried out in the context of armed conflicts at all. Terms like "cyber attacks" or "cyber terrorism" may evoke methods of warfare, but the operations they refer to are not necessarily conducted in an armed conflict. Cyber operations can be and are in fact used in crimes committed in everyday situations that have nothing to do with war. In a nut shell, the researcher argues IHL will apply to cyber operations that are conducted within the framework of an ongoing international or non-international armed conflict in addition to kinetic operations.

THE LEGAL FRAMEWORK

The Conduct of Cyber Attacks

As we know the customary international law of IHL does not prohibit any civilian from participating in an armed conflict, whether international or non-international.

It should be noted that Additional Protocol I39 provides that "members of the armed forces of a Party to a conflict (other than medical personnel and chaplains covered by Article 33 of Geneva Convention III) are combatants, that is to say they have the right to participate directly in hostilities". This provision, applicable in international armed conflict, confirms that combatants enjoy immunity in respect of the acts undertaken a part of the hostilities. It does not prohibit others from engaging in those hostilities. Besides, the Tallinn Manual with regard of the conduct of hostilities stipulates "the law of armed conflict does not bar any category of person from participating in cyber operations. However, the legal consequences of participation differ based on the nature of the armed conflict and the category to which an individual belongs". Needless to mention, the generally accepted understanding of combatant derives from the Hague Regulations. Geneva Convention III adopts this standard in Article 4A with regard to the entitlement to prisoner of war status. Although Article 4A (1), (2), (3), and (6) is textually applicable only to such status, it is universally understood as reflecting the customary international law criteria for being combatant. The notion of combatant is limited to international armed conflict; there is no non-international armed conflict equivalent of either prisoner of war status or combatant immunity rather those who have participated in non-international armed conflict will face criminal prosecution. On top of that the soft-law or Tallinn Manual provides vividly in an international armed conflict, members of the armed forces of a Party to the conflict who, in the course of cyber operations, fail to comply with the requirements of combatant status lose their entitlement to combatant immunity and prisoner of war status. Moreover, Combatants are entitled to treatment as prisoners of war in accordance with Geneva Convention III upon capture. They are also entitled to combatant immunity, that is, they may not be prosecuted for having engaged in belligerent acts that are lawful under the law of armed conflict. For instance, a combatant who conducts cyber operations that violate domestic criminal law may not be prosecuted for such actions so long as they are carried out in compliance with the law of armed conflict. Combatant immunity is a customary international law principle recognized in Article 43(2) of Additional Protocol I.

The Impact against Civilians The term civilian under international humanitarian law is not defined in a very comprehensive way. Albeit, Additional Protocol I 46 defines civilians in negative terms as being all persons who are neither members of the armed forces nor of a Leve'e en masse47. This approach is implicit in Geneva Conventions III and IV. As a general rule, then, during an international armed conflict, civilians are persons who are not members of the armed forces or of groups assimilated to the armed forces. The majority of the International Group of Experts agreed that civilians retain civilian status even if they directly participate in cyber hostilities. Meaning they are civilians irrespective of their participation For instance, consider an international armed conflict in which civilian patriotic hackers independently undertake offensive cyber operations against the enemy's forces. Such individuals may be lawfully targeted, and, unless they qualify as participants in a levée en masse, lack combatant immunity for their actions. The right of non-combatant inter alia civilians is not absolute right since they owe a duty of refraining from participation in warfare generally and cyber warfare particularly. According to Karma Nabulsi, The right of the non-combatant population to protection…involves…a corresponding duty of abstaining from…hostilities. The researcher observes the impact of cyber warfare on civilians from two dimensions. First, from protection point of view they should deserve protection from being targets of attacks since the international legal framework in force obliges to do so. For instance, the civilian population and individual civilians shall enjoy general protection against dangers arising from military operations. By the same vein, civilian objects should be protected from attacks. Albeit, Computers, computer networks, and cyber infrastructure may be made the object of attack if they are military objectives. The possible impacts include among other things are humiliating industries, infrastructures, telecommunications, transportation services and financial systems. For example manipulating civilian air traffic control systems. Thus, the researcher opined that the above civilian facilities should be protected from cyber-attacks. Second, from Participation point of view civilians have no right to participate in the conduct of hostilities yet if they take part on warfare they loss the protection of the law. In Toto, Civilian hackers remain civilians unless they meet the definition of combatants under the law. In the case of states who have signed Additional Protocol I would mean all members of the armed forces and any groups and units etc as defined under the protocol. For those states who are not party to API the older rules set out in the Geneva conventions apply. All other civilian hackers remain civilians—however they lose their protection as civilians for such time as they directly participate in hostilities.

THE IMPACT AGAINST COMBATANTS

With no doubt Additional Protocol I55 provide that "members of the armed forces of a Party to a conflict (other than medical personnel and chaplains covered by Article 33 of Geneva Convention III) are combatants, so that they maintain the right to participate directly in hostilities". The Tallinn Manual Commentary reviewed the issue dictating that, although the law of armed conflict contains no prohibition on participation, it does set forth consequences that result from such participation. Three are of particular importance: combatant immunity, prisoner of war status, and targetability. Entitlement to combatant immunity and prisoner of war status depend on whether the individual concerned is a combatant in an international armed conflict.

By the same token, members of the armed forces of a Party to the conflict who, in the course of cyber warfare, fail to comply with the requirements of combatant status lose their entitlement to combatant immunity and prisoner of war status. In other words, if a person engaged in cyber operations during an armed conflict is a member of an organized armed group not belonging to a Party to the conflict, it does not matter if the group and its members comply with the four criteria of combatancy. That person will not have combatant status and therefore not be entitled to combatant immunity or to be treated as a prisoner of war. Such a person would be an unprivileged belligerent. According to Dr. Harrison, the term combatant has been used to describe both those persons with a right to take direct part in hostilities but also to describe any person who actually engages in hostile acts in an armed conflict on behalf of a party to conflict, whether or not they are permitted to do so. Thus, in international armed conflicts, combatants may be further distinguished in two viz, members of regular armed forces and any other persons actively participated in hostilities57. On the other hand, the researcher argues that the term combatant should be destined to those regular members of armed force otherwise we defeat the very purpose of being combatant.

Still more Unlike civilians, combatants are entitled to directly participate in hostilities and are subsequently immuned from prosecution for acts which are carried out as per the laws of armed conflicts, Given the increasing extent of international and domestic laws prohibiting and criminalizing various forms of computer misuse and network intrusion, the combatant shield is perhaps the most important consequence of being a lawful combatant for cyber operations where combatants are unlikely to face capture and subsequent detention. As mentioned somewhere in this paper, Right now, there is no comprehensive international treaty exists specific to regulate cyber-attacks. Plethora international legal frameworks are not directly aimed at cyber-attacks but however regulate means that may be used in or may be a focus of a cyber-attack. These include particularly, the international law governing telecommunications, aviation, space, and the law of sea.

By similar fashion, these legal regimes were largely formed prior to if not at the infant stage of the emergence of cyber-attacks and therefore and are not comprehensive enough to regulate or prohibit cyber-attacks. Instead, these "means-based" frameworks implicate cyber-attacks only so long as an attack employs the particular means regulated by the agreement. Thus, the jurisprudence on cyber security has suggested that these bodies of international law can be used to regulate cyber-attacks. However, internationally assessing the legality of new weapons is in the interest of all States, as it will help them ensure that their armed forces act in accordance with their international obligations.

In other words, whenever a state study to use, acquire or adopt new weapon, means and methods including cyber such employment in some or all situations is prohibited by this protocol or international law.

In particular, States party to Additional Protocol I must consider the rules under that treaty, as required by Article 36 whenever cyber operation is conducted. These include:

- Prohibition to employ weapons, projectiles and material and methods of warfare of a nature to cause superfluous injury or unnecessary suffering61.
- Prohibition to employ methods or means of warfare which are intended, or may be expected to cause widespread, long-term and severe damage to the natural environment62.
- Prohibition to employ a method or means of warfare which cannot be directed at a specific military objective and consequently, that is of a nature to strike military objectives and civilians or civilian objects without distinction63.
- Prohibition to employ a method or means of warfare the effects of which cannot be limited as required by

Additional Protocol I and consequently, that is of a nature to strike military objectives and civilians or civilian objects without distinction64.

Prohibition of attacks by bombardment by any methods or means which treats as a single military objective a number of clearly separated and distinct military objectives located in a city, town, village or other area containing a similar concentration of civilians or civilian objects.

Prohibition of attacks which may be expected to cause incidental loss of civilian life, injury to civilians, damage to civilian objects, or a combination there of, which would be excessive in relation to the concrete and direct military advantage anticipated. Is Cyber considered as a weapon? Yes indeed! The researcher glanced at the definition of the term weapon by taking three countries experience.

Now after saying that cyber as weapon as well as means and method of warfare, the question is that weather cyber is prohibited under international humanitarian law? The researcher argues cyber is not unlawful. Albeit, A weapon that can be used with due care is going to be used abusively against civilians. In such a case, it is not the cyber per se as a weapon rather as a method or the way in which it is used is prohibited.

However, Cyber operations are not explicitly referred to in existing law of armed conflict treaties. Albeit, in the Nuclear Weapons Advisory Opinion, the International Court of Justice affirmed that "the established principles and rules of humanitarian law…apply to all forms of warfare, and to all kinds of weapons, those of the past, those of the present and those of the future." Finally, the researcher opined that Article 36 of API is backed by ICJ advisory opinion mentioned above on Nuclear Weapons case so that cyber warfare is subject to IHL regulation.

Customary International Law

To begin with, under international law, custom comprises two elements. These are state practice and opinion juris sive necessitates. The first element should be backed by actual practice of states via duration, uniformity and generality. Meanwhile, the second element that is the opinion juris, belief that a state activity is legally obligatory, is the factor which turns the usage into a custom and renders it part of the rules of international law. To put it slightly differently, states will behave a certain way because they are convinced it is binding upon them to do so. Still more, the increasing use of computers and computer networks through the 1970s and 1980s was followed swiftly by the rise of the "network of networks" known as the Internet in the mid-1990s. Ultimately, the Internet spawned an entirely new domain of operations referred to as cyberspace. It is in and through this virtual space that cyber activities occur. So, not only are the activities in cyber new, where cyber actions take place is a unique location. As noted above, customary law does not instantly appear but is developed through state practice and rationale. The cyber practices of states and the thought behind those actions over the past 30 years must be examined to determine if there is customary law in cyberspace. If no principles have been developed, as earlier discussed, cyberspace remains unconstrained under the default customary international regime.

Taking the above explanation in to account, custom as a source of international law is vividly stipulated under the ICJ statute. Thus, the same is true for international humanitarian law in general and Cyber warfare in particular. Despite the law of armed conflict does not expressly regulate cyber activities, regard should be had to the Martens Clause, found in Hague Convention IV, the 1949 Geneva Conventions, and Additional

Protocol I. The text in Hague Convention IV provides that: "Until a more complete code of the laws of war has been issued, the High Contracting Parties deem it expedient to declare that, in Cases not included in the Regulations adopted by them, the inhabitants and the belligerents remain under the protection and the rule of the principles of the law of nations, as they result from the usages established among civilized peoples, from the laws of humanity, and the dictates of the public Conscience." Thus, as far as cyber operations are conducted in the course of an armed conflict is concerned, the Martens Clause, which reflects customary international law, should come in to picture to address the scenarios. At this juncture, the issue worth considering is that cyber warfare is a new phenomenon in the contemporary world due to the advancement of technology. So, instant-customary international law should govern the situations regarding cyber warfare.

General Principles of International Law

The other issue worth considering is that general principles of law, General principles of IHL help to guide belligerents during an armed-conflict, the following are the most dominant principles under IHL;

1) Military Necessity: It is permissible to use those measures not forbidden by international law which are necessary to secure the complete submission of the enemy. In other words, all measures necessary to bring an enemy to complete submission excluding those (as cruelty, torture, poison, perfidy, wanton destruction) that are forbidden by modern laws and customs of war.

   By the same vein, the Tallinn manual stipulates that "a use of force involving cyber operations undertaken by a State in the exercise of its right of self-defense must be necessary…"

2) Humanity: It is forbidden to inflict suffering, injury or destruction not actually necessary to accomplish a legitimate military purpose. This principle is reaffirmed in St. Petersburg conference of 1868. At the conference the delegates affirmed that the only legitimate object of war should be to weaken the military force of the enemy and not to senselessly cause suffering to innocent millions.

3) Proportionality: The collateral damage arising from military operations must not be excessive in relation to the direct and concrete military advantage anticipated from such operations. an action is proportional when it does not cause: a) Too many unintended collateral civilian casualties; b) Unintended damage excessive in relation to the expected military advantage. "Proportionality" does not aim to limit casualties among combatants in war; it seeks to minimize non-combatant losses.

   Proportionality addresses the issue of how much force, including uses of cyber force, is permissible once force is deemed necessary. The criterion limits the scale, scope, duration, and intensity of the defensive response to that required to end the situation that has given rise to the right to act in self-defense. It does not restrict the amount of force used to that employed in the armed attack since the level of force needed to successfully mount a defense is context dependent;

more force may be necessary, or less force may be sufficient, to repel the attack or defeat one that is imminent.

In addition, there is no requirement that the defensive force be of the same nature as that constituting the armed attack. Therefore, a cyber-use of force may be resorted to in response to a kinetic armed attack, and vice versa.

4) Distinction and Precautions: Military Commanders must distinguish between legitimate military targets & civilian objects including the civilian population. Pursuant to Additional Protocol I82 codify the customary international law principle: "in order to ensure respect for and protection of the civilian population and civilian objects, the Parties to the conflict shall at all times distinguish between the civilian population and combatants and between civilian objects and military objectives and accordingly shall direct their operations only against military objectives".

   On the other hand, Precaution is a right hand of distinction principle. Pursuant to first additional protocol which provides in the conduct of military operations, constant care shall be taken to spare the civilian population, civilians and civilian objects.

5) Limitation: The rights of the belligerents to choose methods and means of warfare are not unlimited. This principle is reaffirmed in the first additional protocol I of Geneva conventions, which stipulates in black and white as; "In any armed conflict, the right of the parties to the conflict to choose methods or means of warfare is not unlimited".

   By the same fashion, the Tallinn Manual provides that it is prohibited to employ means or methods of cyber warfare that are of a nature to cause superfluous injury or unnecessary suffering. Finally, the researcher strongly argues that the general principles of IHL mutatis mutandis applies to cyber warfare since such principles from times immemorial guide and regulate the conduct of belligerents.

MONITORING ORGAN

Although the UN so far had took limited action on the issue of cyber-security and on sui generis cyber warfare yet still there are several UN General Assembly resolutions. In August 1999, the United Nations sponsored an international meeting of experts in Geneva to better grasp the security implications of emerging information technologies. A follow-up General Assembly resolution in 2002 called for further consideration and discussion of "information security". Finally, although absurd, these recommendations represent real progress in overcoming a long impasse between the United States and Russia over how to address cyber-security issues. The cooperation may even suggest possibilities for a future multilateral treaty under the auspices of the United Nations, which Russia has been advocating for some time. Now a day, however, the role of the United Nations with respect to cyber warfare remains largely limited to discussions and informational sharing since so far there is no binding treaty governing the issue and absence of commitment by international community thereof. Besides regional moves are encouraging despite cyber plans and capabilities are still emerging and could serve as courage for further actions.

Current Challenges

The emergence of cyberspace adds an additional dimension to warfare: with and without clashes of traditional troops and machines of war. Cyber warfare is not consistently defined across national borders. Further many countries lack laws against it and lack of enforcement coupled with low cost attack allows anyone or any state to initiate cyber-attacks.

The researcher has identified and noted the following critical issues as far as cyber warfare is concerned, needless to say,

- As to the battlefield, there is only one cyberspace, shared by military and civilian users, and everything is interconnected. The key challenge is whether it is feasible to ensure that attacks are directed against military objectives only and that constant care is taken to spare the civilian population and civilian infrastructure.
- Are hackers a legitimate target in cyber warfare? Most hackers would be civilians who remain protected by IHL against direct attack—although they would remain subject to law enforcement and possible criminal prosecution depending on whether their activities violated other bodies of law. The researcher argues that if hackers take a direct part in hostilities by way of a cyber-attack in support of one side in an armed conflict, there is no reason to let them free from being legitimately targeted.
- The other challenge is the inevitable Attitudinal and policy differences between major super powers as to cyber law treaty. For instance, the United States has for many years been an opponent of creating an international treaty for cyber-warfare. It has listed enforceability and accountability as two of its primary concerns. Instead, the US has suggested increasing national cyber-defence technology and increasing the cooperation between law enforcement agencies. Albeit, Russia has been the ardent supporter of an international treaty for cyber-warfare. Beginning in 1998, Russia has been submitting requests to members of the United Nations to back its plan for a global cyber-warfare treaty.
- Finally, there are no centralized monitoring mechanisms to govern cyber warfare so far as the only actors irrespective of the questionable effectiveness are NATO, Council of Europe, Organization of American states and Shanghai Cooperation Organization which are mandated to follow up their respective regions and members

CONCLUSION

Cyber warfare is a new phenomenon and scenario under International Humanitarian law. There is no agreed definition for cyber warfare albeit for the sake of understanding that it is Internet-based conflict involving politically motivated attacks on information and information systems. Cyber warfare attacks can disable official websites and networks, disrupt or disable essential services, steal or alter classified data and cripple financial systems...among many other possibilities. The cyber incidents coupled with lenient legal framework pave the cyberspace for hackers as a playground. Internationally, there is no comprehensive cyber oriented treaty to address the hazards posed by cyber warfare despite attempts towards codification by a group of experts in Tallinn albeit being as a soft law.

RECOMMENDATIONS AND THE WAY AHEAD

To solve the above mentioned challenges, the researcher recommends the following suggestions as a way forward; First and foremost, there should be comprehensive and well organized International legal machinery by enacting separate treaty document to govern cyber warfare. Secondly, from jus in bello point of view since the law of war is based in large part on the provisions of the Geneva Conventions and their customary counterparts so that Some of the fundamental principles underlying law of war are the principle of military necessity (military operations must be intended to assist in the military defeat of the enemy and must serve the intended military purpose) the principle of distinction (military operations may be conducted only against "military objectives" and not against civilian targets), and the principle of proportionality (the expected incidental loss of civilian life, injury to civilians or damage to civilian objects must not be disproportionate to the anticipated military advantage). Thus, the researcher recommends that fore onething, cyber warfare should be conducted to serve military necessity principle fore another thing, even if one cyber dominion, combatants in cyber warfare should spare civilians' and their objects. And with regard to objects having dual purpose that is military as well as civil use effective assessment should be made in light with principle of proportionality. As to should hackers a legitimate target in cyber warfare? Most hackers would be civilians who remain protected by IHL against direct attack—although they would remain subject to law enforcement and possible criminal prosecution depending on whether their activities violated other bodies of law. The researcher recom- mends the notion of direct participation in hostilities should be on pragmatic way (case by case) that is if hackers take a direct part in hostilities by way of a cyber-attack in support of one side in an armed conflict. In such a situation, the hackers will be legitimately targeted. Finally, from monitoring organ point of view, there are no centralized monitoring mechanisms to govern cyber warfare so far only NATO, Council of Europe, Organization of American states and Shanghai Cooperation Organization follow up their respective regions and members. there should be United Nation Special body for Cyber Affairs to come up with centralized monitoring organ.

REFERENCES

1. Clarke, R. (2010). Cyber War. New York: HarperCollins.
2. Dinniss, H. A. H. (2013). Participants in Conflict—Cyber Warriors, Patriotic Hackers and the Laws of War. In D. Saxon (Ed.), International Humanitarian Law and the Changing Technology of War. Leiden: Martinus Nijhoff. http://dx.doi.org/10.1163/9789004229495_013
3. Dinstein, Y. (2010). The Conduct of Hostilities under the Law of International

Armed Conflict. Cambridge University Press.

4. Droega, C. (2008). Elective Affinities? Human Rights and Humanitarian Law. International Review of the Red Cross, 90.
5. Hensel, H. M. (2007). The Law of Armed Conflict: Constraints on the Contemporary Use of Military Force. Ashgate Pub Co.
6. Pictet, J. (Ed.) (1952). Commentary on the Geneva Convention for the Amelioration of the Condition of the Wounded and Sick in Armed Forces in the Field. Geneva: ICRC.
7. Solis, G. D. (2010). The Law of Armed Conflict: International Humanitarian Law in War. Cambridge University Press.

SECTION IV: CYBER TERRORISM

13

CHAPTER

PERCEPTION ON CYBER TERRORISM

Rabiah Ahmad, Zahri Yunos, Shahrin Sahib, Mariana Yusoff

Keywords: Cyber Terrorism Components, Framework, Focus Group

INTRODUCTION

A more holistic way in describing cyber terrorism is useful in understanding the concept of cyber terrorism. Based on literatures review, it is noted that there is no consensus agreement on the concept of cyber terrorism [1-5]. However, to have a common understanding on this term is important in order to get a better apprehension on what constitutes cyber terrorism. While there are many definitions of cyber terrorism, these suggest a trend that further analysis of the phenomena could be further conducted. This is evidence as the study of this concept has been the focus of many policy makers and scholarly studies, but their standpoints and views vary.

Cyber terrorism is about threat perception that makes the concept differ from one to another. This is due to multidimensional structures (or components) of cyber terrorism that made people interprets it differently at different levels. Therefore, understanding similarities and differences in perception of what constitutes cyber terrorism can provide insight to the policy makers and researchers to countering such threats.

METHOD

Background of This Study

The focus group discussion on cyber terrorism conceptual framework was held in

Citation: R. Ahmad, Z. Yunos, S. Sahib and M. Yusoff, "Perception on Cyber Terrorism,"Journal of Information Security, Vol. 3 No. 3, 2012, pp. 231-237. doi: 10.4236/jis.2012.33029.

conjunction with the 3-days cyber terrorism workshop organized by the South East Asia Regional Center for Counter Terrorism (SEARCCT), an agency under the Malaysia's Ministry of Foreign Affairs, in collaboration with the CyberSecurity Malaysia (an agency under the Malaysia's Ministry of Science, Technology and Innovation) and the Universiti Teknikal Malaysia Melaka, Malaysia.

The focus group discussion was held on the last day of the 3-days workshop. The discussion was designed as a platform to address the cyber terrorism framework in a holistic approach. The workshop gave an insight and a basic understanding of terrorism and cyber terrorism, issues and challenges revolving around them and complexity in coming up with one single universal definition before finally embarking to focus group discussion. Speakers from various agencies who are responsible in the area of counter terrorism and counter cyber crimes were invited to provide their thoughts and perspectives on these topics on the first 2-days of the workshop. In addition, detail explanation about the cyber terrorism conceptual framework was presented by the moderator on day 3 of the workshop. The sessions were designed in such a way to trigger the minds of the participants and to channel all relevant issues to the focus group discussion.

Participants

Focus group discussion is often used as an exploratory technique and is one source of data collection method [6]. Normally, it consists of a group of people, typically between 5 to 10 participants and is led by a moderator.

In this study, 30 participants took part in the focus group discussion. However, they were divided into smaller groups consists of 6 participants for each group. This approach is similar to the focus group discussion conducted by Bray, Johns and Kilburn [7]. The background of the participants varies: management, policy, laws enforcement and prosecution, research and technical and the range of working experiences of the participants is between 10 years to 34 years. All participants were from the government agencies whereby all of them were nominated by the SEARCCT.

Procedures

The participants were divided into 5 groups and each group consists of 6 participants who are differed in term of age, organizations and working experiences. The rationale to have small number in a group is to give everyone the opportunity to express their views and opinions.

First, a briefing session was conducted in order to ensure that each focus group followed the same structure and had the same understanding on the key objectives as well as the discussion guidelines. Each group was given a flip chart to write their discussion points during the group brainstorming session. Before the group discussion, the proposed cyber terrorism conceptual framework was explained to the participants: target, motivation, tools of attack, domain, methods of attack and impact. Overall, the discussion and presentation sessions took about 3 hours. Focus group discussion was identified as the appropriate and accessible technique, given the exploratory nature of the research [7]. The objectives of focus group discussion were as follows. Firstly, to discuss factors that make-up the components (or elements) of cyber terrorism and secondly, to evaluate the proposed conceptual framework that describes the components of cyber terrorism. In a nutshell, the focus group discussion was conducted to get consensus on people perception towards the proposed concept of cyber terrorism that was derived from the qualitative study. The proposed cyber terrorism conceptual framework is based on the author's initial study as described in **Figure 1**.

The primary output of this focus group was to gauge the participants view on the proposed cyber terrorism framework. The focus group discussion was facilitated by a moderator to provide guidance to the group and allowing respondents to talk freely and spontaneously in expressing ideas, views and experiences on the given topic. Although the moderator initiated the topic for discussion and thus exercises a certain control over what was to be discussed, he did not offer any viewpoints during the talk-in-process session [6]. As recommended by Bray, Johns and Kilburn [7], a relaxed and conversational method was used during the focus group discussion in order to produce a free flowing discussion with minimum intervention from the moderator.

Kamarulzaman [8] explained that in a focus group, people interacting with each other with the help of a moderator to get more information and to share their own experience. It is noted that the usefulness of focus group data are affected to the extent that the participants are openly communicating their ideas, views, or opinions during the focus group discussions. This is ascertained by Ho [6] whereby the author explained that, people are

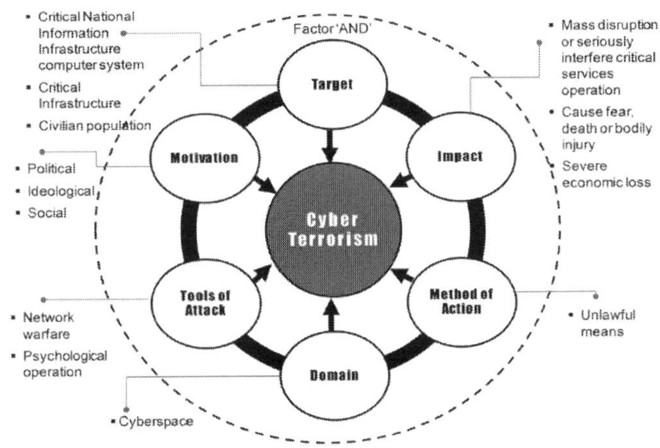

Figure 1. Proposed cyber terrorism conceptual framework.

gathered together to voice their opinions and perceptions about a study topic in a comfortable environment. During the discussion, participants are encouraged to talk to one another, asked questions and exchanged comment on the group's presentation. The focus group study allows a flexible and in-depth exploration of participants' attitudes and experiences as well as reveals differences in perspective between groups of individuals [9].

For context setting, the participants were asked several questions (**Table 1**). The questions did not run in any sequential order, rather to provide guidelines and overviews on the topic under discussion. In order to ensure that the objectives of the focus group discussions were met, the questions were focused on the components of cyber terrorism. The questions were selected from the questionnaires which had been used for the in-depth interviews, which were done prior to the focus group discussion.

Data Collection

In exploratory research, the hypotheses that obtained during the in-depth interview (qualitative data) is useful for enriching and comparing the effectiveness of the initial findings [10]. Besides, the ideas and observations are often used for later quantitative testing [10]. Prior to the focus group discussion, separate in-depth interviews were conducted to explore on the concept of cyber terrorism. Meaning to say, the focus group discussion was conducted on top of the in-depth interview to explore the concept of cyber terrorism. The group discussions were tape-recorded and the discussion points that were noted down on the flip chart were collected at the end of the session.

RESULTS

Similarity in Views on the Proposed Conceptual Framework

The overall result of the focus group discussion is presented in **Table 2**. We included several recommendations

Table 1. Questions for the focus group discussion.

Q1. What are the factors that make up the components (or elements) of cyber terrorism?
Q2. What are the factors that should not be considered as component (or element) of cyber terrorism?
Q3. From the various literatures, a conceptual framework describeing the core components of cyber terrorism can be described as follows (but not limited to): Target, Motivation, Tools of Attack, Domain, Method of Action and Impact. What is your view?
Q4. The components of cyber terrorism are bound or linked to each other to form the concept of cyber terrorism. We need to combine the components with the conjunction "AND", which means that, each of those components is necessary to constitute cyber terrorism. If one or more components are not provided, the statement would not constitute cyber terrorism. What do you think?

from the groups in the findings table. Out of the 5 groups, 3 groups are fully agreed with the proposed framework. The other 2 groups partially agreed with the proposed framework with some recommendations. Group 1 explained, "Overall, our group found that the proposed cyber terrorism framework is sufficient enough. There are a few things we would like to simplify further just in the terms only, not the content. The content is still important." Group 1 further clarified, "Regarding to the impact, I think the examples of 3 elements: mass disruption or seriously interfere critical services operation; caused fear, death or bodily injury; and severe economic loss, I think that are covered."

Group 3 indicated that, "First of all, I would to extend our appreciation to our speaker today for his very comprehensive presentation. In fact, I think that, the presentation today should be brought back to our first day, to give us a basic understanding on the components of cyber terrorism itself." However, Group 3 stressed that "Domain" and "Motivation" should not be too rigid, as they viewed that the components keep changing and have a wide interpretation.

Group 4 pointed out that, "My group agrees on the proposed framework. However, as for the motivation component, we would like to add an economical factor". One of the respondents from Group 4 stated that, "We agree on the term cyber terrorism. We feel we should stick to that. For a simple reason, it looks like international term now where all countries are using this kind of term. If we deviate, we will be different. And secondly, even if it is cyber terrorism, we only looking at the terrorism, the terrorism act itself. Just because the mean of doing is through cyber, it is known as cyber terrorism. Likewise, why we call human trafficking? Drug trafficking? The offence is trafficking but it involves another way. Likewise, I think cyber terrorism is a better word, stick to it."

With regards to statement that the components of cyber terrorism are bound or linked to each other to form the concept of cyber terrorism, all groups agreed with the statement. For example, Group 4 indicated that, "In our discussion, all of the components must be there. In the absence of any of the components, there will be no cyber terrorism. The inner components must be "AND". If you take out target, that is it, no cyber terrorism."

Further question was posed to Group 1. Question: "In order to consider cyber terrorism, we need to combine all factors such as motivation, target and impact. Do you agree with that?" Answer: "Yes, we agree."

Difference in Views on the Proposed Conceptual Framework

Group 5 agreed with most of the proposed cyber terrorism framework (Motivation, Target and Impact). However, they suggested that "Tools of Attacks", "Domain" and "Methods of Attack" should be combined as one component, "Medium". Similarly, Group 1 also suggested combining "Tools of Attack" and "Methods of Action" as one component, "Tools & Methods of Action".

Domain here refers to cyberspace, which is defined as an "interactive domain that made up of digital networks that is used to store, modify and communicate information. It includes the internet, but also the other information systems that support our businesses, infrastructure and services" [11]. In this particular study, "Domain" is similar to "Medium", but not "Tools of Attacks" or "Methods of Attack".

Table 2. Results of the focus group discussion.

Proposed Components	Group 1		Group 2		Group 3		Group 4		Group 5	
Target	Target	Critical National Information Infrastructure computer system Critical Infrastructure	Target	CNII Civil population Critical Infrastructure	Target	Critical National Information Infrastructure computer system Critical Infrastructure Civil population	Target	Critical National Information Infrastructure computer system Critical Infrastructure Civil population	Target	Government Country Corporation CNII
Motivation	Motivation	Political Ideological Social Economic	Initiator 100% personal or group with motiva- tion	The person or group must have the intention to commit the act of cyber terrorism (Refer to Note 3)	Motivation	Political Ideological Social Economic	Motivation	Political Ideological Social Economic	Motivation	Political Ideological Social Economic
Tools of Attack	Tools & Methods of Action	Network warfare Psychological operation The method of action is through unlawful means	Medium	Computer network	Tools of Attack	Network warfare Psychological operation	Tools of Attack	Network warfare Psychological operation	Medium (Tools & Methods) (Refer to Note 5)	Techniques (e.g. recruitment) Domain (e.g. cyberspace)
Domain	Refer to Note 1		Domain	Cyberspace Physical world	Domain	Cyberspace	Domain	Cyberspace		
Methods of Attack	Refer to Note 2		Method	Unlawful means	Methods of Attack	Unlawful means	Methods of Attack	Unlawful means		
Impact	Impact	The target must be impactful	Impact	Mass disruption lead to • destruction • cause-fear, death, instability of country • Severe economic loss • Doc- trinazation	Impact	• Mass disruption or seriously interfere critical services operation • Cause fear, death or bodily injury • Severe economic loss	Impact	• Mass disruption or seriously interfere critical services operation • Cause fear, death or bodily injury • Severe economic loss	Impact	Physical Non Physical National • Security • Economic • Image • Govern- ment to function • Health and safety
							Attempt	(Refer to Note 4)	Perpetrator	Group/ Individual Country

Note: 1) Group 1 excludes "Domain" as the factor which is by default is part of cyber terrorism. 2) Group 1 combines "Tools of Attack" and "Methods of Action" as one component. "Tools & Methods of Action". 3) Group 2 starts the concept of cyber terrorism with initiator, where the person or group has the intention to commit the act of cyber terrorism. The person or group also must have the motivation to do the act of cyber terrorism. 4) Group 4 suggests "Attempt" should be considered as part of cyber terrorism. 5) Group 5 combines "Tools of Attack", "Domain" and "Methods of Action" as one component, "Medium".

"Tools of Attacks" means computers and networks that are used as the weapons through which computers are attacked and exploited (via worms, denial-of-service, bots) [12]. While "Methods of Attack" refers to way and mean the attack was conducted, and in this particular case is referred to unlawful means. As mentioned by Denning [13], cyber terrorism is generally understood to mean unlawful attack against computers, networks and the information stored therein when done to intimidate or coerce a government or its people in furtherance of political or social objectives.

Group 5 also added one new component, "Perpetrator" which consists of group/ individual and country. This is more or less similar with Group 2 where the group identified "Initiator" as one component of cyber terrorism. However, this can be further argued whether "Perpetrator" or "Initiator" is the right component of cyber terrorism. Rollins and Wilson [14] argue that, there are two views in defining cyber terrorism, one of it is the impact (effect-based). They clarify that, effect-based cyber terrorism exists when computer attacks result in effects that are disruptive enough to generate fear comparable to a traditional act of terrorism, even if done by criminals. This implies that, cyber terrorism should focus on the act rather than the doer. Likewise, Tun Dr Mahathir Mohamad [15], a former Malaysia's Prime Minister said, "If we have to determine who a terrorist is and who is not then we have to base it on the act, not on the person, the group, the race or the religion. Once we agree on what constitutes an act of terror, then it would be easy to identify a terrorist."

Although Group 4 agreed with all components of the proposed cyber terrorism framework, they suggested "Attempt" as part of cyber terrorism. One of the participants stated that, "Under the criminal laws, attempt is considered as an offence. What if the terrorist does all this, preparation is done but is unsuccessful in hitting the target? Everything is well prepared but the mission is not achieved. The possibility of causing harm should also be considered as offence in cyber terrorism. Example is murder or manslaughter. The action can cause death, likewise the person conduct whatever action under terrorism, it is possible of causing massive destruction, causing some kind of injury or fear, but the perpetrator did not achieve it. Does is it mean that there is no offence? Does is it mean that he/she is not a terrorist?" One of the objectives of this study is to identify factors that make up the components (or elements) of cyber terrorism. The components then describe the concept and the meaning of cyber terrorism. In this particular case, the authors suggest that an "attempt" should not be considered as factor that make-up the components of cyber terrorism as it is already an offence under the criminal laws. Under the Malaysian law, terrorist means any person who commits, or attempts to commit any terrorist act [16]. It means that, if the components are met with supporting evidence, action by the perpetrator can be classified as cyber terrorism and subsequently the person may be charged under the court of laws. In fact, attempt should be part of any criminal action, including cyber terrorism.

Proposed Future Works in Related to This Study

For future works, the groups have recommended several action plans which can be considered for implementation. The first proposal is amendment to the law. Their argument is that, effective legislation on cyber terrorism is regarded high priority as the countermeasure in countercyber terrorism plans. Group 1 recommended that, "We would like to propose amendment to our laws (to counter threats on cyber terrorism)". This is supported by Group 2, "After this, we need to develop further on the counter action of cyber terrorism. If enforcement is not effective enough, cyber terrorism can easily happen". Group 2 further stated that, "From time to time, we need to revise the laws. If such crimes are becoming more violent and cyber terrorism becoming so developed in times to come, perhaps there is a need specific definition on cyber terrorism."

The second proposal is the preventive measure. One of the participants said, "My views, all of these (the framework) are responsive action. What happen if we want to take preventive measure when it comes to mass disruption or national casualty? We cannot wait the attack to happen and then react. So, we need to think on preventive measure as we don't want to wait until the thing happen, we need to have measure on how to prevent this from happening." Another participant responded that, "For response, a lot of things need to be considered. For root causes, there is mention the origin of attack.

Then, there is non-state issue that gets involve. Also, there are ways and means toward cyber terrorism." In response to this issue, the moderator stated that, "That discussion will be in a different forum. The objective of this research is to provide baseline in understanding the components that make cyber terrorism. After this, we need to come out with response and action plan on how we are going to handle this issue."

The third proposal is the need to have a proper definition on the concept of cyber terrorism. Group 3 stated that, "I think it is crucial for us to have an understanding on the overall definition on the concept of cyber terrorism first before we can approach to the component. There are a few factors that we have to consider in approaching the questions: the perpetrator, the policy of various ministries, the enforcement, and the judicial authority. We think that cyber terrorism is quite similar with other crime. There are starting points and there are ending points. The starting point could be the action itself and the ending points could be the prosecution in court."

Group 3 further explained that, "We would like to admit that there is a need to have a mutual understanding between countries because cyber terrorism is a transboundary issue. It is very crucial for each country to have basic understanding or common understanding on what constitute cyber terrorism." Group 3 continued that, "I would like to take example on Convention on Cyber Crimes. In fact in this convention, we do not have any specific definition or understanding what cyber crimes is, but it provides what constitute cyber crimes. Perhaps in one day, we could have convention on cyber terrorism that would provide understanding to each country or at least common understanding on how or what constitute cyber terrorism."

Research Limitation

This study has several limitations. Therefore, some of the imperfections may lead to the unreliability of the data collected [10]. First, the constraint of this study is that majority of the participants were representatives from the defense & security and the government sectors of the Critical National Information Infrastructure (CNII). In Malaysia, there are 10 CNII sectors: water, banking & finance, defense & security, transportation, information & communication, government, emergency services, food & agriculture, energy and health. Therefore, the participants of the focus group discussion did not represent the CNII sectors as a whole. The second constraint is that from observation, not all participants were participating in the discussion. As a result, not all the participants' viewpoints were heard and well noted.

CONCLUSIONS

Cyber terrorism is a serious matter at the national and international level, and this is demonstrated through the conduct of this workshop. The present study supports our initial research [17] that the cyber terrorism conceptual framework constitutes the following components: target, motivation, tools of attack, domain, methods of attack and impact. This is evident from the overall result whereby 3 out of 5 groups are fully agreed with the proposed framework, while the other 2 groups agreed with the proposed framework with some recommendations. Although there are differences in opinions on some of the components, but their views are not that critical and can be further justified. These results suggest that the proposed cyber terrorism framework is acceptable.

Further research can be conducted to test or verify the conceptual framework. The outcome can be achieved by using quantitative method to quantify them and then applied statistical method to test the dynamic relationship of components of the cyber terrorism framework. Additionally, future research from this study could be used to help better in defining and adopting the concept of cyber terrorism in a holistic manner.

ACKNOWLEDGEMENTS

The authors would like to thank Sazali Sukardi and Zaleha Abd Rahim of CyberSecurity Malaysia who provided valuable input to this paper. The authors also would like to thank the Center for Advanced Computing Technology, Faculty of Information Technology and Communication, Universiti Teknikal Malaysia Melaka (UTeM) that provided research grant for this project.

REFERENCES

1. J. Matusitz, "Social Network Theory: A Comparative Analysis of the Jewish Revolt in Antiquity and the Cyber Terrorism Incident over Kosovo," Information Security Journal: A Global Perspective, Vol. 20, No. 1, 2011, pp. 34-44.
2. M. Dogrul, A. Aslan and E. Celik, "Developing an International Cooperation on Cyber Defense and Deterrence against Cyber Terrorism," 2011 3rd International Conference on Cyber Conflict, Tallinn, 7-10 June 2011, pp. 1-15.
3. M. Conway, "Against Cyberterrorism," Communications of the ACM, Vol. 54, No. 2, 2011, pp. 26-28. doi:10.1145/1897816.1897829
4. Z. Yunos, S. H. Suid, R. Ahmad and Z. Ismail, "Safeguarding Malaysia's Critical National Information Infrastructure (CNII) Against Cyber Terrorism: Towards Development of a Policy Framework," IEEE Sixth International Conference on Information Assurance & Security, Atlanta, 23-25 August 2010, pp. 21-27.
5. P. A. H. Williams, "Information Warfare: Time for a Redefinition," Proceedings of the 11th Australian Information Warfare & Security Conference, Perth Western, 30 November-2 December, 2010, pp. 37-44.
6. D. Ho, "The Focus Group Interview: Rising to the Challenge in Qualitative Research," Australian Review of Applied Linguistics, Vol. 29, No. 1, 2006, pp. 1-19. [Paper reference:3]
7. J. Bray, N. Johns and D. Kilburn, "An Exploratory Study into the Factors Impeding Ethical Consumption," Journal of Business Ethics, Vol. 98, No. 4, 2011, pp. 597-608.doi:10.1007/s10551-010-0640-9 [Paper reference:3]
8. Y. Kamarulzaman, "A Focus Group Study of Consumer Motivations for e-Shopping: UK versus Malaysia," African Journal of Business Management, Vol. 5, No. 16, 2011, pp. 6778-6784. [Paper reference:1]
9. F. Saleem, M. Hassali, A. Shafie, S. Bashir and M. Atif, "Perceptions of Disease State Management among Pakistani Hypertensive Patients: Findings from a

Focus Group Discussion," Tropical Journal of Pharmaceutical Research, Vol. 10, No. 6, 2011, pp. 833-840. doi:10.4314/tjpr.v10i6.18 [Paper reference:1]

10. D. R. Cooper and P. S. Schindler, "Business Research Method," McGraw-Hill Companies, Inc., New York, 2008. [Paper reference:3]
11. UK Cabinet Office, "The UK Cyber Security Strategy— Protecting and Promoting the UK in a Digital World," 2011. http://www.cabinetoffice.gov.uk/sites/default/files/resources/The UK Cyber Security Strategy-web ver.pdf [Paper reference:1]
12. N. Veerasamy and J. H. P. Eloff, "Application of NonQuantitative Modelling in the Analysis of a Network Warfare Environment," World Academy of Science, Engineering and Technology Conference, Paris, 2008. [Paper reference:1]
13. D. E. Denning, "Cyberterrorism," Testimony given to the House Armed Services Committee Special Oversight Panel on Terrorism, 23 May 2000. [Paper reference:1]
14. J. Rollins and C. Wilson, "Terrorist Capabilities for Cyberattack: Overview and Policy Issues," CRS Report for Congress, 2007. [Paper reference:1]
15. M. Mohammad, "The Need to Identify Terrorists and Remove the Causes of Terrorism," In: H. Makaruddin, Ed., Terrorism and the Real Issues, Pelanduk Publications (M) Sdn Bhd, Subang Jaya, 2003, pp. 29-40. [Paper reference:1]
16. ACT 574 Penal Code, "Chapter VIA—Offences Relating to Terrorism. Section 130B (1)-(5)," Zul Rafique & Partner Report, 1997. [Paper reference:1]
17. R. Ahmad and Z. Yunos, "A Dynamic Cyber Terrorism Framework," International Journal of Computer Science and Information Security, Vol. 10, No. 2, 2012, pp. 149- 158. [Paper reference:1]

14

CHAPTER

DEVELOPING A CYBER TERRORISM FRAMEWORK

Rabiah Ahmad, Zahri Yunos

Keywords: Mixed Method Research, Methodology, Data Analysis, Data Collection, Cyber Terrorism

INTRODUCTION

Methodology can be simplified as a plan of action where the method used brings to the desired outcome. The context of methodology as described by Crotty [1] cited in Levy [2], defines methodology as "the strategy, plan of action, process or design lying behind choice of particular methods and linking the choice and use of methods to the desired outcome". Methodology refers to the theoretical arguments that researchers use in order to justify their research methods and design [3]. The purpose of this paper is to describe the application of mixed method in developing a cyber terrorism framework. This project has two primary goals, firstly is to discover a theory and then develop a conceptual framework that describes the phenomena by using qualitative method. Secondly is to verify the conceptual framework that describes the phenomena by quantitative method. By utilizing both techniques within the same study, the researcher is able to incorporate the strength of both methodologies and fit together the insights into a workable solution.

LITERATURE REVIEW

Cyber Terrorism

In this digital age, the concept of cyber terrorism or the use of cyberspace to carry

Citation: R. Ahmad and Z. Yunos, " Developing a Cyber Terrorism Framework," Journal of Information Security, Vol. 3 No. 3, 2012, pp. 209-214. doi: 10.4236/jis.2012.33026.

out terrorist activities has emerged. The convergence of physical terrorism and new advancement of ICT have spawned a new term called cyber terrorism [4]. It can be summarized that cyber terrorism is the perpetration of attack through the cyberspace and the virtual world. However, there is no universally accepted definition of cyber terrorism, which seems to be a fundamental issue and challenge in countering threats from cyber terrorism.

At the international front and among the researchers, there is no common agreement on the concept of cyber terrorism [5-10]. While there are many definitions of cyber terrorism, these suggest a trend that in-depth analysis of this concept can be conducted. This can also be evidence that the study of this concept has been the focus of policy makers and scholarly studies, but their standpoints and views vary. Due to multidimensional structure (or components) of cyber terrorism, we can say that the concept of cyber terrorism is a contested concept whereby various parties interpret it differently.

The concept of cyber terrorism has several attributes (or components) such as motivation, impact and target [11]. Due to complexity of various interacting variables in the concept of cyber terrorism, to formulate a framework in describing its influential components would be beneficial. Therefore, accurate knowledge of the context of cyber terrorism enhances clarity and helps to avoid obscuring intent. Thus, there is a need for a more structured approach in understanding the various components of cyber terrorism. The outcome of this study serves the basis for various strategic decisions for policy and decision makers as well as useful foundation for academic research in understanding the context of cyber terrorism.

Mixed Method Research

One important way to strengthen a study design is through triangulation, or the combination of qualitative and quantitative approaches in the study of a situation or a certain phenomenon [12]. Usually, the researchers triangulate the two methods in order to check on the accuracy of the data gathered by each method, to make the choices available more concrete, to amplify strengths and lessen weaknesses in a study, and to answer broader and more complete range of research problems [13].

Currall et al. [14] study the use of qualitative and quantitative methods and conclude that the mixed methods promoted both theory development and theory evaluation (or verification). Srnka and Koeszegi [15] conclude that qualitative studies are accepted in the social sciences as exploratory or triangulation efforts that complement quantitative studies, which provide quality checks for each of these stages for result's validity and reliability. A detailed study that examine the ways in which quantitative and qualitative research were integrated and combined in practice was conducted by Bryman [16]. He defines triangulation as traditional view where quantitative and qualitative researches are combined to triangulate findings in order to be mutually corroborated.

KNOWLEDGE MANAGEMENT ARCHITECTURE IN DEVELOPING CYBER TERRORISM FRAMEWORK

Knowledge management is a matter of managing analytical process to transform data into information, and information into knowledge, and knowledge into wisdom [17]. Recent research suggests that architectural knowledge, such as design decisions, is important and should be recorded alongside the architecture description [18]. In this research, the conceptual framework describing cyber terrorism is developed by using the grounded theory method. In grounded theory, the main source of data collection are interviews conducted with participants and observed by the researcher, whereby the researcher looks for common patterns among the sets of data [19]. Grounded theory is a rigorous process that involves generating a conceptual model (or theory) that is grounded in the data [20].

Egan [21] recommended five steps in the process of grounded theory research; initiating research, data selection, initiation and ongoing data collection, data analysis and concluding the research (**Figure 1**). Jones and Alony

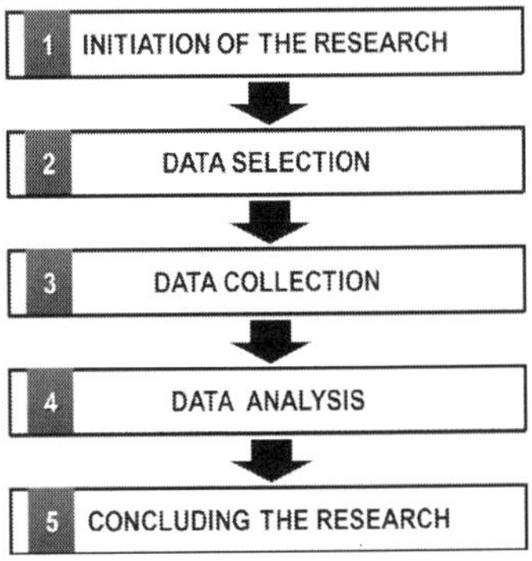

Figure 1. Grounded theory process (adapted from Egan [21]).

[22] suggest five steps in grounded theory approach: acknowledgement of researchers' bias, data selection, data collection, data coding & analysis and compilation of results. Likewise, the grounded theory method employed by Esteves et al. [23] composed of the following phases: research design phase, data collection phase, data analysis phase and comparison phase. Overall, the steps of grounded theory approach discussed above are more or less similar with each other. For this research, we adopted Egan's recommendation.

The first level, initiation of the research involves the selection of an area of inquiry. The research begins with an awareness of the context of the research by reviewing literatures relevant to the area of inquiry. In the second level, data selection, involves the identification of potential data sources (individuals and organizations they represent) associated with the research questions. The respondents are chosen from various expert positions to reflect variety of expertise. The third level is initiation of data collection from targeted respondents. Data collection is an ongoing process, whereby the researcher can return to the interviewees for clarification and elaboration besides comparing related documents or records with data collected during initiation of the research. In the fourth level, data analysis, involves a constant comparison method for generating and analyzing data. Data analysis is defined as a process of systematically searching and arranging the interview transcripts, field notes and other materials with the objectives to increase the understanding and to enable researcher to present what have been discovered. Lastly, concluding the research, involves documenting the grounded theory based on researcher observation of the data saturation and sufficient theory which has emerged from the data. Data saturation is the evident when data collection no longer contributes to elaboration of the phenomenon being investigated.

CONCEPTUAL FRAMEWORK OF THIS STUDY

Two research methods that are commonly used are qualitative research and quantitative research. It is suggested that when the goal of a research is to develop a conceptual model for the purpose of building theory around a particular phenomenon or process, an interpretive approach utilizing a qualitative methodology may be more appropriate [2]. On the other hand, if the primary goal of a research problem is to test the validity of a model where all the variables of influence a phenomenon or process is already known, then quantitative methodology may be appropriate [2]. In summary, qualitative research approaches seek to explore phenomena while quantitative research approaches seek to confirm hypothesis about phenomena.

This research is about exploring the context of cyber terrorism, focusing on the attributes or components of cyber terrorism. Since this project is exploratory in nature, a qualitative research by using a grounded theory method is adopted for this study. The phrase grounded theory refers to theory that is developed from a corpus of data through literatures, interviews and observations [24]. In this method, the objectives are to investigate the phenomena under study, to identify and construct attributes of the phenomena, and to develop a conceptual framework that describe the phenomena.

Once the theory discovery and conceptual framework have been developed, the next stage is to test or verify the conceptual framework. The outcome can be achieved by using quantitative method to quantify them and then applied statistical test to conduct the hypothesis test. In this method, the objectives are to evaluate the framework and to test the dynamic relationship of attributes (or components) of the framework.

In short, we believe that a mixed method approach is appropriate to be used in this study in order to accomplish both theory discovery and verification within a single research project. Theory discovery is achieved by using qualitative data to sharpen our theoretical ideas about the phenomena under investigation, while verification is achieved by using quantitative data to quantify them and then applied statistical test to conduct hypothesis test. The combination of qualitative and quantitative techniques within one research study able to incorporate the strength of both methodologies. The framework of research methodology is described below (**Figure 2**).

The approach discussed in this paper is well described by Srnka and Koeszegi [15] where they state that the combination of two separate studies, one collects and analyzed qualitative and quantitative data sequentially, has been acceptable to researchers in the social science. By conducting qualitative method in a preliminary stage, the objective is for the researchers to develop a conceptual framework (or to generate hypothesis) for the quantitative study. Thus, when qualitative data collection precedes the quantitative data collection, the intent is to first explore the problem under study then follow up on this study with quantitative data that are amenable to studying a large sample so that results might be inferred to a population [25]. We believe that by merging the results provides an overall picture of the research problem.

FRAMEWORK OF DATA COLLECTION AND DATA ANALYSIS

In this study, mixed method research involves both collecting and analyzing quantitative and qualitative data in sequential order. The first stage in the analysis cycle is to frame a theory or hypothesis from the literatures which can be used as initial guidance for data collection and data analysis. Once the theory or hypothesis has been generated, the researchers develop questionnaires to get in-depth understanding on the phenomena under investigation. Data collection is a semi-structured method by using in-depth interviews. Interviews are part of most

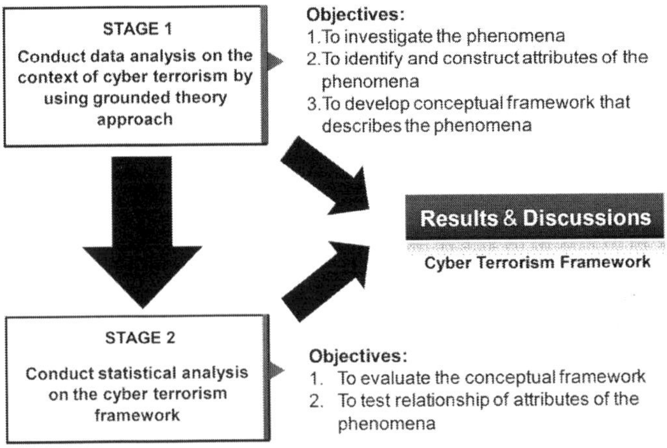

Figure 2. The framework of research methodology.

interpretive studies and as a key way of accessing the interpretations of informants in the field [26]. Since the first stage is explanatory in nature, data analyses are done by using grounded theory approach. Qualitative research includes a variety of methodological approaches and one example is grounded theory [27]. As have been mentioned earlier, the phrase grounded theory refers to theory that is developed from a corpus of data through literatures, interviews and observations.

In the next stage, quantitative approach is applied to corroborate the researcher's initial discovery. A survey with close-ended questions format are used for data collection to determine the views and opinions of the population that represents various groups in the society. In this phase, the researcher's goal is to test the theory or hypothesis, which finding is generalized from a larger representative sampling. Statistical analysis is performed to test the validity of the theory or hypothesis. The numerical findings help to interpret the results, where clearer interpretations of the statistical results are obtained. **Figure 3** shows the summary on how the data are collected and analyzed.

SUITABILITY OF MIXED METHOD IN THIS RESEARCH

All the relevant methodological issues discussed in this paper provide justification and practical approach on how the research is conducted. The methodology explained in this paper provides the researchers with the right direction and understanding in conducting the research by choosing the right research design. Research design as defined by Cooper and Schindler [27] is a plan and structure of investigation so conceived as to obtain answers to research questions. It includes an outline on what the researcher will do from initiation of the research to the final analysis of the data.

In this study, we suggest that a mixed method research approach is appropriate to be applied. The motivation factors in applying the mixed method (as opposed to a single method) are due to the following reasons. Firstly, the nature of the research is exploratory and explanatory in nature, and is grounded in theory. The goals are to discover theory and to develop a conceptual framework that describes the phenomena (qualitative method); and to test or verify the conceptual framework that describes the phenomena (quantitative method). As noted by Yauch and Steudel [13], the mixed method research complements each other, which explains the results of analyses. The qualitative research is interpretive, which allow for the discovery of new ideas and unanticipated occurrences. Qualitative research aims to achieve an in-depth understanding of a situation or a certain phenomenon [27]. Focus of the research is to explore (understand and interpret) of a situation or a certain phenomenon. On another hand, quantitative research aims to achieve precise measurement of something such as participants behavior, knowledge or opinion [27]. Focus of the research is to confirm (describe and explain) hypothesis about a situation or a certain phenomenon. Therefore, by utilizing a mixed method research, we believed it would bring conclusive findings on outcome of this study.

Secondly, mixed method approach helps to answer questions that cannot be answered by qualitative or quantitative approaches alone, thus, provide breadth and depth to the study [28]. Researchers who conduct mixed methods research are more likely to select methods and approaches with respect to their underlying research questions in ways that offer the best opportunity for answering important research questions [28]. In this research, a survey questionnaire using qualitative in-depth interviews is conducted as a way to tap into participants' perspectives and insights. During analysis, the qualitative researcher uses content analysis of written or recorded materials drawn from participants' expressions and observations [27] or documents review [2]. Qualitative research study via questionnaires interview, and supplement with close-ended survey systematically provide

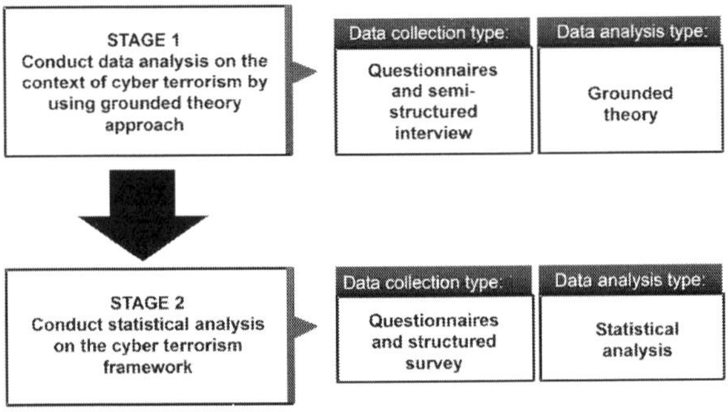

Figure 3. Framework for data collection and data analysis.

breadth and depth to the research [12]. Quantitative research looks at the frequency [27] or any kind of research that produces findings arrived at by means of statistical procedures [2]. Through this approach, it is believed that the findings are corroborated across different approaches, thus provide greater confidence in the conclusion.

Lastly, the research framework of mixed method is chosen to apply the concept of triangulation. As noted by Paton [12], one important way to strengthen a study design is through triangulation, or the combination of methodologies in the study of a situation or a certain phenomenon. Paton [12] also argues that triangulation provides accuracy of the data gathered while Olsen [29] argues that triangulation provides validation besides deepening and widening one's understanding. Triangulation is a term derived from navigation and surveying where different bearings are taken in order to arrive at a precise location. In this study, triangulation involves locating a true position by referring to two or more other coordinates [12]. As noted by Yauch and Steudel [13], triangulation corroborates data and obtains convergent validity. Moreover, triangulation reduces biasness besides be able to heighten the validity of the data collection and analysis.

CONCLUSIONS

The study on the context of cyber terrorism is quite complex as it is about threat perception which makes the concept differ from one to another. Understanding similarities and differences in perception of what constitutes cyber terrorism can provide insight on the concept of cyber terrorism. The outcome of this study serves the basis for various strategic decisions for policy and decision makers as well as useful foundation for academic research in understanding the context of cyber terrorism. Detail focus analysis can be conducted to investigate and analyze the context of cyber terrorism.

This paper provides information on how this research is conducted. It also describes the framework of research methodology, where we have recommended that the study to be conducted by using a mixed method research: qualitative data and quantitative data are collected and analyzed respectively in a separate phase. This paper also established the conceptual framework that guides the data collection and data analysis techniques. Finally, the research methodology explained in this paper provides the researchers with the right direction by choosing the right research design. The mixed method improves the rigor and explanation of the results, thus bring conclusive findings to the research outcome. By utilizing qualitative and quantitative techniques within the same study, a mixed method research should be able to incorporate the strength of both methodologies and fit together the insights into a workable solution.

ACKNOWLEDGEMENTS

The authors would like to thank the following individuals who provided valuable input to this paper: Dr. Solahuddin Shamsuddin and Zaleha Abd Rahim of CyberSecurity Malaysia. We also would like to thank the Center for Advanced Computing Technology, Faculty of Information and Communication Technology, Universiti Teknikal Malaysia Melaka (UTeM) that provided research grant for this project.

REFERENCES

1. M. Crotty, "The Foundation of Social Research: Meaning and Perspective in the Research Process," Allen and Unwin, St Leonards, 1998.
2. D. Levy, "Qualitative Methodology and Grounded Theory in Property Research," Pacific Rim Property Research Journal, Vol. 12, No. 4, 2006, pp. 369-388.
3. J. M. Case and G. Light, "Emerging Methodologies in Engineering Education Research," Journal of Engineering Education, Vol. 100, No. 1, 2011, pp. 186-210.
4. D. A. Simanjuntak, H. P. Ipung and C. Lim, "Text Classification Techniques Used to Facilitate Cyber Terrorism Investigation," Proceeding of Second International Conference on Advances in Computing, Control, and Telecommunication Technologies (ACT 2010), Jakarta, 2-3 December 2010, pp. 198-200. doi:10.1109/ACT.2010.40
5. M. Dogrul, A. Aslan and E. Celik, "Developing an International Cooperation on Cyber Defense and Deterrence against Cyber Terrorism," 3rd International Conference on Cyber Conflict, Tallinn, 7-10 June 2011, pp. 1-15.
6. M. Conway, "Against Cyberterrorism," Communications of the ACM, Vol. 54, No. 2, 2011, p. 26. doi:10.1145/1897816.1897829
7. Z. Yunos, S. H. Suid, R. Ahmad and Z. Ismail, "Safeguarding Malaysia's Critical National Information Infrastructure (CNII) against Cyber Terrorism: Towards Development of a Policy Framework," IEEE Sixth International Conference on Information Assurance & Security, Atlanta, 23-25 August 2010, pp. 21-27.
8. P. A. H. Williams, "Information Warfare: Time for a Redefinition," Proceedings of the 11th Australian Information Warfare & Security Conference, Perth Western, 30 November-2 December 2010, pp. 37-44.
9. C. Czosseck, R. Ottis and A. M. Taliharm, "Estonia after the 2007 Cyber Attacks: Legal, Strategic and Organisational Changes in Cyber Security," International Journal of Cyber Warfare and Terrorism, Vol. 1, No. 1, 2011, pp. 24-34. doi:10.4018/ijcwt.2011010103
10. J. Matusitz, "Social Network Theory: A Comparative Analysis of the Jewish

Revolt in Antiquity and the Cyber Terrorism Incident over Kosovo," Information Security Journal: A Global Perspective, Vol. 20, No. 1, 2011, pp. 34-44.

11. R. Ahmad and Z. Yunos, "A Dynamic Cyber Terrorism Framework," International Journal of Computer Science and Information Security, Vol. 10, No. 2, 2012, pp. 149- 158.

12. M. Q. Paton, "Qualitative Evaluation and Research Methods," 2nd Edition, SAGE Publications, Thousand Oaks, 1991.

13. C. Yauch and H. Steudel, "Complementary Use of Qualitative and Quantitative Cultural Assessment Methods," Organizational Research Methods, Vol. 6, No. 4, 2003, pp. 465-481. doi:10.1177/1094428103257362

14. S. C. Currall, T. H. Hammer, L. S. Baggett and G. M. Doniger, "Combining Qualitative and Quantitative Methodologies to Study Group Processes: An Illustrative Study of a Corporate Board of Directors," Organizational Research Methods, Vol. 2, No. 1, 1999, pp. 5-36. doi:10.1177/109442819921002

15. K. J. Srnka and S. T. Koeszegi, "From Words to Numbers: How to Transform Qualitative Data into Meaningful Quantitative Results," Schmalenbach Business Review, Vol. 59, No. 1, 2007, pp. 29-57.

16. A. Bryman, "Integrating Quantitative and Qualitative Research: How Is It Done?" Qualitative Research, Vol. 6, No. 1, 2006, pp. 97-113.

17. R. J. Chenail, "Conducting Qualitative Data Analysis: Qualitative Data Analysis as a Metaphoric Process," The Qualitative Report, Vol. 17, No. 1, 2012, pp. 248-253.

18. A. Tang, P. Avgeriou, A. Jansen, R. Capilla and M. Ali Babar, "A Comparative Study of Architecture Knowledge Management Tools," Journal of Systems and Software, Vol. 83, No. 3, 2010, pp. 352-370. doi:10.1016/j.jss.2009.08.032

19. R. Hoda, J. Noble and S. Marshall, "Using Grounded Theory to Study the Human Aspects of Software Engineering," Proceeding of HAoSE 10 Human Aspects of Software Engineering, Nevada, 17-21 October 2010.

20. A. A. Singh, A. Urbano, M. Haston and E. Mcmahan, "School Counselors' Strategies for Social Justice Change: A Grounded Theory of What Works in the Real World," American School Counselor Association, Vol. 13, No. 3, 2010, pp. 135-145.

21. T. M. Egan, "Grounded Theory Research and Theory Building," Advances in Developing Human Resources, Vol. 4, No. 3, 2002, pp. 277-295.

22. M. Jones and I. Alony, "Guiding the Use of Grounded Theory in Doctoral Studies—An Example from the Australian Film Industry," International Journal of Doctoral Studies, Vol. 6, 2011, pp. 95-114.

23. J. Esteves, U. Politécnica and J. Carvalho, "Use of Grounded Theory in Information Systems Area: An Exploratory Analysis," European Conference on Research Methodology for Business and Management, 2000, pp. 129- 136.

24. J. W. Creswell, "Qualitative Inquiry and Research Design: Choose among Five Traditions," Sage Publications, London, 1998.

25. J. M. Azorin and R. Cameron, "The Application of Mixed Methods in Organisational Research: A Literature Review," Electronic Journal of Business Research Methods, Vol. 8, No. 2, 2010, pp. 95-105.
26. G. Walsham, "Doing Interpretive Research," European Journal of Information Systems, Vol. 15, No. 3, 2006, pp. 320-330. doi:10.1057/palgrave.ejis.3000589
27. D. R. Cooper and P. S. Schindler, "Business Research Method," McGraw-Hill Companies, Inc., New York, 2008.
28. R. B. Johnson and A. J. Onwuegbuzie, "Mixed Methods Research: A Research Paradigm Whose Time Has Come," Educational Research, Vol. 33, No. 7, 2004, pp. 14-26.doi:10.3102/0013189X033007014
29. W. Olsen, "Triangulation in Social Research: Qualitative and Quantitative Methods Can Really Be Mixed," In: M. Holborn, Ed., Development in Sociology, Causeway Press, Ormskirk, 2004, pp. 1-30.

15
CHAPTER

AUTOMATIC DETECTION OF CYBER-RECRUITMENT BY VIOLENT EXTREMISTS

Jacob R Scanlon and Matthew S Gerber

Keywords: Cyber, Recruitment, Extremist, Terrorism, Darkweb, Machine learning, Natural language processing

INTRODUCTION

In the last decade, the modern landscape of extremism has expanded to encompass the Internet and online social media [1],[2]. In particular, extremist organizations have increasingly used these technologies to recruit new members. Recent research by Torok shows that cyber tools are most influential at the onset of a future member's extremist activity—the recruitment and radicalization phase [2]. Terrorist groups use the free and open nature of the Internet to form online communities [3] and disseminate literature and training materials without having to rely on traditional media outlets which might censor or change their message [2],[4]. Terrorist organizations engage in directed communication and advertisement, recruiting members on social websites like Second Life, Facebook, and radicalized religious web forums [1],[2],[5]. The intelligence community would benefit from knowledge of how terrorist organizations conduct online recruitment and whom they may be targeting.

The investigation report on FBI counterterrorism intelligence failures leading up to the Ft. Hood shooting on November 7, 2009 cited a "data explosion" and "workload" as contributing factors to analyst and agent oversights. At "nearly 20,000 Aulaqi-related [electronic documents]," keeping up with workload demands was clearly a challenge for the two reviewers assigned to the case at the time [6]. Considering this large volume of possibly relevant text data requiring review by a limited number of FBI agents,

Citation: Jacob R Scanlon and Matthew S Gerber, Automatic detection of cyber-recruitment by violent extremists, doi:10.1186/s13388-014-0005-5.

automated classification methods would be useful for pre-screening text documents—reducing the workload of human analysts.

Within this article, a violent extremist (VE) group is an organization that uses violent means, like terrorism, to disrupt a legitimate authority, whereas insurgents and terrorists are common types of violent extremist groups that act with the specific goal of influencing public opinion or inciting political change. A radical religious group organizing inflammatory yet peaceful protests or a politically motivated person engaging in civil disobedience are not considered violent extremists under these definitions. Many modern groups, like the Westboro Baptist Church, have radical religious views, but these beliefs are neither necessary nor sufficient to classify them as violent extremists without the intent to carry out or advocate for specific acts of violence. Within this article, VE recruitment is any attempt by a group or individual involved in VE to recruit, radicalize, or persuade another person to aid a violent movement. Cyber-recruitment is therefore recruitment activity that makes use of computers and the Internet.

This article presents data and analytic methods for automatically identifying recruitment activities of violent extremist organizations within online social media. Specifically, these methods identify messages recruiting individuals for participation in violent extremism. For these classification purposes, a VE cyber-recruitment message is any message that attempts to persuade the reader to join a violent extremist organization. These recruitment messages must assist readers in finding violent movements to join, or describe ways to become more active or provide material aid. By developing and evaluating an automatic system for identifying such messages, we demonstrate an important and feasible method for identifying the intention/incitement of violent activity within online communities.

The rest of this article is organized as follows. In the section "Related work", we compare offline violent extremist recruitment with the recent increase in cyber-recruitment efforts. Additionally, we discuss previous counterinsurgency efforts and contemporary research that outlines the challenges associated with analyzing VE activities, like recruitment; we emphasize the specific gaps that our article addresses. The "Data collection and annotation" section describes our data requirements and the specific data sources we used, followed by the pre-processing and annotation steps required for supervised learning of VE recruitment. Following the annotation steps, we present our agreement analysis results of the VE recruitment annotations. In the section "Analytic approach", we propose a probabilistic model employing natural language features for automatically classifying VE recruitment in forum posts. We also describe the classification functions used in our supervised learning experiments, such as naive Bayes, logistic regression, and support vector machines. A description of the results obtained from the experiments along with our interpretation is provided in the "Results and discussion" section. Finally, "Conclusions and future work" section discusses future directions and potential for our proposed techniques along side privacy concerns related to automated monitoring and analysis of ubiquitous communication.

RELATED WORK

Offline recruitment and manual social network analysis

The modern jihadist insurgencies in Iraq and Afghanistan operate among the local civilian population and engage in both legal and illegal activities in order to achieve their strategic and political goals. However, the illegal acts are only effective when carried out by an organized and well-manned group [7]. Recruiting new members is thus a critical activity for both daily operations and the underlying political cause. An average terrorist group has a life expectancy of less than a year, so groups wishing to extend their lifespan must replace members lost through arrests, deaths, and defections [3]. Several studies have tried to understand why some people join violent rebellions [8]–[12], while others only sympathize or cooperate in a non-violent capacity [13]–[16]. This article facilitates such understanding by providing methods that identify examples of active recruitment activity within a population of individuals who may passively sympathize with violent groups.

Ralph McGehee observed VE recruitment first hand during his 1967 work to identify communist insurgents in the rural villages along the northern border of Thailand. His efforts enabled the joint CIA-Thai counterinsurgency (COIN) to provide targeted aid to at-risk villages and persons, and in doing so simultaneously thwart communist recruitment efforts and improve regional support for the Thai government. The success of McGehee's program can be attributed to his intelligence teams collecting information on nearly every person in the villages, not just the communist sympathizers he was specifically targeting. This provided a more complete picture of the community and allowed this early social network analysis (SNA) effort to better infer the community's support for the communists and successfully identify active members of the insurgency [17]. Although our research problem specifically targets online communities, strong parallels exist between these virtual worlds and the physical communities addressed by McGehee because both contain violent extremist groups that operate within, hide among, and recruit from a passive majority population.

Cyber-recruitment, social network analysis, and data mining

The primary danger of cyber-recruitment is its ability to quickly expose large online communities to a substantial amount of engaging, multimedia content [2],[18],[19]. COIN experts are increasingly concerned with the potential of these cyber-communities for illegal purposes. Most literature has focused on how violent extremist groups use legitimate social networking websites along with online discussion forums for recruitment and other activities. This prior research largely provides evidence and case studies of real online VE activity and suggests ways that virtual worlds may be used by these groups in the future [4],[5],[19]–[22]. Recent research has evaluated the use of political tools for shutting down websites or shaming material supporters [23]. Some researchers have suggested the use of web-crawling and analysis techniques to monitor for VE activities including recruitment [2],[24],[25]; however, we are not aware of any implementations of such techniques on recruitment specifically. This article presents new research that fills this gap, addressing the need to detect cyber-recruitment in online social media forums.

Computer-based social network analysis is a large field of research, one objective of which is to identify the organizational structure of VE networks [1],[26]–[29]. With objectives similar to McGehee's manual SNA work, present research hopes to detect the presence of VE groups and their influence within large-scale networks based on the number of interconnections among VEs and influential community members. There have also been preliminary attempts to profile individual users using text mining techniques [30]. However, this prior research has typically focused on violent extremist activity in general without focusing on a particular activity like recruitment. Although much COIN literature has covered cyber-recruitment, and data/text mining techniques have been used in an early capacity to collect/analyze Internet data, no published research has applied such techniques to specifically examine the cyber-recruitment activities of extremist groups in online environments. The present research complements the research surveyed above by building on recent data collection efforts, focusing on online recruitment specifically, and applying current techniques from natural language processing to automatically identify recruitment activities.

DATA COLLECTION AND ANNOTATION

The need for cyber-COIN tools has increased interest in methods that analyze so-called "dark web" content. Dark web content is defined as information from typically private social websites where extremists interact. Many early efforts focused on locating, accessing, extracting, and storing data from dark web forums [1],[22],[24],[31],[32]. The present research builds on these key efforts. In the section "Data requirements and sources", we describe requirements that must be met by data sources supporting our objectives along with specific data sources used in our study. In the "Data pre-processing and annotation" section, we describe our manual annotation effort, which analyzed individual posts for recruitment content.

Data requirements and sources

This article leverages prior data collection efforts by using pre-compiled forum post data to model violent extremist recruitment within online social media. The following data requirements are needed to support our research objectives.

Violent extremist activity - The collected data should come from sources that are popular among violent extremist groups and their sympathizers and contain overt recruitment for such groups.

Contemporary time-frame - The collected data should cover a contemporary time-frame (e.g., the last decade) in order to be considered relevant to contemporary anti-extremist efforts.

Language - The collected data must use the English language or be translatable to English using an automatic process like Google's machine-translation service [33]. We identified the Dark Web Portal Project [31],[34] as an ideal data source according to the requirements described above. The Dark Web Portal is a repository of social media messages compiled from 28 different online discussion forums. These forums focus on extremist religious (e.g., jihadist) and general Islamic discussions, many of which are sympathetic to radical Islamic groups. Most of the thirteen million collected messages come from Arabic sources, but the Dark Web Project provides translation services and compiles information from at least seven dedicated English-language forums. The most relevant forums come from the Ansar AlJihad Network, which we summarize in Table 1 and describe in more detail below.

Table 1 Forums used in our study, extracted from the Ansar AlJihad Network via the Dark Web Portal

	AsAnsar	**Ansar1**
Time-frame	11/2008 - 5/2012	12/2008 - 1/2010
Messages	269,548	29,492
Members	5,034	382
Language	Arabic	English

The Ansar AlJihad Network is a set of invitation-only jihadist forums in Arabic and English that are known to be popular with western jihadists [35]. The Dark Web Project compiled 299,040 total messages posted on Ansar AlJihad between 2008-2012. Fewer posts are compiled from the English forums, called Ansar1, than from the Arabic portion of the site; however, the English subset was sufficiently large for our study and contained contemporary, original-English discussions between jihadists and jihadist sympathizers. We used this subset in all of our experiments. The structured data annotations discussed below are the only data elements not originating from this pre-compiled Ansar AlJihad source.

Data pre-processing and annotation

We collected and pre-processed the Ansar1 data as follows:

- We read in a sample of raw Ansar1 forum posts and compiled the message text and respective message IDs into an initial corpus. We then automatically removed duplicates (same message ID) and empty documents (no message text) from the corpus.
- Most posts contain exclusively English text as Asnar1 is the English-language forum for the Ansar AlJihad Network. However, occasional posts include non-English words or phrases; these are commonly Arabic passages from the Koran. In these cases the non-English passages were converted to English using Google Translate [33]. We left slang words written in latin characters intact under the assumption that they were meant to be readable by an English language speaker. For example, "Kuffar" is a derogatory Arabic term for unbeliever.

The Dark Web Portal project does not indicate which messages contain VE recruitment content and which do not. Thus, we manually annotated this information within the data. We provided two independent judges with the following instructions:

1. You have been provided with 192 forum posts sampled from a Jihadist forum.
2. Read each post carefully and determine whether that post has the intent to recruit violent extremists to some group or movement. For the purpose of annotation, violent extremist recruitment is defined as any attempt by a group or individual to recruit, radicalize, or persuade another person into aiding a violent movement aimed at disrupting a legitimate authority.
3. Annotate each post by marking it as either (a) contains violent extremist recruitment, or (b) does not contain violent extremist recruitment.

The forum posts' message text had a wide range of sizes with an average of 246 words among the samples (352-word standard deviation); examples of annotated posts are shown in Table 2. We then used Cohen's κ[36] to validate the labeled data for consistency. Agreement, κ, is the proportion of agreement between the judges after chance agreement has been removed. The value of κ is bounded on [– 1,+1] with zero indicating that observed agreement equals chance agreement. Therefore a positive κ indicates non-random agreement between judges, and a negative κ indicates conflicting annotation between judges. The following terms are used to calculate κ:

Table 2 Example text of Ansar1 forum posts and the respective annotations

Annotation	**Sample text****
Recruitment	A Golden chance to join Jihad in Somalia. Abo Dojana invited those who want to participate in jihad to join the militants in Somalia to form what he called a base of martyrdom-seekers who would from there spread to the entire world. Somalia could actually be an ideal base for physical and weapons training...
Recruitment	Representing the militant Islamic group Shebab, Abu Mansour makes a pitch for new overseas recruits after praising one militant fighter killed in an apparent ambush. 'So, if you can encourage more of your children and more of your neighbors and anyone around to send people like him to this jihad (holy war), it would be a great asset for us,' he says.
Not recruitment	I have now added him as a friend on Facebook. But something tells me that he isn't going to answer to my request. LOL, you had me rolling on the floor man!!!!! So this attack was done my 'Jaish al Mujihadeen' How it that possible?, did they have problems with bounced-checks from the US?
Not recruitment	A court in the German city of Koblenz sentenced a German of Pakistani origin to eight years in prison Monday on a conviction of assisting the international Al-Qaeda terror network. The man gave the group financial aid and tried to recruit new members in German territory, according to the indictment
Not recruitment	Did Mansoor join the emerat? I heard he is still fighting for Ichkira Republic

**Incorrect spellings and grammar of original posts have been left as is throughout the table.

$$\kappa = \frac{p_o - p_c}{1 - p_c}$$

p_o= proportion of observations for which judges agree (see Table 3), p_c= proportion of observations for which agreement is expected by chance (see Table 3)

Table 3 Agreement matrix of proportions for recruitment categories

		Judge A		
	Category	**No**	**Yes**	p_{iB}
Judge	**NO**	0.82 (0.74)*	0.04	0.86
B	**YES**	0.03	0.11 (0.02)	0.14
	p_{iA}	0.85	0.15	∑pi=1.00
	p_o=0.82+0.11=0.93			
	p_c=0.74+0.02=0.76		$\kappa = \frac{0.93-0.76}{1-0.76} = 0.70$	

*Parenthetical values are proportions expected due to chance association.

Table 3 shows the agreement results for our manually annotated Ansar1 data. As shown, the two judges found that approximately 11% of the posts contained VE recruitment. The two judges agreed on the labels for 93% of the posts, with an expected chance agreement of 76%, producing a κ of 70% (see Table 3 for details). Significant non-random agreement was observed with a confidence interval of (0.5,0.7) at p=0.01; however, interpreting strength of agreement is a common problem with agreement metrics. Some studies have attempted to provide a scale and would describe κ=0.70 as "substantial" strength of agreement [37],[38], but despite considerable debate among statisticians this issue has never been definitively addressed. Considering both the significance and magnitude of agreement, these results adequately justify using the annotated Ansar1 messages in our analytic approach. To increase the final size of our experimental dataset, one of the judges annotated an additional 100 posts from the Ansar1 collection following the same protocol described above. In total, we observed that 13% of forum posts contained recruitment according to our definition.

Analytic approach

We developed a binary classifier that labels forum posts as either containing or not containing VE recruitment. We used the following probability model:

$$Pr[\,Recruitment = True \mid d_i] = F[\,w_1(d_i), \ldots, w_n(d_i)] \quad (1)$$

In Equation 1, Recruitment is a binary classification label, $d_i \in D$ is a forum post, and w_j is a feature function of d_i. In the following section, we discuss the features used and then we present different formulations of the classification function F.

Text classification features

We employed a bag-of-words, or unigram only, feature space by parsing each forum post in the corpus into a term-by-document matrix. This matrix of term frequency (tf) features was created using the RTextTools and tm text mining packages in R [39],[40] which also performed basic normalization and feature reduction through the removal of URL web addresses, numbers, punctuation, stopwords, and whitespace. The number of features was further reduced through stemming using the Porter Stemming Algorithm [41]. Under this representation, $w_j(d_i)$ is equal to the raw frequency of a stemmed word form, with n (the number of feature functions) equal to the number of distinct words remaining after document processing.

We then normalized each term frequency (tf_j) and weighted each by its inverse document frequency (IDF_j), producing the logarithmically scaled TF-IDF feature function shown below [42]:

$$w_j\left(d_i\right) = \frac{\left(\log_2\left(tf_j\right)+1\right)\cdot IDF_j}{\sqrt{\sum_{j'} w_{j'}\left(d_i\right)}} \tag{2}$$

where the denominator is a normalization of the feature vector for unit length, and the formula for IDF is shown below:

$$IDF_j = \log_2\left(\frac{|D|}{\sum_{d_i \in D} \mathbb{I}\left[w_j \in d_i\right]}\right)$$

|D|, corpus cardinality, is the total number of posts in the training corpus, and the denominator represents the number of posts containing at least one occurrence of the jth feature (i.e. word). In order to keep the test data unbiased we used IDF terms computed only from posts in the training portion of the corpus.

Classification functions

We conducted supervised learning over our annotated posts using a variety of classification functions: naive Bayes, logistic regression, classification trees, boosting, and support vector machines (SVM).

Naive Bayes

Our application of a naive Bayes classifier is described below as an example of how we applied the probability model in Equation 1 to the various classification algorithms mentioned in this section. We calculated the posterior probability of VE recruitment $Pr(Rec_j \mid d_i)$, where$Rec_j \in \{+1,-1\}$, by building upon Bayes' rule and the generic probabilistic model defined above [43]:

$$Pr\left[Rec_j \mid \mathbf{w}(d_i)\right] = \frac{Pr[\mathbf{w}(d_i) \mid Rec_j]\ Pr(Rec_j)}{Pr[\mathbf{w}(d_i)]}$$

$$= \frac{Pr[\mathbf{w}(d_i) \mid Rec_j]\ Pr(Rec_j)}{\sum_{r \in Rec} Pr[\mathbf{w}(d_i) \mid Rec_r]\ Pr\left(Rec_r\right)}$$

The naive Bayes independence assumption reduces the joint probability to the product of component probabilities Pr[$w_k(d_i) \mid Rec_j$], giving us the posterior probability estimator F[$w_1(d_i)$,..., $w_n(d_i)$] from Equation 1. Since the denominator is a constant with respect to classRec_j, the posterior function F can be further reduced to the following proportion:

$$\left[\ Rec_j \mid w_1(d_i), \ldots, w_n(d_i)\ \right] \propto Pr(Rec_j)\ \prod_{k=1}^{n}\ Pr\left[\ w_k(d_i) | Rec_j\ \right] \tag{3}$$

Our implementation of naive Bayes was adapted from the R package e1071 for use with the sparse training data typical in a term-by-document matrix [44]. We fit a naive Bayes model using the default settings of Laplace (add one) smoothing and priors taken from the training data.

Logistic regression

We used our probability model from Equation 1 with a two-class logistic regression model. Given VE recruitment class labels Rec={+1,−1}, we applied the following generalized linear model (GLM) using the logit function [45].

$$Rec_j = \pm 1 \mid \mathbf{w}(d_i)\ ] = \frac{1}{1+\exp\left[-Rec_j\left(\beta_0 + \sum_{k=1}^{n} \beta_k \cdot w_k\left(d_i\right)\right)\right]}$$

We estimated parameters $\beta_0, \ldots, \beta_k$ from training data by minimizing the L2-regularized log-likelihood:

$$\frac{1}{2}\beta^T\beta + C\sum_{i=1}^{n} \log\left(1 + e^{-Rec_i\ \beta^T d_i}\right) \tag{4}$$

where C>0 is the regularization cost parameter.

We used the LiblineaR package in R to minimize Equation 4 and then to predict the VE recruitment classification of testing data [46]. All GLM results shown in the "Results and discussion" section are for L2-regularized logistic regression models fit with the default settings for this R package and an L2-regularization cost parameter C equal to the ratio of negative to positive class labels.

Classification trees

We applied the probability model in Equation 1 to a classification tree by calculating the posterior probability of the recruitment classes at each node of the tree. The R package tree was used to train classifiers grown using recursive partitioning with a deviance criterion to select features at each node [47]. We used the default package parameters to control tree growth, including: minimum within-node deviance $=0.01(\text{deviance}_{root})$, minimum allowable node size = 10, and minimum observations to a candidate child node = 5.

Logit boosting

We applied an ensemble of the tree classifier to this recruitment classification problem using the LogitBoost algorithm implemented in the R package caTools[48]. The boosting results shown in the "Results and discussion" section were produced using the package's default weak learner, decision stumps, and 101 boosting iterations. Logit boosting is an application of the original boosting algorithm, AdaBoost, except with the binomial log-likelihood as the minimized loss function (logistic loss) shown below [49]:

$$\sum_{i=1}^{n} log\left(1 + e^{-2Rec_i\ F(d_i)}\right) \tag{5}$$

Support vector machines

Finally, we trained a recruitment classifier using the support vector machine (SVM) algorithm implemented in the R package e1071[44]. SVMs do not fit into a probability model like Equation 1; however, the R package provides a method for estimating class probabilities if they are required for things like performance comparisons with receiver operating characteristic (ROC) curves. All SVM results shown below were produced using default package parameters, constraint violation cost = 100, and a radial basis function as the kernel.

RESULTS AND DISCUSSION

To make full use of the annotated data available for training and testing, we randomly segmented the data into ten folds and applied cross-validation. The statistics shown in this section come from the aggregated results of those ten models trained on mutually exclusive training data. We evaluated the classification methods using ROC curves, which show trade-offs between the metrics in the contingency table shown in Table 4. Specifically, ROC curves show the trade-offs between the False Positive Rate (FPR) and True Positive Rate (TPR) at various classification thresholds θ, as generated using Equations 6 and 7. We also employed area under the ROC curve (AUC) to compare each method's performance along the entire curve using a single measure.

$$FPR(\theta) = \frac{FP}{FP+TN} = \frac{FP}{N} \quad (6)$$

Table 4 Confusion matrix used to assess the recruitment model's classification performance

Model classification			
Observed classification	$Pr(Rec_i \mid d_i) \geq \theta$	$Pr(Rec_i \mid d_i) < \theta$	
Recruitment = True	True positives	False negatives	P=TP+FN
	(TP)	(FN)	
Recruitment = False	False positives	True negatives	N=FP+TN
	(FP)	(TN)	
	^P=TP+FP	^N=FN+TN	I=P+N

$$TPR(\theta) = \frac{TP}{TP+FN} = \frac{TP}{P} \quad (7)$$

A comparison of five VE recruitment classifiers using the annotated Ansar1 data can be seen in Figure 1. These are mean ROC curves averaged over the ten fold cross-validation experiment. Results show all the classifiers performing better than a random-guess model (the diagonal), with the SVM classifier performing best at an AUC of 0.89. A comparison of bootstrap results estimating the mean cross-validated AUC can be seen in Figure 2. These bootstrap results were obtained by re-sampling 10,000 times from each testing fold, calculating the AUC on each bootstrapped sample, and then averaging each of those bootstrapped AUCs across the ten cross-validation folds. This resulted in 10,000 mean AUCs for each of the classification models described above. The box-plots provide a similar graphical performance comparison to Figure 1, but also provide a reference for how widely each method's accuracy varies. All the methods range between 0.2 and 0.3 AUC with SVM having the smallest performance variance and boosting having the widest. A statistical comparison of the five classification methods using the bootstrapped mean AUCs is shown in Table 5. We used Tukey's range test to determine if the difference in mean AUC between the models is statistically significant [50]. The 95% confidence intervals in Table 5 show a significant difference between each of the classification methods' mean AUC. Therefore, as shown by the ordering of model results in Figure 2 and Table 5, the SVM classifier returned the best performance and classification trees returned the worst mean AUC performance ($p<0.05$).

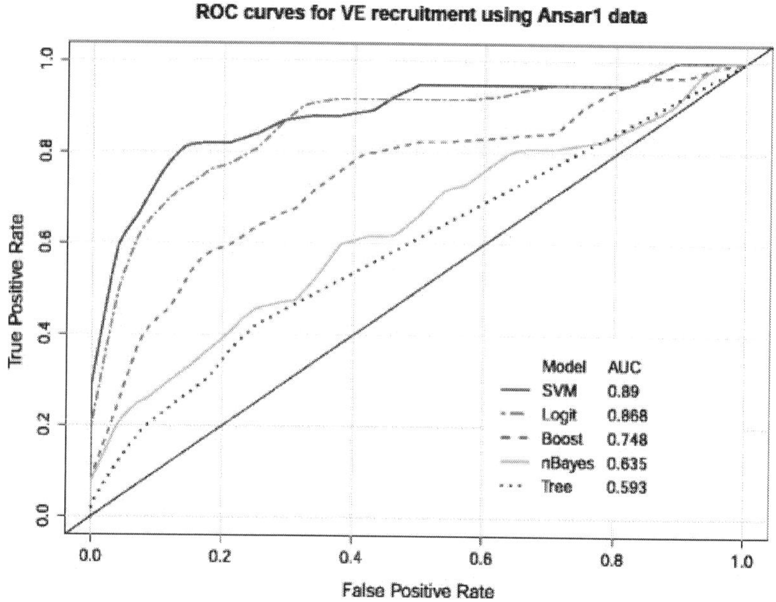

Figure 1 Comparison of VE recruitment classifiers using ROC curves. Curves are averaged over ten cross-validation folds showing classification results for the models.

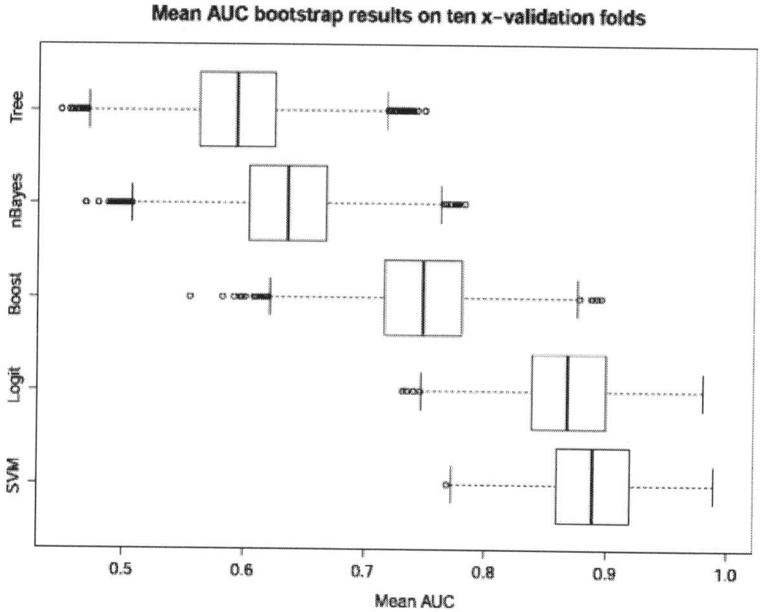

Figure 2 Comparison of VE recruitment classifiers using mean AUC bootstrap results.Box-plots of 10,000 bootstrapped AUCs averaged over ten cross-validation folds.

Table 5 95% confidence intervals for multiple comparisons of bootstrapped mean AUCs using Tukey's range test

	95% CI	
Tukey's test comparisons	**Upper**	**Lower**
SVM – Logit	0.019	0.023
SVM – Boost	0.139	0.143
SVM – nBayes	0.252	0.256
SVM – Tree	0.294	0.297
Logit – Boost	0.119	0.122
Logit – nBayes	0.232	0.235
Logit – Tree	0.273	0.276
Boost – nBayes	0.111	0.115
Boost – Tree	0.153	0.156
nBayes – Tree	0.040	0.043

The computational complexity of these methods is well documented; however, their runtime performance on this VE recruitment task is not well known. A comparison of time performance benchmarks for two different tasks can be seen in Table 6. The training task results are obtained from trials of each supervised learning algorithm applied to 294 annotated posts per trial. The classification task is the application of each pre-trained classifier to a set of posts resulting in an average classification time per post. Comparing the results in Table 6, we can see that all the methods train in under 30 seconds with SVM, Logistic Regression, and naive Bayes learning two orders of magnitude faster. SVM and logistic regression perform the best on the classification task, but all the methods classify posts in well under a second. Therefore any of these methods is a feasible VE recruitment classifier if the average time between posts is greater than a tenth of a second; a reasonable assumption for many online forums.

Table 6 Time performance benchmark results* (a) training time using 294 posts, and (b) mean classification time per post

	Training (s)		**Classification (ms/post)**
SVM	0.450		0.18
Logit	0.049		0.22
Boost	29.790		0.27
nBayes	0.987		128.57
Tree	11.140		28.18

*Hardware: Intel®; Core™ i5 CPU M 480 @ 2.67 GHz; 8 GB RAM.

Typically classification research compares results against prior methods as a benchmark for improvements in accuracy; however, we were unable to find any previously published methods for the specific task of identifying violent extremist recruitment using text classification techniques. Thus, our results serve as initial performance benchmarks against which future methods can be compared.

To provide some understanding of how the best performing classification models are being trained to recognize VE recruitment, Table 7 shows a list of the top-weighted features in the logistic regression model. It is clear from the table that posts relating to the escalating conflicts in Nigeria and Somalia were primary topics in the Ansar1 data—an intuitive finding considering the 2009 timeframe of the sampled data. The importance of such terms hints at the Logit model's potential for over-fitting this particular time period. Running the same model on other time periods would likely produce lower performance scores, since different wording is likely. Other important terms like "jihad", "allah", and words stemming from "milit" exemplify the algorithm's ability to recognize typical features of Islamic violent extremism. Perhaps surprisingly, none of the top ten terms are particularly indicative of recruitment. This may be due to the abundant presence of terms like "recruit" and "join". These terms are among the top 30 most frequent, appearing in our corpus 178 and 126 times respectively. High frequency makes these terms more likely to occur in both recruitment and non-recruitment posts and therefore diminishes their discriminating power. Regardless of how they work, performance metrics show that the best models (SVM and Logit) detect VE recruitment with considerable accuracy (mean AUC>0.85).

Table 7 The most discriminating term features as weighted by the cross-validated logistic regression models

Feature	Weight	Feature	Weight
nigeria	0.90	jihad	0.61
hamas	0.72	alandalus	0.61
foreign	0.67	milit (ant,ary,...)	0.60
somalia	0.66	american	0.60
may	-0.65	allah	-0.54

CONCLUSIONS AND FUTURE WORK

This work was motivated by increasing online activities of violent extremist organizations along with the lack of automated approaches to analyze such activity. Our research built upon recent data collection and analysis efforts to develop supervised learning and natural language processing methods that automatically identify cyber-recruitment by violent extremists. The results presented in this article support the conclusion that automatic VE recruitment detection is a feasible goal. As the first reported results on this task, our classifiers serve as initial performance benchmarks against which future VE recruitment classifiers can be compared.

In the future, our VE recruitment detection methods could be improved by including support for non-English languages. Whether such future methods use automatic translation or non-English features, support for other languages is an important task considering that violent extremist groups frequently operate in non-English speaking communities. Incorporating non-English text and features could be accomplished through the use of experts to perform the manual annotation. Expert judges might also improve annotation quality if agreement remains strong. Future work could also analyze classifier behavior in depth, and test the effectiveness of more advanced feature selection and modeling techniques. Methods like latent semantic analysis perform singular value decomposition transformations on the feature space and may be employed to further reduce both dimensionality and the effect of non-discriminating terms [51]. Latent Dirichlet allocation may be used to substitute the terms in a high-dimensional feature space with a smaller set of latent topics that represent the major subjects appearing in the corpus [52]. Such latent variable modeling techniques could serve as feature selection and replacement methods while preserving the statistical relationships that are essential for text classification tasks.

By testing the effectiveness of our methods in a proxy for real-world settings we demonstrated that such automated classification tools would clearly fit into the workflow of counterterrorism intelligence teams like the FBI's information review analysts. The current workflow tasks human analysts with manually reviewing and annotating "the ever-increasing [volume of investigative] information" stored in data warehouses like the Electronic Surveillance Data Management System (DWS-EDMS) used by the FBI [6]. An automated classification system using our methods for detecting VE recruitment could serve as a pre-screening step in the current review workflow tasked with reducing the volume of documents requiring human attention. Our automated approach could also complement current lead management systems like eGuardian by automatically detecting potential terrorist recruitment events so they can be efficiently compiled into leads for current investigations or used as evidence to open new terrorism-related investigations.

More generally our automated classification methods could be used as part of a VE recruitment identification and tracking methodology that would enable the study of recruitment efforts and the membership dynamics of violent organizations. Such a method might be able to measure the effectiveness of extremist and counterinsurgency efforts on new membership by correlating specific recruitment activities and current events with changes in the VE population of a community. As a future research path, this proposed methodology requires (1) an automated system for classifying whether a forum user is a member of a violent extremist group, and (2) time series methods for analyzing recruitment and membership along a timeline.

In light of the still unfolding news regarding the NSA's Boundless Informant and PRISM programs [53], we address some ethical implications of our work. Given that such a comprehensive and intrusive source of text data does exist, there is clearly a potential for abusing a recruitment and membership classification method to target non-combative individuals. Such tracking methods could thwart perfectly legal recruitment efforts of peaceful protesters, or radical yet law-abiding religious sects. These groups might fit the profile of a VE organization in every way except the critical ingredient of violence. Furthermore, recruitment alone rarely necessitates a violent act even though a recruiter may refer to or even encourage such acts. Because of these possible unethical repercussions, we proposed classification methods that target not just extremist groups, but specifically violent groups engaged in acts like terrorism. We hope that tuning the learning algorithms in this way will reduce some risk of misuse.

REFERENCES

1. LA Overbey, G McKoy, J Gordon, S McKitrick, Automated sensing and social network analysis in virtual worlds, in Intelligence and Security Informatics (ISI) (IEEE Vancouver, BC, Canada, 2010), pp. 179–184
2. R Torok, "Make A Bomb In Your Mums Kitchen": Cyber Recruiting And Socialisation of 'White Moors' and Home Grown Jihadists, in Australian Counter Terrorism Conference (School of Computer and Information Science, Edith Cowan University Perth, Western Australia, 2010), pp. 54–61
3. M Rogers, ed. by A Silke, Chapter 4: The Psychology of Cyber-Terrorism, in Terrorists, Victims and Society: Psychological Perspectives on Terrorism and its Consequences (John Wiley & Sons Chichester, West Sussex, England, 2003), pp. 77–92
4. S O'Rourke, Virtual radicalisation: Challenges for police, in 8th Australian Information Warfare and Security Conference (School of Computer and Infomation Science, Edith Cowan University Perth, Western Australia, 2007), pp. 29–35
5. S Mandal, E-P Lim, Second life: Limits of creativity or cyber threat, in IEEE Conference on Technologies for Homeland Security (IEEE Waltham, MA, 2008), pp. 498–503
6. WH Webster, DE Winter, L Adrian, J Steel, WM Baker, RJ Bruemmer, KL Wainstein, Final report of the William H.Webster Commission on the Federal Bureau of Investigation, counterterrorism intelligence, and the events at Fort Hood, Texas on November 5, 2009. Technical report, Federal Bureau of Investigation (2012)
7. RR Tomes, Waging war on terror relearning counterinsurgency warfare. Parameters. 34(1), 16–28 (2004)
8. F Gutiérrez, Recruitment in a civil war: a preliminary discussion of the colombian case, in Santa Fe Institute, Mimeo, (2006)
9. M Humphreys, JM Weinstein, Who fights? the determinants of participation in civil war. Am. J. Pol. Sci. 52(2), 436–455 (2008)
10. MI Lichbach, The Rebel's Dilemma. (University of Michigan Press, Ann Arbor, 1998)
11. K Peters, P Richards, 'Why we fight': Voices of youth combatants in Sierra Leone. Africa. 68(02), 183–210 (1998)
12. JM Weinstein, Inside Rebellion: The Politics of Insurgent Violence. (Cambridge University Press, New York, 2007)
13. RD Petersen, Resistance and Rebellion: Lessons from Eastern Europe. (Cambridge University Press, New York, 2001)

14. S Popkin, The rational peasant. Theory Soc. 9(3), 411–471 (1980)
15. JC Scott, The Moral Economy of the Peasant: Rebellion and Subsistence in Southeast Asia. (Yale University Press, New Haven & London, 1976)
16. EJ Wood, Insurgent Collective Action and Civil War in El Salvador. (Cambridge University Press, New York, 2003)
17. RW McGehee, Deadly Deceits: My 25 Years in the CIA. (Sheridan Square Publications, Inc., New York, 1983), pp. 95–116
18. M Conway, Terrorism and the internet: new media–new threat? Parliamentary Aff. 59(2), 283–298 (2006)
19. R Torok, Developing an explanatory model for the process of online radicalisation and terrorism. Secur. Informatics. 2(1), 1–10 (2013)
20. L Bowman-Grieve, A psychological perspective on virtual communities supporting terrorist & extremist ideologies as a tool for recruitment. Secur. Informatics. 2(1), 1–5 (2013)
21. EF Kohlmann, Al-Qaida's MySpace: terrorist recruitment on the internet. CTC Sentinel. 1(2), 8–9 (2008)
22. LA Overbey, G McKoy, J Gordon, S McKitrick, Jr MH, L Buhler, L Casassa, S Yaryan, Virtual DNA: Investigating cyber-behaviors in virtual worldsL. Technical Report 33-09 E, Space and Naval Warfare System Center Atlantic Charleston, SC (2009)
23. GS McNeal, Cyber embargo: Countering the internet jihad. Case West. Reserv. Univ. J. Int. Law. 39, 789–826 (2008)
24. H Chen, S Thoms, T Fu, Cyber extremism in web 2.0: An exploratory study of international jihadist groups, in IEEE International Conference on Intelligence and Security Informatics (ISI) (IEEE Taipei, 2008), pp. 98–103
25. M Yang, M Kiang, H Chen, Y Li, Artificial immune system for illicit content identification in social media. J. Am. Soc. Inf. Sci. Technol. 63(2), 256–269 (2012)
26. A Basu, Social network analysis of terrorist organizations in India, in North American Association for Computational Social and Organizational Science (NAACSOS) Conference (NAACSOS Notre Dame, Indiana, 2005), pp. 26–28
27. KM Carley, Destabilization of covert networks. Comput. Math. Organ. Theory. 12(1), 51–66 (2006)
28. M Chau, J Xu, Using web mining and social network analysis to study the emergence of cyber communities in blogs, in Terrorism Informatics (Springer New York, 2008), pp. 473–494
29. J Diesner, KM Carley, Using network text analysis to detect the organizational structure of covert networks, in Proceedings of the North American Association for Computational Social and Organizational Science (NAACSOS) Conference (NAACSOS Pittsburgh, 2004) 30. Z Chen, B Liu, M Hsu, M Castellanos, R Ghosh, Identifying intention posts in discussion forums, in Proceedings of NAACL-HLT (Association for Computational Linguistics Atlanta, Georgia, 2013), pp. 1041–1050

30. H Chen, W Chung, J Qin, E Reid, M Sageman, G Weimann, Uncovering the dark web: A case study of jihad on the web. J. Am. Soc. Inf. Sci. Technol. 59(8), 1347–1359 (2008)

31. T Fu, A Abbasi, H Chen, A focused crawler for dark web forums. J. Am. Soc. Inf. Sci. Technol. 61(6), 1213–1231 (2010)

32. Google Inc., Google Translate (2014). http://translate.google.com/

33. H Chen, E Reid, J Sinai, A Silke, B Ganor (eds.), Terrorism Informatics: Knowledge Management and Data Mining for Homeland Security. (Springer, New York, 2008)

34. Artificial Intelligence Laboratory, University Of Arizona, Dark Web Forum Portal: Ansar AlJihad Network English Website (2014). http://cri-portal. dyndns. org

35. J Cohen, A coefficient of agreement for nominal scales. Educ. Psychol. Meas. 20(1), 37–46 (1960)

36. JR Landis, GG Koch, The measurement of observer agreement for categorical data. Biometrics. 33(1), 159–174 (1977)

37. JL Fleiss, B Levin, MC Paik, The measurement of interrater agreement. Stat. Methods Rates Proportions. 2, 212–236 (1981)

38. I Feinerer, K Hornik, Tm: Text Mining Package. (R Foundation for Statistical Computing, 2014). R package version 0.5-10. http://CRAN.R-project.org/ package=tm

39. TP Jurka, L Collingwood, AE Boydstun, E Grossman, W van Atteveldt, RTextTools: Automatic Text Classification Via Supervised Learning (2014). R package version 1.4.2. http://CRAN.R-project.org/package=RTextTools

40. CJ Van Rijsbergen, SE Robertson, MF Porter, New Models in Probabilistic Information Retrieval. (British Library Research and Development Dept, 1980)

41. W Cavnar, ed. by DK Harman, Using an n-gram-based document representation with a vector processing retrieval model, in Overview of the Third Text Retrieval Conference (Computer Systems Laboratory, National Institute of Standards and Technology Gaithersburg, MD, 1995), pp. 269–277

42. RO Duda, PE Hart, DG Stork, Pattern Classification, 2nd edn. (John Wiley & Sons, Inc, New York, 2001), p. 62

43. D Meyer, E Dimitriadou, K Hornik, A Weingessel, F Leisch, E1071: Misc Functions of the Department of Statistics (e1071), TU Wien (2014). R package version 1.6-2. http://CRAN.R-project.org/package=e1071

44. C-J Lin, RC Weng, SS Keerthi, Trust region newton method for logistic regression. J. Mach. Learn. Res. 9, 627–650 (2008)

45. T Helleputte, LiblineaR: Linear Predictive Models Based On The Liblinear C/ C++ Library (2013). R package version 1.80-7. http://CRAN.R-project. org/web/ packages/LiblineaR

46. B Ripley, Tree: Classification and Regression Trees (2014). R package version

1.0-35. http://CRAN.R-project.org/package=tree

47. J Tuszynski, caTools: ROC AUC Tools, Moving Window Statistics (2013). R package version 1.16. http://CRAN.R-project.org/package=caTools
48. J Friedman, T Hastie, R Tibshirani, Additive logistic regression: a statistical view of boosting. Ann. Stat. 28(2), 337–407 (2000)
49. AP Fenech, Tukey's method of multiple comparison in the randomized blocks model. J. Am. Stat. Assoc. 74(368), 881–884 (1979)
50. S Deerwester, ST Dumais, GW Furnas, TK Landauer, R Harshman, Indexing by latent semantic analysis. J. Am. Soc. Inf. Sci. 41(6), 391–407 (1990)
51. DM Blei, AY Ng, MI Jordan, Latent dirichlet allocation. J. Mach. Learn. Res. 3, 993–1022 (2003)
52. G Greenwald, NSA Collecting Phone Records of Millions of Verizon Customers Daily (2013). http://www.guardian.co.uk/world/2013/jun/06/ nsa-phone-records-verizon-court-order

16
CHAPTER

A PSYCHOLOGICAL PERSPECTIVE ON VIRTUAL COMMUNITIES SUPPORTING TERRORIST & EXTREMIST IDEOLOGIES AS A TOOL FOR RECRUITMENT

Lorraine Bowman-Grieve

Keywords: Psychology, Terrorism, Extremism, Virtual communities, Recruitment

BACKGROUND

Understanding terrorism: a group phenomenon

Terrorism is, first and foremost, a group phenomenon [1], the dynamics of which have traditionally been difficult to assess due to the predominantly clandestine nature of these organisations. However, the Internet and its use by terrorist movements, individual members, and potential supporters and recruits afford new avenues for accessing information about terrorist groups and their activities.

Crenshaw (1990) [2] argues that because terrorist behaviour cannot be labelled as pathological or irrational due to the lack of empirical evidence to support such notions, it must therefore be considered a choice which is made following a process of logical reasoning. As such terrorist activity can be described as rational and comprehensible in light of the circumstances and contexts in which it occurs. Individual psychological processes toward involvement can be described as rational and logical because of the primarily psychological benefits associated with involvement in terrorism for example, a sense of belonging, status, or power; perceptions of excitement or empowerment.

Citation: Bowman-Grieve: A psychological perspective on virtual communities supporting terrorist & extremist ideologies as a tool for recruitment. Security Informatics 2013 2:9. doi:10.1186/2190-8532-2-9

Individual reasons why people become involved are many and varied, with no single catalyst event that explains involvement [3], however research indicates that involvement is a gradual process that occurs over time. This gradual process of becoming involved is mediated by 'group' factors, the social aspects of which provide justifications and support for increasing involvement over time.

Despite the clandestine nature of terrorist movements and their predominant incompatibility with first-hand research our understanding of involvement and recruitment processes has increased in recent years. For example, it has been noted in numerous studies that inter-personal bonds play an important role in this recruitment process. Della Porta (1992) [4] for example, from empirical research with Italian militants, suggests that an important stage in the socialisation process, which leads to involvement in a terrorist or underground movement, is the construction of peer groups during adolescence. Similarly, in a more recent study Post, Sprinzak and Denny (2003) [5], based on semi-structured interviews with incarcerated Middle Eastern terrorists, found that peer influence was cited as a dominant reason for joining a terrorist group. Furthermore recent studies relating to Islamic fundamentalist recruitment indicate that kinship and social bonds also play a key role in this process. Sageman (2004) [6] for example, in an analysis of 400 terrorist biographies, found that sixty-eight percent had pre-existing friendship bonds to others involved in the Jihad or joined the Jihad as a collective decision, while a further twenty percent joined through kinship bonds, meaning that the individual had a close relative in the Jihad.

Passy (2000) [7] states that social networks play an important role in influencing the behaviour of the individual and their readiness to take part in collective action because of their inherent functions, such as socialising, recruitment and decision shaping; success or failure in the recruitment process ultimately is dependent on the relationship formed by the recruiter with the potential recruit. According to Starks and Sims Bainbridge (1980) [8] the recruiter must 'bond' with the potential recruit for the process to be successful. The Internet and virtual communities in particular may aid in facilitating this process. For example, Back (2002) [9] draws attention to the use of websites and virtual communities to recruit new members, by providing contact information and details on how to join and contribute to support activities. Encouraging Internet users to become involved in online support activities serve to draw supporters further into the movement. Members can also use virtual communities to make contact with other supporters within their localities, forming both on and offline communities, networks and bonds through the Internet. Arguably the most potent combination will be involvement online and identification with the terrorist group, in addition to exposure to recruiters and opportunities to engage in support behaviours in the physical world.

CASE DESCRIPTION

The internet, virtual communities, recruitment & processes of involvement

While the effectiveness of the bomb remains essential to the terrorist movement in terms of the psychological element of terrorism and to draw attention to the movement and their goals, the Internet provides a safe, easy and cheap means of communicating, disseminating propaganda, gathering intelligence, promoting support, demonising the enemy and raising funds. Terrorist use of the Internet and the communicative value the use of this technology brings, are wide ranging and far-reaching. In essence the Internet provides a new solution to the old problem of communication; where once terrorist movements were reliant on 'traditional' forms of media to bring their 'cause' to the public, the Internet now facilitates a broad spectrum of communication possibilities, from websites to virtual communities.

The term 'virtual community' can be used here as an anchor, an already formulated notion of shared online space and communicative interaction between users [10], from which it is possible to examine the content and nature of online communities in support of terrorist movements and extremist ideologies. Virtual communities of this nature have important functions for the individual and the group, providing a 'safe haven' for supporters of extremist ideologies, a forum of validation and support and the means to become knowledgeable and increasingly involved within the movement over time. Analysis and interpretation of online interactions within virtual communities [11] indicate that community interaction may play a role in the earlier phases of the recruitment process particularly those relating to initial support and involvement.

The discourses created and sustained within virtual communities can be used to disseminate information, to communicate ideologies, to promote and propagandise, to encourage involvement and throughout all of these to potentially facilitate the recruitment of individuals to specific groups. The sustenance of discourses that seek to dehumanise the enemy and justify the ideology of the movement contributes to a community of validation that exists for members and potential members of the movement. It can be argued that virtual community members exist in some kind of a pre- or semi-radicalized state; they are groups of members, potential members, recruiters and recruits.

DISCUSSION & EVALUATION

Recruitment online: some examples from the radical right

As early as 2001 Ray and March II [12] investigated the use of Internet by white extremists for recruitment purposes. These authors found that white extremist movements were indeed using the services and facilities provided by the Internet to recruit new members and encourage investment and further online involvement in the activities of the organisation. The ease of access to material provided by the Internet has increased the likelihood of both adults and young people searching online to find something to believe in or to reaffirm their already existing beliefs, as such the Internet can be used as a gateway into the particular culture, ideals and beliefs of a movement in question [13]. The following quote from a member of the radical right virtual community of Stormfront illustrates the important role the Internet can play in recruitment and involvement processes - "*It was the Internet that got me interested: checking out sites like the Hammerskins and Combat 18/Screwdriver.net in particular. Then after a few emails etc., I got contacts and then was able to meet up with like minded people in the flesh...it all just grew from there. Never underestimate the power of the Internet when it comes to recruiting new folk to our movement.*"

The availability of White Power music and white supremacist computer games online (made available through websites and virtual communities), are used to target youths specifically in an attempt to interest them in the movement with the aim of recruitment. Similarly 'white' dating services can function effectively in the promotion and sustenance of right wing networking [14].

White power music

The significance of White Power music to the recruitment process involving young people is worthy of mention particularly in light of the many websites that exist to promote such music. The White Power music scene remains one of the fundamental links promoting a wide radical right (in particular neo-Nazi/skinhead) network, with music and lyrics used not only to promote violence against minorities but also to reflect the socio-economic issues and grievances of importance to the movement, such as immigration policies, the 'Jewish conspiracy' and belief in the inevitability of a race war [15]. According to Cotter (1999) [15], the lyrics of such music reinforce the White Power rhetoric and acts as an important recruitment tool; representing primarily the youth sub-culture of the movement.

In the following example a user of the radical right virtual community 'Stormfront' refers to the role of White Power music and the Internet in his involvement process - "*I was on the Internet one night looking for a song on some file sharing program. I came across one called "White Power" by a band called Skrewdriver. I hated negroes, spics, gays, etc. and decided to download it. The second Ian Stuart shouted out "White Power 1,2,3,4" i was HOOKED.*" In this case the music downloaded from the Internet lead to this individual 'surfing the net' further to find the website of a White Power record label and subsequently the purchasing of David Duke's book 'My Awakening' which is in turn cited by many individuals as playing an important role in becoming involved in support of the radical right.

Computer games

The increasing popularity and sophistication of computer games is being utilised by extremist elements online to draw in potential new recruits, targeting primarily the youth demographic [12]. The increasing sophistication of these games and their potential as a propaganda and recruitment tool should not be ignored. For example according to the Anti-Defamation League (2002) [16] Resistance Records (owned by The National Alliance and considered the main distributors of White Power rock), have widened their product base to include racist and anti-Semitic games such as 'Ethnic Cleansing'. This particular game is based on other more mainstream games such as Doom and Quake. It is a city-based game and the player can choose his attire, with KKK robes or Skinhead garb as the options. The player moves through the game murdering 'predatory sub-humans' and their Jewish 'masters' in order to save the white world. Throughout the game National Alliance signs and posters can be seen in the background while White

Power rock bands provide the background music. In the final stages of the game the player is confronted by the 'end boss' (Ariel Sharon) who shouts statements such as "We have destroyed your culture", when the Sharon character is killed he says "Filthy white dog, you have destroyed thousands of years of planning" (reflecting the conspiracy theory of the Jews being the Master planners plotting the downfall of the white race) [16]. Ethnic Cleansing is just one of the games promoted and sold by the National Alliance and affiliate Resistance Records. Another game White Law is also for sale from the site and is reminiscent of The Turner Diaries[a] (which had been rumoured to be planned for release as a computer game in 2002). The associated blurb for 'White Law' claims, "More weapons, more levels, much more challenging than Ethnic Cleansing". (These games can be purchased for just US$10 each). While the link between right wing inspired online gaming & computer gaming in general remains tentative at best it continues to serve an important propaganda dissemination function for Right Wing extremist movements in general [11].

Online dating service – 'Whites Only'

In relation to the facilitation of interpersonal bonds online, some Radical Right communities (and websites) have set up dating services. Such services target white men and women who desire contact on a personal level, and can have an impact on lifestyle choices for members of the movement making it easier for them to meet a partner with similar political/ideological views. For example, a number of websites are dedicated purely to 'White Pride' dating services, such as euro datelink (http://www.eurodatelink.com/). The Stormfront discussion forum also provides a forum section dedicated to white singles seeking dates, this section of the board is divided into two subsections, one dedicated to 'talk', the other dedicated to 'dating advice'. These facilities are popular among single users and appear to be well used. They provide information and links to other white dating services, for example this information posted by one of the moderators:

"*Dating web sites are very popular on the Internet. There are many dating sites for many different ethnic groups -- Jewish, Black, Indian, Native American, Arab, and Asian. However, if you look for White singles, there isn't much. We needed a dedicated dating site for normal White people of European descent who would like to meet people with a similar background. Therefore we decided to launch Eurodatelink.net. Eurodatelink is for people of European descent wherever they may live, rich or poor, Christian, pagan, or atheist who share one common desire: to meet other White people for dating, romance, or friendship.*http://www.eurodatelink.net/*is a real dating site for White heterosexual people looking to meet singles or who just want to make new friends.*"

The use of the Internet, particularly websites and discussion forum services, to promote in-group networking and 'dating' services for whites only, are noteworthy not simply because they represent a means for individuals to meet other like minded individuals but also because they can arguably be seen as facilitating increased involvement. For example, in encouraging others to date within their own race group members promote the ideology of the group as important in relation to life decisions outside of the virtual realm. Similarly, such services provide a way for people to become involved in this movement and to become acquainted with others within the movement on a more personal level. The fostering of personal relationships with others involved within extremist movements has been identified as a contributing factor toward increasing involvement over time. The potential for relationships formed online to contribute to the involvement process of individuals has not been empirically studied and perhaps warrants further investigation, particularly given the large number of Internet and community members who apparently avail of this service.

CONCLUSIONS

The radical right represents a factionalised movement with dispersed networked organisational structure which primarily adheres to the notion of 'leaderless resistance'. While the radical right have not actively orchestrated a large-scale terrorist campaign to achieve their aims they continue to retain an interested body of supporters and promoters, as exemplified by their online presence, in particular sophisticated virtual communities of support with large number of registered members.

Essentially virtual support communities facilitate social interaction and the formation of social bonds, which in turn can lead to changes in attitudes and behaviour over time. These changes in attitude might include adopting the most prevalent ideology expressed within the community. Similarly changes in behaviour might include involvement in a range of both on and off line activities in support of the ideology/organisation. Just as individuals who may be open to supporting an organisation do not necessarily become further involved, so is the case for virtual community members. Although virtual community members may freely express their opinions online, not all of them will take the next step and become new members or recruits (of either the online or offline organisations), similarly not all individuals become increasingly involved.

However given that virtual communities promote discussion, interaction and the formation of interpersonal bonds and relationships, which often occur when individuals use the communities regularly, they are potential recruiting grounds and should be recognised as such. This is particularly the case in light of research that suggests this may be an important factor in the recruitment process [12]. Limited numbers of people decide to become members of terrorist organisations however the Internet has the potential to facilitate at least some level of recruitment. Arguably this will be most apparent where there is a strong online presence that encourages and promotes involvement in support related activities such as donating funds, distributing fliers, supporting Prisoners of War and/or engaging in online support activities (with the potential to later engage in offline support activities). With this in mind it is important to continue investigating how and why terrorist movements and their supporters use the Internet and to consider that these uses are open to innovation and change reflecting the dynamic nature of modern technology.

ENDNOTES

[a]The Turner Diaries (1978), written by William Pierce (former leader of the National Alliance) under the pseudonym Andrew Macdonald, provide a blueprint for the organisation and strategic development of a clandestine terrorist group.

ACKNOWLEDGEMENTS

Journal instruction requires an Acknowledgements section however none was provided. In this regard, please provide the missing section. Many thanks to Alison Torn and EISIC reviewers who commented on earlier drafts of this paper.

REFERENCES

1. N Friedland, Becoming a terrorist: Social and individual antecedents, in Terrorism: Roots, impact, responses, ed. by L Howard (Praeger, New York, 1992), pp. 81–94
2. M Crenshaw, The logic of terrorism: Terrorist behaviour as a product of strategic choice, in Origins of terrorism: Psychologies, ideologies, theologies, states of mind, ed. by W Reich (Cambridge University Press, Cambridge, 1990), pp. 7–24
3. J Horgan, The Psychology of Terrorism (Routledge, Oxon, 2005)
4. Dd Porta, Political socialization in left-wing underground organizations: Biographies of Italian and German militants, in Social movements and violence: Participation in underground organizations, ed. by Dd Porta (JAI Press, Greenwich, CT, 1992), pp. 259–290
5. J Post, E Sprinzak, L Denny, The terrorists in their own words: Interviews with 35 incarcerated Middle Eastern Terrorists. Terrorism & Political Violence 15(1), 171–184 (2003)
6. M Sageman, Understanding terrorist networks (University of Pennsylvania Press, Philadelphia, 2004)
7. F Passy, Socialization, recruitment, and the structure/agency gap. A specification of the impact of networks on participation in social movements, 2000. Retrieved June 20th, 2011 from http://www.nd.edu/ ~dmyers/lomond/passy.pdf
8. R Starks, W Sims Bainbridge, Networks of faith: Interpersonal bonds and recruitment to cults and sects. The American Journal of Sociology 85(6), 1376–1395 (1980)
9. L Back, Aryans reading Adorno: Cyber-culture and twenty-first century Racism. Ethnic & Racial Studies 25(4), 628–651 (2002)
10. S Jones, Cybersociety: Computer Mediated Communication and Community (Sage Publications, Thousand Oaks, 1995)
11. L Bowman-Grieve, Exploring Stormfront: The Virtual Community of the Radical Right. Studies in Conflict & Terrorism 32(11), 989–1007 (2009)
12. B Ray, & GE Marsh II, Recruitment by extremist groups on the Internet. (Electronic version) First Monday, 6 (2), 2001. Retrieved June 20th, 2011 from http://firstmonday.org/htbin/cgiwrap/bin/ojs/index.php/fm/article/view/834/743
13. L Bowman-Grieve, Irish Republicanism and the Internet: Support for new wave dissidents. Perspectives on Terrorism 4(2), 22–34 (2010)
14. R Ezekiel, The racist mind (Viking, New York, 1995)
15. JM Cotter, Sounds of Hate: White Power rock and roll and the Neo-Nazi Skinhead subculture. Terrorism and Political Violence 11(2), 111–140 (1999)

16. Anti-Defamation League. Racist Groups Using Computer Gaming to Promote Violence against Blacks, Latinos and Jews, 2002. Retrieved June 20th, 2011 from http://www.adl.org/videogames/default.asp

17

CHAPTER

DEVELOPING AN EXPLANATORY MODEL FOR THE PROCESS OF ONLINE RADICALIZATION AND TERRORISM

Robyn Torok

Keywords: Foucault, Psychiatric power, Online radicalization, Power relations, Norm alization, Terrorism

INTRODUCTION

The use of the internet for terrorist recruitment and operations has increased significantly in recent years. Part of that expansion is an embracing of Western social media including Facebook, Twitter and YouTube. While this phenomenon is well documented, what is more difficult to determine due to limited research, are the mechanisms and power relations that underlie this phenomenon of online media used to promote radicalization which in some cases can develop into terrorism. Currently, more traditional models are utilized that look at concepts such as psychological warfare, propaganda, indoctrination and data mining [1]. Furthermore, narratives are viewed as an important aspect of seduction for radicalization [1, 2].

This paper examines these mechanisms and power relations using the analytical framework from historian and philosopher Michel Foucault; in particular, his earlier work on psychiatric power [3]. Foucault's approach on psychiatric power focused on the asylum as an institution in order to modify and normalize extreme behaviors of those who were deemed as 'mad'. What is particularly significant from Foucault's work is that terms such as 'madness' and psychiatric discourses are historically constituted

Citation: Torok: Developing an explanatory model for the process of online radicalization and terrorism. doi:10.1186/2190-8532-2-6.

through power relations [4]. Naturally the term 'jihad', should also be subject to historical contextualization. However, it is not the intention of this paper to reproduce what others have done, such as a genealogy of Islamic ideas [5]. Rather, this paper looks at how the institutional context for these discourses has shifted, particularly in light of the 'war on terror'. Traditional 'institutions' such as training camps are becoming increasingly difficult to operate given the fact that they are continually targeted. In response, terrorists have had to create new forms of institutions to recruit, radicalize and train. Most significant is the use of the online institution.

This shift to an online institution reflects one of the most important strategic shifts and considers Foucault's methodology which relies on examining historical and strategic shifts in practices as part of his methodological approach [6, 7]. Furthermore, these strategic shifts reflect a transformation in power dynamics where the weaker party in asymmetrical warfare can further disperse relationships through a giant open network. Coupled with these shifts, it is also useful to include Foucault's discourse of a 'game' when conceptualizing how either discourses or practices change over time, and very much parallels the online cyber environment that has its own set of 'rules' [7]. Consequently it is expected that a shift in practices will also involve a shift in the nature and type of threat posed by terrorist groups.

The recent case of Arid Uka reveals a disturbing new trend in online terrorism, that of the loner, with no clear organizational affiliations or connections [8]. It marks a shift away from training camps and small group affiliations towards the online institution [9]. In other words, 'The terrorists we should fear most are self-recruited wannabes who find purpose in terror and comrades on the Web.' [9], p. 37]. So the key question is, what drives this new breed of recruit? It is not poverty, not even necessarily religion, but a sense of marginalization and a search for significance [9]. What is most concerning is that the internet has become an online institution for gathering and coordinating these marginalized individuals.

In recent years there has been an increasing reliance on internet technologies primarily because they allow good targeting of marginalized individuals, anonymity and decentralization [10]. Originally the focus has been on terrorist created web sites, now the focus has shifted and spread to Western social media sites and forums such as Facebook, Twitter, YouTube and Yahoo groups [10]. These forums offer distinct advantages in that they enable terrorists to attract or lure individuals to a cause as well as creating a mechanism to coordinate attacks [10]. These media forums have become the new institutions of radicalization and terrorism. It is within these institutions where attitudes are shaped, rationalities are developed and individuals reshaped for the path of jihad.

METHODOLOGY

This paper used qualitative data collection and analysis. Specifically, it followed a grounded theory model of cyclic development in terms of hypothesis generation, testing and refinement [11]. The final explanatory model can be considered the result of hypothesis generation resulting from a guiding theoretical framework in conjunction with a literature analysis on current research, social media research and post fact terrorist cases. Grim and others utilize the idea of qualitative hypothesis testing in focus group interviews in order to test a generated hypothesis [12]. In like fashion, this study utilized several terrorist case profiles coupled with ten extremist groups using their social media group pages on Facebook over a period of three months in order to confirm, refine or modify the analytical framework developed. The internet is regarded by researchers as a cultural domain in its own right [13], and this is harmonious with the exploratory notion of the internet as an institution. Due to ethical boundaries, analysis was restricted to public domain group pages and did not focus on personal profile pages. Continual data generation, hypothesis refinement and checking were conducted in order to achieve data saturation [12].

This study combined both pre terrorism data through social media analysis of radicalized groups coupled with post fact data of well-known terrorism cases. Together, these formed a more comprehensive profile of extremist and terrorist sociology that was used to develop concepts in comparison with Foucault's analytic of psychiatric power. Points of agreement and disagreement were both actively sought in order to refine the hypothesis generated.

RESULTS OF GROUNDED THEORY ANALYSIS

In developing a substantive model for radicalization and terrorism, data generation was subdivided into several areas using Foucault's analytic framework of psychiatric power. From this, a preliminary hypothesis was proposed, which was then further developed.

The online environment as an isolating influence

An obvious starting point for exploring the nature of the online environment is its role in terrorist cases. Consider Faisal Shahzad, the accused Time Square bomber. His profile classifies him as a loner, only going out at night and focusing on activities on his computer (also has university background in computing) [14]. Likewise, Nidal Hasan, the Fort Hood killer was also classified a very quiet and was also found to have spent extensive time on the internet [15]. Numerous other cases also support extensive online engagement [9]. From these case studies the following hypothesis was generated:

- H1: The online environment becomes a self-imposed institution, whereby individuals become isolated in terms of developing rationalities.

Although, individuals in these terrorism cases were not completely separated from the rest of the world, they did exhibit a withdrawal from interaction with others. The word institution was chosen because it specifically captures the nature of this isolation. An institution has walls and boundaries that separate it from the rest of the world. Typical institutions that can powerfully reshape individuals include prisons, schools and mental institutions. In contrast to traditional institutions, the online institution is one chosen by the individual rather than one that a person is forced into.

In a search for disconfirming data, it was found that the nature of institutions did vary and were not always online. For example there were cases of small splinter groups that first met in mosques such as the Detroit Sleeper Cell [16] and the Benbrika Case [17]. Additionally, prisons have also become another institution for recruiting and radicalizing [16]. In addition, institutions have been combined to include both small groups coupled with online material such as the Madrid Train Bombers [9]. Nonetheless, the online environment has proven to be a salient institution for terrorism. Therefore, the next point of investigation lies with describing the nature of this institution.

Commentators have noted a move toward more open online access to extremist material [18]. An analysis of Facebook revealed that groups were set up with varying levels of openness: open access, requested access and hidden. As a general trend, more extreme groups tend to be less open, thus layering access to the level of extremism on social media. However, there are disconfirming cases where extreme material has open access, but is also reproduced; it seems with the expectation of having this material deleted (See following subsection). Additionally, members of extremist groups are cautioned about being infiltrated by intelligence agents with warnings posted.

Sample posts highlighting security concerns. Here a number of sample posts illustrate the concern over viewing by intelligence agencies.

- [Do not accept or invite any more than 10 friends a day] [VR05]
- [Just so everyone knows, some of you are coming up as being online twice. Be careful I think they are hacking our accounts. In particular, call to jihad members] [SFA09]
- [Someone has hacked our group] [SFA08]
- [Allah protect out accounts] [PA08]
- [... then I'll get disabled again in 2 or 3 weeks al hamdulillah ala kulli kaal] [SFA08]

Source: Group pages including Voice of Islamic Resistance 4

The number 4 after the name indicates that the page has been previously shut down three times. What is also very evident is the large number of Islamic extremist groups and pages present on Facebook and these keep reappearing even after being shut down.

Another issue in exploring the online institution is the way that individuals interact with it. In exploring the link between internet use and depression with terrorism, it is difficult to make generalized comments. However, cases do exist that link emotional issues, online use and terrorism. The most notable being Nidal Hasan whose profile reveals that he was disturbed through his dealing with veterans [15]. Similarly, Mohamed Mohamud (Portland bomb plot) harbored high levels of anger and resentment towards his family [19]. While, there has not been any formal diagnosis of depression, these cases clearly show that the perpetrators were disaffected and harbored emotional issues.

The online environment used to influence thoughts and behaviours

Perhaps one of the most important aspects of this investigation is the way that the online institution is used to influence ways of thinking and ways of viewing the world. Given the fact that many terrorist cases are correlated with high exposure to the internet [9, 14, 15, 20], the following hypothesis was proposed:

- H2:The online environment is a critical mechanism used by terrorists to change thoughts and behaviors, with the specific aim of increasing radicalization.

Despite a strong correlation effect, establishing a stronger cause and effect relationship through a better understanding of mechanisms at work is more difficult. In an attempt to explore these mechanisms, the focus was on exploring social media data. Using Foucault's analytic as a guide, investigation centered on exploring how forms of knowledge are transferred and propagated as well as what dimensions of the soul, terrorists are targeting (i.e. rational or affective). Media and in particular social media are an important tool for the propagation of the relationship between religion and terrorism [21]. Analysis of group pages revealed consistent discursive schemas. Some key schemas are summarized in Table 1 There were a number of common themes that emerged.

Table 1 Discursive schemas on facebook

Discursive element	Sample Posts[a]
Oppression/ Blaming of the West	*[There's a 9/11 and 7/7 happening more than once a day in muslim[b]countries, afghanistan, pakistan, iraq, palestine, chechneya, etc., etc.,] [UFWM0303]*
	["Because of my Islamic conscience I could not just sit back and watch the Jews while they were shooting the Muslims like someone shooting birds." (12 year old boy)]
[Some more moderate elements subscribe to conspiracy theories]	*Quoted by [HGB0621]*
	[what about the killing of palestinian,bosnian... is it justified ?] [AA0313]
	[OSAMA did not blow up the 2win towers them illuminati pple did it nd bush is 1 of them. 3.Osama isnt a terrorist Americans, them Jew nd the british they kill thousands of our bros nd sis in iraq, gaza... 5.Osama was a muslim my bro] [AA0309]
Defends actions of terrorists [Osama bin Laden]	*[islam is sweet, and yes it is not osama obviously, for he too is a servant of Allah who can say on the day of judgement h... ow he helped other muslims, how he had raised the banner of islam, with no shame, for look at how many witnesses he has for his actions] [UFWM 0307]*

Unity of Islam	*[However he [bin Laden] is a brother in islam, and as muslims we are one body! where pain may hit one part, affects the rest. You cannot judge, especially as you do not even begin to even try to understand our religion, why do you think islam is the worlds greatest and fastest growing religion in the world.] [UFWM0308]*
Restoring the glory of Islam	*[and upholding islam, returning it to its glory, inshallah only by the will of Allah] [UFWM0311]*
Embracing of death	*[Earth is a prison for believers and a paradise for unbelievers] [DF0601]*
	[We're just a traveler in this dunya[c] and this dunya is just a trial for us.] [GBAM0603]
	[O ALLAH GRANT ME MARTYRDOM IN YOUR PATH AND OCCUR MY DEATH IN THE CITY OF YOUR PROPHET.] \HGB0608]

a. Sources: Facebook Group Pages linked to Sheikh Anwar Al Awlaki et. al.

b. Incorrect spellings and grammar of original posts have been left as is throughout the table.

c. Dunya is an Arabic word meaning 'temporal world'.

First, extremists do not view themselves as the aggressors, rather they merely respond to Western occupation and aggression. Second, terrorist figures are esteemed and regarded as hero's and/or martyrs. Third, the unity of Islam is a key discursive mechanism used to normalize the actions of extremists and prevent alienation from moderates. Further, it is used as a mechanism to try and swing moderates toward more extreme thinking. Fourth, restoring the glory of Islam is a key goal and is linked to the first point where it made clear that it is Islam (not terrorism) that is being attacked by the West and once again this seeks to unify Muslims. Finally, extremists are keen to contrast their different views on death to the West especially the concept of 'dunya' (Table 1). This list is by no means exhaustive but is does illustrate that common discursive schemas can be found across a wide variety of group pages.

In terms of targeting, the affective dimension is crucial for fuelling extremist views. As a case in point, the Voice of the Islamic Resistance 4 group page contains graphic images of dead Muslims designed to incite anger. Additionally, the choice of the word resistance is congruent with the first point in Table 1 of the discursive schema, Western oppression. Clearly, this discursive schema (Table 1) is designed to target the affective dimension highlighting that the West is against Islam. Another source of inspiration is interaction with western people on Islamic extremist sites that tend to harden their views. Here, westerners are allowed to discuss issues and as the following subsection illustrates they are baited due to extremist support of Osama bin Laden and other terrorists. Furthermore, extremists make it a war against Islam and in a sense they win by stirring up the Americans to be disrespectful to Allah, further reinforcing their alienation (see last post on in the following subsection).

Sample posts showing interactions to harden views. Interactions show high levels of polarization.

- [You're a stupid, ignorant sand nigger. Your buddy osama is dead, your next towel-head.] [ER0328]
- [@ethan you r dead wrong OSAMA is not dead just giving ya self alittle hope hahahaha!!!] [FI0329]
- [he is though… so? denial?] [ER0329]
- [Stop abusing sheikh anwar and Osama is a HERO OUR HERO. Get it.] [FI0329]
- [You're hypocrites. You think Americans are tyrants, you beat your women, and blow yourselves up and think your going to paradise.] [ER0330]
- [Wow wat about u superpowers yet you cant stop storms from destroying you. Allah is punishing u for your deeds you want 2 finish ISLAM No u cant just fooling yo self.] [FI0330]
- [yo fatimah if you're so tight with allah, once you blow yourself up along with innocent men, women and children in exchange for 72 dunegook virgins, tell him i say go fuck yourself] [CC0331]

FI : Islamic extremist, ER and CC: Americans

Source: Facebook Group Page linked to Sheikh Anwar Al Awlaki

THE ONLINE ENVIRONMENT ALLOWS FOR A MORE DISTRIBUTED FORM OF POWER

The targeting of training camps and the shift towards online forms of recruitment and training has resulted in a corresponding shift in power structures. This represents a shift towards more distributed network structures and a more 'leaderless' jihad [9, 22]. Arid Uka is just one such case of a loner terrorist [8]. Others such as Tsouli start as isolated individuals and then become part of a group [9]. Consequently, the following hypothesis is proposed.

- H3: Online power relations follow a more distributed network structure, rather than a top down hierarchical structure.

Data from terrorist cases support this network structure without necessarily having specific forms of leadership. Nonetheless, there are cases that show some aberrance to this trend, most notably, the Benbrika case [17]. Here, one individual was clearly identified as the leader and guiding influence of the group. Nonetheless, there were no formal wider connections to a specific Islamic terrorist group. This case demonstrates that in small group structures there can exist a more formal hierarchical power structure. Yet such a power structure does not hold up well beyond small groups. Despite this, such small seemingly disconnected groups are part of a larger power structure or mechanism that warrants investigation.

Use of discourse to maintain power

Evidence suggests that cohesion of world-wide Islamic terrorism is maintained through discursive schemas. While there are clearly divergences between groups, each with its own particular ideology and focus, there are important concepts or rationalities that unite them to form the framework of this global power structure. Table 1 illustrates some of these common discursive features that have been collected from extremist groups on Facebook. Researchers in the field of Islamic terrorism will look at this table and see that it contains nothing new. It simply recreates well known discursive fields. However, this in and of itself is significant. The very fact that researchers are able to easily and clearly recognize common discursive elements of Islamic terrorism lend support to a model that holds the discursive framework as integral to the power structure of Islamic terrorism.

Islamic propaganda and discursive formations are rampant on the internet; this is a well known fact. However, this in and of itself is insufficient as a power structure to create radicalization and terrorism. The internet is filled with a vast variety of discursive schemas with many of them regarded as nothing more than fiction. Essentially, discursive schemas must be supported with some sort of normalizing process. In other words, the discourse in question must be presented as 'normal' and correct and discourses that run counter to it as false and abnormal. So the question becomes, how does this normalizing process work? Social media analysis of groups provides the best insights here.

Shifting the 'norm' to the radical extreme

After an initial focus on radical Islamic groups, I decided to broaden my focus to also encompass more moderate groups. This decision led to some significant findings. Several moderate Islamic groups tended to have input from more radical members. Consider the following example in the following subsection that challenges the views of a moderate. It seems that more radical Islamic elements are searching out and trying to influence more moderate Muslims thus shifting the normality of Muslim discourse in the more extreme or radical dimension. Note how the third post in the following subsection seeks to shift the notion of 'balance'.

Sample posts showing the challenging of a moderate by an extremist. Demonstrates a clear delineation with Western media.

- [Osama was d reason y many muslims were called terrorist] [SS0303]
- [i think you have been brain washed by the media . Listen before you say something you should think,concerning osama you need 2 do more research as to why he did that] [FI0322]
- ["Every muslim considers himself as balanced BUT the balance is according to the Prophet sallallahu alayhi wa salaama, so if he has participated in jihad 27 times in his life and we have not done this action even once, how then can we say we are balanced and that we follow the way of the Prophet sallallahu alayhi wa salaamh" (Masood Al Benin).] [HGB0517]

Source: Facebook groups

1. a. A well-known Islamic prophet

Another important aspect of the normalizing process is not just the discursive schemas but also where they come from and who authors these discourses. As an offshoot of social media, the extreme 'Inspire' magazine features articles from prominent terrorist leaders including Usama bin Laden. Quotes from prominent prophets, sheiks and terrorists are also common in Facebook postings. Interestingly, these terrorist leaders share certain physical characteristics as a symbol of their authority. These include long beards and classic Islamic robes. Such characteristics run contrary to much of the modus operandi presented that recommends its terrorist operatives to 'blend in' to Western culture in all aspects especially appearance. This paradox illustrates the importance of symbolic authority in the discursive formations of jihad. Additionally, group posts as illustrated below demonstrate high levels of respect for sheiks and their discursive schemas.

Sample posts illustrating loyalty to radical sheiks. Defending of extremist leaders is clearly evident here:

- [May Allah tala protect our sheikh and keep him away from all evil and harm, May he make his affairs easy for him ameen. When the disbeliever plot and plan Allah too plans and plots against them and Allah is the best of plotters and planners allahu akbar] [SB0332]
- [Mansha Allah, sheikh Anwar al Awlki may Allah reward him.] [AL0333]
- [salam, i just want us to know that victory is ours. i have heard sheikhs but nothing like you. Allahs promise is binding on Him and he will protect you both in duniya and akhira INSHA ALLAHU. salam and sakinah for you till we meet in Jannah either as a shaheed or whatever Allah decides for us] [AS0334]

Source: Facebook groups linked to Anwar Al Awlaki

In spite of this symbolic authority, actual authority is does not belong to any particular individual or cleric. This is evident in social media groups that tend to focus on the discourse rather than on the authority of particular terrorists or sheiks.

DISCUSSION: DEVELOPING AN EXPLANATORY MODEL OF ONLINE RADICALISATION

Having generated preliminary hypothesis and then further investigated aspects covering the normalization of radicalization and terrorism, it was confirmed that Foucault's analytic utilizing concepts of psychiatric power was an invaluable guiding framework for developing an explanatory model of online radicalization and terrorism. Consequently, this section will outline in detail this newly applied model in addition to some of its original theoretical foundations.

Power is reconceptualized as a move away from the use of force and coercion to affect change and a move towards more carefully planned, subtle, methodical, tactical routines [3]. To parallel radical Islamic extremism, it is a shift away from conversion by the sword, away from threats and forced action, and a move towards a disciplined, subtle and constant training; it is an immersion of the individual within this nebulous online context.

Although this online context has varying effects on different individuals with users having different motivations for online social interaction and engagement [23], forms of power are more subtle and widespread being a technique used to effect change. In other words, it is a method, a means to alter the attitudes and behaviors of users. Of course it is not always successful, but in the case of reproducing terrorism it does not have to be. Even changes in very small population sets can have devastating consequences. So the key question arises, how do forms of power work to promote radicalization and terrorism? This will be answered by looking at the key elements of psychiatric power as it relates to this topic.

SELF IMPOSED ISOLATION OF INDIVIDUALS LEADS TO RADICALIZATION

To begin outlining this model, the internet or online environment will be contextualized an an institution. That said, the institutional does not necessarily need the traditional four walls, yet at the same time it does need to possess certain characteristics that define it.

Social isolation

First, an institution does need to possess a degree of social isolation [3]. This isolation is critical for normalizing behaviors and will be discussed in detail shortly. However, it is important to establish that this form of isolation is not a type of solitude, but rather insulation from pervasive outside influence, particularly alternative ideas and competing rationalities. In the case of radicalization, this seems to be a case of self imposed social isolation where individuals spend large amounts of time online engaging with radical materials.

Disciplined regularity

Second, an institution is a regulated and disciplined environment which stems historically from the ascetic exercises of the monastic tradition [3]. Research illustrates that terrorist's use of the internet parallels significant levels of regularity and discipline. This ranges from the use of the internet to coordinate and plan attacks as well as recruit and train individuals [10]. Most importantly, terrorist activity of the internet reflects elements of the master/servant type relationships of the monastic tradition as well as the expert/trainee relationships from the psycho-social sciences. A case in point are chat room forums where 'experts' train others in the specific tactical details of planning and conducting terrorist attacks including bomb creation skills, ambush skills and computer hacking [10].

Access to normalizing discourses

Thirdly, and perhaps most importantly is the use of the internet as an institution to normalize and reinforce behaviors. Research indicates that online users often actively seek out those who support their views and also interpret evidence in light of their belief and expectations [24]. Furthermore, this corroborating of opinion and beliefs often causes increases in opinion extremity [24]. This evidence, even if only true for a small subgroup of the population, demonstrates the actual and potential strength of the online institution in normalizing and strengthening attitudes and opinions. Other research has also shown that the internet does not increase participation in the political process [25], reinforcing its potential isolating affects. Overall, it is this isolation that forms the foundation of the online context.

Online environment as a castle

Perhaps one of the most salient symbols of institutional isolation is that of the castle. Specifically, the isolation and disciplinary regulation of a castle, its activities, timetable and even its surroundings 'imprints itself on the brain.' [3], p. 2]. Parallel to a physical castle, the internet is like a self-imposed virtual castle, a self-imposed form of isolation and training where one enters the institution both willingly and with a habitual, some may even say obsessive regularity. These virtual castles are particularly appealing to the disaffected young who seek fantasy narratives more so than religious or theological rigor [9].

To some, the internet as a castle is counterintuitive to what it represents, namely, diversity of opinion. While exposure to multiple viewpoints is critical to promoting diversity, group polarization is a phenomenon both in real world and online contexts when group exposure to debates simply results in the reinforcing of current beliefs in addition to a shift towards a more extreme position [24]. Group polarization stems from homophily, where like-minded individuals seek each other out, resulting in a mutual reinforcing of beliefs and opinions [24]. This phenomenon is well suited to recruiting and radicalizing individuals on the path to jihad and terrorism.

Given this phenomenon of group polarization coupled with the diverse and cosmopolitan nature of the internet, we have an interesting paradox. A place with a multitude of opinions and viewpoints while no doubt for some leads to promoting tolerance and diversity, but for others merely presents a choice of a multitude of self-imposed castles or virtual institutions. These online institutions are ready and waiting to reinforce current beliefs and opinions and even take them to a more extreme place. So the question arises, how do the disaffected and marginalized find and enter these radical Islamic virtual castles?

Previously, it was common for jihadi forums to be closed and password protected, only allowing those screened and chosen to enter [10]. Metaphorically, this meant that the gates of the castle were closed. This choice was made to protect those working within the institution from outsiders, namely intelligence agencies. However, this also meant that not only were the gates closed to unwanted intruders, they were also closed to new and potential recruits which was a significant disadvantage.

Access to online 'castles' of radicalization

Given the increasing emphasis on the use of Western social media, there has been a corresponding shift in the need to open up the virtual institution [10]. Many terrorist organizations now have open Facebook groups, which makes it much easier for radicals to enter these virtual institutions without the previous restrictions [10]. In addition, many of these sites are becoming much more media savvy, targeting and appealing to marginalized and disaffected youth. Despite these benefits, there is also the increased risk that terrorist organizations face of being infiltrated by intelligence agencies, and even prominent jihadi figures have warned their members and recruits about these potential dangers [10]. Nevertheless, given the enormous membership of social media sites such as Facebook (more than 500 million active users) and Twitter (more than 40 million active users) these are an important tool for finding and recruiting subjects for the virtual castle. These facts, in conjunction with the shift toward loner jihad wannabes targeting heroic fantasies [9], make this risk a necessary one for terrorist organizations to take.

Marginalized and disaffected individuals join interest groups that allow terrorists to specifically target individuals in a manner similar to the way a marketing group would target consumers [10]. Many of these are young males and females who are socially isolated and hence are seeking an identity. The danger here is that these individuals are voluntarily entering a virtual castle with a high degree of disciplined regularity. This disciplined or obsessive regularity is better known as problematic internet usage (PIU).

There have been a number of studies conducted on PIU especially in relation to loneliness and isolation. In terms of predictors of PIU on a group of university students: loneliness, depression and computer self-efficacy were the main predictors with loneliness then depression being the most significant [26]. For a younger cohort of secondary students, a strong relationship was found between hours of internet engagement and levels of loneliness [27]. This relationship in itself is problematic; nonetheless, other research studies also suggest that a negative spiral can occur. Those who were lonely or had poor social skills could develop PIU and this in turn had negative impacts on lifestyle factors such as home, school, work and relationships leading in further social isolation and loneliness [28]. Another study also supported the link between high internet use and poor social ties [29]. Consequently, those most likely to enter the obsessive regularity of the virtual castle are also those most vulnerable with problematic psychological antecedents. Others have also found that PIU is associated with low psychological wellbeing [23].

To further elaborate on the vulnerability of the disaffected, online interaction becomes a form of compensation for an individual's poor social skills [28]. Furthermore, the freedom of online interaction without the need for non-verbal cues often compounds the problems of real world interactions reinforcing the attraction of internet usage [23]. Unfortunately such individuals, in addition to those who shown sympathy to terrorist causes, are particularly vulnerable for recruitment and training given that they actually prefer online interaction.

THE ONLINE ENVIRONMENT IS AN IMPORTANT CONTEXT TO NORMALISE RADICAL THINKING AND BEHAVIOR

Once terrorists have targeted sympathizers, the vulnerable or disaffected, their next task is to achieve a transformation; to 'normalize' the way in which they should think and ultimately act. Discipline and regularity are essential elements in order to normalize aberrant behaviors [3]. Online users achieve this order and socialization through their own regular or compulsive internet use that has a narrow focus on a particular group of rationalities.

A key aspect of engagement is facilitating the individual to self-disclose; however this is a very natural process online, with the internet promoting higher levels of self disclosure [23]. Furthermore, online users are generally more uninhibited [23], making them increasingly subject to forms of power. Specifically, this allows individuals to better self monitor and regulate their own behaviors using self subjectification [4]. Here individuals can compare their own frameworks against those of the extremist or terrorist group.

Group polarization

Homophily and group polarization are important concepts where like-minded individuals seek each other out and further strengthen their mindsets and even take them to more extreme levels [24]. A key dynamic of group polarization is group identity where individuals categorize themselves and others as in-group or out-of-group [24]. Group identification is particularly salient in political and ideological contexts [24]. For terrorist or extremist groups, this group identity is particularly important where individuals continually compare themselves against group categorizations and norms. Furthermore, threats to group identity tend to strengthen the homogeneity of the group [24]. This is particularly the case with terrorist groups, many of which highlight threats to their identity such as war crimes and maltreatment, bombing of civilians, as well as cases of discrimination and prejudice. Equally dangerous to strengthening group identity is the publication of victories against terrorists who are subsequently turned into heroes and martyrs [9]. Therefore, a strong group identity is imperative within the virtual institution.

Social media forums are battlegrounds for the hearts and minds of the vulnerable and disaffected. In fact the key to the success of radicalization is the victory of one idea over another [3]. This is an important objective of online radicalization, to replace moderate ideas with extreme ideals. Sageman is adamant that this is a battle for the hearts and minds of young Muslims which regularly go online to share their dreams and grievances [9]. Moreover, this is where terrorists attempt to suppress the realities and horrors of war and replace them with fantasy and heroic narratives [9]. These narratives are designed to give purpose, fulfillment and glory, in addition to providing an avenue for their grievances. What is particularly critical about these narratives is the way they capture the affective dimension.

Targeting the affective dimension

Monitoring and dealing with feelings is just as important as analyzing thoughts with many psychotherapeutic approaches also targeting the affective dimension [4]. Critically, for terrorists, Sageman argues that the affective dimension is more important than the rational dimension in explaining behavior and further links actions to a type of moral outrage over perceived injustices [9]. What is more concerning is that the virtual castles found through online social media are important forums to discuss issues that involve emotional triggers [24]. This is particularly so around political or controversial issues. These provide an important opportunity for terrorist recruiters to play on the feelings of disaffected young Muslims, with the aim of engendering radical feelings of injustice and hatred. To achieve this goal, terrorist leaders and radical clerics have carefully devised schemas or frameworks which they exercise.

Schemas of knowledge

A key aspect of normalizing behavior is the development of a prescriptive schema where forms of knowledge are combined with training, surveillance, monitoring and testing to ensure their adaptation by those within the institution [3]. In the case of institutions, frameworks of knowledge and expectations are developed about how to behave. In addition, these schemas were not value free but leaders have a clear body of theoretical knowledge about normality and how abnormality needs to be addressed [4]. In the virtual institution, radical Islamic leaders use their extreme views as the prescriptive schema that impose order, training and discipline upon those within this social media institution. Perhaps one of the most famous terrorists to make use of this concept was Younis Tsouli, also known as Terrorist 007, who produced a multitude of YouTube propaganda videos [10]. These videos were specifically designed to impose forms of knowledge about the path of jihad.

An important element in making up schemas is the concept of dispersion. This concept recognizes that diverse ideas make up a body of knowledge. A case in point is the concept of jihad that has a variety of divergent interpretations. However, a schema can and is still created by recognizing that: different variations make up a single discursive object; statements that make up a discourse are organized by form and connection; discourse is determined by more permanent and coherent concepts; and statements are grouped and regrouped according to themes [7]. The key point here is that extremist schemas while diverse are marked by prominent themes and persistent concepts that are echoed by many leaders and groups.

THE DISTRIBUTED NATURE OF POWER IN THE ONLINE ENVIRONMENT HELPS THE PROCESS OF RADICALIZATION

Power to radicalize, in addition to being founded on schemas of knowledge, is a very meticulous and calculated power; with the modern asylum being one of disciplined and sophisticated routines rather than brute force [3]. This is critical in online environments as maintaining extremist or terrorist recruits is a difficult process, it is often gradual and slow. Also, although key leaders may be influential, power is not possessed by any individual; it is a circular relation that flows through many networks and individuals that make up that network [3]. Essentially, it is perfectly suited to the online environment. Further, this dispersion of hierarchies allows for a more tactical functioning of power [3], and is well suited to terrorist causes.

The illusion of servanthood

To explore this tactical functioning further, it is necessary to explore the illusion of servant hood. Terrorists on many online forums appear as servants giving their fellow radicals any assistance with tactical tools or moral support they need in order to carry out the global jihad. Fundamentally, what often occurs is high ranking and experienced terrorists become the servant of the novice radical while simultaneously exercising a form of power over them through their disciplined training regimes and schemas of radicalized thinking. As a consequence, new radicals become embedded within a framework of power. It is the locating within this framework of power that is critical in order for such power to be effective at transforming behaviors [3].

Slow, structured and disciplined form of power

When locating an individual within a framework of power, it is imperative not to conceptualize this as a repressive or controlling form of power. Rather, psychiatric power is a structured and productive power aimed at normalizing thoughts and behaviors contained within an institutions schema of knowledge [4]. Clearly, repressive forms of power would be very ineffective given the structure and dynamics of the online environment. However, a productive power that works in a subtle, regular and disciplined fashion is well suited to a network environment. To become effective this productive power must be created by what Foucault terms an 'apparatus of power' [3], p. 13].

The relationship between power and discourse

The key question in devising a framework is '... to what extent can an apparatus of power produce statements, discourses and, consequently, all the forms of representation that may then derive from it?' [3], p 13]. Overall, it is discourse that is the true leader of the online jihad [9]. Such discourses have been created by an apparatus of power and now seek to encompass all who enter the virtual castle. This apparatus of power seeks to suppress alternative forms of discourse that can compete or undermine it [7]. In the case of jihad, notions such as peace, compromise and moderacy must all be suppressed and categorized as ills while notions such as victory, war, martyrdom and sacrifice must be embraced.

Power does not belong to an individual

A final point on the flow of power is the disindividualisation of power. This is where power is decentered and not focused on one individual [4]. Online jihads are inspired, taught and trained by a wide variety of radical clerics, terrorists and terrorist groups. Despite this disindividualisation of power coupled with the circular and network relations of power, still present are forms of power dissymmetry through recognized symbolic authority [3]. In the traditional asylum, doctors symbolized their authority through a variety of physical features such as long white coats, white hair, expressive voice and prominent features [3]. For the online jihad, clerics also maintain a form of authority through physical appearance such as long beards, wearing of robes and the strong aggressive tone of voice. These forms of authority are a critical part of the apparatus of power that create the dominant schemas of knowledge use to regulate thoughts and behavior.

CONCLUSION

Given the rise of the online jihad as the third wave of radicals [9], it is critical to gain an understanding of the mechanisms of this process of radicalization. Through a grounded theory analysis of both terrorist cases and social media sites promoting jihad, Foucault's analytic on psychiatric power provides a solid analytical model for this process. Additionally, aspects of this model are also supported by findings from other researchers. In particular, this model encompasses the discourses of power and their interrelationship with schemas of knowledge that are carefully combined to normalize behavior. It is this transformation of ideology and behavior that is critical for producing terrorist acts. Of most concern is the way that radical Islamic elements seek to influence and transform more moderate and disaffected individuals including those within more moderate group forums.

Given the difficulty of data collection and the 'gap' between online radicalization and post terrorism case data, any model developed should be viewed as a partial, yet significant step in understanding the mechanisms that result in an individual or group undertaking terrorist acts. This paper has given another perspective that can add to the growing body of research on perhaps the most important tool used by Islamic extremists: the internet and in particular social media. Clearly, more research is needed in this vital area with the need to further explore mechanisms of radicalization and de-radicalization in order to prevent the spread of Islamic extremism and terrorism.

AUTHORS' INFORMATION

Dr Robyn Torok is currently undertaking her second PhD in security science. Her main research focus is online terrorism and in particular the use of social media to propagate terrorism.

REFERENCES

1. K von-Knop, Countering web-based Islamist narratives: conceptualizing an information war and a counter-propaganda campaign, in Hypermedia seduction for terrorist recruiting, ed. by B Ganor, K von-Knop, CAM Duarte (IOS Press, Amsterdam, 2007), pp. 169–187
2. C Mbakwe, D Cunliffe, Hypermedia seduction: further exploration of the process of "seductive" online user interactions, in Hypermedia seduction for terrorist recruiting, ed. by B Ganor, K von-Knop, CAM Duarte (IOS Press, Amsterdam,

2007), pp. 207–230

3. M Foucault, Lectures at the College de France 1973–1974, in Michel Foucault: psychiatric power, ed. by J LaGrange (Palgrave MacMillan, New York, 2006). Davidson AI (Series Editor)]
4. M Roberts, The production of the psychiatric subject: power, knowledge and Michel Foucault. Nurs Philos 6, 33–42 (2005)
5. Q Wiktorowicz, A genealogy of radical Islam. Studies in Conflict & Terrorism 28, 75–97 (2005)
6. M Foucault, Nietzsche, genealogy, history, in Language, counter-memory, practice: selected essays and interviews, ed. by DF Bouchard (Cornell University Press, Ithaca, 1977)
7. D White, Foucault at work: archaeology, genealogy, and the dispositions of power. Eur Leg 14, 317–324 (2009)
8. J Burke, Islamist terrorism: the rise of the loners. http://www.guardian.co.uk/commentisfree/2011/mar/04/islamic-terrorism-frankfurt-shooting-arid-uka
9. M Sageman, The next generation of terror. Foreign Policy March/April, 36–42 (2008)
10. G Weimann, Terror on facebook, twitter, and youtube. Brown Journal of World Affairs 16, 45–54 (2010)
11. CD Sutton, M David, Social research: an introduction, 2nd edn. (Sage Publications, London, 2011)
12. BJ Grim, AH Harmon, JC Gromis, Focused group interviews as an innovative quanti-qualitative methodology (QQM): integrating quantitative elements into a qualitative methodology. The Qualitative Report 11, 516–537 (2006)
13. C Hine, Internet research as emergent practice, in Handbook of emergent methods, ed. by SN Hesse-Biber, P Leavy (Guilford Press, New York, 2008), pp. 525–542
14. T Leonard, A Yusufzai, Times square bomb: Faisal shahzad profile. http:// www.telegraph.co.uk/news/worldnews/northamerica/usa/7678771/TimesSquare-bomb-Faisal-Shahzad-profile.html
15. Profile: major nidal malik hasan. http://news.bbc.co.uk/2/hi/8345944.stm
16. T Johnson, Threat of homegrown Islamist terrorism. http://www.cfr.org/ terrorism/threat-homegrown-islamist-terrorism/p11509
17. Benbrika & Ors v The Queen [2010] VSCA 281 (25 October 2010). http://www.austlii.edu.au/au/cases/vic/VSCA/2010/281.html
18. G Weimann, Terror on the Internet: the new arena, the new challenges (United States Institute of Peace, Washington, 2006)
19. C Brooks, Portland's Bomb plot: Who is Mohamed mohamud?. http://www. time.com/time/nation/article/0,8599,2033372,00.html
20. BM Jenkins, The al Qaeda-inspired terrorist threat: an appreciation of the current situation. http://www.rand.org/content/dam/rand/pubs/testimonies/ 2010/RAND_CT353.pdf

21. T Stanley, B Karl, H Jurgen, Transcendental aporias of global civil society. Political Theology 9, 477–502 (2008)
22. M Sageman, Understanding terror networks (University of Pennsylvania Press, Pennsylvania, 2004)
23. S Kang, Disembodiment in online social interaction: impact of online chat on social support and psychosocial well-being. Cyberpsychol Behav 10, 475–477 (2007)
24. S Yardi, D Boyd, Dynamic debates: an analysis of group polarization over time on twitter. Bull Sci Technol Soc 30, 316–327 (2010)
25. W Zhang, TJ Johnson, T Seltzer, SL Bichard, The revolution will be networked. Soc Sci Comput Rev 28, 75–92 (2010)
26. AA Ceyhan, E Ceyhan, Loneliness, depression, and computer self-efficacy as predictors of problematic internet use. Cyberpsychol Behav 11, 699–701 (2008)
27. L Deniz, Excessive internet use and loneliness among secondary school students. J Instr Psychol 37, 20–23 (2010)
28. J Kim, R LaRose, W Peng, Loneliness as the cause and the effect of problematic internet use: the relationship between internet Use and psychological well-being. Cyberpsychol Behav 12, 451–455 (2009)
29. CE Sanders, TM Field, M Diego, M Kaplan, The relationship of internet use to depression and social isolation among adolescents. Adolescence 35, 237 (2000)

INDEX

R

S

T

V

W